OXFORD THEOLOGICAL MONOGRAPHS

OXFORD THEOLOGICAL MONOGRAPHS

THE PRINCIPLE OF RESERVE IN THE WRITINGS OF JOHN HENRY NEWMAN
By R. C. Selby. 1975

THE COSMIC CHRIST IN ORIGEN AND TEILHARD DE CHARDIN
A Comparative Study
By J. A. Lyons. 1982

THE HIDDEN GOD
By Samuel E. Balentine. 1983

PROTESTANT REFORMERS IN ELIZABETHAN OXFORD
By C. M. Dent. 1983

REVELATORY POSITIVISM?
Barth's Earliest Theology and the Marburg School
By Simon Fisher. 1988

THE COMMUNION OF SAINTS
Radical Puritan and Separatist Ecclesiology 1570–1625
By S. Brachlow. 1988

PROBABILITY AND THEISTIC EXPLANATION
By Robert Prevost. 1990

VERBAL ASPECT IN NEW TESTAMENT GREEK
By Buist M. Fanning. 1990

'WORKING THE EARTH OF THE HEART'
The Messalian Controversy in History, Texts, and Language to AD 431
By Columba Stewart, OSB. 1991

The Lordship of Christ

Ernst Käsemann's Interpretation of Paul's Theology

DAVID WAY

CLARENDON PRESS · OXFORD
1991

Oxford University Press, Walton Street, Oxford OX2 6DP
Oxford New York Toronto
Delhi Bombay Calcutta Madras Karachi
Petaling Jaya Singapore Hong Kong Tokyo
Nairobi Dar es Salaam Cape Town
Melbourne Auckland
and associated companies in
Berlin Ibadan

Oxford is a trade mark of Oxford University Press

Published in the United States
by Oxford University Press, New York

British Library Cataloguing in Publication Data
Way, David
The lordship of Christ.
1. Christian theology
I. Title
230
ISBN 0–19–826742–8

Library of Congress Cataloging in Publication Data
The lordship of Christ: Ernst Käsemann's interpretation of Paul's theology / David Way.
(Oxford theological monographs)
Revision of the author's thesis (doctoral)—University of Oxford 1987.
Includes bibliographical references and index.
1. Käsemann, Ernst—Contributions in interpretation of Paul's theology. 2. Bible. N.T. Epistles of Paul—Theology—History 20th century. I. Title. II. Series.
BS2651.W39 1991 225.9'2—dc20 90–24241
ISBN 0–19–826742–8

Typeset by Hope Services (Abingdon) Ltd
Printed in Great Britain by
Bookcraft (Bath) Ltd., Midsomer Norton, Avon

Acknowledgements

In the writing of a work of this nature, I have inevitably built up a number of debts of gratitude. A Major State Studentship from the Department of Education and Science allowed me to make a substantial start on the doctoral thesis which underlies this work and which was accepted by the University of Oxford in October 1987. My research has profited greatly from several periods of study in West Germany. A grant from the *Deutscher Akademischer Austauschdienst* enabled me to improve my German in the Goethe-Institut in Bremen. I am particularly grateful for the stimulus which I received from studying in Bonn in the autumn of 1983. This was a product of the Bonn–Oxford theological exchange and was facilitated by Professor G. Sauter. Grants from the World Council of Churches (through the Evangelisch-Lutherische Landeskirche Hannovers) and the Hall-Houghton and Squire-Marriott Funds allowed me to spend 1984/5 in the excellent libraries of the University of Göttingen. Professor Käsemann did me the honour of showing interest in my work and generously allowed me free access to his library and papers during an unforgettable fortnight in Tübingen in May 1985. My work also benefited from the comments of my examiners, Mr J. Ashton (Oxford) and Professor Dr W. Schrage (Bonn). Above all I am indebted to Revd R. Morgan, who suggested the subject, shared his knowledge of Käsemann's work and of the traditions of German Protestant theology and historical criticism, and provided criticism, encouragement, and support along the way.

Contents

Bibliographical Note

SYSTEM OF REFERENCE

Käsemann's work is cited by abbreviated title (*Römer*, *EVB*, *PP*, etc.; the abbreviations are listed before ch. 1) or with a full reference to minor works. The page references are given to the latest German edition and to the ET, where available, in that order (e.g., *Römer* 113/119).

Other works are cited (according to the Harvard system) by author and date only (e.g., Barrett 1962); or, if there is more than one significant edition, with the date of first publication and the latest edition (e.g., Althaus 1938/1951).

Fuller details of the cited works will be found in the bibliography which is subdivided into sections on (1) Käsemann's work, (2) general.

TRANSLATION POLICY

One of the aims of this study is to make Käsemann's thought more accessible to the English-speaking theological world. I have quoted Käsemann and other authors in English, trusting that the loss of Käsemann's concise and vivid German will be accepted as the price of an English route into his thought. The existing ETs of Käsemann's work have been utilized, and corrected or modified as indicated. 'ET modified' means that while the ET is not actually incorrect, the translation given is closer to Käsemann's German. Where no translation is available I have supplied my own. The original has been reproduced in the few places where substantial quotations have been made from sources which are not publicly available.

Abbreviations

KÄSEMANN'S WORKS

'Abendmahl'	'Das Abendmahl im Neuen Testament' (1937)
'Baur'	'Einführung' in *F. C. Baur: Historisch-kritische Untersuchungen zum Neuen Testament* (1963)
'Entmythologisierung'	'Zur Frage der Entmythologisierung: Vortrag am 7.12.1949 in Darmstadt'
ENTT	*Essays on New Testament Themes* (ET of essays from *EVB* i)
'Epheserbrief'	'Epheserbrief' (1958)
'Erwiderung'	'Erwiderung an Ulrich Asendorf' (1967)
EVB	*Exegetische Versuche und Besinnungen*, i (1960), ii (1964)
'Frau'	'Der Dienst der Frau an der Wortverkündigung nach dem NT' (1942)
Freiheit	*Der Ruf der Freiheit* (1968/1972)
'Geist'	'Geist IV. Geist und Geistesgaben im NT' (1958)
'Gemeinde'	'Vom Leben der paulinischen Gemeinde: Referat im Propädeutikum am 21.6.1949'
Gottesvolk	*Das wandernde Gottesvolk: Eine Untersuchung zum Hebräerbrief* (1939)
KK	*Kirchliche Konflikte*, i (1982)
'Legitimität'	'Die Legitimität des Apostels: Eine Untersuchung zu II Korinther 10–13' (1942)
Leib	*Leib und Leib Christi: Eine Untersuchung zur paulinischen Begrifflichkeit* (1933)
'Leiblichkeit'	'Das Motiv der Leiblichkeit bei Paulus' (n.d.)
NTQT	*New Testament Questions for Today* (ET of essays from *EVB* ii)
PoP	*Perspectives on Paul*; ET of *PP*
PP	*Paulinische Perspektiven* (1969)
'Probleme'	'Probleme neutestamentlicher Arbeit in Deutschland' (1952)
Römer	*An die Römer* (1973/4)

'Römer 13'	'Römer 13, 1–7 in unserer Generation' (1959)
'Theologie'	'Theologie des Neuen Testaments, Vorlesungsnachschrift' (n.d.)
'Vaterunser'	'Die zweite Bitte des Vaterunsers' (1952)
'Versöhnung'	'Erwägungen zum Stichwort "Versöhnungslehre im Neuen Testament"' (1964)
'Zusammenbruch'	'Die evangelische Kirche im deutschen Zusammenbruch: Vortrag vor evang. Akademikern Gelsenkirchen am 4.12.1945'

OTHER WORKS

Abbreviations of German language material follow S. Schwertner, *Internationales Abkürzungsverzeichnis für Theologie und Grenzgebiete: Zeitschriften, Serien, Lexica, Quellenwerke mit bibliographischen Angaben* (Berlin, 1974).

ABR	*Australian Biblical Review*, Melbourne
ASNU	Acta Seminarii Neotestamentici Upsaliensis, Stockholm
AThANT	Abhandlungen zur Theologie des Alten und Neuen Testaments, Zurich
BEvTh	Beihefte zur evangelischen Theologie, Munich
BFChTh	Beiträge zur Förderung christlicher Theologie, Gütersloh
BHTh	Beiträge zur historischen Theologie, Tübingen
Bib	*Biblica: Commentarii periodici ad rem biblicam scientifice investigandam*, Rome
BJRL	*Bulletin of the John Rylands Library*, Manchester
BNTC	Black's New Testament Commentaries, London
BZNW	Beihefte zur Zeitschrift für die neutestamentliche Wissenschaft, Berlin
ChW	*Die christliche Welt*, Gotha
CNT	Commentaire du Nouveau Testament, Neuchâtel
CuW	*Christentum und Wissenschaft*, Leipzig
DLZ	*Deutsche Literaturzeitung für Kritik der internationalen Wissenschaft*, Berlin
EKK	Evangelisch-Katholischer Kommentar zum Neuen Testament, Neukirchen
ET	English translation
EvK	*Evangelische Kirche*
EvQ	*Evangelical Quarterly*, London
EvTh	*Evangelische Theologie*, Munich

EvTh	*Evangelische Theologie*, Munich
ExT	*Expository Times*, Edinburgh
FGLP	Forschungen zur Geschichte und Lehre des Protestantismus, Munich
FRLANT	Forschungen zur Religion und Literatur des Alten und Neuen Testaments, Göttingen
Gn	*Gnomon: Kritische Zeitschrift für die gesamte klassische Altertumswissenschaft*, Munich
GPM	*Göttinger Predigt-Meditationen*, Göttingen
GTA	Göttinger theologische Arbeiten, Göttingen
HJ	*Heythrop Journal: A Quarterly Review of Philosophy and Theology*, Oxford
HNT	Handbuch zum Neuen Testament, Tübingen
HThK	Herders theologischer Kommentar zum Neuen Testament, Freiburg
HTR	*Harvard Theological Review*, Cambridge, Massachusetts
HUNT	Hermeneutische Untersuchungen zum Neuen Testament, Tübingen
ICC	The International Critical Commentary on the Holy Scriptures of the Old and New Testaments, Edinburgh
Int	*Interpretation: A Journal of Bible and Theology*, Richmond
JBL	*Journal of Biblical Literature*, Philadelphia
JSNT	*Journal for the Study of the New Testament*, Sheffield
JTC	*Journal of Theology and Church*, New York
JTS	*Journal of Theological Studies*, Oxford
JusEcc	Jus Ecclesiasticum: Beiträge zum evangelischen Kirchenrecht und zum Staatskirchentum, Munich
KBRS	*Kirchenblatt für die reformierte Schweiz*, Basle
KEK	Kritisch-exegetischer Kommentar über das Neue Testament. Begr. v. Heinrich August Wilhelm Meyer, Göttingen
KuD	*Kerygma und Dogma*, Göttingen
LR	*Lutherische Rundschau*, Stuttgart
LW	*Lutheran World*, Geneva
MThSt	Marburger Theologische Studien, Marburg
NBl	*New Blackfriars*, London
NovT	*Novum Testamentum*, Leiden
NTA	Neutestamentliche Abhandlungen, Münster
NTD	Das Neue Testament Deutsch. Neues Göttinger Bibelwerk, Göttingen
NTF	Neutestamentliche Forschungen, Gütersloh
NTS	*New Testament Studies: An International Journal Published under the Auspices of Studiorum Novi Testamenti Societas*, Cambridge

NZSTh	*Neue Zeitschrift für systematische Theologie und Religionsphilosophie*, Berlin
ÖF	Ökumenische Forschungen, Freiburg
RB	*Revue biblique*, Paris
RGG	*Die Religion in Geschichte und Gegenwart*, Tübingen
RHPhR	*Revue d'histoire et de philosophie religieuses*, Strasbourg
RSR	*Religious Studies Review*, Waterloo, Ontario
RV	Religionsgeschichtliche Volksbücher für die deutsche christliche Gegenwart. 1: Religion des Neuen Testaments
SBS	Stuttgarter Bibelstudien, Stuttgart
SBT	Studies in Biblical Theology, London
SEÅ	*Svenk exegetisk årsbok*, Lund
SJT	*Scottish Journal of Theology*, Edinburgh
SNTSMS	Studiorum Novi Testamenti Societas Monograph Series, Cambridge
StNT	Studien zum Neuen Testament, Gütersloh
StUNT	Studien zur Umwelt des Neuen Testaments, Göttingen
TDNT	*Theological Dictionary of the New Testament*, Grand Rapids
TEH	Theologische Existenz Heute: Eine Schriftenreihe, Munich
ThBl	*Theologische Blätter*, Leipzig
ThHK	Theologischer Handkommentar zum Neuen Testament, Leipzig
ThLZ	*Theologische Literaturzeitung*, Leipzig
ThPh	*Theologie und Philosophie: Vierteljahresschrift für Theologie und Philosophie*, Freiburg
ThR	*Theologische Rundschau*, Tübingen
ThSt	Theologische Studien, Zurich
ThZ	*Theologische Zeitschrift: Theologische Fakultät der Universität Basel*, Basle
TS	*Theological Studies: St Louis University*, New York
TU	Texte und Untersuchungen zur Geschichte der altchristlichen Literatur, Berlin
TynB	*Tyndale Bulletin*, London
UNT	Untersuchungen zum Neuen Testament, Leipzig
VF	*Verkündigung und Forschung: Theologischer Jahresbericht* (Evangelische Theologie), Munich
WBC	Word Biblical Commentary, Waco and Dallas
WdF	Wege der Forschung, Darmstadt
WMANT	Wissenschaftliche Monographien zum Alten und Neuen Testament, Neukirchen
WUNT	Wissenschaftliche Untersuchungen zum Neuen Testament, Tübingen

ZNW	*Zeitschrift für die neutestamentliche Wissenschaft und die Kunde der älteren Kirche*, Berlin
ZRGG	*Zeitschrift für Religions- und Geistesgeschichte*, Cologne
ZThK	*Zeitschrift für Theologie und Kirche*, Tübingen
ZZ	*Zwischen den Zeiten*, Munich

I

The Theological and Historical-Critical Context of Käsemann's Interpretation of Paul's Theology

PAULINE THEOLOGY: THE CENTRE OF KÄSEMANN'S LIFE AND WORK

In the English-speaking world Ernst Käsemann's name is associated primarily with the renewed quest of the historical Jesus which he helped to initiate in the mid-1950s. In addition he is well known for his passionate theological commitment, and for the highly polemical character[1] and sheer difficulty of his writing. There is less appreciation of the breadth of Käsemann's interests, the system of his thought, and the key role of his understanding of Pauline theology within the whole.

Käsemann's life and work

Käsemann's career can be outlined in a few sentences. Born in the Dahlhausen area of Bochum, Westphalia, on 12 July 1906, he studied at Bonn, Tübingen, and Marburg. His dissertation, written under Bultmann in Marburg, was submitted in 1931, and he then worked as a pastor in Gelsenkirchen in the Ruhr. After war service he became Professor of New Testament in Mainz (1946–51), from where he moved to Göttingen (1951–9) and finally to Tübingen (1959–71), where he has continued to live in retirement. The movement from parish to university gives an important clue to the nature of his work. From the

[1] This is well summed up in the title of G. Haufe's essay, 'Exegese als Provokation; (1971). In his recent monograph (1986) B. Ehler, writing from within the German context, points out that many of the debates with Käsemann have merely taken issue with his 'exaggerated' slogans. Consequently he seeks to understand Käsemann's work as a whole by focusing on the problem of 'the centre of scripture'.

first Käsemann has been interested in the theological significance of the New Testament, not just its historical interpretation. For him the task of interpreting scripture is closely related to the ministry of preaching.[2] This stance was in keeping with the prevailing theological climate of the time, and the role of theological faculties in the education of pastors for the Protestant church in Germany. Thus, it was natural that his work should issue in contributions to church life.

Within the sphere of New Testament studies, Käsemann's interests are very wide-ranging,[3] although there is a clear predilection for Paul. This holds true both for his publications[4] and in his teaching.[5] The main topics of his research are the history-of-religions background of the New Testament;[6] history-of-traditions research, with a particular focus on hymnic or

[2] In the preface to the German edition of his first collection of essays, Käsemann justifies the inclusion of short pieces, first published in *Göttinger Predigt-Meditationen*, which are intended to give theological background for the writing of sermons, with the view that he sees the 'beginning and culmination of all theological work in preaching' (*EVB* i. 8).

[3] This is reflected in the series of articles which survey NT studies in *Verkündigung und Forschung* (1949/50–1963/5). Cf. also 'Probleme neutestamentliche Arbeit in Deutschland' (1952), and 'Neutestamentliche Fragen von heute' (1957; ET 1969), the only survey to be translated into English. Despite the passage of time these articles are still of interest because Käsemann is at his best when commenting on the historical and theological trends of the times.

[4] A bibliography up to 1975 is given in the Käsemann Festschrift (Lang 1976). To this should be added Käsemann's review of H. W. Bartsch, *Gnostisches Gut und Gemeindetradition bei Ignatius von Antiochen* (1940) (*VF* 3 (1946/7), 131–6). Since 1975 Käsemann has published one academic piece, a review of B. Ulrich, *Zur frühchristlichen Theologiegeschichte* (1976) (*ThLZ* 105 (1980), 432 f.), and a number of more popular addresses, some of which are collected in *Kirchliche Konflikte*, i.

[5] The reasons for Käsemann's popularity as a lecturer are not difficult to divine, even from the duplicated transcripts of his lectures: instead of the highly compressed style, epigrammatic debate with fellow professionals, and attention to detail of his published work, in the lectures subjects are dealt with in broad outline, enlivened with the characteristic polemic, and related to great theological concerns. According to official lecture lists he lectured on every book of the NT with the exceptions of Heb.—which is surprising given his monograph of 1939—and Philem. He returned repeatedly to Rom., 1 Cor., Matt., John, Acts, and NT theology. Approximately one third of his seminars were on specifically Pauline topics, especially Romans. Apart from his interest in Paul, the other notable feature is the concentration of courses in the area of 'early catholicism' in his years at Göttingen, including a series of five seminars on the literature of the apostolic fathers.

[6] Käsemann pursued the question of the gnostic background of the NT in his doctorate (*Leib und Leib Christi*, 1933), his monograph on Hebrews (*Das wandernde Gottesvolk*, 1939; ET 1984), and in the essays of 1949 and 1950 on pre-Pauline hymnic tradition in Col. 1 and Phil. 2. On his change of view on the history-of-religions question, see pp. 122 f. below.

credal material in the epistles;[7] the history of the Lord's supper; the quest of the historical Jesus; the theologies of Paul and John; the emergence of 'early catholicism' within the New Testament period; and the question of the canon. However, these are not a list of unconnected topics, and it will be seen that they fit within Käsemann's view of the New Testament as a whole.

Before embarking on this survey, it will be useful to note the wider theological contribution made by Käsemann up to the end of the war. In his later publications he frequently mentions the importance of the conflicts within the German churches in the Hitler years. However, with very few primary sources from this period, it is difficult to make more than a few points.[8] Käsemann's monograph on Hebrews was not concerned merely with history-of-religions questions but with the theology of the letter. Recently he has summed up its coded message to the then contemporary struggles: 'By describing the church as the new people of God on its wandering through the wilderness, following the Pioneer and Perfecter of faith, I of course had in mind that radical Confessing Church which resisted the tyranny in Germany, and which had to be summoned to patience so that it could continue its way through endless wastes' (*KK* i. 17; ET in the ET of *Gottesvolk*, 13). This theme of exodus is combined with that of the clash of the aeons in his report on 1936 for the Westfalian Gustaf Adolf-Stiftung and becomes the basis for implied criticism of the 'German Christians': the church of Jesus, unlike the Jewish synagogue, has no true homeland (*Heimat*) on earth,

[7] Apart from examples in the seven commonly accepted Pauline epistles, Käsemann studied the baptismal hymn of Col. 1: 15–20 ('Eine urchristliche Taufliturgie', 1949; ET 1964), the 'ordination paraenesis' in 1 Tim. 6: 11–16 ('Das Formular einer neutestamentlichen Ordinationsparänese', 1954), and the Johannine prologue ('Aufbau und Anliegen des johanneischen Prologs', 1957; ET 1969). For his form-critical studies in the gospels, see n. 12 below.

[8] Käsemann was arrested by the Gestapo in 1937 on account of his use of Isa. 26: 13 ('O Lord our God, other lords besides thee have ruled over us, but thy name alone we acknowledge' [RSV]; *KK* i. 36; Ehler 1986: 1 n. 1). The first draft of his study of Hebrews was written in prison (preface to the 2nd edn. of *Gottesvolk*). Käsemann's relationship with the Confessing Church was in itself not uneventful. In a letter to Bultmann, dated 11 Jan. 1941 (Bultmann Nachlaß), he explains his resignation from the Westfalian Confessing Church on the grounds of its decision to work with the German Christians in Synod. For Käsemann this indicated that it saw itself as merely a 'party' (*Fraktion*) within the church.

and the seed of the divine word always stands in conflict with the powers of ruin which attack it from all sides (1936: 15 f.).[9]

In 1941–2 Käsemann participated in a theological commission which was set up to examine the question of the participation of women 'curates' (*Vikarinnen*) in the ministry of preaching, a debate which had arisen due to the shortages of pastors.[10] In this commission, headed by J. Schniewind and E. Wolf, Käsemann attempted to break the deadlock caused by conservative Lutherans who regarded Paul's injunction to silence in 1 Cor. 14: 34 as an absolute bar on the participation of women in the ministry of preaching. Although by today's standards Käsemann's views seem very traditional,[11] he pointed to the role of women pneumatics and prophets in the Pauline churches and argued for a differentiated view of the ministry on the basis of Paul's doctrine of the charismata (*KK* i. 13 f.).

Käsemann's later theological work can be summarized as a comprehensive, historical and theological, attempt to interpret the New Testament in the light of two leading ideas. At the historical level, he sketches an outline of the New Testament period around the category of 'apocalyptic', by which he means the imminent expectation of the end. Simultaneously, he evaluates the various theologies which can be reconstructed from the study of the New Testament in the light of a theological criterion which is summarized in a number of catch-phrases, 'the justification of the ungodly', 'the theology of the cross', and 'the primacy of christology'. While he never published a New Testament theology organized in this way, the basis for such a work is outlined in essays of 1960–3[12] and

[9] Cf. Haufe 1971: 259.

[10] The papers from this commission, which include Käsemann's account of the place of women in the preaching ministry of the NT church ('Der Dienst der Frau an der Wortverkündigung nach dem NT'), and which are marked as 'missing' in the Käsemann bibliography, have recently been rediscovered.

[11] Käsemann notes that, at the time, the question of permanent women ministers (*Pastorin*, *Pfarrerin*, as opposed to *Vikarin*) was not even discussed (*KK* i. 15 f.).

[12] As early as 1937 Käsemann used eschatology as the theme around which the history of the eucharist in the NT period is to be understood ('Das Abendmahl im Neuen Testament'). This approach to early Christian history appears to have been further stimulated by his form-critical work in 'Sätze heiligen Rechtes im Neuen Testament' (1955; ET 1969) and by his interest in the prophetic character of the earliest Christian ministry. (For his call for a new approach to primitive Christian history, see *EVB* ii. 239 n. 1/236 n. 1.) His programme is outlined in 'Die Anfänge

is clear in his unpublished lectures on the theology of the New Testament.[13] In these lectures Käsemann argues that eschatology is the decisive category for the historian of the New Testament. Christology on its own will not suffice because, as W. Bousset showed, the history of christology is the history of borrowings from the cultural environment. Rather, the various christologies only came to expression in connection with the prevailing eschatologies ('Theologie' 41 f.). Käsemann summarizes his approach to the New Testament thus: 'The New Testament contents itself with the statement that Jesus as the Christ is the end-time revelation of God, and expresses this in many ways' (44).

Within this approach the starting-point is John the Baptist's message of imminent judgement. While Jesus made John's message his point of departure, 'his own preaching . . . did not bear a fundamentally apocalyptic stamp but proclaimed the immediacy of the God who was near at hand' (*EVB* ii. 99/101).[14] More precisely, Käsemann argues that Jesus preached an inaugurated eschatology, and cites the evidence of the parables (*EVB* i. 212/44 f.).

At this point the historical survey can be interrupted to note Käsemann's contribution to the debate about the historical Jesus.[15] His essay is a response to the apparent deadlock

christlicher Theologie' (1960; ET 1969) and 'Zum Thema der urchristlichen Apokalyptik' (1962; ET 1969), and is followed up in 'Paulus und der Frühkatholizismus' (1963; ET 1969) and 'Einheit und Vielfalt in der neutestamentlichen Lehre von der Kirche' (1963; ET 1969). Mark's gospel is included within this perspective in *Der Ruf der Freiheit* (73–8/55–8).

[13] These were duplicated for circulation among students. Judging by the books discussed in them, the undated copy I have consulted stems from the early 1960s. They are divided into 11 sections of which the last 3 are missing: the theological meaning of academic (*wissenschaftlich*) theology; the task and structure of NT theology; the problem of the canon; *sola scriptura* in current exegesis (in the work of H. Schlier, J. Jeremias, and H. Riesenfeld); NT eschatology as a hermeneutical problem (eschatology and history in the work of R. Bultmann, O. Cullmann, and W. Pannenberg); the problem of the historical Jesus; early Christian confession; early Christian enthusiasm; the theology of Paul; the gospels and gospel questions; and roads to early catholicism (and the theology of John).

[14] Cf. the important modification of this in 1962: the authentic Jesus material does not emphasize the apocalyptic element very strongly, 107 f./111 f.

[15] Robinson 1959 provides an initial survey of this debate. For the studies of Käsemann's contribution, see n. 39 below. Käsemann's influence on the revival of interest in the historical Jesus should not be overstated. Within the circle of Bultmann's pupils, but outside Germany, N. Dahl was working on this subject at the same time, though at first his essay appeared only in Norwegian (Dahl 1953).

brought about by Bultmann's view that Jesus is to be understood as part of 'late Judaism', and thus his life and teaching are merely a precondition for the study of New Testament theology.[16] In coming to this judgement Bultmann was giving historical support to M. Kähler's theological argument, directed at nineteenth-century liberal research into the life of Jesus, that Christian faith has as its object, not the Jesus of historical research, but the Christ who is preached.[17] While Käsemann does not wish to return to a liberal theology, he finds Bultmann's solution to the problem equally unsatisfactory in that it relegates Jesus to the side-lines of Christian theology. Noting that historical criticism, while hoping to find the historical Jesus behind the gospels, has found only the earliest community kerygma (*EVB* i. 194/22 f.), his solution is to argue that our only access to the historical Jesus is through the kerygma itself. 'The historical Jesus meets us in the New Testament . . . *not* as he was in himself, *not* as an isolated individual, but as the Lord of the community which believes in him' (194/23). The importance of eschatology re-emerges at this point: the gospels are, in the main, not interested in Jesus' biography, but in him as the eschatological event (200/30). But there is also a particularity about revelation: the eschatological event is tied to this human being from Nazareth (200/31). After reviewing further theological reasons for the gospel writers' interest in history, Käsemann argues that, despite theological variety among the evangelists, there is agreement 'that the history of Jesus [*die Historie Jesu*; ET: 'life history'] was constitutive for faith, because the earthly and the exalted Lord are identical' (203/33 f.).

Käsemann concludes with a brief sketch of the distinctive elements in the mission of Jesus as they can be ascertained by using the criterion of dissimilarity, i.e., by appealing only to material which does not show the influence of either Judaism or early Christianity.[18] Firstly, he highlights Jesus' authority over the law (206 f./37 ff.) and his abolition of the division between the sacred and the profane (207 f./39 f.). On these key points Käsemann sees a fundamental agreement between

[16] Bultmann 1948: 3, and 1949. [17] Kähler 1892/1896.

[18] Among many discussions of this criterion, see Dahl 1953, Perrin 1967, Barbour 1972.

Jesus and Paul: 'Because Jesus allies himself with the ungodly in the name of God, the Spirit permits the justification of the ungodly to be proclaimed and believed' (*PP* 284/165)—the 'justification of the ungodly' being Käsemann's favourite summary of Paul's theology. Secondly, Jesus is marked by a consciousness of inspiration, an immediate assurance of knowing and proclaiming the will of God (*EVB* i. 210/42). Thirdly, in Matt. 11: 25 f., Jesus pays John the Baptist the honour of being the initiator of the new age and yet gives himself a higher mission, presumably as the one who brings in the kingdom itself (210 f./42 f.). He does this, not as messiah (in line with Jewish expectation), nor as son of man (as he was to be understood by the earliest Christianity), but as the one who put his work, not his person, at the forefront of his preaching. (Post-Easter Christianity was therefore correct to acknowledge him as son of God and messiah; 211/44.) Thus, on the basis of this admittedly short sketch, Käsemann takes a middle line between the liberals and Bultmann on the question of the significance of the historical Jesus, and locates his distinctiveness in his preaching. This is available to us, in a modified but not unrecognizable form, in the tradition handed on by the early church. Käsemann sums up: 'The question of the historical Jesus is, in its legitimate form, the question of the continuity of the Gospel within the discontinuity of the times and within the variation of the kerygma' (213/46). He defends this position in a second article[19] against, on the one hand, the more conservative views of J. Jeremias and, on the other, the restatements of Bultmann's position by Bultmann himself and H. Braun.

After Easter, Jesus' message is replaced, in a certain sense, by a new 'apocalyptic' (*EVB* ii. 99 f./101 f.). This consists of imminent expectation of the end and a variety of concrete eschatological scenarios, and was closely connected with primitive Christian enthusiasm. Even the very earliest Christianity was marked by 'very severe theological tensions' and 'something very like a confessional controversy' among competing groups (83/83). The first group which Käsemann describes is the Jewish Christianity which can be detected

[19] 'Sackgassen im Streit um den historischen Jesus' (1964; ET 1969). Cf. also 'Die neue Jesus-Frage' (1975).

behind Matt. 5: 19, 10: 5 f. It took over the Jewish eschatological hopes of the restoration of the twelve tribes and of the pilgrimage of the nations to Zion. (Käsemann later added that the central feature of their hope was the return of Jesus as the son of man, 110/114.) Their conception of community order located the power of the spirit exclusively in the teaching office, and thus in an emerging Christian rabbinate. Secondly, there is a group who attack this ecclesiology in Matt. 23: 8–10 and who in turn are attacked for their enthusiastic piety in 7: 22–3 (84 f./84 f.). This second group are to be identified with the hellenists, and especially Stephen and the seven. For them temple and Torah have been superseded because of the gift of the spirit. (At the least they disregarded the cultic law in favour of the Gentile mission; 86 f./86 f.) This group was driven out of Jerusalem to Antioch and was ultimately dissolved into Pauline Christianity. A third group is Jewish Christian in ethos but, not being under the influence of Jerusalem, they preserved the enthusiastic traditions which were eventually deposited in the synoptic gospels and John (88 f./89 f.). They survived with itinerant prophetic leadership in small congregations on the borders of Palestine and Syria (91/92).

By contrast, the dominant ethos at Corinth was hellenistic enthusiasm which turned Christianity into a form of mystery religion. The key to their beliefs lies in realized eschatology (125/131): they proclaimed that the general resurrection had already occurred (cf. the situation opposed in 2 Tim. 2: 18). The enthusiasts deny the future, corporeal resurrection (which Paul affirms in his response to them in 1 Cor. 15), believing instead that they already partake in the resurrected Christ through the sacraments. The christology of this group is to be found in the pre-Pauline fragments in Phil. 2: 6 ff., Eph. 2: 5 ff., 5: 14; Col. 2: 12 f.: 'As participants in the Cross of Christ, the baptized are at the same time participants in his Resurrection and Enthronement, liberated from the old aeon of death and the powers and translated into the new aeon of the Kingdom of Christ' (120/125).

It is into this context that Paul's gospel comes as a critical power: he curbs hellenistic enthusiasm by his proclamation of the crucified Christ and through the 'apocalyptic' character of his theology (126/132). In the earthly sphere the Christian does not share in the resurrection of Christ; rather, participation in the heavenly life means that the *nova oboedientia* is made possible, the living out of justification by faith. Participation in the resurrection is a future hope. Secondly, the content of the resurrection is not primarily anthropological (i.e., it does not primarily affect the status of believers) but christological: it is Christ who is risen, it is he who reigns. But even his lordship is limited by the hope of the final lordship of God (1 Cor. 15: 28). Thus, it is in the course of Käsemann's use of eschatology as the key theme for the understanding of early Christianity that he made his now famous statement: 'Apocalyptic was the mother of all Christian theology—since we cannot really class the preaching of Jesus as theology' (100/102).[20] Within this perspective he argues that 'Even as a Christian Paul remained an apocalyptist'[21] (193/181, ET modified).

Käsemann made several contributions to wider debates on the basis of his view of Paul's theology, including the question of the ministry of women already noted. Thus, while agreeing with Bultmann on the need for demythologization in the task of interpreting scripture, he argues that Bultmann's error is to use, as the standard of that demythologization, a view of the human being simply as an individual (cf. Käsemann's criticism of a '*private* self-understanding', *PP* 48/25, my emphasis; cf. 65–7/34 f.; for a more formal statement, see 'Probleme' 144–6). For Käsemann the theology of the cross is the criterion for the whole theological enterprise, including demythologization. Much later it was Käsemann's

[20] Käsemann's essay of 1960, summed up in this statement, sparked off an immediate debate. For E. Fuchs the present is the source of God's revelation, according to Jesus, and thus it is this question which is the abiding source of theology (1961: 73). G. Ebeling was also critical: 'the ground on which we are authorized to think God and history together in the *right* way (that is, differentiatingly) lies not in apocalyptic, but the unapocalyptic fact of Jesus' (1961: 64) Bultmann himself responded in 1964: it is not apocalyptic but eschatology which is the mother of Christian theology. It was Paul's achievement to anchor and limit apocalyptic in present eschatology, which for him was more important—and not as Käsemann had argued, to anchor and limit present eschatology in apocalyptic. Paul raised belief in the presence of salvation from the sphere of speculation and enthusiasm to that of authentic human existence (1964*b*: 479 f.).

[21] E. Lohse (1971) replied by seeking to give 'apocalyptic' a much more limited role in Paul's theology.

understanding of the person and death of Christ, in addition to differences over the question of the correct approach to the interpretation of the Bible,[22] that caused so much offence to the pietists at the 1967 Kirchentag at Hanover. In 'Die Gegenwart des Gekreuzigten', based closely on his views of the theologies of Matthew, Paul, and Hebrews, Käsemann attacked the ghetto mentality, 'edifying' tendency, and overwhelmingly bourgeois character of much modern Christianity, and proclaimed the Christ who lived and died for the God, not of the pious, but of the godless. This Christ's existence is orientated solely to the first commandment. Correspondingly, the Christian life is to be understood as the discipleship of the crucified, in which we are called to exodus, the breaking out of our fixed encampments into the earthly no man's land in which true service can occur. Käsemann responded to the pietists' criticisms[23] of his address in his highly polemical writings of this period.[24]

The post-Pauline period in the New Testament is marked by a variety of responses to the problems of the Pauline period, the most important of which is the growth of 'early catholicism' (*Frühkatholizismus*).[25] The question of eschatology is again a key feature here. In an essay on 2 Peter,[26] Käsemann argues that this letter is not a true apology for early Christian eschatology. In it eschatology has been distorted into a blatant (*handfest*; ET: 'straightforward')

[22] Käsemann went over on to the offensive on this issue in 'Vom theologischen Recht historisch-kritischer Exegese' (1967). See also the earlier essay, 'Zum gegenwärtigen Streit um die Schriftauslegung' (1962; ET 1969).

[23] The tone of much of this debate can be judged from title 'Wie christlich ist Ernst Käsemann?' (Kopfermann 1967); cf. Asendorf 1967 and 1971—Käsemann replied to his former student in 'Erwiderung an Ulrich Asendorf', *Lutherische Monatshefte*, 6 (1967), 595–7; Findeisen *et al.* 1967. Klappert 1967 introduces and brings together articles from this debate which is discussed from an arbitrating standpoint in Jentsch 1968.

[24] Käsemann's ire erupted in the first edition of *Der Ruf der Freiheit* (1968); in later editions the polemic is tempered and redirected to more general targets, and additional chapters were added, making a more complete survey of the NT in the 5th, expanded and 'final', edn. of 1972 (the ET is of the 3rd, revised, edn. of 1968). The same polemical note characterizes many of the asides in *Paulinische Perspektiven* (1969; ET 1971) and is a major theme of his recent addresses collected in *Kirchliche Konflikte*, i. See also 'Das Evangelium und die Frommen' (1975; ET 1982).

[25] On the history of this concept see Schmitz 1977 and the forthcoming collection of articles, K. Kertelge, '*Frühkatholizismus*', Wege der Forschung (Darmstadt).

[26] 'Eine Apologie der urchristlichen Eschatologie' (1952; ET 1964).

doctrine of retribution. Thus, 2 Peter represents early catholicism because in it eschatology is only tenuously connected with christology; instead of being concerned with Christ's lordship, it is primarily concerned with the fate of Christians (*EVB* i. 146/181).

However, the most important witnesses to early catholicism in the New Testament are Acts, Ephesians, and the Pastoral Epistles. For Luke 'there is salvation only within the Church, whose history, thanks to divine guidance, shows a continuous progression'. He adapts the story of Paul's mission to this scheme so that Paul is seen as working under the authority of the mother church at Jerusalem (*EVB* ii. 243/240).[27] The central Pauline motif of an imminent expectation of the end is replaced with a scheme of salvation history. In Ephesians[28] another fundamental change takes place: Paul's concentration on the crucified lord, made present by his spirit, is replaced by the related but fundamentally different view of 'the sacramental presence of Christ in the Church for the world'. In this view the church becomes an integral factor in the salvation event (246/243). The difference between Paul and his later followers is clearest in their view of ministry. For Paul every Christian is a charismatic and shares in the priesthood of all believers. There is no mention of ordination and presbyterate; nor, strictly speaking, is there a cult because the gospel destroys the distinction between the sacred and the profane. Luke and the Pastorals replace this with written instructions for church order, which, according to Käsemann, include ordination, the monarchical bishop surrounded by presbyters, deacons, and co-workers, and apostolic succession (249/246 f.). 1 Clement and the Ignatian epistles are merely further important milestones on the road to 'a fully developed cultic praxis'.

The Gospel of John is in turn understood as a reaction to early catholicism: 'it contains no explicit idea of the Church,

[27] See also the articles 'Ephesians and Acts' (1966) and 'Die Johannesjünger in Ephesus' (1952; ET 1964).

[28] In addition to the first item in n. 27, see the dictionary article 'Epheserbrief' (1958) and especially the extended reviews of F. Mussner's *Christus, das All und die Kirche: Zur Theologie des Epheserbriefes* (1955; review, 1956) and H. Schlier's Ephesians commentary (2nd edn., 1958; review article, 'Das Interpretationsproblem des Epheserbriefes', 1961).

no doctrine of ministerial office, no developed sacramental theology' (264/255). It again strongly expresses the *solus Christus* theme and redefines the church as the company of those living under the word. These themes are developed at greater length, with the famous essay on the docetic nature of John's christology, in the Schaffer lectures of 1966.[29] Similarly, 3 John[30] represents the response by 'the presbyter', a Christian gnostic, to Diotrephes, a representative of early catholicism (*EVB* i. 178, 182). Salvation comes, not from sacraments nor legitimate church order, but from remaining under the word (184, 186). Thus the presbyter is both 'heretic', on account of his lack of interest in the tenets of early catholicism, and 'witness', on account of his promulgation of *simul iustus, simul peccator* (182), his stand against docetism—the point which divided him from gnosticism (178), and his retention of the early Christian belief that every Christian, and not just the ordained, possesses the spirit (186).

Käsemann's view of the New Testament as a whole naturally becomes clear in his studies of unity and diversity in the canon.[31] For him the question of the canon is bound up with the view of the church in the New Testament. He argues against the widespread assumption that the New Testament presents the theologian with a canon marked by theological unity, upon which the unity of the church is based. The New Testament kerygma is not in itself invariable; rather there is an extraordinary wealth of theological positions within primitive Christianity, and, furthermore, some of these positions are theologically incompatible (*EVB* i. 221/103). As a result, the New Testament, far from being the basis of the unity of the church, is the basis of the multiplicity of the confessions, each of which can find some justification for their own stance within its pages (22/103 f.).

[29] *Jesu letzter Wille nach Johannes 17* (1966, ET 1968; rev. German edn., 1971). Käsemann wrote some notable reviews in the sphere of Johannine studies, among which his review article of Bultmann's commentary (1941; review, 1946/7) and 'Zur Johannes-Interpretation in England' (1956/7) are particularly important.

[30] 'Ketzer und Zeuge. Zum johanneischen Verfasserproblem' (1951).

[31] See especially 'Begründet der neutestamentliche Kanon die Einheit der Kirche?' (1951/2; ET 1964) and *Das Neue Testament als Kanon: Dokumentation und kritische Analyse zur gegenwärtigen Diskussion* (1970).

Käsemann's solution to this problem is theological. The interpreter is called on to 'discern the spirits', to evaluate the statements of the New Testament theologically. The standard by which the theology of a writing, an author, or a group is to be judged is the doctrine of justification. In the interpretation of scripture this is expressed in the dialectic of letter and spirit, the Pauline motif Käsemann interprets in an essay of 1969.[32] It is the gospel (not the canon of scripture) which is the sole basis of the unity of the church, and the gospel cannot be identified with the scripture or the canon. The gospel is heard by the believer who is led by the spirit. The spirit manifests itself in scripture, but scripture without the spirit merely becomes 'letter', the claim on human beings to earn their own salvation by works of the law (221 ff./104 ff.). It is clear that this theological principle of evaluation or 'canon within the canon' (*PP* 282/165) is based on Käsemann's understanding of Paul's gospel, the centre of which is the doctrine of justification.

On the basis of this view of the New Testament Käsemann made a controversial and important contribution to the ecumenical movement at the Fourth World Conference for Faith and Order in Montreal in 1963. His address, 'Unity and Multiplicity in the New Testament Doctrine of the Church', which again emphasized the diversity of views of the church within the New Testament itself, and which regarded the unity of the church as an eschatological quality, ran counter to the then dominant view of the World Council of Churches which had taken as a model the supposedly unified church of the New Testament (*KK* i. 241).[33]

Since his retirement Käsemann's interests have widened to questions of social and economic justice on a world-wide scale. This development was undoubtedly accelerated by personal tragedy: his daughter Elisabeth, who had been working in Latin America for nearly a decade, was murdered in an Argentinian jail on 24 May 1977, fourteen months after the

[32] 'Geist und Buchstabe' (1969; ET 1971). Ehler takes this as his starting-point for his exposition of Käsemann's theology (1986: 71 ff.).

[33] Käsemann gave his own account of the conference in 'Einheit und Wahrheit: Bericht über die Faith-and-Order-Konferenz in Montreal 1963' (1964).

military take-over.[34] In the same year, apart from attempting to disentangle the truth about his daughter's fate from the disinformation put out by the military regime, and criticizing the passivity of the foreign office in Bonn, he took up the cause of left-wing Christian students in the University of Tübingen who had fallen foul of conservative church leaders.[35] His argument for the freedom of the young to make mistakes, coupled with his threat to leave the church over the issue, resulted in extensive coverage in the national press. Finally, Käsemann notes that his participation at the World Conference for Mission and Evangelization in Melbourne in 1980 convinced him that Christianity is no longer determined by the white man (*KK* i, 242). Many of the addresses collected in *Kirchliche Konflikte*, i (1982), reflect these new interests, as does the as yet unpublished 'Gottesgerechtigkeit bei Paulus', in which a very clear development can be observed in comparison to the essay of the same title of 1961.

Two main themes have emerged from this review of Käsemann's life and work. Firstly, it has been shown that his exegetical work, while often having the appearance of being concerned with individual problems of exegesis, is carried out within the framework of a coherent interpretation of the New Testament as a whole. As has been seen the two central themes are, on the one hand, eschatology, the theme around which the history of New Testament Christianity is reconstructed, and, on the other, the 'theology of the cross', which acts as a theological criterion by which the various understandings of Christianity within the New Testament are judged. Secondly, it has been seen that Käsemann's view of Paul's theology is the centre of the entire construction. (Apart from any other considerations, it is in Paul that Käsemann finds these two themes in the theologically correct relationship to one another.) Other writings contribute key themes to Käsemann's theology (the 'wandering' or pilgrimage of the people of God, and the church as the community under the word, being

[34] 'Tod im argentinischen Dschungel: Geschichte und Deutung einer Ermordung' (1977); see also Käsemann's preface to Thun 1985 (*Menschenrechte und Aussenpolitik: Bundesrepublik Deutschland-Argentinien 1976–1983*).

[35] Earlier Käsemann, with H. Gollwitzer, was one of the few professors to support the students in the unrest of 1967–8, though he was also criticized for not taking a radical enough stance (*EvK* 1 (1968), 241, 293, 344 f.).

based on Hebrews and John respectively), but these do not effect the structure of the whole. Thus, if Käsemann's view of Paul's theology is the centre-piece and orientation point of his interpretation of the New Testament,[36] a detailed study of it will shed light on his contribution to New Testament studies and modern theology.

Käsemann's interest in Paul is not, however, reflected in the discussion of his work.[37] The published monographs[38] include sections on the interpretation of Paul, but, like the unpublished dissertations, though with one exception,[39] their focus of interest lies elsewhere. It is also noticeable that none of the longer studies analyses the relationship between historical and theological concerns, nor do they discuss the problems which arise from this dual interest.

The approach of this study

In the light of these points the aims and scope of the present study, which is intended as a contribution to the history of the interpretation of the New Testament, can be outlined.

36 So also Scroggs 1985: 261.

37 A similar lack of attention to Pauline interpretation is noted by W. G. Kümmel with regard to studies of Bultmann (Kümmel 1984, 174), although in Bultmann's case, Paul does not dominate his life's work to the same extent.

38 P. Gisel studies Käsemann with a view to answering the question of what theology is, with particular reference to the question of its place and function, concluding that it is the theological interpretation and practice of history (1977: 30, 653). B. Ehler (1986) keeps much closer to Käsemann's own concerns in expounding Käsemann's understanding of the question of the centre of scripture. Thus both these monographs are primarily concerned with Käsemann as a theologian and not as an exegete, although Ehler is concerned with Käsemann as an interpreter of scripture. Cf. also H. Häring, *Kirche und Kerygma. Das Kirchenbild in der Bultmannschule* (1972), 293–355, and H. J. Schmitz, *Frühkatholizismus bei Adolf von Harnack, Rudolph Sohm und Ernst Käsemann* (1977), 145–201.

39 The exception is G. Ince, 'Creation, Justification, Resurrection: An Exposition and Critique of Käsemann's Romans' (1987), which, however, deals only with Romans and focuses heavily on ch. 4. See also W. J. Close, 'The Theological Relevance of History. The Role, Logic and Propriety of Historical Understanding in Theological Reflection. Considered in the Context of the Debate on the Historical Jesus between Rudolf Bultmann and Ernst Käsemann' (1972); S. A. Foster, 'The Canons of Historical Authenticity in the Writings of R. Bultmann, G. Bornkamm and E. Käsemann' (1976); D. W. Sandifer, 'History and Existential Interpretation: The Debate between Ernst Käsemann and Rudolf Bultmann' (1979). Other shorter studies will be noted below.

The basis of this study is a systematic account of Käsemann's interpretation of Paul.[40] His exegetical work has been divided into two periods: in Chapter 2 Käsemann's publications up to 1950 are discussed and the work of the period after 1960 is treated in Chapters 3–5. While there are many points of continuity and overlap between the two periods, there are also important differences:

1. In the first period the New Testament is read primarily against the history-of-religions background of hellenism and gnosticism; in the second, against the background of Jewish 'apocalyptic'.[41]

2. In the first period Käsemann focuses primarily on Paul's participatory themes (baptism, the spirit, the 'in Christ' formula, the body of Christ, etc.); in the second on the doctrine of justification and its ramifications throughout Paul's theology. (The theme of eschatology is a constant concern in both periods.)

3. Käsemann is consistently concerned with the theological, as opposed to the merely historical, interpretation of Paul, but the concern to defend a particular doctrinal position through the interpretation of the apostle's theology becomes a dominating factor only in the second period.

4. In the second period Käsemann makes his theological and exegetical debate with Bultmann explicit.

5. The periods can be called pre-1950 and post-1960 although Käsemann published one, relatively unimportant, essay on Paul in the 1950s ('Eine paulinische Variation des "amor fati"'; 1959, ET 1969). During this decade his attention was taken up with the problems of the historical Jesus and early catholicism. It is also the case that, while a letter of 1949 shows the direction in which Käsemann's thinking on the history-of-religions question was going, the move from a 'gnostic' to an 'apocalyptic' Paul was not completed before the end of the 1950s.

[40] Although Käsemann never explicitly discusses the question of how many of the Pauline letters are authentic, he accepts the consensus of the Bultmann school (1 Thess., Gal., 1 and 2 Cor., Phil., Philem., and Rom.: so Bornkamm 1969: 241 f.).

[41] On this point it needs to be emphasized that the division into pre-1950 and post-1960 periods refers to the dates of publication of Käsemann's work. For an earlier indication of Käsemann's change of view on the history-of-religions question, see pp. 122 f. below.

One major change in Käsemann's views predates the division outlined here. In his dissertation, published in 1933, the centre of Paul's thought is found in the themes of baptism, the Lord's supper, the spirit, and the 'in Christ' motif; in short, in the participatory themes. In all his other work, though with particular emphasis after 1960, the doctrine of justification is seen as the centre of Paul's theology. There is, however, despite this change, a remarkable degree of consistency in Käsemann's views. Under the catch-phrase 'the lordship of Christ' he presents a unified view of Paul's theology in which all the individual themes are integrated. The insights of the pre-1950 studies, which deal with the participatory themes, are neither rejected nor left on one side, but are integrated into an interpretation which centres on the doctrine of justification. Käsemann's solution to the problem of the unity of Paul's thought is to interpret the major elements of his thought in the light of one another: the participatory themes are interpreted in the light of the doctrine of justification, and vice versa. At the same time it is maintained that Paul's thought as a whole is determined by his eschatology.

This analysis can be related directly to the history of interpretation. The dominant interpretation in German Protestant historical-critical circles at the end of the nineteenth century saw Paul's religion as comprising two or three disparate elements. By contrast, in the period between the wars, Barth, Schlatter, and Bultmann, each in his own way, presented a unified view of Paul's theology. Käsemann has roots in both these traditions and seeks to resolve the conflict between them. Thus, his lifelong commitment to the interpretation of Paul's theology[42] is not to be understood merely as a defence of the traditional Lutheran interpretation in which justification by faith is regarded as the central doctrine. Rather, it is an attempt to overcome the fragmented view of nineteenth-century critical exegesis—precisely by integrating the insights of that exegesis into a view of Paul which is fundamentally

42 With Barth, Schlatter, and Bultmann, Käsemann presupposes that the subject of Pauline studies is the apostle's theology, and not merely his religion (cf. Käsemann's comments on Romans, *Römer* p. iv/p. vii), as will become clear later in this chapter.

indebted to the Lutheran doctrinal tradition, as expounded by Barth, Schlatter, and Bultmann.[43] Secondly, with regard to Käsemann's place in the history of interpretation, as is well known, he attempts to correct Bultmann's view of Paul's theology at certain key points. Käsemann's criticisms of other types of interpretation will also be noted.

Turning to questions of hermeneutics, it will be argued that the phrase 'the lordship of Christ' is not to be understood as an interpretation of particular Pauline words, for example, *κύριος* or *βασιλεία*; nor is it the result of the exegesis of passages in Paul's letters which deal explicitly with the theme of lordship. Rather, it is a construct, arising out of the interpretation of a large number of individual Pauline motifs and themes. Chapter 2 will show how this construct arises in Käsemann's work, and the remaining chapters how other major themes of Paul's theology are incorporated within this approach.

On a wider front, attention will be paid to the question of the relationship between historical and theological interpretation of New Testament texts. For the most part this question, which has posed a constant problem since the emergence of historical criticism, has been discussed in relation to the question of New Testament theology.[44] However, the same issues arise with any part of the New Testament, and particularly with those parts which have been influential in the doctrinal history of Christianity. Given the importance of Paul's theology for the Lutheran tradition, it is not surprising that the interpretation of Paul's religion and theology has been a major focus of exegetical and theological debate among scholars of this tradition.[45] With reference to the interpretation of Paul, this study analyses how Käsemann's exegetical

[43] The interpretations of these theologians can be called 'Lutheran' in the sense that they emphasize the doctrine of justification in Paul (even though Barth and Schlatter were not Lutherans). However, they also relate this doctrine to eschatology, thereby modifying the traditional Lutheran interpretation and allowing Barth and Schlatter to introduce a Reformed emphasis on the sovereignty of God.

[44] It is discussed in Morgan 1973 with particular reference to the exemplary positions of Wrede and Schlatter, and the major contribution of Bultmann. Cf. also the introduction and collection of articles in Strecker 1975. It is noticeable that these discussions (and that of Merk 1972) all focus on the German Protestant tradition, where these questions have been pursued most vigorously.

[45] See Morgan 1982.

and theological interests are related to each other. Thus, it is a case-study of how one interpreter interprets scripture historically *and* theologically.[46]

In order to distinguish between, and relate, various types of interpretation it has proved useful—particularly with reference to Käsemann's earlier work—to speak of different 'levels' of interpretation. Thus 'level 1' interpretation refers to the individual techniques of historical-critical exegesis: philology, text criticism, form criticism, history-of-religions work, and the like. These individual techniques are to be distinguished from the historical reconstructions to which they contribute. In these 'level 2' interpretations, the interpreter attempts to reconstruct Paul's religion or theology on the presupposition that there is a connection between the various subjects of his occasional letters. Finally, 'level 3' interpretation refers to contemporary theological statements which are based on level 1 or 2 interpretations.

In the tradition of interpretation in which Käsemann stands, which received powerful expression in the prefaces to Barth's Romans, this third level of interpretation is closely connected with level 2, the interpretation of Paul's thought. According to Barth, the interpreter can or does know, or at least can discover, something of the 'subject-matter' (*die Sache*) of the text. (The precise relationship between the subject-matter and the text became a matter of debate, as will be seen.) Thus, as the final subject-matter of Romans is held to be God, interpretation along these lines claims to be talk of God, not merely an account of what Paul believed. Here the interpreter does theology by interpreting the historical text. The relationships between these levels of interpretation will be a subject of this study.

Finally, the task of charting the reception of Käsemann's views is begun and exegetical criticisms are offered at some points.

[46] From the different perspective of systematic theology, Kelsey 1975 presents case-studies of the types of decisions which theologians take when they take scripture to be authoritative for theology.

KÄSEMANN'S INTERPRETATION OF PAUL: A SUMMARY

In order to set Käsemann's interpretation of Paul's theology within the history of interpretation, and in particular to indicate the historical-critical and theological context in which his views arose, it will be useful to provide a summary of his view of Paul's theology. In the following chapters a historical account will be given, which will trace the development of his views; here a general summary will be sufficient.

Käsemann is constantly concerned with the question of the centre of Paul's theology and the illumination of the whole by identifying that centre. Until the contrary is proved, it is presupposed that Paul's theology has a dominating centre and an inner unity. This centre is the motif of God's righteousness (*δικαιοσύνη θεοῦ*), or, to state the point in doctrinal terms, the doctrine of justification. God's righteousness is understood simultaneously as his gift and his power, and the whole of Paul's theology is determined by the gift–power dialectic.

The theme of God's righteousness determines Paul's understanding of who God is: he is the one who justifies the ungodly, gives life to the dead, and calls into existence the things which do not exist (Rom. 4: 5, 17). Here the eschatological orientation and cosmic scope of Paul's theology can be seen. The doctrine of justification is not restricted to the individual. To understand it in this way is to miss the fundamental point that God's righteousness is his lordship, his kingdom, which makes its claim on the world. It is his 'right' or rightful claim on a creation which has been made subject to the lordship of sin. (The cosmic scope of Paul's theology is expressed in terms of a conceptuality based on the gnostic aeon in Käsemann's interpretation of Paul up to about 1950, and in terms of the 'apocalyptic' character of Paul's theology in the post-1960 period.)

A human being is a 'piece of world' and a representative of the world; God makes his claim on the world through this 'piece of world'. This has the corollary that it is human beings in their corporeality with which God has to do: corporeality is the goal of all God's activity. Here again Paul's theology does not focus on the individual but on human beings in their solidarity with the world.

The salvific revelation of God's righteousness reveals a unity in the divine activity: there is a correspondence between God's action in the primal time (creation) and the end-time (eschatological new creation). However, the temporal framework of Paul's thought must not be limited to creation and the present: Paul also looks forward to the parousia when God will be all in all. The present experience of salvation is incomplete and subject to constant attack, and it is only at the end that the creation will know the freedom of the children of God. Thus, there is a *future* hope. At the same time the character of this future *hope* must be respected: the kingdom of God is not yet fully realized on earth, nor in the church. This 'eschatological reservation' has profound implications for the understanding of the church and the Christian life.

Paul's understanding of salvation history is also determined by the doctrine of justification; to reverse this relationship is to misunderstand Paul fundamentally. Salvation history is the history of the hearing of God's word, either before Christ, as promise, or as the gospel. Salvation history, thus defined, is always accompanied by its opposite, the history of perdition. The gospel calls forth faith, but is also met by disbelief and superstition, and by misappropriation in the forms of legalism and enthusiasm. Thus salvation history cannot be understood in terms of an immanent continuity within history. The only continuity in history is that created by God's activity, an activity which is to be designated as 'miracle'. In addition, salvation history is characterized by the conflicting spheres of Adam (fall), Moses (law), Abraham (promise), Christ (gospel), and the future hope (God's unopposed reign). With the exception of the last named, these spheres are not simply consecutive stages in the history of salvation, but overlapping and conflicting spheres of power. Human beings are not free agents who make their own choices; rather they are caught up in the conflict between the various lordships, and confirm or deny the lordship under which they stand.

Similarly Paul understood the Old Testament in the light of his doctrine of justification. In fact he was the first in Christian history to develop a theological hermeneutic. This is summed up in the opposition of the spirit and the letter: under the former, the Old Testament is understood as the promise of the righteousness of faith; under the latter, the divine intention laid down in the Old Testament (and particularly in the law) is understood as a demand for works.

If the doctrine of God is determined by the theme of justification, the same is also true of the understanding of human beings and of salvation. Human beings are fallen creatures who try to attain salvation by their own efforts or achievement. Because of their fallen status, this effort leads to either pride or despair. The only hope is God's righteousness which reduces human beings to nothing and creates them anew. Thus God's righteousness issues in the justification of the ungodly which is his free gift to those who have no works or achievement of their own. God's gift is received by faith, and consequently is called the righteousness of faith; as such it stands in radical opposition to the righteousness of works.

It is correct to understand Paul's theology in terms of God's righteousness, but only if it is constantly borne in mind that concretely this is revealed in the gospel, whose content is Jesus Christ. Thus, the content of the righteousness of God is the lordship of Christ, and the latter is marked by the same gift–power structure. Concretely, it is Christ's lordship which is preached, experienced (as grace and judgement) in the worship of the church, and made visible in the life of the Christian. Christ's lordship only disappears from view at the end when God becomes all in all.

As noted, the lordship of Christ is itself defined by God's righteousness, or the doctrine of justification. Paul's takes up the christological and soteriological traditions of hellenistic Christianity but modifies them to express his own theology of justification. The soteriological motifs of the earliest hellenistic Christianity (sacrifice, forgiveness of sins, expiation, reconciliation) are used by him only to indicate that human beings cannot achieve salvation by themselves. His own understanding of soteriology and christology is formulated in terms of the antithetical sovereignty (lordship) of Adam on the one side and Christ on the other. When human beings are confronted by the gospel and accept it in faith they are transferred from one sphere of sovereignty to another; they undergo a change (or exchange) of lordship. This understanding of soteriology coheres with Paul's anthropology in which human beings are not understood as isolated individuals, free to choose from a variety of possibilities. Human beings are always under a lord; their actions merely ratify or deny the lordship under which they stand. In Paul's christology Adam and Christ determine the destiny of their respective worlds and, consequently, they are not merely models but prototypes. As both are cosmic figures Christ is the *cosmocrator*, or better, the designated *cosmocrator*, as his world rule is not yet uncontested.

The church is primarily understood as the body of Christ, the sphere in which he is lord on earth before the parousia. Paul only uses the people of God motif to indicate the place of the church in salvation history, and in debate with Jewish Christianity. Christ is present in the church through the spirit but first and foremost he remains its lord and judge. In the supper the community is confronted with the lord in grace and judgement—and thus, in Paul's thought, even the cultic sphere is understood in the light of the doctrine of justification. Further, the body of Christ motif again expresses the cosmic scope of Paul's theology: in and through his body Christ reaches out for the whole world. Baptism and the Lord's supper incorporate people into the body of Christ.

The key to this part of Paul's theology is the virtual identity of 'in Christ' and 'in the spirit'. However, Paul guards against enthusiasm by insisting that the work of the spirit issues in the *nova oboedientia* (the living out of the doctrine of justification in everyday life), and in standing fast in the face of temptation and suffering. Even the spirit is set under the eschatological reservation: the present experience of the spirit is only the pledge of future glory. Thus, before the parousia, the church and the believer are never removed from the sphere of temptation and weakness. They remain the disciples of the crucified; it is their lord alone who has been removed from the earthly sphere. This is the case even in the worship of the church. Glossolalia, which to the enthusiast is the sign of angelic status, is seen by Paul as evidence of the church's weakness and of its continuing solidarity with the unredeemed world.

The central idea in Paul's view of ministry is his doctrine of charismata. A charisma is the concretion and individuation of grace, the specific part that an individual has in the lordship of Christ. Consequently, it too has the character of gift and power: the Christian is enabled by the gift, and claimed by God for service. Because a charisma is God's gift, it frees human beings from the nexus of the law and the attempt to earn salvation by their own achievement. In this way the charisma doctrine is the projection of the doctrine of justification into the sphere of ecclesiology. Further, because a charisma is a specific gift, it carries with it a limit. Boundaries are set on the ministry of the charismatic who thereby becomes dependent on the gifts of others, which in turn leads to the building up of the community. The charisma doctrine is the basis of the priesthood of all believers. Authority within the community is not based on office but exists in the concrete act of service. Even apostleship is no more, and no less, than the particular calling in which the apostle experiences the determining power of the gospel as a compelling destiny.

Christian ethics can be summed up as 'lived justification'. Sanctification is not a separate stage of the Christian life, in which human beings can fall back into legalism by attempting to earn their own salvation by works. Rather, it is living in the light of God's justifying grace, afresh in each new situation. As God's action does not take place in a special sacred sphere, and does not create such a sphere—because, in Paul's eschatological perspective, the whole world is the place of God's presence and thus the idea of sacred places, times, and people is abolished—Christians are called to daily obedience in everyday life. This is the sphere in which Christians confirm Christ's lordship by their action. Worship and ethics coincide.

Christian life before the parousia is the place of the conflict between the old and new aeons, and thus the Christian and the church are constantly assailed or tempted. To pretend to escape from this—even on the grounds of having received the spirit—is enthusiasm. Again, as Christians do not already experience the full liberty of the children of God, they still have to pay due respect to earthly realities, including earthly authority. However, the obligation of obedience to earthly authorities is not absolute. It no longer applies if the situation is such that the obedience of the Christian no longer retains the character of service. God's righteousness and the entire Christian life are summed up in the first commandment and in the first beatitude, both of which proclaim the dialectic of absolute grace and absolute claim.

In the following sections the theological and historical-critical context of Käsemann's interpretation of Paul's theology will be sketched. It will not, of course, be possible to give a full account of the history of Pauline interpretation, nor even to deal comprehensively with the views of those relevant to the present line of enquiry. Attention will be paid to those aspects of the theological and intellectual background which are important for Käsemann's interpretation of Paul's theology.

MARTIN LUTHER AND THE LUTHER RENAISSANCE

Although Käsemann makes very few explicit references to the reformer Martin Luther (1483–1546), it is his theology and interpretation of Paul which determine Käsemann's position most fundamentally. Not only was Käsemann brought up within this tradition (*KK* i. 241); it was also reinforced by the 'Luther renaissance'[47] (*KK* i. 9) which contributed to the change in direction in German-language theology in the 1920s. Käsemann does not discuss Luther's interpretation of Paul, nor the newly rediscovered lectures on Romans (cf. *Römer* p. iii/p. vii); rather, he takes certain fundamental theological doctrines from Luther. First among these is the conviction that the doctrine of justification is the centre of Paul's theology and of Christian theology. It is this conviction about the centrality of the doctrine of justification in Paul that is intended by the phrase 'the Lutheran view of Paul'.[48] Luther understood Romans as 'the gospel in its purest expression',[49] and argued that the theme of God's

[47] Böhmer 1905/1918 and Wolf 1933, 1934 give accounts of the Luther renaissance.

[48] On this subject, see now Watson 1986: 2–10.

[49] Luther 1522: 19.

righteousness is the centre of the epistle.[50] As is well known, he connects the radical change in his own theology with the interpretation of this theme.[51] God's righteousness is not 'the righteousness whereby God is righteous and deals righteously in punishing the unrighteous' but 'that righteousness whereby, through grace and sheer mercy, he justifies us by faith'.[52] Both the focus on this theme as found in the epistle to the Romans, and Luther's interpretation of righteousness as the righteousness which is valid before God because it it given by him, are important to Käsemann.

The interpretation of Luther's theology played an important role in the debate in the 1920s on the question of the nature of theology itself. This debate between dialectical[53] and liberal theologians is exemplified in the exchange between F. Gogarten (1887–1967) and K. Holl (1866–1926). Gogarten, one of the principal exponents of dialectical theology, takes Holl's celebrated essays on Luther[54] as typical of liberal misunderstanding of the reformer. The misunderstanding does not concern Holl's unrivalled detailed knowledge of Luther but the theological presuppositions from which he interprets his theology. For Holl, Luther's theology is fundamentally orientated to morality, in the tradition of Kant where the moral is the highest value. Consequently theology is said to be science (*Wissenschaft*) which must respect its limits and speak about human knowledge of the religious and the moral.[55] By contrast, for Luther, in Gogarten's view, theology must protect its own special concern, the gospel. Theology is a proclamation of the gospel, not the taking of a historical or psychological inventory.[56] Here one of the fundamental principles of dialectical theology—that theology has a subject-

[50] Luther 1515/16: 17 f. and n. 40.

[51] In the preface to his lectures on Galatians, Luther calls the doctrine of justification the 'one solid rock', and links this with faith in Christ: 'For the one doctrine which I have supremely at heart, is that of faith in Christ, from whom, through whom and unto whom all my theological thinking flows back and forth day and night.' (1535: 16) Cf. Bruce 1963: 59.

[52] Bruce 1963: 59. On Luther's understanding of the righteousness of God, see McGrath 1986: 3–19.

[53] Important early essays in dialectical theology are collected in Moltmann 1962 and 1963.

[54] Holl 1921. See also Holl's reply to Gogarten (Holl 1924).

[55] Gogarten 1924: 34 f.

[56] Ibid. 37–9.

matter of its own—comes into view. This is the basis of its criticism of nineteenth-century liberal theology, and a cause which Käsemann has championed down to the present day (*KK* i. 233 ff.).

Two particular points in Gogarten's view of Luther are also of importance. Firstly, he agrees with Holl that the first commandment sums up Luther's theology: in the first commandment God passes the deepest judgement on human beings and yet simultaneously promises to maintain covenant with them; God destroys and yet allows to live.[57] This interpretation of the first commandment with its dialectic of grace and judgement (the *ad nihilum redigi*)[58] is fundamental to Käsemann's view of Paul. Secondly, Gogarten argues that Christ is not secondary in Luther's piety as Holl had claimed. It is true that Luther does not develop a 'Christ piety' or 'mysticism', nor does he speak of an I–Thou relationship between Christ and the believer. However, Christ is and remains the revelation of the divine act of redemption. Whereas Holl starts from Jesus the human being whose divinity lies in his peculiar consciousness of God, Luther starts from Christ as God who becomes incarnate in this human being, Jesus Christ. Käsemann does not take up the details of Luther's christology and soteriology as expounded by Gogarten[59] but the christological determination of theology does become a major concern of his.

In the understanding of christology, Käsemann is indebted to H. J. Iwand's (1899–1960)[60] study of Luther's lectures on Romans. Iwand argues that the mutual relationship (*gegenseitige Aufeinanderbezogensein*) between christology and justification is the sign of authenticity in Christian faith.[61] This becomes a key point in Käsemann's view of Paul's theology. In a characteristic argument on two fronts, he maintains that the

[57] Ibid. 40.

[58] Käsemann acknowledges the influence of Gogarten's view of the young Luther on this point ('Erwiderung' 596).

[59] Ibid. 70–6. In particular Käsemann does not take up the metaphysical structure of Luther's theology, nor the soteriology of the 'exchange of qualities' in which Christ takes on humanity's sin while human beings take on Christ's sonship.

[60] Käsemann and Iwand were colleagues, briefly, at Göttingen and he is among those to whom *Kirchliche Konflikte*, i. is dedicated.

[61] Iwand 1930: 7.

mutual relationship between the two themes ensures that christology does not become a doctrinal abstraction, and that justification is not 'reduced' anthropologically or individualistically. The justification of the individual believer must not be separated from the controlling theme of the lordship of Christ.

Luther's understanding of this last theme, the *regnum Christi*, is summarized in a study by W. Trillhaas. For Luther, Jesus Christ is my lord because he redeemed me and won me from sin, death, and the power of the devil. The lordship of Christ is opposed to the power (*Gewalt*) of the devil, not the rule of earthly rulers. Most important of all, however, is the point made in the interpretation of Ps. 2 in 1519. Here the idea of the lordship of Christ is put under the ruling theme of the *theologia crucis*.[62] It is the suffering Christ who is acknowledged as lord. He is lord as the crucified one. Thus, his kingdom is paradoxical, beyond our conception (*unanschaulich*), and can only be recognized in faith. Further, because Christ's lordship is the lordship of the crucified one, it provides a way through temptation (*Anfechtung*), the constant situation of the Christian in this life.[63] Salvation does not remove the Christian or the church from temptation and attack, and any attempt to escape this reality is to succumb to 'enthusiasm'.

Finally, Käsemann also takes up from Luther the notion of the gospel being at war on two fronts. The gospel is under constant attack from the dual tendencies of nomism (the attempt to win salvation by one's own works and thus have a claim against God) and enthusiasm (the attempt to use God's gifts to win autonomy from him).[64] These two tendencies are embodied ecclesiologically in Catholic and sectarian Christianity respectively.[65] Theology itself is involved in the war on

[62] Cf. also the argument, summed up in the title of M. Kähler's book, *Das Kreuz: Grund und Maß für die Christologie* (1911).

[63] Trillhaas 1967: 42–5.

[64] For Luther, enthusiasm (*Schwärmerei*) is rooted in the attempt by Christians to avoid the tension of living simultaneously in two realms, the realm in which fallen creation is preserved by God's laws of creation and the natural orders of government, family, etc., and the realm of the new creation in Christ. In this life, Christians are and remain sinners, and as such continue to be subject to the judgement of law; to claim that they are not under the powers of law, sin, and death is enthusiasm (Krodel 1965). For enthusiasm as a history-of-religions category, see p. 143 below.

[65] Thus, for example, in the Preface to Galatians, Luther criticizes the Papacy and the Anabaptists (1535: 17–19). For both Luther and Käsemann the concrete

two fronts and has an inherently polemical character. In keeping with the critical power of the gospel, the theologian's task is to distinguish between the spirit and the letter, to unmask nomism and enthusiasm wherever they may be found.

In the following sections the question of the correct interpretation of the theological heritage of the Reformation (and its relationship to Paul's theology) will never be far from the surface. This issue was particularly acute in the latter part of the nineteenth century when the traditional Lutheran interpretation of Paul came under severe attack from (Lutheran) historians seeking to give a historical interpretation of Paul.

ASPECTS OF THE HISTORICAL-CRITICAL STUDY OF PAUL FROM F. C. BAUR TO A. SCHWEITZER

If Käsemann's view of Paul is indebted to Luther for some key theological themes, his interpretation also stands in the tradition of the historical-critical study of Paul's religion and theology going back to F. C. Baur (1792–1860).[66] Baur is important to Käsemann, not only on account of the impetus he gave to historical-critical study in general, but because he attempts to interpret the New Testament theologically and sets Paul's theology at the centre of that project.[67] In Käsemann's introduction to the volume of Baur's selected works devoted to historical-critical studies of the New Testament, he notes that Baur was the master of detailed study and offered a total interpretation ('Baur' p. xi) which is marked by powerful logical consistency (p. xiv).

However, Baur's theology embodies much of what Käsemann rejects in nineteenth-century liberalism, despite Baur's own

opponents in the war on two fronts may change, and the two fronts become general tendencies in theology. When Käsemann debates with 'Catholic' interpretation, this is sometimes with a stereotyped model of Catholic theology but at other points very specifically with the work of his fellow Bultmann pupil and contemporary H. Schlier (1904–82), who converted to Roman Catholicism. On the second front, Käsemann debates with pietism and its interpretation of the NT.

[66] On Baur, see Kümmel 1958, part IV *passim* and Hodgson 1966; for his view of the nature of NT theology, Bultmann 1953: 244 f. and Morgan 1977 and 1985.

[67] Morgan 1977, especially 203 f.

appeal to the Reformation (p. xvi). Käsemann argues that he failed to distinguish adequately between his Reformation heritage and the premisses of a Protestantism influenced by rationalism. Instead of using the gospel of the righteousness of faith as the criterion of his theology, he used 'the self-manifestation of the spirit in its totality on the road to immanent historical progress' (p. xxiv). With Barth and others, Käsemann rejects this understanding of revelation with its Hegelian sense of progress in history.

With respect to the interpretation of Paul,[68] Käsemann notes that Baur understood the apostle as a very important representative of the hellenistic church whose specific contribution is in the sphere of anthropology (*EVB* ii. 125/131; *PP* 17/6). In addition, he highlights the point that, in his attempt to understand Romans historically, Baur regarded chapters 9–11 as the peak and thematic centre of the epistle. By doing so he put his finger on the weakest point in the Lutheran interpretation of Paul, the tendency to regard these chapters as an excursus, a weakness which was challenged by Wrede and Schweitzer (*PP* 110/61; *Römer* 244/253). Käsemann takes up the challenge of this question: how can Paul's theology be understood within its historical context while holding on to the central insight of the Lutheran interpretation? Alternatively the question can be put in terms of the interpretation of Romans: what is the relationship between the first eight chapters and chapters 9–11? In theological terms this becomes the question of the relationship of justification and salvation history.

The second major influence on Käsemann originating in the nineteenth century is the work of the group of scholars known as the history-of-religions school.[69] Like Baur, they

[68] Morgan 1978 gives an account of Baur's major study of Paul (1845) and reports on the section on Paul in his lectures on NT theology (Morgan 1977: 203–5). He shows that Baur's view of Paul, with its focus on the antithesis of works and faith, applied to Judaism and Christianity, owes more to the Lutheran tradition than is generally realized (1978: 6).

[69] The members of the school in the first generation were A. Eichhorn (1856–1926), H. Gunkel (1862–1932), W. Bousset (1865–1920), W. Heitmüller (1869–1926), W. Wrede (1859–1906), and J. Weiss (1863–1914). On the school, see Kümmel 1958: part V; Ittel 1958; on Gunkel, Klatt 1969; and on Bousset and the whole school, Verheule 1973; and, most recently, Lüdemann 1987, and Lüdemann and Schröder 1987.

took up the quest of a thoroughgoing historical account of the New Testament. Wrede argued that the discipline of New Testament theology should be transformed into the study of the history of primitive Christian religion and theology. Historical study ought not to observe the traditional, dogmatically determined and historically arbitrary limits of the canon. Its task was to give an account of the living religion of the earliest Christianity as a historical appearance, and its boundaries should be drawn as that history dictates.[70] The concern of the historian is not with the doctrinal concepts of the various books of the New Testament but with the flow of history which lies behind the books. With regard to the understanding of the history of the New Testament period, the school introduced the new concept of a primitive hellenistic church between the primitive Jewish Christian community and Paul,[71] and consequently understood Paul, not as the initiator in a process of hellenization, but as one who already stood in this tradition and made a particular contribution within it. This periodization was taken up by Bultmann and Käsemann.

In order to study New Testament Christianity as a historical phenomenon, the school, as its name implies, attempted to set primitive Christianity within a wider history of religion. In the first period of the school (1888–1903),[72] primitive Christianity was set within the context of what was called 'late Judaism', and particular attention was paid to the Old Testament apocrypha and pseudepigrapha. In the second period (1904–29),[73] some members of the group followed the

[70] Wrede 1897: 70 ff., 115 f.

[71] Heitmüller 1912; Bousset 1913/1921; the relationship between these works is discussed in Verheule 1973: 184 f.

[72] i.e. the period from the publication of Gunkel's monograph on the spirit to Bousset's textbook on the religion of Judaism in the late hellenistic age. Holmström (1926: 37; followed by Ittel 1958: 68) gives 1895 as the starting date (Gunkel's *Schöpfung und Chaos im Urzeit und Endzeit*) but Gunkel's earlier work is informed by the same methodology.

[73] Verheule (1973: 309) argues that the change of direction followed the publication of Reitzenstein's *Poimandres* (1904) and the consequent discussions between Reitzenstein and Bousset. The latter outlined a series of topics for future study in 'Das Neue Testament und die Religionsgeschichte' (1904). However, Heitmüller's article on the Lord's supper in Paul, which belongs to the second period, and Gunkel's programmatic study, arguing for the importance of the oriental

lead of the orientalist R. Reitzenstein (1861–1931), and sought to understand primitive Christianity against the background of hellenistic and oriental religion. The school has come to be identified with this line of enquiry, and particularly with the hypothesis of the gnostic redeemed redeemer which was believed to lie behind much New Testament (including Pauline) christology.[74] For Käsemann the attempt to understand primitive Christianity against the background of the wider history of religion is one of the fundamental methods of historical interpretation. In terms of the derivation of Pauline theology he followed both the major suggestions of the school, if in reverse chronological order: up to about 1950 he argued for the gnostic and hellenistic background of Paul's thought; in his later work he turns, primarily, to its 'apocalyptic' background.

A second aspect of the history-of-religions method was the study of the way religion functioned and evolved in the New Testament period. This approach was developed in opposition to the tendency to focus on the theological concepts of the New Testament. Proceeding from the liberal axiom of the distinction between religion and theology,[75] these scholars distinguished between popular, living, religious experience; the judgement of a prominent individual; and fixed doctrinal systems.[76] In line with their liberalism they elevated living religious experience over doctrine and investigated areas such as the sacraments (Heitmüller) and Christ as the centre of the Christian cult (Bousset). This is part of the background to Käsemann's interest in Paul's understanding of the church, the sacraments, and Christ as the object of Christian worship and acclamation.

In this area both Bultmann[77] and Käsemann looked to Gunkel's work on the spirit as being of the greatest exegetical

religions, had already appeared in 1903. Holmström (1926) sees Reitzenstein's *Die Vorgeschichte der christlichen Taufe* (1929) as the school's 'swan-song'.

[74] This theory was developed by Reitzenstein (1904, 1921) and Bousset (1907, 1913/1921).

[75] Ittel 1958: 61.

[76] Gunkel 1888: 13–15; Eichhorn 1898: 23 f.; Heitmüller 1911, 29. The same approach was utilized outside the school by A. Deissmann and M. Dibelius.

[77] Bultmann 1929*a*: 318 f. For Bultmann's appreciation of the history-of-religions school in general, see Bultmann 1926*a*; 1939; 1953: 247; 1956: 336–8; and his preface to the 5th edn. of Bousset's *Kyrios Christos* (1913/1921).

and theological importance. The spirit is not to be understood as a doctrine but as experience. 'Belief in the Spirit is not for the purpose of grasping God's plan for the world [as in Hegel and Baur] but for the purpose of explaining the presence of certain, above all, inexplicable phenomena by means of the transcendent.' The human recipient of the spirit is not the actor but passive, for the spirit is 'the supernatural power of God which works miracles in and through the person'.[78] Käsemann emphasizes that with this insight Gunkel destroyed the idealist interpretation of the spirit, thereby undermining Baur's view of Paul in which the spirit was the central concept. Equally, Gunkel's findings came to be theologically important because in them Bultmann and Käsemann found exegetical and historical support for the critique of the theology inspired by the philosophy of German idealism[79] which took place after the first world war.

This line of approach naturally raised the question of whether Paul's thought was to be understood as religion or as theology. Heitmüller's position was typical of the period: the sacramental and cultic character of Paul's religion is emphasized, though at the same time this is compared unfavourably with the 'simple' ethical teaching of Jesus, and with Paul's own ethics.[80] On the other hand, Wrede argued for the theological character of Paul's religion. For him Paul's christology and doctrine of redemption are products of his previous Jewish beliefs, and not of the influence of the personality of Jesus. Paul is not a 'disciple of Jesus', but 'the second founder of Christianity'.[81] Wrede's view is of particular importance because it was taken up by Bultmann,[82] and then by Käsemann. However, despite this basic decision and despite his hostility to the notion of religion, it ought not to be assumed too quickly that Käsemann has no interest in aspects

[78] Gunkel 1888: 13 f.; the two quotations are from 32 f. and 35 respectively.

[79] An introduction to this movement of thought from Kant to Schelling is provided by Ewing 1934.

[80] Heitmüller 1911, 38.

[81] Wrede 1904: 87. Weiss took a middle line and regarded the teaching of Paul as 'the theological expression . . . of a religious attitude directly derived from the teaching of Jesus' (Weiss 1909: 14; quoted in Furnish 1964/5: 355, which provides a survey of the Jesus–Paul question).

[82] Bultmann argues that, like Barth, Wrede saw that Paul's theology is not orientated to experience but to faith (1929*a*: 324).

of the religion of the Pauline congregations. At least in the period up to 1950 his choice of research topics indicates that this is not the case. This then raises the question of how these aspects of Paul's religion are incorporated into Käsemann's view of Paul's theology.

Nineteenth-century research into Paul's religion also led to a questioning (specifically by German Lutheran scholars) of Paul's status as the precursor of the Reformation. Wrede argued that the doctrine of justification of faith was no more than a 'polemical doctrine' forged in the debate with Judaism and Jewish Christianity—which to this extent was historically important and characteristic of Paul.[83] The centre of Paul's theology was not here but in his doctrine of redemption. Heitmüller and Bousset laid emphasis on the sacramental and cultic character of Paul's religion. Heitmüller even marked the occasion of the celebration of the 400th anniversary of the Reformation by arguing that, in some respects, Paul was the father, not of the Reformation, but of the ancient and medieval church.[84] Agreeing with Wrede that the doctrine of justification grew out of Paul's missionary experience and served to protect the law-free Gentile mission,[85] he contrasted the understanding of justification in Luther, where the focus is on the individual, and in Paul, where it is on humanity. For Luther, faith is the source of the new life, or the new life itself; in Paul, the supernatural gift of the spirit brings new life, and alongside faith there stands enthusiasm, inspiration, and mysticism, as in the later church. Thus, for Heitmüller, the Reformation is not a renewal of Paulinism but a putting aside of the Pauline elements which the Catholic church took up.[86]

Notwithstanding the Luther renaissance and the restatement of the Lutheran interpretation of Paul at the beginning of the twentieth century, the history-of-religions school's views on the relationship between Luther and Paul are of significance for understanding Käsemann's work. On the one hand,

[83] Wrede 1904: 67. From outside the school, A. Schweitzer came to the conclusion that the doctrine of justification was merely a 'subsidiary crater' within the main crater of the 'mystical' doctrine of redemption through the 'being in Christ' (1930: 224 f.).

[84] Heitmüller 1917: 21; Bultmann drew attention to this argument in his review of the history of Pauline interpretation (1929*a*: 198).

[85] Heitmüller 1917: 19.

[86] Ibid. 20–2.

Käsemann argued specifically against Wrede on the place and significance of the doctrine of justification in Paul. On the other hand, he takes over many of the features of the Catholic Paul from the history-of-religions school. These include the 'real', as opposed to the symbolic, understanding of the sacraments, the emphasis on the spirit and on what was called 'mysticism', and the influence of the context of worship on the doctrinal history of the earliest Christianity. It will be seen that Käsemann integrates these elements into a view of Paul in which the doctrine of justification is the centre.

The same tendency to integration and towards a unified view of Paul's theology will be seen in Käsemann's response to another key feature of the nineteenth-century interpretation of Paul. In his monograph of 1872, H. Lüdemann (1842–1933) argued that Paul has a 'physical' and an 'ethical' anthropology. In the physical anthropology, which is hellenistic in origin, Paul distinguishes between the inner and the outer human being (*σάρξ* as material); in the ethical anthropology, which is Jewish in origin, he speaks of human beings as being under the lordship of the *σάρξ* (cf. *PP* 17/6). Corresponding to the two types of anthropology are two understandings of redemption, a Jewish, juridical view, in which Christ's vicarious death is appropriated in the righteousness of faith, and a hellenistic, 'realistic' view, in which righteousness is acquired by identification with Christ in baptism, and in the life of the spirit. Lüdemann's view was that Paul's theology develops: the Jewish view present in Rom. 1–4 is merely pedagogical and propaedeutic; it is superseded by the hellenistic view of chapters 6–8.

The far-reaching ramifications of Lüdemann's work are summarized concisely by Kümmel:

> This downgrading of the doctrine of justification by faith, a doctrine regarded by others as central, raised the question, as had the hypothesis of a bifurcated Pauline proclamation, of the inner coherence and the central content of Pauline theology and, at the same time, the question of the relation of this theology to the background of ancient religions, so that Lüdemann's study, which also referred to the importance for Paul of the expectation of Christ's return, raised all the basic problems of further Pauline research.[87]

[87] Kümmel 1958: 189.

The question of the place and significance of the doctrine of justification has already been touched on. Lüdemann's bifurcation of Pauline theology, and the consequent question of the unity of Paul's theology, was also taken up and became a stock question for interpretation.[88] Thus, for example, Heitmüller contrasted Paul's 'realistic' view of the sacraments, which worked *ex opere operato* in the Catholic sense, with his inner, spiritual understanding of faith.[89]

The tendency towards an understanding of Paul's theology marked by differing lines of thought is conveniently summarized in A. Schweitzer's (1875–1965) much delayed study of Paul of 1930.[90] Schweitzer, while arguing for a unified view of Paul's theology, speaks of the eschatological, juridical, and 'mystical' elements within it. This last category is in fact very wide, including the concepts of the community of saints, the body of Christ, dying and rising with Christ, suffering, the spirit, and the sacraments. (Schweitzer's own studies led him to emphasize the eschatological element, which was a new departure in the study of the various elements of Paul's thought.) This threefold division has recently been taken up again in E. P. Sanders's influential studies of Paul, in which he gives the third category the more satisfactory title of 'participation'.[91] Thus, for Käsemann to present a unified view of Paul's theology he must overcome these divisions and account for the eschatological, juridical, and participatory elements of Paul's thought. In summary, Käsemann takes up the challenge to the Lutheran view of Paul which was raised by the historical studies of Baur, Lüdemann, and the history-of-religions school.

[88] Bultmann 1929*a*: 312 f.

[89] Heitmüller 1903: 14 f.

[90] Schweitzer tells how his study goes back to a first draft of 1906 and was originally intended to follow his study of the history of Pauline interpretation (1911) immediately. As he had not been involved in the academic study of the NT in the intervening years, his book responds to the state of the debate at the end of the nineteenth century. Cf. Kümmel 1976: 287, on the book's history and reception.

[91] Sanders 1977: 440.

KARL BARTH

The publication of Karl Barth's (1886–1968) commentary on Romans[92] marks the beginning of a new era in the understanding of the task of interpreting scripture and in the interpretation of Paul.[93] With regard to the question of interpreting scripture, Barth is highly critical of the type of interpretation practised by the exponents of the critical orthodoxy of the day, arguing that they fail to get beyond the level of a historical commentary. In the preface to the first edition he says that while Paul did, of course, speak to his contemporaries, it is far more important that as prophet and apostle of the kingdom of God he speaks to all people of every age. Historical criticism has its rightful place, to prepare the intelligence, but Barth's goal is to see through the historical into the spirit of the Bible which is the eternal spirit.[94] This brief, general statement of his understanding of the task of interpretation is filled out in the preface to the second edition. Barth complains that commentaries have become no more than an ascertaining of what is present in the text, a series of philological, grammatical, and archaeological notes, with a more or less plausible ordering of the individual points by the means of psychological and historical categories. Such interpretation is far from being an exact science and cannot be called more than the first primitive attempt at explanation—and there are numerous indications that these scholars[95] wish to get beyond this type of interpretation.

Barth's concern is that of Luther and Calvin and some modern commentators[96] who set out to understand (*verstehen*), explain (*erklären*), and rethink or think through (*nach-denken*) what Paul meant. He contrasts the work of Jülicher and

[92] Barth's Romans commentary appeared in 1919 and was completely rewritten for the edition of 1922. The prefaces of these and subsequent editions contain extremely important reflections on Barth's aims and methods, and respond to criticisms.

[93] Kümmel 1958: 363; Strecker 1975: 12.

[94] Barth 1922: p. v.

[95] Among more recent scholars Barth mentions the work of A. Jülicher, H. Lietzmann, T. Zahn, and E. R. T. Kühl.

[96] Barth mentions J. C. K. von Hofmann, J. T. Beck, A. Godet, and A. Schlatter.

Calvin as typical examples. Jülicher stays close to the wording of the text which remains like undeciphered runes. Yet, at the same time, he is content either to reject much of Paul's teaching by regarding it as Paul's peculiar view or to claim to have interpreted him by reference to the general and banal categories of his own religious thought (experience, feeling, conviction, etc.). In addition, he attributes responsibility for the text to the Damascus experience, late Judaism, hellenism, antiquity, or other demi-gods.[97] It is not only liberals who are censured by Barth: the lack of real understanding is merely better concealed among 'positive', orthodox commentators.

By contrast, Calvin thinks through what stands in the text, he debates with it until the walls of the intervening centuries become transparent: Paul speaks and the audience of the sixteenth century hears. The conversation between the text and the reader is concentrated on the 'subject-matter' (*die Sache*). Barth outlines how the subject-matter is to be approached. He calls for 'the most open and willing investigation of the inner tension of the concepts which are given with greater or lesser clarity in the text'.[98] With respect to a historical text, κρίνειν means the measuring of the words and groups of words which it contains by the subject-matter of which it clearly speaks, if it does not deceive altogether. The key point here is the notion of measuring all by the subject-matter (*das Messen . . . an der Sache*). Or, to put it in other words, the interpreter needs to relate all the answers of the text to the questions it asks, and then to relate all these questions back to the one cardinal question. The relationship of the words to the word in the words must be uncovered. The interpreter must press on until he (or she, as we would now say) is faced by the riddle of the subject-matter (not just the riddle of the text) so that he can almost forget that he is not the author and can speak in his own name. The question which Barth puts to liberal commentators is whether they know that there is a cardinal question, a word among the words. This he has learnt, not from the university with its

[97] Barth 1922: pp. x–xi.

[98] '. . . durch ein *tunlichst* lockeres und williges Eingehen auf die innere Spannung der im Text mit mehr oder weniger Deutlichkeit dargebotenen Begriffe' (ibid., p. xii; Barth's emphasis).

'reverence before history', but from the experience of having to preach and thus of having to understand and explain the Bible.[99]

In an attempt to explain the 'inner dialectic of the subject-matter' further, Barth first replies that he does not have a system which he has imposed on the Bible. He wants to speak of 'the infinite qualitative distinction' between time and eternity (Kierkegaard), of the theme that 'God is in heaven and you are on earth'. The relationship of this God to this human being, and vice versa, is both the theme of the Bible and the sum of philosophy. The origin of this final question for philosophy is the 'crisis of human knowledge' (*diese Krisis des menschlichen Erkennens*). For the Bible this 'crisis' or 'crossroads' (*Kreuzweg*) is Jesus Christ. When Barth approaches a text like Romans he does so under the presupposition that, in the formation of his concepts, Paul knows at least as much about this relationship as he does. This is Barth's working hypothesis which he compares with the working hypothesis of the historian and which can only be confirmed by the interpretation itself. Thus, Barth approaches Romans with the presupposition that Paul genuinely speaks of Jesus Christ, and not of any other. He has found no reason to deviate from this belief. In fact, he believes that Paul knows something about God which we in general do not know, but which we could know. This belief is his 'system' or 'dogmatic presupposition'.[100] As Strecker says, Barth calls for an 'unconditional listening to the revelation of God to which the New Testament witnesses'. The exegete is no longer the enquiring subject but the object of questioning: the exegete is questioned and grasped by God's self-revelation.[101]

Barth then responds to the charge of 'biblicism'. P. Wernle listed eight 'uncomfortable points' which Barth had avoided in his interpretation. These were elements of Paul's religion, as understood by liberal research, which did not square with a liberal understanding of Christianity (Paul's low estimation of the value of the earthly life of Jesus, his sacramentalism, etc.). For Barth a historical discussion of these subjects does not constitute a commentary. Rather than avoiding these points

[99] Ibid., pp. xii–xiii. [100] Ibid., pp. xiii–xiv.

[101] Strecker 1975: 12 f., quotation on 13.

which are said to wound modern consciousness, he has thought them through to the point where some of his most outstanding insights were made. Whether his views are correct is another matter. For the rest, he claims that the same method of interpretation could be applied to Goethe or Lao-tzu, although he would have trouble applying it to some other parts of the Bible. He does not expand on these last enigmatic points.[102]

Barth concedes that he is concerned with the 'true', rather than the 'whole', gospel. By this he means that he is not concerned with a comprehensive account of the Christian faith where all elements are assigned to their correct positions but with the subject-matter, the theological centre of the gospel. His concern is with the 'true' gospel because there is no way to the whole gospel except through the 'true' gospel. Paulinism is always on the borders of heresy and is dangerous—because of its radical concentration on the centre of the gospel—and it is remarkable how harmless most books on Paul are. Although the book might have a fatal effect on immature spirits, the counter question of how to bring the dangerous aspect of Christianity into the open has to be faced.[103] Barth goes on to comment on the charge that his interpretation is Marcionite,[104] but argues that there is no similarity at decisive points.

The prefaces to Barth's Romans are of the greatest importance for the formation of Käsemann's views on the task of interpretation. From Barth, he takes up the insistence on interpreting Paul's letter in the light of its ultimate subject-matter, i.e., God, and thus, theologically. He also agrees with Barth on the dialectical understanding of the nature of theology. The single most important point for his interpretation of Paul is the focus on the centre of the gospel, and the consequent interpretation of all other elements in the light of

[102] Barth 1922: pp. xv–xvi.

[103] In introducing the 2nd edn., Barth takes one of his many side-swipes at liberal theologians: 'This time I myself . . . would like to exhort the theological children—I mean, of course, the students— . . . to read the book very carefully' (ibid.).

[104] Jülicher had made this point (1920) and then certain parallels struck Barth himself on reading the first reviews of Harnack's monograph on Marcion (Harnack 1921; Barth 1922: pp. xvi–xvii).

that centre.[105] Käsemann also emphasizes the dangerous character of Paul's theology and defends Marcion's approach to the question of gospel and tradition. Marcion is Paul's successor in that he criticizes tradition (here the contents of the canon) by the standard of 'pure doctrine'; his mistake was to practise theological criticism by excision.[106]

While Barth claims to have seen through the historical to the underlying dialectic or spirit of the Bible (and thus can pour scorn on Wernle's history-of-religions and -traditions questions), Käsemann, in his approach to the New Testament, attempts to integrate historical-critical exegesis[107] and theological interpretation. At this point Käsemann sides with Bultmann against Barth. However, with Bultmann, he does reflect Barth's conviction that Paul knows something about God which in general we do not know, and thus there is a very close relationship between Käsemann's interpretation of Paul and his understanding of the Christian faith.

While Käsemann is indebted to Barth for some individual points of importance in the interpretation of Paul, his greatest influence in this area is his emphasis on and theological appropriation of Paul's eschatology. The significance of eschatology in Paul's thought had already been emphasized by R. Kabisch and Schweitzer[108] at the level of historical interpretation. However, for liberal research, eschatology was one of the elements of Paul's religion which could not be assimilated theologically. Barth's concern is not with the actual eschatological schemes of the New Testament: 'Christian eschatology is not interested in the last things for their own sake. Conversely, here man is confronted with the mystery of the future for the sake of revelation . . . because the

[105] A similar programme was adopted by J. Schniewind who, like Käsemann, regarded the theme of God's righteousness as the centre of Paul's theology and wished to interpret all the elements of his theology (even the worship of the community) in the light of this.

[106] See *Das Neue Testament als Kanon* (1970), especially 354–7, 399, 408–10 and *Römer* 251/261.

[107] It is entirely characteristic of Barth that, when he met Käsemann in 1960 to discuss 'the problem of the relationship between exegetical and "systematic" theology, which evidently disturbs us both', he put the question, 'Tell me, what does "historical" mean? And "critical"? And what is the significance of the hyphen between the two words?' (Busch 1975: 447 f.)

[108] Kabisch 1893; Schweitzer 1911 and 1930.

revelation which constitutes the Word of God is in itself eschatological.'[109] Barth can equally well express this with reference to christology: 'Christianity which is not eschatology, totally and without remainder, has nothing whatsoever to do with *Christ*.'[110] It is this connection between eschatology and christology—and hence with the doctrine of justification—which made eschatology a subject of central theological significance in the 1920s and beyond.[111]

Finally, Käsemann is also clearly indebted to Barth for some of the connotations of the theme of lordship of Christ itself. While his Lutheran background has been emphasized, this theme, which Käsemann expounds in terms of sovereignty, omnipotence, and ubiquity, is also indebted to the Reformed tradition.[112] Thus, Barth's profound influence on Käsemann ranges from individual exegetical points through the renewed insistence on, and new understanding of, the theological interpretation of Paul, to major theological themes.

ADOLF SCHLATTER

Although Käsemann rarely mentions those who have influenced him by name, on several occasions he has made a point of paying tribute to the work of Adolf Schlatter (1852–1938).[113] With regard to his overall approach, Schlatter is praised by Käsemann for his focus on christology and

[109] Quoted from a Münster lecture in Busch 1975: 166.

[110] Barth 1922: 298 (his emphasis). Barth later commented on this exaggerated passage: 'Well roared, lion!' (Busch 1975: 120)

[111] Beker speaks of a collapse of eschatology into christology in the neo-orthodoxy inspired by Barth (1980: 139; cf. 142 f.). For the connection between christology and justification in Luther, see above.

[112] Barth began to work this theme out in the interpretation of Romans. 'God's *kingdom*, God's sphere of *lordship* and *power* is the new world' (1922: 166, Barth's emphasis). 'Grace is the kingdom, the lordship, the power and the rule of God over humanity' (196).

[113] The more important references are *ThLZ* 64 (1939), 412; letter to Bultmann, dated 18 Apr. 1949; *VF* 4 (1949/50), 209; *EVB* ii. 14 f./4 f., 23/14; *NTS* 19 (1972/3), 239 f. where Käsemann speaks of Schlatter as 'Bultmann's one and only peer'; *Römer* p. iv/p. vii, 244/254. On Schlatter, see Morgan 1973 and Stuhlmacher 1978. His own autobiographical sketch (1952) provides a good introduction to his theological concerns which he described as finding a middle way between liberalism and pietism in the understanding of the New Testament (ibid. 101, cf. 171).

Käsemann follows in Schlatter's footsteps when he argues that the New Testament is to be understood as 'the history of Jesus, continued and caught up in the kerygma of his disciples' (*NTS* 19 (1972/3), 239). This christological approach is further to be defined by 'the Cross of Jesus and the justification of the godless' (240). This theological starting-point is explicitly championed by Käsemann after 1960.

With respect to the interpretation of Paul, Käsemann singles out Schlatter (along with 'dialectical theology') as having striven to overcome the supposed tensions within Paul's theology, particularly with reference to the relationship of the themes of justification and salvation history (*Römer* 244/254). Most significant is Schlatter's focus on the theme of 'God's righteousness' (*Gottes Gerechtigkeit*), the title he gave to his major commentary on Romans (1935). This title summarizes his main point in the debate over the interpretation of Paul within German Protestantism: Paul's theology is primarily concerned with *God's* righteousness, and only then with the righteousness of faith and the justification of the individual.[114] Consequently, he focuses on the genitive in 'God's righteousness' (understood as a subjective genitive) and makes this the starting-point for the investigation of the doctrine of justification. The righteousness of faith ought not to be emphasized so much that it becomes a work, and exegesis of Romans can end with 5: 1. God's righteousness is his faithfulness and his right (*Recht*); faith is God's work, as is the obedience of the righteous (chs. 6–8), the fate of his people (chs. 9–11),[115] and what happens in the community (chs. 12–15). It is only from this perspective that the unity of the epistle can be maintained.[116] All these

[114] Schlatter's extensive comparison between the theologies of the reformers (especially Luther and Calvin) and of Paul is expounded and discussed by Althaus. Two points are relevant here. (1) For the reformers the saving act is the forgiveness of sins, so that God disappears under his mercy, whereas, for Paul, the saving act is justification, the positive act of setting human beings in relationship with God. (2) For the reformers the doctrine of salvation is anthropocentric, i.e., it is our need which drives us to God (with the consequent danger of synergism); for Paul the doctrine of salvation is theocentric since 'God's work originates in God's work' (Althaus 1938/1951: 21–3, with reference to Schlatter 1917 and 1935). Cf. also the phrase *Gottheit Gottes*, which Käsemann associates with Schlatter (letter to Bultmann, 18 Apr. 1949; the phrase occurs in Schlatter 1935: 36, 302, 310, 392).

[115] Schlatter specifically criticizes Barth for replacing the topic of Israel with that of the church in the interpretation of Rom. 9–11 (Schlatter 1922: 144).

[116] For this understanding of Schlatter's Romans, see Klaiber 1978: 10–15.

points are taken up by Käsemann. Further, like Barth, Schlatter argues for the eschatological orientation of Paul's theology and relates this directly to Paul's doctrine of God:

> It is clear that every sentence of the letter [Romans] is meant 'eschatologically' since God's message proclaims Christ through whom God's lordship [*Gottes Herrschaft*] occurs; it proclaims the deliverer from whom the faithful will receive acquittal in the judgement and who will confer life on them. Because the reception of the message is the reception of the deliverer, it proclaims the judgement and gives the faithful the hope which is certain of life.[117]

Here God's lordship is understood in terms of the gospel which proclaims Christ, and the message of salvation is not abstracted from the God who initiates it through Christ. Further, Christ is experienced simultaneously as judgement and life. This theme is also present in Barth. Grace is gift, even the epitome of all divine gifts, but it is this in that the giver himself, and thus God himself, becomes gift. 'Gift' is not a third entity between God and the creature but the being and act of God.[118] As will be seen, the gift–giver theme underlies Käsemann's interpretation of Paul as a whole.

Against this background Schlatter argues that, parallel to God's wrath and power, δικαιοσύνη θεοῦ means God's own righteousness. The central category in Paul's theology is God's activity, and God's righteousness, wrath, and power are not to be thought of as 'qualities'. In every statement about God Paul thinks of the creator who creates right (*Recht*) and brings human beings into the relationship with himself which he desires.[119] This complex of themes is important for Käsemann who also brings together the idea of God as creator and the doctrine of justification. Schlatter's emphasis on the theocentric character of Paul's theology influences Käsemann, and leads to one of the major points of his critique of Bultmann's theology.

117 Schlatter 1935: 10.

118 Barth 1940: 2, 1, 397, commenting on Rom. 1: 5.

119 Schlatter 1935, 36. While no attempt has been made here to outline even the main points of disagreement between Käsemann and those who influenced him, in the light of the current reappraisal of Paul, Judaism, and the law, it is noteworthy that Schlatter's view of Judaism, which is much more sympathetic than the mainstream of German scholarship, and was based on a first-hand knowledge of Jewish sources, appears to have had no influence on Käsemann.

RUDOLF BULTMANN

The immediate context of Käsemann's interpretation of Paul and of his own theology is the work of his *Doktorvater*, Rudolf Bultmann (1884–1976). Bultmann's own views are of particular importance but he also represents a synthesis of the historical-critical tradition stemming from Baur and the renewed emphasis on theological interpretation associated with Barth.

A superficial reading of Käsemann's work might suggest that his relationship to Bultmann is fundamentally negative. While it is true that he is often in debate with Bultmann, the strength of his polemic masks the large area of agreement between them. Three such areas will be surveyed here: the task of interpreting scripture, the existential approach to the New Testament, and the interpretation of Paul.

Bultmann entered the debate about the interpretation of scripture in the aftermath of the publication of Barth's Romans commentary of 1919/1922.[120] He agrees with Barth that the interpreter must measure all that is in the text by the standard of the subject-matter. Philological and historical techniques are necessary but so is an inner relationship with the subject-matter. However, in Bultmann's view, Barth has fallen short of his own ideal and done violence to Romans and to Paul.[121] Bultmann makes two types of criticism. Firstly, Barth makes the untenable assumption that the subject-matter is adequately expressed in Paul's words and phrases. Even these must be judged by the standard of the subject-matter if one is not to espouse a modern dogma of inspiration. This type of (theological) criticism is far more radical than historical criticism, and, in Bultmann's view, does not originate from outside the text. Nor does this show a lack of reverence to Romans because the subject-matter is greater

[120] Bultmann takes up this issue in his extended reviews of Barth's commentaries on Romans (Barth 1922; Bultmann 1922*a*) and 1 Corinthians (Barth 1924; Bultmann 1926*b*), and in his essay on the problem of the theological interpretation of the New Testament (1925*a*; the English translation of this essay should be used with caution; some corrections are made in Morgan 1973). For the correspondence between Barth and Bultmann, see Jaspert 1971 and Thyen 1984.

[121] Bultmann 1922*a*: 140.

than the interpreting word.[122] If the task of historical (*zeitgeschichtlich*) interpretation is to ask what is said, the task of theological exegesis (*Sachexegese*)[123] is to ask what is meant. Theological criticism (*Sachkritik*) distinguishes between what is said and what is meant. It does not, however, divorce the two, as theological criticism can only arrive at what is meant through what is said. It is, therefore, in a peculiarly ambiguous and contradictory situation, comes to no 'results', and is always in motion.[124]

In a second major criticism of Barth's understanding of the task of interpretation, Bultmann argues that history-of-religions work, the ascertaining of Paul's dependence on Jewish, primitive Christian, or hellenistic views, is a necessary part of theological exegesis. No one, not even Paul, speaks only of the subject-matter, and 'Spirits other than the *pneuma Christou* come to expression in it [the text]'.[125] It is precisely in the task of theological exegesis that historical work can reach its final goal. It here converges with systematic theology so that both lead to reflection on the foundations of our existence (*Selbstbesinnung*).[126] Thus, Bultmann is critical of Barth for not allowing either theological criticism or historical criticism its full scope.[127] On both these points Käsemann follows Bultmann.[128]

122 Bultmann 1922*a*: 141.

123 The ET renders *Sachexegese* with 'objective exegesis' which is highly misleading. The translation 'theological exegesis' is chosen because, for Barth and Bultmann, the *Sache* in the study of New Testament is God. These concepts and Bultmann's view of the task of interpreting the New Testament are discussed in Morgan 1973: 36–52.

124 Bultmann 1925*a*: 253–7.

125 Bultmann 1922*a*: 142.

126 Ibid.

127 In the preface to the 3rd edn. of his Romans commentary Barth replied that it is not that the spirit of Christ speaks through some passages and not others, but that the whole is under the 'crisis' of the spirit of Christ. The other spirits serve Christ. Otherwise one is left with a commentary *on* Paul's letter, not a commentary, so far as is possible, *with* him. Barth allows that the words should not be approached too rigidly, and that the letter must be judged by the spirit, but not that Paul's concepts or beliefs are sometimes inappropriate to the subject-matter (Barth 1922: pp. xix–xxi).

128 This is particularly clear in the debate between Käsemann and Conzelmann on the place of primitive Christian creeds in Pauline (and Christian) theology. Conzelmann proposed to make the creeds, formulated in, and understood as obligatory by, the NT, central to the task of understanding its message (Conzelmann 1966*b*, with particular reference to 1 Cor. 15: 3–5). Incensed by this view, because of its apparent equation of the NT credal formulae and the truth of the gospel, which as a consequence uses objectified language of God, Käsemann objects that Conzelmann has failed to note Bultmann's criticism of Barth's programme: 'Historical criticism without this theological criticism is shadow boxing' ('Konsequente Traditionsgeschichte?' *ZThK* 62 (1965), 150).

As is well known, Bultmann interprets the New Testament through the analysis of its understanding of human existence.[129] He criticizes the approaches of orthodox Lutheranism, rationalism, and idealism for imposing their own systems on the text: the text is not to be inspected, but should determine the existence of the reader. The question for the interpreter is 'What is the content [*Sache*] of what is said, and to what kind of reality does it lead?'[130] As has been seen, the final purpose of historical and theological study is to lead to reflection on the foundations of our existence.

Käsemann's debate with Bultmann does not concern the necessity or the legitimacy of this type of interpretation but the theological convictions and philosophical presuppositions which he believes control Bultmann's view of New Testament (and contemporary) theology. Two issues in particular come to dominate the debate: the interpretation of primitive Christian eschatology, and the relative theological significance of christology and soteriology in primitive Christian (and contemporary) theology.

For Bultmann, primitive Christian eschatology is to be existentially interpreted so that it reveals its understanding of human existence:[131]

> According to the New Testament, *Jesus Christ is the eschatological event*, the action of God by which God has set an end to the old world. In the preaching of the Christian church the eschatological event will ever again become present and does become present ever and again in faith. For the old world has reached its end with the fact that he himself as 'the old man' has reached his end and is now 'a new man', a free man.[132]

The eschatological event is not to be understood as a dramatic cosmic catastrophe but as a happening within history, the event of Jesus Christ which is continued in preaching, and which results in a new self-understanding. Käsemann agrees that primitive Christian eschatology has to be demythologized and that Bultmann's programme has its roots in the theology of the Reformation. However, Bultmann's view of human

[129] Bultmann 1953: 251.

[130] Bultmann 1957: 151.

[131] On Bultmann's understanding of myth, see, among many discussions, Johnson 1974 and Thiselton 1980: 252–63.

[132] Bultmann 1925*a*: 253.

existence is too individualistic and, at times, does not regard a human being as a whole. He is still under the sway of German idealism. This philosophical difference leads into extensive debate about Paul's anthropology and the 'apocalyptic' nature of his theology. Secondly, the interpreter must not allow the hermeneutical question to dominate but must pursue the theological question of 'how God becomes our lord, and what it means if God becomes lord over us'—which, for Käsemann, is the common theme of Jesus' proclamation of the kingdom of God, Paul's message of God's righteousness, and the Book of Revelation ('Entmythologisierung' 7; cf. 'Probleme' 142–6; *PP* 48 f./25, 65–7/34 f.). Thus, he believes that Bultmann has been drawn away from the essential theological task by his hermeneutics.

On the question of the relative theological significance of christology and soteriology in primitive Christian and contemporary theology, Bultmann argues that the cross of Christ was the saving event for the first disciples (who had personally known the earthly Jesus), because it was the cross of *Christ*. However, for all later believers, 'it is not because it is the cross of Christ that it is the salvation event; it is because it is the salvation event that it is the cross of Christ'.[133] For Bultmann, christology is subordinate to soteriology, and he quotes Melanchthon's dictum to this effect: 'hoc est Christum cognoscere, beneficia eius cognoscere'.[134] Responding to this, Barth criticizes Bultmann for putting the accent in the wrong place. 'That *Christ* is the kerygma is what the New Testament appears to say, not that Christ is the *kerygma*.'[135] Thus, while Barth and Bultmann agree that Paul's christology and soteriology are closely linked, they differ on which is the controlling theme. On this issue Käsemann takes up Barth's line in his own debate with Bultmann.

With respect to the interpretation of Paul, Bultmann's views are again the immediate context of Käsemann's work. On the one hand, Käsemann takes over Bultmann's views, and occasionally refines them; on the other hand, he devotes much of his work to debate with Bultmann. As the relationship between their views will be kept constantly in view in the

133 Cf. Bultmann 1941*b*: 36.

134 Bultmann 1933*a*: 279, 285.

135 Barth 1952*b*: 96.

following chapters, it is necessary to note here only the most important points. With regard to Paul's position within primitive Christian history, Käsemann initially followed Bousset, Bultmann, and Erik Peterson (1890–1960): Paul is a representative of hellenistic Christianity[136] who borrows from both Jewish-apocalyptic and gnostic sources. From the former comes Paul's consistent eschatological outlook, from the latter his primal-man christology. (Later Käsemann abandoned this view in favour of reading Paul against an 'apocalyptic' and, to a lesser degree, hellenistic, but now not a specifically gnostic, background.)

Paul's relationship to primitive Christianity can be further defined by the investigation of the fragments of pre-Pauline creeds or hymns embedded in the extant letters. Following the lead of E. Norden, E. Peterson, and E. Lohmeyer,[137] Bultmann made some seminal suggestions concerning traditional liturgical or credal material in the Pauline epistles[138] and Käsemann helped to confirm this approach with several detailed studies.[139] This historical enterprise bears theological fruit as it allows a glimpse into Paul's understanding of, and modifications to, earlier Christian tradition.

With Wrede, Bultmann is emphatic that Paul can only be properly understood as a theologian.[140] With regard to the question of the centre of Paul's thought, Bultmann rejects the

[136] Käsemann specifically mentions the influence of Peterson, his first teacher in Bonn, in leading him to understand the NT against a hellenistic background (*KK* i. 8). On Peterson, see Fellechner 1978.

[137] Norden 1913: 380–7 and Peterson 1926 were followed by Lohmeyer's substantial study of Phil. 2: 6–11 (1928*a*).

[138] Bultmann's major work of historical reconstruction in this area is the section on the pre-Pauline hellenistic church in his *Theologie des Neuen Testaments* (1948). The textual basis of this section is the traditional elements of Paul's thought (as reconstructed by Bultmann).

[139] 'Kritische Analyse von Phil. 2, 5–11' (1950; ET 1968); 'Zum Verständnis von Römer 3, 24–26' (1950/1); 'Erwägungen zum Stichwort "Versöhnungslehre im Neuen Testament"' on 2 Cor. 5: 18–21 and 1 Cor. 1: 30 (1964; ET 1971); 'Konsequente Traditionsgeschichte' on 1 Cor. 15: 3–5 (1965); and the Romans commentary on 1: 3–4, 3: 24–6, 4: 25. See also the dictionary articles 'Formeln II: Liturgische Formeln im NT' (1958); 'Liturgie II: Im NT' (1960).

[140] 'If Paul is to be understood on his own terms he must be understood primarily as a theologian, precisely like Luther'—and not as a hero of piety (*contra* A. Deissmann; Bultmann 1926*c*: 273). In the same period, though from a very different theological perspective, Lohmeyer also presented a theological account of Paul (Lohmeyer 1929*a*).

view that the doctrine of justification is merely a polemical doctrine. However, to regard Bultmann's view of Paul simply as a statement of the traditional Lutheran view, in which justification by faith is the central doctrine, would be to miss his main point. He is not primarily concerned with Paul's theology as a system with a particular doctrinal centre.[141] He organizes his material under the headings of 'human being outside of faith' and 'human being in faith',[142] and thus describes and analyses these two understandings of existence. (Of course, the new self-understanding of the 'human being in faith' is a result of being justified by faith.) Again, Bultmann focuses on the existential meaning of Paul's anthropological terms, and mythological and doctrinal beliefs, not on the doctrinal shape of his theology. This leads to the major areas of debate between Bultmann and Käsemann in which Käsemann argues that Bultmann has misinterpreted Paul's theology by reducing it to a theological anthropology[143] at the expense of its 'apocalyptic' orientation (ch. 3 below) and christological and theological content (ch. 4). Thus, Bultmann is both the interpreter and theologian with whom Käsemann shares the most common ground and the principal target of his criticisms.[144]

The theological and historical-critical context of Käsemann's interpretation of Paul can now be summed up:

1. From the prefaces to Barth's commentary on Romans, Käsemann takes up the call to interpret Paul in the light of his final 'subject-matter', i.e., theologically. An appropriate interpretation involves more than the solving of historical problems.

2. However, in contrast to Barth, Käsemann attempts to bring together theological and historical interpretation. The

[141] Cf. his description of the task of New Testament theology, and of Paul's place within it (Bultmann 1953: 251).

[142] Bultmann 1941*b*: 15–20, and 1951.

[143] Käsemann recalls a discussion on the concept 'cosmos' in Bultmann's seminar in which Bultmann argued that 'humanity' (*Menschheit*) does not exist but is an abstraction. Käsemann says that he had to learn that it is rather the concept 'individual' which is an abstraction, and points to the early influence of Peterson and then Schlatter in this process (*KK* i. 241).

[144] Käsemann's work is also characterized by constant debate with other views of Pauline (and Christian) theology which will be noted below.

latter concern goes back ultimately to Baur, but Käsemann is particularly influenced by the attempt to set Paul against a wider history-of-religions background. Here he is indebted to the approach of the history-of-religions school, mediated to him primarily through Bultmann.

3. The theological model which is employed for interpretation is derived from Barth, and from Gogarten and Iwand's understanding of Luther. The doctrines of christology and justification are interrelated and summed up under the catchphrase of the lordship of Christ. To have faith in Christ is to submit to his lordship and not to seek to justify oneself by works of the law; conversely, justification is not merely an individual matter but points to Christ's and, ultimately, God's, lordship over the world. This complex then acts as a centre for a Pauline theology.

4. Standing in the tradition which understands Romans as a summary of Paul's teaching, Käsemann learned from Schlatter to interpret the entire epistle in the light of the theme of God's righteousness. Like Schlatter, Käsemann relates this theme to the idea of God as creator, who claims his 'right' over his fallen creation. These themes are brought together with Barth's idea of lordship as God's (or Christ's) sovereignty. 1 Cor. 15: 28 is therefore a key text which speaks of the lordship of Christ which will be handed over to God at the end.

5. Käsemann takes up three major challenges which arise from the historical interpretation of Paul in the nineteenth century. Firstly, he attempts to demonstrate the underlying unity of Paul's thought, contesting the view that it is made up of three supposedly disparate (eschatological, juridical, and participatory) elements. This approach to Paul was pioneered by Lüdemann's study of Paul's anthropology and is exemplified in Schweitzer's work.

6. Similarly, Käsemann seeks to demonstrate the unity of Romans. Here the key issue is the relationship of chapters 1–8 and 9–11, summed up under the headings of justification and salvation history. For Käsemann, Baur's view that the climax of the epistle lies in chapters 9–11 is both a historical advance (because the epistle is read as a whole, and these chapters are no longer regarded as an excursus) and a

theological challenge (because the doctrine of justification is no longer regarded as the epistle's central concern). Käsemann's solution is to adopt Schlatter's argument that the theme of God's righteousness is the key to the whole letter. By this means the theme of salvation history can be affirmed but firmly subordinated to the doctrine of justification.

7. Käsemann's interpretation of Paul also attempts to bring together two major lines of interpretation which were current in German Protestantism in the 1930s. Here the issue is the status of Paul's thought: on the one hand, the predominant view of the late nineteenth century spoke of Paul's *religion*, in which the key themes were the spirit, the sacraments, and the *ἐν Χριστῷ*; on the other hand, the 1920s saw the revival of interest in Paul's *theology*, in which the doctrine of justification (interpreted within an eschatological framework) is central. Käsemann seeks to integrate the insights of the former into a Pauline theology based on the latter.

8. The immediate background to Käsemann's interpretation is the classic synthesis of the trends outlined above in Bultmann's interpretation of Paul. With the aid of categories drawn from Heidegger's existentialist philosophy, Bultmann seeks to meet the double demand for *historical* and *theological* interpretation. Against the background of fundamental agreement on this issue, Käsemann conducts a wide-ranging, theologically inspired, debate with him. To sum up: Käsemann's interpretation of Paul is to be understood against the background of the debates about the correct understanding of the theological heritage of the Reformation which took place within the sphere of the historical-critical interpretation of Paul from Baur to Bultmann.

2

The Lordship of Christ: The Origins of a Construct (1933–1950)

Käsemann's work on Paul in the period up to 1950[1] comprises his dissertation, written under Bultmann, *Leib und Leib Christi*,[2] and a number of essays on themes which are, in the main, ecclesiological: the body of Christ as sacrament and as church, the acclamation of the *cosmocrator* in the Christ hymn of Phil. 2, apostleship, charisma, and the question of pre-Pauline tradition in Rom. 3: 24–6.[3] The dissertation itself covers a wide range of topics in the areas of Pauline anthropology and ecclesiology. While Käsemann does not consciously use the lordship of Christ as a theme to unite these early pieces into a Pauline theology, it will be shown that they all contribute to what will be called the lordship of Christ construct. It is a 'construct' because it is made up of elements from a wide variety of exegetical discussions, while at the same time being the theologoumenon which stands at the centre of his interpretation. In later chapters it will be seen that this construct is modified by new insights while retaining most of the themes from this earlier period. This is one of the senses in which the lordship of Christ is the centre of Käsemann's interpretation of Paul both before and after 1950.

[1] For the reasoning behind this division, see p. 20 above.

[2] Käsemann's dissertation was submitted in 1931 and published in 1933.

[3] Käsemann's main articles on Paul in this period are 'Das Abendmahl im Neuen Testament' (1937); 'Die Legitimität des Apostels. Eine Untersuchung zu II Korinther 10–13' (1942); 'Anliegen und Eigenart der paulinischen Abendmahlslehre' (1947/8; ET 1964); 'Kritische Analyse von Phil. 2, 5–11' (1950; ET 1968); 'Zum Verständnis von Römer 3, 24–26' (1950); and 'Amt und Gemeinde im Neuen Testament' (1960; ET 1964). The article on Rom. 3: 24–6 will be discussed in ch. 4 below.

THE BODY: *ΣΆΡΞ*, *ΣΩ̃ΜΑ*, AND *ΠΝΕΥ̃ΜΑ*

Before the contents of *Leib und Leib Christi* can be discussed, it is necessary to note its approach and aims. Despite its title it is not primarily concerned with detailed exegetical discussion of the Pauline passages in which *σῶμα* and *σῶμα Χριστοῦ* occur.[4] In the first half of the study Käsemann portrays the history-of-religions background of the term 'body', and concludes that the idea of the gnostic aeon, which was thought to encompass a person like a giant body, lies behind Paul's thought.[5] The second aim is summed up by the subtitle, 'an investigation of Pauline conceptuality'. To this end Käsemann covers a large number of topics including the 'concepts' flesh, body, spirit, sin, death, law, baptism, sacrament, charisma, hope, and spiritual body. Against the two main traditions of interpretation then current in German scholarship, he criticizes, on the one hand, the use of the antithesis of finite and infinite (as in the idealist tradition including Baur), and, on the other, at least so far as Paul's anthropology is concerned, Lüdemann's use of the distinction between a Jewish, 'ethical' line of thought and a hellenistic, 'physical' line. Instead, following Bultmann's recently published views,[6] Paul is best understood in terms of 'historicity' (*Geschichtlichkeit*, *Leib* 111, cf. 118), i.e., existentially.[7] Käsemann's two lines of enquiry merge in the question of whether Paul is influenced by Old Testament (existential) anthropology or gnostic (material, metaphysical) anthropology. It is worth noting again that Käsemann's subtitle, which draws attention to the search for an appropriate conceptuality, and his approach to the state of the question just outlined, both point to his interest in the *theological* interpretation of Paul. Despite the appearance that his

4 These terms, as they occur in Paul's authentic letters, are dealt with in seven and (on a generous count) nineteen pages respectively.

5 In Bultmann's view this was the most important result of Käsemann's study (1936: 21).

6 Bultmann 1929*a*: 337; 1930*a*: 153.

7 The terms *Geschichtlichkeit*, *geschichtlich*, etc. pose a problem for translators. As 'historical' is potentially misleading for English readers, 'existential' has been preferred. For an introduction to Heidegger and Bultmann's use of these terms, see Macquarrie 1955: 150 ff.

dissertation is primarily concerned with history-of-religions questions, in fact theological questions concerning the conceptuality and structure of Pauline theology motivate his research. There is always a concern, even in this first, apparently historical work, for the implications for contemporary theology and preaching of a particular interpretation of a Pauline theme or word. It is important to bear this in mind before entering the often complex exegetical argument, partly at least because one expects detailed demonstration of the history-of-religions hypothesis that Paul is influenced by gnosticism, a demonstration which is not forthcoming.

After the review of the term 'body' in ancient literature noted above, the themes of body and body of Christ in Paul are discussed in the second and third parts of the thesis. The section on 'body' treats the terms *σάρξ*, *σῶμα*, and *πνεῦμα*. With Bultmann,[8] and in criticism of earlier idealistic interpretation, Käsemann argues that the distinction in 1 Cor. 15: 39 between the substance of the flesh and the form of the body is not typical of Paul's view; in fact this is a singular usage (101). Rather, to take the first of the three anthropological terms just listed, *σάρξ*, is always related to 'the human being and his sphere' and is 'the mode of appearance of human life *per se*' (*die Erscheinungsweise des menschlichen Lebens schlechthin*, ibid.). Thus, *σάρξ* and life are connected in Gal. 2: 20, and the term is used virtually for the individual life of a person (Gal. 4: 14; Rom. 6: 19; 2 Cor. 7: 5; Rom. 7: 18).[9]

Secondly, following Old Testament tradition, *σάρξ* refers to relationships in which human beings belong together: it is the bearer of human association (Phil. 1: 24), and of the ties of relationship (e.g., Rom. 9: 8), race (e.g., Rom. 1: 3), and people (e.g., Rom. 9: 3). All these differentiations allow Paul

[8] Bultmann 1926*c*: 161; 1930*a*: 153.

[9] Cf. Bultmann's argument that all the anthropological terms can at times be translated with 'I' (1930*a*: 153). The use of *εὐ τῇ σαρκί μου* in Gal. 4: 14 is generally referred more specifically to Paul's illness (e.g., Betz 1979: 235). Rom. 6: 19 scarcely relates to the individual lives of the addressees as it concerns the state of humanity in general. 2 Cor. 7: 5 again refers to a group but here *σάρξ* could well refer to individuals (*ἡ σὰρξ ἡμῶν* = 'we'; Bultmann 1930*a*: 156; Barrett 1973: 207). Rom. 7: 18, where Käsemann points to the parallel between *ἐν ἐμοί and ἐν τῇ σαρκί μου*, does refer, at least in the first instance, to an individual. However, Käsemann's claim, that the term is used 'virtually' for the individual life of a human being, cannot be sustained.

to take up the Old Testament formula 'all flesh' (e.g., Rom. 3: 30; *Leib* 101 f.). Thirdly, as there is a connection between *σάρξ* and 'world' in this last formula, *σάρξ* can mean 'worldly' in the sense of lacking divine insight. Here the Old Testament sense of the distance between God and 'all flesh' is foremost. Thus, there is a human (1 Cor. 2: 5) or worldly wisdom (1 Cor. 1: 20) which is also of the flesh (2 Cor. 1: 12; *Leib* 102).

Moving on to the phrases *ἐν σαρκί* and *κατὰ σάρκα*, Käsemann builds on this last result and finds that the former means 'standing in, as it were, a cosmic sphere' (105). The latter expresses the influence of a cosmic power. Indeed, with regard to Gal. 5: 17 it is said: '*Spirit and flesh are here set over the human being in such a sharp dualism that he does not appear as the subject but as the object of the struggle between two worlds*' (104, Käsemann's emphasis). Further, *σάρξ* not only appears as a power but is also personified (ibid.). These two points, and particularly the former, are important in that they constitute the starting-point for Käsemann's later explicit criticism of Bultmann's understanding of Paul's anthropology. He concludes that Paul understands *σάρξ* along the lines of a gnostic aeon:[10] 'Man relates to it [the flesh] neither by being the aeon [i.e., of the flesh] nor by it having him, rather he is in it in the manner of *κατέχεσθαι*' (105). In this way the idea of possession by an external power becomes a feature in Käsemann's understanding of lordship, even though the theme of lordship is not prominent in *Leib und Leib Christi*.

Käsemann next asks how the term *σάρξ*, understood along the lines of a gnostic aeon, can have anthropological and existential significance. This presents itself as a problem because of the individualistic character of the theological anthropology then current, for example, in Bultmann's work, and the determinism of gnostic anthropology. By contrast to Bultmann,

[10] This blunt assertion is typical of the way that Käsemann handles the history-of-religions questions in *Leib*. Throughout the Pauline section of his dissertation he uses the model of the gnostic aeon heuristically without demonstrating its validity in individual cases. He does not spell out the stages of his argument which is certainly not based on particular words, phrases, or theological themes common to Paul and the gnostic texts. The case is presumably that, having postulated the spatial and dynamic characteristics of the gnostic aeon concept, he finds the same conceptuality appropriate for the interpretation of Paul. However, the appropriateness of this conceptuality for the interpretation of Paul's anthropological terms is repeatedly asserted, not demonstrated.

through his gnostic interpretation of Paul, Käsemann defines a person as 'the concrete manifestation of the world which concretely determines his activity and suffering' (111 f.). This puts the emphasis not on the individual but on the 'world' which determines him or her, while maintaining the human being's capacity for decision over against gnostic determinism. At the contemporary theological level he formulates this view polemically against theologies which speak positively of the possibility of the individual:[11] 'The "possibility" of the individual is the necessity of his world, the "predestination" from his world' (112).

Having established that the aeon concept can be existentially significant, he now turns to the question of how Paul can combine Old Testament and gnostic anthropologies. Human beings are not free agents but are under the influence of an aeon. But if they are further characterized, not by the body or by 'soul substance', as in gnostic thought, but existentially, by their acts, then their determination is no longer metaphysical but existential. Thus, Paul takes up gnostic metaphysics and sees behind them a true existential approach in line with the Old Testament (ibid.). This finding in turn vindicates an existential approach to interpretation (118). Summing up, σάρξ means 'being in the world' (*in-der-Welt-sein* or *Sein in der Welt*) or 'worldliness' (*Weltlichkeit*, 112), and κατὰ σάρκα, human beings determined by their 'worldliness' (115).

Turning to the term σῶμα, Käsemann finds two senses, the first of which runs parallel to the meaning of σάρξ. Σῶμα is the 'mode of appearance of human life' and can mean the physical body (e.g., Gal. 6: 17). Again 1 Cor. 15: 35 is a singular exception in which the Greek sense of 'form' is present. Elsewhere Paul follows the Old Testament tradition in which life is connected to the body. Thus, a human being does not have a body, a human being *is* one,[12] just as a human being *is*

[11] Käsemann frequently criticizes views which represent an uncritical adoption of existentialist ideas. These criticisms ought not to be misunderstood as criticism of Bultmann but as criticism of real or possible trends in interpretation.

[12] This antithetical formulation is associated with Bultmann ('man does not *have* a *soma*, he *is soma*'; 1951: 194). Although he does not use the formulation in this period, this view is implied in 1930*a*: 153. Käsemann appears to be the first to use this formulation in print. Curiously, he does not actually make the point that a human being *is* flesh in the section on σάρξ, but he builds on this argument in this discussion of σῶμα.

flesh (119). Like σάρξ, σῶμα can refer to humanity and not just to the individual, and thus comes to mean the earthly sphere as such, especially in the phrase ἐν (τῷ) σώματι (2 Cor. 5: 6 ff., 12: 2 ff.). Finally, like σάρξ, σῶμα refers to the whole person,[13] and not to a part of the person. Thus, in this first meaning, σῶμα runs parallel with, in fact, is identical with, the meaning of σάρξ (119 f.).

In its second sense σῶμα refers to creatureliness (*die Geschöpflichkeit*).[14] Käsemann begins by drawing on Rom. 1: 20 ff: '*in this context body clearly*[15] *means the being* [*Sein*] *of man as the non-objectified* [*nicht vorfindlich*] *divine creation, and which, as a whole, including his sexuality, is the bearer of divine promise*' (121, Käsemann's emphasis). Secondly, as σῶμα a human being is faced with decision for or against God (Rom. 12: 1; 1 Cor. 3: 16;[16] 1 Cor. 6: 12 ff.; *Leib* 121). Käsemann brings the results of his investigation of the term σῶμα together so that creatureliness comes to mean 'being faced with decision for or against God' (122). In this way a further step towards an existential, theological interpretation of the creation theme is taken. He goes on to investigate the terms σῶμα τῆς ἁμαρτίας and σῶμα πνευματικόν and comes to the conclusion that they are

[13] This key point of Bultmann's interpretation is mentioned for the first time here with reference to Bultmann 1928: 160 f. and 1930*a*: 153. See further, p. 156 below, and Thiselton 1980: 279 f.

[14] So Bultmann 1930*a*: 155.

[15] It is anything but 'clear' that this is what σῶμα means in this passage. Käsemann's point is that the punishment of the Gentiles (that God gave them up to the dishonouring of their bodies) is necessarily connected with the nature of their sin (the isolation of the creation from its creator). The argument depends on an implied connection between 'creation' and 'body'. But Käsemann has picked the word σῶμα out of a passage which also mentions the effects of God's judgement on human thinking (vv. 21 f.), on sexual relationships (vv. 26 f.) and, again, on thought and consequent behaviour (vv. 28–31). Thus, one would have to say that a human being as νοῦς and as subject to πάθος is also 'non-objectified creation and the bearer of the promise'. But this would be damaging to Käsemann's argument and indicates the arbitrary nature of his focusing on τὰ σώματα in v. 24. It also weakens the general point that Paul's anthropological terms refer to a human being as a whole in a particular orientation. Here Paul refers to several parts of a human being. This interpretation of 1: 20 ff. is dropped in the later Romans commentary (*Römer* 44/48) but without recognition that this is one of Käsemann's two key passages for the interpretation of σῶμα.

[16] By citing 1 Cor. 3: 16 Käsemann presupposes that the temple metaphor in that verse is to be interpreted in the light of 1 Cor. 6: 19 in which the body is the temple of the spirit. But this is most unlikely, as Paul uses the metaphor in different ways in the two passages.

metaphysically opposed to one another as the earthly and divine spheres (124), though the metaphysical tradition is interpreted existentially by Paul. To sum up, in this second sense, σῶμα means '*the human being tempted by the objectified world, who in this world is secretly claimed by God to be "pleasing to him"*. It is the creatureliness which, robbed of its character, can become the "body of sin", but which alternatively should become the "*pneuma*-body"' (125; Käsemann's emphasis). As with the term σάρξ, the interpretation of σῶμα is related to the idea of lordship, here in the sense of God's claim: as σῶμα, humanity is claimed by God in the world (*die von Gott her beanspruchte Menschlichkeit in der Welt*, 133). Again there is a corresponding divergence from Bultmann's view: the central point is not that 'man is "body" in his temporality and historicity';[17] rather, a human being is claimed by an external power.

This interpretation of σῶμα is developed in Käsemann's article on the Lord's supper of 1947/8. Greater emphasis is laid on corporeality itself: σῶμα denotes 'the corporeality of existence as a member of creation, claimed by God and threatened by the powers' (*EVB* i. 29/129, ET modified). At a more general level, it is maintained that corporeality is the end of all God's ways, a theme which will be emphasized more strongly after 1960. In addition, the new point is added that σῶμα denotes the possibility of communication, with other people, the powers, and God (32/133). No exegetical arguments are presented to back up these important points.

The third term which Käsemann focuses on is πνεῦμα. Viewed in terms of the history of religion, πνεῦμα is a power, the power of miracle (*Leib* 99 f.),[18] and should be understood under the category 'mana' (125). Further, the spirit is thought of 'materially and substantially' (*stofflich und substanzhaft*), and, therefore, there is a close connection between the spirit and the sacraments (ibid.).[19] As in Stoic thought, the spirit is believed to penetrate the entire world; but Paul's view is not

[17] Bultmann 1930*a*: 153; later Bultmann argues that 'man . . . can be called *soma*, that is, *as having a relationship to himself*' (1951: 195 f., Bultmann's emphasis).

[18] Käsemann continues to hold to Gunkel's point ('Abendmahl' 75; *EVB* i. 111/66; 'Geist' 1272; *EVB* ii. 84/84; *PP* 212/122 f.; *Römer* 204/212).

[19] This connection was emphasized by those who investigated the hellenistic background of the NT (e.g., Heitmüller 1903: 17–21).

Stoic when he goes on to contrast the spirit and the flesh dualistically. The spirit is a 'world determining power' (*weltbestimmende Macht*), and like *σῶμα*, a type of aeon. One is set in the '*pneuma* aeon' by baptism (1 Cor. 6: 11; 12: 13; 2 Cor. 1: 22) and confirmed in it by the Lord's supper and proclamation of the word (126). Paul has a 'sacramental ethic'[20] in that the virtues appear necessarily with the new creation. They are not the result of human action but are the charismata of a miracle world (127). Thus, in this first section, Käsemann stresses Paul's 'naturalism' and the influence of hellenism. Paul's theology is ruled by sacramentalism, a point which has rightly been emphasized by Catholic exegesis against Protestant-idealistic thought (128).

However, Paul also understands the spirit existentially and eschatologically. The spirit is given by God and is itself divine (e.g., Rom. 5: 5); it stands over against the life of the human soul as life-creating. At this point Käsemann reflects on the place of the spirit in relation to other key themes of Paul's theology: as the divine revelation is always related to eschatology, and the eschatological event has dawned for the cosmos in Christ, the spirit must be understood in the light of Paul's eschatology and his christology. Following Lüdemann, Käsemann argues that Paul 'reserves' the spirit for christology.[21] Thus it is not the ethical deepening of the spirit concept which is characteristically Pauline (Gunkel)[22] but the consistently eschatological approach. As a result, life as a whole is understood 'pneumatically and eschatologically': 'It is no longer the singular and miraculous which is "charismatic" but the entire Christian existence of all Christians' (129). As a consequence a charisma is not a special *χάρις* but a 'particularisation [*eine Besonderung*] of *χάρις*' (ibid.). In this convoluted line of argument the neo-orthodox merging of eschatology and christology (ch. 1 n. 111 above) is all too evident.

Finally, the sacramental and eschatological lines of interpretation are brought together and into connection with other major themes in Paul. The sacramental spirit is an eschatological reality, issuing in the new covenant and in the

[20] *Leib* 127, quoting von Soden 1931: 376.

[21] *Leib* 129; Lüdemann 1872: 105.

[22] Gunkel 1888: 90.

opposition of the cosmic-historic powers, the letter and the spirit. The letter is the law, understood 'Judaistically' (*judäistisch*), as a demand arising out of a contract relationship. Its opposite is the obedience of faith which is, therefore, the true pneumatic act. This last statement is given lengthy exposition in which Käsemann draws the Lutheran understanding of the *nova oboedientia* under the heading of the 'pneumatic'. In the obedience of faith, it is no longer the human being but non-human *pneuma* who acts, and God, who alone is the eschatological reality, alone remains active (*Gott als der eschatologisch allein Wirksame auch allein wirksam bleibt*, 130). True life consists in allowing God the creator to act without hindering him through one's own achievement (*Leistung*). Thus, Paul's dualism and naturalism are interpreted existentially: the human being of achievement and the believing child of God have nothing in common. Neither the activity resulting from Paul's 'sacramental ethic', nor the spirit, are ever a human possession (*menschlicher Besitz*), faith is always new hearing and new obedient receiving (131 f.). In Paul's doctrine of the spirit, the existential is the meaning of the sacramental.

This interpretation of πνεῦμα shows that, from the first, Käsemann attempts to overcome the supposed divisions in Paul's thought. Here the spirit is related to the sacraments, ethics, and, most notably, the doctrine of justification. In addition, his interpretation of πνεῦμα also contributes to the lordship construct: human beings are set in a larger entity, the *pneuma* aeon, which determines them. This entity penetrates the entire world and is a 'world determining power'. Further, key theological themes from the neo-orthodox Protestant agenda are very prominent in this interpretation.

It is difficult to determine exactly to what extent Käsemann was critical of Bultmann's interpretation of Paul's anthropology in *Leib und Leib Christi*, his earliest work. Certainly he does not argue that 'the essence of the unredeemed man is to be . . . split';[23] rather, a human being is seen as under a power or, as he will say later, under a lord. Recently Käsemann has remarked that Bultmann never took up this debate, even

[23] Bultmann 1930*a*: 155.

though it is clear where the two views divide (*KK* i. 10 f.). However, there is much in the anthropological section in the dissertation which Bultmann would have agreed with and which, indeed, came from him. With hindsight it can be seen that Käsemann's own insights stand in an uneasy juxtaposition with Bultmann's views. Thus, for example, Käsemann agrees that it is not Rom. 5 (with its 'objective', i.e., supraindividual, anthropology), but Rom. 7 (with its focus on the individual) which gives the truly Pauline view of sin. Rom. 5 wards off the danger of dissolution into 'psychology', while Rom. 7 prevents the 'objective' view of Rom. 5 dissolving into metaphysics (*Leib* 113). While Käsemann continues to hold to this second point, the first one is in tension with his own finding that in Paul's theology human beings are always thought of as under a power.

THE BODY OF CHRIST: CHURCH, SACRAMENT, AND CHRISTOLOGY

In this earlier period Käsemann discussed the subject of the body of Christ on three occasions.[24] These discussions can best be dealt together as they share a great deal in common, while the development of Käsemann's views will also be noted.

The church as the body of Christ

It is surprisingly difficult to give a clear account of Käsemann's understanding of the church as the body of Christ from his pre-1950 work. The only prolonged discussion occurs in his dissertation where the argument is focused on exegetical debate with H. Schlier to such an extent that it is difficult to see Käsemann's main point, which is that Paul's understanding of the body of Christ (like that of Colossians and Ephesians) presupposes the gnostic doctrine of the primal man, whose gigantic body fills the cosmos, and into which believers are incorporated.

[24] *Leib* 159–62, 168–71, 174–86; 'Das Abendmahl im Neuen Testament' (1937); 'Anliegen und Eigenart der paulinischen Abendmahlslehre' (1947/8; ET 1964).

Schlier[25] had argued that the gnostic primal-man myth is the background to the use of the body of Christ motif in Colossians and Ephesians, but that the myth is absent from the authentic Pauline letters. In the latter the Stoic organism idea is employed to explain the relationship of believers to one another. In the authentic letters the 'head' belongs entirely to the body and is not given a particular role, whereas in gnostic usage the head–body motif is of decisive importance. Consequently, the enigmatic **οὕτως καὶ ὁ Χριστός** of 1 Cor. 12: 12*c* is to be translated 'thus it is, where Christ is' (*so steht es auch, wo Christus ist*), avoiding the implication that the church *is* Christ's body. Finally, in 1 Cor. 12: 13, 27, rather than the body *being* Christ's, it *belongs* to Christ.[26] Thus, for Schlier, Paul's understanding of the body of Christ does not go beyond the Stoic organism idea of one body and many members applied to a community.

Before outlining Käsemann's own views it is worth noting his refutation of Schlier's detailed objections to the hypothesis of gnostic influence on Paul's use of the body of Christ (168 f.).

1. While the body myth is more concrete and pictorial in the deutero-Pauline epistles than in Romans and 1 Corinthians, this is not due to gnostic influence on later epistles, but to Paul having modified the gnostic myth to a greater degree. (It is worth noting the two unverifiable hypotheses here: that Paul knew the gnostic myth, and that he then modified it to the point where it can no longer be recognized.)

2. While Rom. 12: 4 and 1 Cor. 12: 27 do not make a direct equation between the body of Christ and the church, the use of 'we' and 'you' in these passages can only be related to the church.

3. While 'one body *in* Christ' (Rom. 12: 5) is not compatible with Ephesians or with the myth which speaks of Christ and the church in juxtaposition, nevertheless the 'one body *in* Christ' of Rom. 12: 5 is not really emphasized. Rather this verse is to be understood as 'We, the many, are one body, in that we are in Christ'. Similarly, 1 Cor. 12: 13 is to be translated 'in Christ one is simultaneously body of Christ'. In

[25] Schlier 1930, which was also a thesis written under Bultmann.
[26] Ibid. 40 f.

other words ἐν Χριστῷ and σῶμα Χριστοῦ are understood as being virtually synonymous. Käsemann agrees with Schweitzer that 'in Christ' is an abbreviation for 'participation in the mystical body of Christ' (162).[27]

4. Schlier argued that in Ephesians the writer is concerned with the relationship of Christ to the body, whereas Paul focuses on the relationship between believers. In reply Käsemann maintains that the question of the unity of the members is not Paul's only concern. The members become a body on account of their relationship with Christ: 'It is from Christ that the members become one body'.

5. Schlier's main objection is that the gnostic myth only occurs with the head–body scheme which is lacking in Paul. However, Schlier has drawn the wrong inference in that in *Eclogae Propheticae*, 56: 2 f., the head has no particular significance (*Leib* 80, 169).

Having responded to Schlier's arguments, Käsemann makes his own case for the importance of the primal-man myth and the aeon conceptuality for interpreting Paul's theology. He does this by arguing that, while the Stoic organism idea is present in Rom. 12 and 1 Cor. 12, it only explains the details of Paul's use of the body of Christ theme. It does not account for the line of thought in 1 Cor. 12–14, nor the relationship of the body of Christ to Paul's anthropology, doctrine of the sacraments, and christology (*Leib* 161). Thus, Käsemann does not claim to show a direct correlation between gnostic and Pauline theologies; rather he makes a case from the nature of Paul's theology (as he understands it) which he believes can best be understood against a gnostic background.

1. In Paul's anthropology the body is not normally seen as the unity of the members (as in the organism idea), but as under the lordship of either God or sin. Thus, the unity of the body is not the unity of the person as opposed to the multiplicity of the members, but the unity of creation which faces the double

[27] Schweitzer 1930: 122. Surprisingly Käsemann does not register a protest against the use of the word 'mystical'. Schweitzer and Käsemann both argue that the church as the body of Christ is cosmic, corporate, christologically determined, and 'real', despite deriving the motif from different history-of-religions backgrounds (apocalypticism and gnosticism respectively).

opportunity of decision, for God or for sin (161). For Käsemann, an approach to the body of Christ theme from the organism idea divorces it from its proper context in Paul's anthropology and theology (*Leib* 161).

2. Church and sacrament are held tightly together by Paul; in fact the centre of Pauline and deutero-Pauline thought lies here. The sacraments are the basis of the activities of the spirit and the 'being in Christ'. In baptism, 'natural personality' is destroyed and the 'Christ nature' is conferred. It is precisely in this way that the plurality of subjects become one, i.e., become Christ and his body. This sacramental naturalism does not fit with the organism idea and, *contra* Schlier, excludes the view that the church belongs to Christ. Thus, the crux in 1 Cor. 12: 12*c* is to be translated 'This is also the case with Christ' (*So verhält es sich auch mit Christus*, 161 f.).

3. Paul's understanding of the Lord's supper also rules out the use of the organism idea as the key to interpretation. It is not the assembling of the congregation which creates or establishes (*konstituieren*) the body of Christ but the sacramental food (162). Thus, Käsemann's first three arguments turn on the inappropriateness of the organism idea to express Paul's theology.[28]

4. Like Paul's other concepts, the body of Christ is to be understood along the lines of a gnostic aeon (ibid.). In order to support this point Käsemann reviews the evidence for gnostic influence on Paul's christology. The key passages are simply listed (Rom. 5: 12 ff.; 1 Cor. 15: 21 f., 45 ff.; Phil. 2: 6 ff.) as evidence for a well-established hypothesis. 'Here Christ is the second Adam who restores the creation' (163). The further discussion is concerned with possible hints of an aeon theology in a wide variety of passages. This is of particular interest because a connection is made between the christological passage in Phil. 2: 6 ff. and the confession of the lord in 1 Cor. 12: 3; in this way the general theme of lordship is broached. It is worth noting that for the concept of confession or acclamation, Käsemann uses a transliteration (*die Exhomologese des Kyrios*), a practice which paradoxically is often a signal that he has a wider theological theme in mind.

[28] Cf. the theological criticism of the organism idea by Barth (1922: 427).

At this point he builds extensively on Peterson's view[29] that acclamations are inspired shouts with legal connotations: 'In acclamation the people of God submit themselves'. Consequently, one can go further than Bousset and argue that the title 'lord' is connected not only with the cult but with myth. If, in addition, the *anthropos* theme is interchangeable with that of lordship (Käsemann cites the deutero-Pauline passages, Col. 2: 6, 4: 1; Eph. 6: 9), a number of verses in the letters (1 Cor. 2: 8, 6: 16 f., 8: 5, 2 Cor. 3: 18) and the phrases ἐν Χριστῷ, ἐν κυρίῳ, and ἐν πνεύματι can be interpreted in the light of the gnostic primal-man myth (163–5). Paul's christology, like his ecclesiology, is to be understood against a gnostic background, and is expounded in terms of lordship.[30] It is worth noting in passing that one of the key stages in this complex argument depends on exclusively deutero-Pauline texts.

5. Whereas in Rom. 12: 5 ff. and 1 Cor. 12: 4 ff., 28 ff. the reader would expect Paul to say that the body of Christ is the unity of the χαρίσματα, in fact he makes a jump and says that Christians are the body of Christ. This is in line with the gnostic tendency to replace 'charismatic powers' with 'soul powers' (169).

6. The organism idea has its place in indicating to the Corinthians that the χαρίσματα have their value, not on account of their mere existence or heavenly origin, but in their service to the church. Thus, 1 Cor. 12: 15–21 is not to be regarded as the centre of Paul's conception of the body of Christ, but is an auxiliary line of thought. The emphasis in 1 Cor. 12 falls on the οὕτως καὶ ὁ Χριστός of v. 12 and the sacramental action in v. 13*a* (170 f.).

7. As will be seen in the next section, in the course of his interpretation of the Lord's supper, Käsemann argues that the

[29] Peterson 1926: 147 n. 1.

[30] This is only extended discussion centred around the concept of lordship in *Leib*. In this earliest work the concept is significant for a number of themes: christology (as above); dualistic world-views in the Old Testament and gnosticism (21, 51, 57); the rule of sin, or the demonic powers, as opposed to God's, or Christ's, rule (113; cf. 126 f., 138, 161, 167); the interchangeability of *kyrios*, *pneuma*, and church in relation to charisma (171); κοινωνία as 'falling under a lord' (176); and the Lord's supper as the proclamation of the ascended, enthroned *kyrios* (178). (The concept is also mentioned on 108, 124, 155, 179, 182, 184 f.) However, lordship is conceptually subordinate to the aeon (e.g., 126, 171, 181) and does not form a central theme of the dissertation.

church as the body of Christ is the new order of salvation, and thus assumes a central place in Paul's theology as a whole.

8. Against Barth,[31] the theme of 1 Corinthians is not the resurrection of the dead but the body of Christ. The function of 1 Cor. 15 is to indicate the scope (*Tragweite*) of the body of Christ theme. At the same time it makes it clear that Paul is not concerned with a metaphysical but an existential state. Käsemann defines this as a state in which the 'here and now' has significance but is also conditioned by the hope of God becoming all in all, a view he will emphasize after 1960. To sum up: the sacrament inaugurates a new history or existence, God's new order of salvation, which is contained 'thoroughly really and concretely' in the church. However, this new order is not objectifiably present, it does not come in by a process of development (*Entwicklungsprozess*), as was understood under the influence of idealism. It stands and falls with the grace of the creator (182 f.).

With these arguments Käsemann puts forward his case that the body of Christ in Paul is to be interpreted along the lines of (an existentially interpreted) gnostic aeon, and in connection with his primal-man christology. As an aeon the body of Christ encompasses the cosmos. Christians are incorporated into it by baptism and the Lord's supper. The body-members idea is secondary to this and Paul employs it only for paraenetic purposes. This implies, as Käsemann argues explicitly later, that the body of Christ is not an image or a metaphor. Indeed, it was a dislike for this type of formulation in liberal exegesis that was one of the driving forces in the search for the gnostic interpretation of the body of Christ (*ThLZ* 81 (1956), 588 f.).

The Lord's supper

It is in the discussion of the Lord's supper that Käsemann's work of 1933, 1937, and 1947/8 both repeats itself most often and undergoes minor and major modifications. To avoid repetition this topic can be dealt with under six main headings. But first it is worth noting the different aims of the

[31] Barth 1924 *passim*.

three accounts. In the dissertation the discussion is focused on the 'concepts' κοινωνία, καινὴ διαθήκη, and ἀνάμνησις. By contrast, the article of 1937 reviews the understanding of the primitive Christian meal in the New Testament as a whole, and argues that the view of the meal is primarily determined by different eschatologies. Finally, the essay of 1947/8 searches for the distinctively Pauline understanding of the Lord's supper,[32] particularly in comparison with the view of the pre-Pauline hellenistic church.

The attempt to understand the Pauline Lord's supper historically, by setting it in a hellenistic history-of-religions context, is to be credited to the history-of-religions school, and in particular to Eichhorn and Heitmüller.[33] Although Käsemann never refers to these scholars,[34] their work is of great importance for him. He takes over some of Heitmüller's basic points, specifically rejects others, and attempts to resolve certain theological problems posed by Heitmüller's (and to a lesser extent, Eichhorn's) interpretation.

The exalted Christ-spirit christology and the hellenistic context of the Pauline Lord's supper

With Heitmüller, Käsemann sets Paul's view of the Lord's supper within the context of a particular strand of his christology which for convenience can be called an exalted Christ-spirit christology. Interpreting the typology of 1 Cor. 10: 3 f., Heitmüller argued that βρῶμα πνευματικόν and πόμα πνευματικόν refer in the first instance to the elements of the Lord's supper, and then to the Old Testament events mentioned in the passage. The elements originate from the spirit and convey the spirit. The rock is the pre-existent Christ because Paul here transfers the Jewish belief in pre-existent wisdom to Christ. He concludes that the exalted Christ is the food and the drink of the Lord's supper.[35] More fundament-

[32] Käsemann's interest in the 'special concern and character' (*Anliegen und Eigenart*) of the Pauline Lord's supper is not conveyed by the ET of the title ('The Pauline Doctrine of the Lord's Supper').

[33] Eichhorn 1898; Heitmüller 1903, 1908, 1911. Cf. Kümmel 1958: 253–7.

[34] This is doubly remarkable, not only on account of the importance of their works, but because of the direct line back to Heitmüller via Bultmann.

[35] Heitmüller 1903: 24 f. His argument ignores the point that the Israelites drank *from* (ἐκ) the rock; it is the rock (and not the water) which was Christ. Cf. von Soden 1931: 366.

ally, he argues that, for Paul, *ἐν Χριστῷ* and *πνεῦμα* are related key concepts, citing 2 Cor. 3: 17, *ὁ δὲ κύριος τὸ πνεῦμά ἐστιν*.[36] Käsemann takes up this exalted Christ-spirit christology and combines it with his view of Paul's debt to the gnostic primal-man myth. Thus, *πνεῦμα* is *a* rather than *the* key concept in Käsemann's view of the Lord's supper.[37]

The idea of the exalted Christ-spirit who is present and gives himself in the Lord's supper is emphasized for the first time in 1937. Christians feed on and drink the power of the resurrection corporeality of Christ in the Lord's supper ('Abendmahl' 75). In contrast with the synoptic gospels, the elements of the supper assume a new importance as they are the bearers of the heavenly 'spirit-substance' (76). This change comes about because of the move into a hellenistic environment where the Lord's supper can be compared with Jewish and pagan (sacrificial or cult) meals. According to Käsemann this can be seen by the way Paul chooses *κοινωνία* as the *tertium comparationis* in 1 Cor. 10: 14 ff. (77). However, in a judgement which implies criticism of Heitmüller, he does not accept that pagan ideas are present in the Lord's supper, even though they were present in the surrounding religious culture (ibid.).[38]

In the essay of 1947/8 Käsemann discusses the Lord's supper in the context of a review of Paul's debt to and modification of earlier hellenistic Christianity. The latter regarded spirit as a rarefied heavenly substance and within this tradition Paul understood it as the substance of resurrection corporeality, the mode of being of the resurrected one. However, his own view is that the spirit is primarily the gift which simultaneously gives participation in the giver. Through the spirit believers are brought into the *praesentia* of the exalted lord and 'stand before his face' (*EVB* i. 19 f./117 f.):

In the *pneuma* the *kyrios* comes to us, takes possession of us and claims us for his own . . . With Paul everything depends on the point[39] that,

[36] On the identification of the lord and the spirit, cf. Bousset 1913/1921: 160–3.

[37] *Contra* Neuenzeit 1960: 185.

[38] For Heitmüller, the Pauline Lord's supper is a sophisticated version of the type of meal in which eating connects the devotee to the god, or in which, by bodily eating of the god, the devotee achieves union with the god (1903: 40–52).

[39] The ET brings out Käsemann's point overdramatically by translating 'Bei Paulus steht und fällt alles damit, daß' (translated above) with 'it is Paul's *articulum*

wherever he describes *pneuma* as a sacramental gift, there he is speaking most radically of the revelation of Christ himself, of his self-manifestation and his presence [*praesentia*]. (20/118, ET modified; cf. 'the spirit is the earthly *praesentia* of the exalted lord'; 'Geist' 1274)

Thus, the phenomenon of the presence of the spirit in primitive Christian worship gives way to the doctrinal centrality of Christ, and Käsemann is only one step from a contemporary theological affirmation.

In the same way Paul builds on and interprets the major themes of the hellenistic theology he inherited. In the hellenistic view a human being is the object of the struggle between the powers of the flesh and the spirit: 'He [man] came into being when earthly matter managed to seize for itself elements of the heavenly world and thus acquired life: similarly he finds redemption when the *pneuma* invades his earthly nature and recaptures him for the heavenly world' (18/116). Again Paul both agrees with this view and develops it theologically: 'Human existence is for him [Paul] no longer autonomous, it is determined by its involvement in its world [*Welt*; ET: 'universe']; it is both the object and the arena of the strife between heavenly and earthly powers. It is conditioned by the answer to the question: "To which power do you belong? Which Lord do you serve?"' (19/117) Redemption is no longer a metaphysical transformation (*Verwandlung*) brought about in a naturalistic way. Rather, because the lord who determines human existence can change, there is the possibility of an existential transformation (ibid.).[40] The Corinthians appear to have regarded the sacrament as a *φάρμακον ἀθανασίας* (Ignatius, Eph. 20: 2) which guaranteed salvation.[41] Paul, while agreeing that the sacrament was 'material' (*naturhaft-stofflich*) and that it transforms its recipient, understood it as 'a call to obedience, the possibility of decision for

stantis et cadentis ecclesiae that', i.e., the theologically essential point is that Christ himself (understood with reference to the doctrine of justification) is the centre of the Lord's supper, and thus of Christian worship and theology.

[40] Cf. Käsemann's later use of the phrase 'change of existence as change of lordship' (*Existenzwandel als Herrschaftswechsel*; e.g., *EVB* ii. 188/176; *Römer* 39/43).

[41] This interpretation, based on exegesis of 1 Cor. 10: 1–13, was well established in the history-of-religions school and goes back at least to Rohde 1890: 298, 307. Cf. Eichhorn 1898: 24; Wernle 1901: 81 (cited in Kümmel 1958: 290); also Lietzmann 1907: 120.

faith and against the temptation to disobedience' (*EVB* i. 19/117).

Finally, as has been seen, Paul did not understand the body of Christ as the sum of its members on the Stoic model, nor metaphysically as in gnosticism. Rather, the body of Christ is to be understood in terms of a sphere of lordship, this idea being used explicitly in the essay of 1947/8:

It [the body of Christ][42] is the Lord himself in the radiation of his power which encompasses the world, and the embodiment [*Inbegriff*] of all that belongs to him—in short, Christ's sphere of lordship. Wherever the *Kyrios* becomes present in the *Pneuma* he claims man for his sphere of lordship. But this is neither a natural event nor a mystical process. The *Kyrios* reaches out for me by claiming my will for himself and makes me serviceable for his will, thus making me a member of his lordship. Obedience is the Christian's new mode of being in which he has been put by the sacramental epiphany of Christ. (*EVB* i. 20/118 f., ET modified)

Here again a history-of-religions analysis and a theological statement are combined: the body of Christ is interpreted as Christ's sphere of lordship (*der Herrschaftsbereich des Christus*),[43] and this is then expounded in theological and existential terms. In the meal human beings are claimed for Christ's lordship by the presence of Christ in the spirit. Käsemann can speak about the 'claim' on the believer because, in terms of the dynamics of the meal, the spirit claims or possesses the participant. This understanding of the meal is transferred to a theological level when it is said that the *kyrios* claims the will of the believer and the result is obedience as the new mode of being. Like Bultmann,[44] Käsemann supports his own theological and existential interpretation by arguing that Paul himself systematically demythologizes the hellenistic conceptuality which he received from the church.

However, it is important to note that this entire discussion of the body of Christ is not based on discussion of the passages

[42] The ET is confusing here because it translates *er*, referring back to *der Christusleib*, as 'he'. In general the translation given above is more literal that the ET.

[43] The importance of the lordship theme is obscured in the ET because of the number of translations of *Herrschaft* and cognates: dominion, kingdom, realm, lordship, etc. For example, the element of lordship is seriously weakened in the sentence 'The Body of Christ is the *realm* [*Herrschaftsbereich*] . . .' (29/130).

[44] See, e.g., Bultmann's interpretation of the resurrection in 1 Cor. 15 (1926*b*).

in Paul's letters in which the body of Christ theme occurs, but on the 'sacramental epiphany' of Christ in the meal. As such it presupposes the argument, still to be outlined, that the idea of the church as the body of Christ is central to Paul's understanding of the Lord's supper.

Κοινωνία: participation in a sphere of power

In his dissertation Käsemann deals with 1 Cor. 10:1 ff. by focusing on the 'concept' *κοινωνία*. Although he was soon to abandon this approach to the passage, his interpretation of this word is of continuing significance. Following Lohmeyer,[45] he argues that *κοινωνία* does not mean community among believers but participation (*Teilhabe*, *Anteil*) in objective realities such as the spiritual food and drink of 1 Cor. 10: 3 f., and ultimately in the *pneuma*-Christ. The underlying idea is that of existence which is determined by having fallen under the power of something (*Verfallensein*). In a cryptic but important footnote it is said that this *Verfallensein* materially underlies the *kyrios* concept which is connected with the myth (*Leib* 176 n. 4). (Käsemann is presumably referring to the primal-man myth.) Thus, the theme of lordship emerges again and is picked up in 1937 and 1947/8: *κοινωνία* means falling under a sphere of power ('Abendmahl' 78); it is 'the experience of forcible seizure, of the overwhelming power of superior forces' (*EVB* i. 25/124, ET modified).

Once again it is a category taken from the study of the phenomena of early Christian worship which contributes to the lordship construct. A sphere of power is what is experienced by a devotee in the cult. Heitmüller argued that *κοινωνία* with the demons (1 Cor. 10: 20 f.) was understood as close and 'real', and not symbolic: 'one truly came into contact with them [the demons] and their sphere of power [*Machtsphäre*] through the meal and sacrifice.'[46] In turn Käsemann's view of a sphere of power is couched in terms of his understanding of an aeon. 'Their community [the participants in the Lord's supper] is not based on their own,

[45] Lohmeyer 1928*b*: 17; *Leib* 174.

[46] Heitmüller 1903: 27. Again it is remarkable that Käsemann makes no reference to Heitmüller's views here; he goes as far as to say that only Lohmeyer has attempted to put this concept in a historical setting ('Abendmahl' 77).

independent activity or will, but on the outworking of a stronger power or sphere [*Macht oder Sphäre*] which is set over them all and which makes them all its participants on account of its dynamism which alone determines and dwells in them' ('Abendmahl' 77). In short, for Käsemann, *κοινωνία* means participation in a sphere of power.

The eucharistic body of Christ and the church as the body of Christ (1 Corinthians 10: 17)

In his dissertation Käsemann had argued, without putting emphasis on these points, that primitive Christian tradition underlies 1 Cor. 10: 16 (*Leib* 176)[47] and that in v. 17 'the meal coincides in some sense with the body of Christ' (177).[48] These points are developed and refined in the discussions of 1937 and 1947/8, the latter being summarized here. Verse 16 contains pre-Pauline sacramental terminology[49] which Paul takes up and interprets in v. 17 (*EVB* i. 13/110). While v. 16 assumes the agreement of the Corinthians, v. 17 begins to make assertions, and it is because Paul wished to interpret the bread word that the traditional order of bread and wine is reversed in v. 16 (ibid.). Paul's own point comes in v. 17: 'Through the element called the *σῶμα Χριστοῦ* we are incorporated into the *σῶμα Χριστοῦ* as church, so that, according to 1 Cor. 12: 12 f., we are members of the body, whose head is Christ.'[50] ('Abendmahl' 80; cf. *EVB* i. 13/110; Käsemann has stood by this interpretation: *EVB* ii. 187/174 f.; *PP* 194/111; *Römer* 26/28; 'Leiblichkeit' 7.) Thus, as has been noted before, it is not merely the assembling of the people

[47] It contains the Jewish 'flesh and blood' concept which Paul has altered to 'body and blood' because the former was unusable within Paul's anthropology. For criticism of this, see Robinson 1952: 57 n. 1. Heitmüller's argument for pre-Pauline tradition in v. 16 is on different grounds (1903: 22–33).

[48] Käsemann here refers to Bousset 1915: 59 n. 1.

[49] Käsemann lists the Jewish expression *ποτήριον τῆς εὐλογίας*, the use of *εὐλογεῖν* instead of *εὐχαριστεῖν*, the phrase 'the breaking of bread', and, probably, the formulae *κοινωνία τοῦ αἵματος/τοῦ σώματος τοῦ Χριστοῦ* (*EVB* i. 12/109).

[50] The head–body motif is not present in the text. Other serious objections can be raised against Käsemann's interpretation of 10: 17. The focus of the verse is not the (eucharistic and ecclesiological) 'body of Christ' but the motif of 'oneness': neither the church, nor the eucharistic element are called *σῶμα Χριστοῦ* here; the terms are *ἓν σῶμα* and *οἱ πάντες* for the former, and *εἷς ἄρτος* for the latter. Paul's concern is not how participants *become* the body of Christ but the relationship of the (already *existing*: the verb is *εἰμί*) one and the many.

which creates the body of Christ; rather, the one bread which is 'taken in bodily' (*sich einverleiben*) incorporates (*einverleiben*) the many into the body of Christ ('Abendmahl' 80). Presupposing his interpretation of 1 Cor. 11: 24 ff. (see below), Käsemann concludes that the theologoumenon of the body of Christ is central to Paul's understanding of the Lord's supper, and of baptism (*EVB* i. 13/111).

Καινὴ διαθήκη: the body of Christ as the new order of salvation

In order to understand Käsemann's interpretation of 1 Cor. 11: 23 f. it is necessary to follow the argument in *Leib und Leib Christi*. If 1 Cor. 10 is centred on the κοινωνία concept, the same is true of 1 Cor. 11 and διαθήκη. With Lohmeyer and Behm,[51] διαθήκη is translated 'order' and, thus, καινὴ διαθήκη is 'the new order of salvation' (*die neue Heilsordnung*) which came into force with the death of Jesus. From a wider Pauline perspective the combination of Rom. 7: 4 and 2 Cor. 3 is used to fill out the interpretation.[52] The law was the old order; but by the body of Christ we have been 'killed' to it, so that we might belong to another, i.e., to the resurrected one. The body of Christ is now not the 'killed' body but the body of the resurrected one, the church (*Leib* 177). Whoever becomes a member of this body leaves the previous order. The law is 'killed' in the church, and the world—which belonged to it—is crucified to the Christian. Now there is no longer Jew, nor Greek, etc. but only members of Christ who cleave to him bodily (*leiblich*, ibid., citing 1 Cor. 6: 15 f.), as previously believers belonged in the flesh to the world. Just as Christ's death 'dissolved' (*auflösen*) his body and the resurrection gave him a new body, so for the Christian the σάρξ, the body of the world and its order of law, is 'dissolved'. As a member of the new body of Christ, the Christian is now dependent on the church. Käsemann concludes: 'The Lord's supper sets one in the new order of salvation, it connects one bodily with the order of salvation of the church' (178).[53] Thus, via an

[51] Behm 1912; Lohmeyer 1913; cf. Bultmann's review of these books (1915).

[52] The following section has been reproduced in a literalistic manner so that the steps in Käsemann's interpretation remain visible.

[53] This hypothesis is the forerunner (and later, companion) of Käsemann's argument of 1937 that the eucharistic σῶμα Χριστοῦ incorporates human beings into

interpretation of Rom. 7: 4 and 2 Cor. 3, Käsemann is able to equate the new covenant and the body of Christ. On the strength of this, he uses the phrase the body of Christ, not merely as an ecclesiological term, but in connection with Paul's soteriology (law, justification, new life).

For Käsemann, the body of Christ is the central motif of the eucharistic passages in 1 Cor. 10 and 11, and thus of Paul's view of the Lord's supper. With this argument he solves one of the principal problems posited by Heitmüller. For the latter, there is a theological tension between a sacramental understanding of the meal in 1 Cor. 10 (communion with the exalted lord brought about by sacral eating and drinking) and a symbolic understanding in 1 Cor. 11 (a meal which brings to memory and proclaims the death of Christ, and institutes the new covenant which is to be interpreted symbolically).[54] Käsemann resolves this problem by arguing that the body of Christ—which is both 'real' and is interpreted existentially—is the central motif of both passages. This discussion is also important for Käsemann's view of the coherence of Paul's theology. If the body of Christ is a general term for the new order brought by Christ, Christ's sphere of lordship, then it can be argued that there is no divide between the ecclesiological and soteriological sides of Paul's theology.

Ἀνάμνησις: the proclamation of the exalted lord

A third point in Käsemann's interpretation of the Lord's supper in his dissertation concerns the meaning of ἀνάμνησις. Rejecting the current views that this refers to the memory of the death of Jesus[55] or is to be regarded as evidence for drawing a parallel with the Greek memorial meals for the dead,[56] he argues that Paul himself explains this word in the following *καταγγέλλειν*. In turn the latter is understood, with Dittenberger,[57] as an official proclamation, and is to be connected with the *kyrios* concept. The *Sitz im Leben* of the

the ecclesiological *σῶμα Χριστοῦ*. However, it should be noted that the 1933 argument is an interpretation of 1 Cor. 11: 25, the 1937 argument of 1 Cor. 10: 17.

[54] Heitmüller 1911: 68 f.

[55] J. Weiss, 1910/1925: 289.

[56] Lietzmann 1907: 58.

[57] Dittenberger 1915/1924: 635. 32; 695. 41; 797. 5; 1903/5: 319. 13; 456. 10. Käsemann also refers to Lohmeyer 1929*b*: 86.

hymn in Phil. 2: 6 f. is the Lord's supper[58] and this indicates what underlies ἀνάμνησις: it is the proclamation of the enthronement of the lord. In fact proclamation is the *raison d'être* of the body of Christ: 'By being constituted as the body of Christ in the Lord's supper [*Herrenmahl*],[59] the community of Christians solemnly proclaims—through its reality, its actual objective presence [*faktisches Vorhandensein*]—the new order of life through God in Christ for the world' (*Leib* 178). Words are not necessary: the Lord's supper is itself a proclamation. It leads to epiphany, acclamation, and enthusiasm. Because it is this kind of event Paul lays great stress on order; otherwise the difference between the old 'order of the world' and the new 'order of salvation' is not observed and those involved open themselves to judgement (179). Finally, this proclamation is only meaningful until Christ's return: the coming day is the limit and meaning of church proclamation and sacramental activity (ibid.). Thus, the supper is a juridical act and this accounts for the legal language in the passage ('Abendmahl' 86). This last point is expanded and becomes very important in the 1947/8 essay.

The epiphany of Christ in grace and judgement

If Käsemann repeatedly stresses that the lord is present in the meal, the 1947/8 essay takes this theme further by arguing that he comes, not only as saviour, but as judge. He begins by pointing to the numerous legal concepts and phrases in 1 Cor. 11: 17 ff.: συνέρχεσθαι is the term for the assembling of the *demos*; the strong antithesis between κυριακὸν δεῖπνον and ἴδιον δεῖπνον recalls the constitutional use of the first adjective;[60] the use of κρίνειν and its derivatives; ἀναξίως, 'not appropriate' and ἔνοχος; καταγγέλλειν and διαθήκη in the sense of 'to proclaim a decree or ordinance'; and the pair, παραλαμβάνειν

[58] Käsemann follows Lohmeyer 1928*a*: 65, here. In 1950 he came to the conclusion that a *Sitz im Leben* in baptism is slightly more probable (*EVB* i. 95/88).

[59] Considering that this word is a literal translation of Paul's own phrase (κυριακὸν δεῖπνον) and fits so well with Käsemann's focus on lordship, it is surprising that he does not use it regularly, preferring the contemporary ecclesiastical term *Abendmahl*.

[60] This usage is very far from the Pauline world. On ἴδιος, see now Theissen's hypothesis: the richer participants provided for all ἐκ τῶν ἰδίων while at the same time enjoying a private, better meal (ἴδιον δεῖπνον) with their peers (Theissen 1974*a*: 148–51).

and *παραδιδόναι*, the equivalents of the rabbinic terms denoting tradition, *qibel* and *masar* (*EVB* i. 21 f./119 f.). Käsemann then argues that the account of the Lord's supper is a binding 'formula of holy law'.[61] The phrases 'in the night in which he was betrayed' and 'until he comes' are to be seen, not as a rather threadbare narrative, but as the *terminus a quo* and *terminus ad quem* which mark off the formula. The naming of the lord indicates on whose authority the eucharistic action is based. Within this context *ἀνάμνησις* is again understood as an obligation to proclaim the redemptive meaning of the death of Jesus which issues in a confession of faith (22/121).

Käsemann combines this analysis with a second point: the underlying conflict between Paul and the Corinthians concerns eschatology.[62] 'The Corinthians are obviously celebrating the Eucharist as an earthly anticipation of the banquet of the blessed in heaven just as, according to ch. 15, they hold that the day of *ἀνάστασις* has already dawned. They are conscious of themselves as the redeemed and fondly imagine themselves to be no longer *in via*' (23/122). Against these views Paul reminds them that they stand between Jesus' death and the parousia (and thus judgement). To bring them to order Paul formulates a law whose validity will only be disclosed on the last day, and thus the *ἔσται* of v. 27 refers to eschatological judgement. Drawing on earlier arguments Käsemann says that the presence of Christ in the supper means that worshippers either unite with the community in proclaiming the death of Jesus, or with the world in bringing about his death, and consequently become 'guilty'. Thus, both the cross

[61] Käsemann had already touched on this subject in *Leib* and developed it in 'Sätze heiligen Rechtes im Neuen Testament' (1954) and 'Die Anfänge christlicher Theologie' (1960). In these essays form-critical arguments (as opposed to vocabulary tests) are used to detect 'sentences of holy law'.

[62] As already noted, the relation between eschatological and sacramental beliefs is a constant point of enquiry in Käsemann's discussions of the Lord's supper and is the main theme of the article of 1937. It is through this that he resolves a tension posited by A. Eichhorn between the last supper and the cult meal of the primitive Christian community: 'Whatever Jesus may have said or done on that evening I find it impossible to understand the cult meal of the community—with the sacramental eating and drinking of the body and blood of Christ—from this beginning' (Eichhorn 1898: 31). In response Käsemann argues that an eschatological outlook unites the two meals: the last supper looks forward to the coming kingdom; in the Lord's supper Jesus' death is understood as the beginning of the new eschatological order ('Abendmahl' 87).

and the parousia (judgement) are encountered in the sacrament and it is with these that Paul confronts the enthusiasts (24/123). Within a *theologia crucis* a sacrament does not provide a guarantee of salvation but the possibility of obedience and a life of trial (*der Stand in der Anfechtung*). Christian life is set between the cross and the parousia and is to be understood within a *theologia viatorum* (24/123). Thus, in this context, Paul's eschatology is the basis of his (and Käsemann's) criticism of enthusiasm. Secondly, a strong unifying tendency can again be seen in Käsemann's interpretation: the sacramental and eschatological lines of thought are integrated.

In his dissertation and the article of 1937, Käsemann took the ambiguous μὴ διακρίνων τὸ σῶμα of 1 Cor. 11: 29 to refer to the church as the body of Christ, but without discussion (*Leib* 179; 'Abendmahl' 86 f.). However, in the essay of 1947/8 he emphatically takes the opposite view: 'It does not seem to me to be possible to refer τὸ σῶμα to anything other than the sacramental element of the bread of the Lord's supper' (*EVB* i. 27/127).[63] He supports this view with an explanation of why Paul fails to mention the blood of Christ here: as in 10: 16 f. the bread word is more significant for Paul than the cup word. Paul's 'enigmatic brevity' in this verse is intended to bring all participants in the Lord's supper under judgement: 'The self-manifestation of the *Kyrios* is, of course, at the same time that of the universal Judge' (25/125, ET modified).[64] The gift cannot be separated from the giver himself. His presence does not become absence because of irreverence. In the supper the worshipper meets either salvation or judgement: 'salvation despised is [ET: "becomes"] judgement . . . Wherever the Saviour is scorned; the Judge of the world nevertheless remains and manifests himself in that very place as the one from whose revealed presence [*Epiphanie*] we can find no way of escape' (ibid.). This is what the Corinthians have in fact

[63] Theissen offers two interpretations of this phrase: some do not distinguish between the food which belongs to the κυριακὸν δεῖπνον and that which belongs to the ἴδιον δεῖπνον (1974*a*: 153), and, secondly, some do not distinguish the bread, 'the body of Jesus', from another kind of σῶμα, a possible allusion to the σώματα of animals (Jas. 3: 3; Theissen 1974*a*: 159). Against the first is the point that σῶμα does not normally mean 'food', but 'corpse' or 'body'.

[64] The ET does not carry the force of the German, achieved by conciseness of expression: *Epiphanie des Kyrios ist ja zugleich die des Weltenrichters.*

experienced (1 Cor. 11: 30), and all are called to judge themselves (v. 31) so as not to fall into the hands of the judge (26/126). Stated in more general terms, Käsemann's point is that the supper issues in the self-manifestation of Christ as saviour and judge.

Consequently, the frequency of legal terminology in this passage is not accidental but arises directly out of Paul's christology. The sacrament is a 'kind of anticipation of the Last Day within the community' (26/125):[65] 'Here we encounter him, in whom election and rejection encounter us' so that, according to our attitude to him, we choose one or the other for ourselves' (ibid.). The play on the verb *κρίνειν* and its derivatives in vv. 29 f. is designed to bring out the dialectic of grace and judgement. Käsemann sums up with reference to the theme of lordship:

> The self-manifestation of Christ calls men to obedience and this means that, at the same time, it calls them to account before the final Judge who is already today acting within his community as he will act towards the world on the Last Day—he bestows salvation by setting men within his lordship and, if they spurn this lordship, they then experience this act of rejection as a self-incurred sentence of death. (26/126)

This brings the second theological theme of this essay to a climax. If Paul systematically demythologizes the motifs which he inherited from the hellenistic church, he also rejects their false understanding of eschatology and puts his own critical christology in its place. Here Käsemann is clearly in the tradition of Luther and Barth, where Christ is both saviour and judge, and where both election and rejection are encountered in him.[66]

The words of institution in tradition and Pauline interpretation

In a final section of the essay of 1947/8 Käsemann seeks to elucidate the specifically Pauline understanding of the words of institution. Here again he finds the doctrine of the body of Christ to be the key for interpretation.

[65] Cf. Theissen 1974*a*: 166.

[66] 'Grace is not grace unless the one who is graced is the one who is judged'; 'Grace is the power of obedience . . . because it is the power of death' (Barth 1922: 166; cf. 194).

Dealing with the words over the cup first, he argues, as before, that the central idea is the new covenant taken in an eschatological sense: it is 'the form of the βασιλεία τοῦ θεοῦ inaugurated by Christ as an already present reality' (28/128, ET modified). The eucharistic cup gives a share in this. Paul's version of the cup word is derived from Mark's (*τὸ αἷμά μου τῆς διαθήκης*) and not vice versa, as *καινὴ διαθήκη* is a Pauline theologoumenon (2 Cor. 3). (The background to Paul's version is to be found in Jer. 31: 31 and not Exod. 24: 8.) In fact Paul has taken the components of the tradition and rearranged them: the new covenant has the body of Christ as its content which portrays the *βασιλεία*, brought in by Christ, in its present form. Käsemann continues that even if this reconstruction is not accepted it must be recognized that the tradition in 11: 23 f. touches directly on the special concern of the Pauline doctrine of the Lord's supper. In the tradition the new covenant is based on the death of Jesus, in Paul its content is the lordship of Christ. The believer gains a share in this and thus in the *kyrios*, the exalted one himself (30 f./131). Whereas in Mark the sacramental gift is a share in the body and blood of Christ, and therefore in his death, in Paul the gift puts the believer into the body of Christ and thus under Christ's lordship (31/131 f.).

Before discussing the words over the bread Käsemann draws attention to a disparity between the two sets of words: the blood is spoken of only with an interpretative gloss (*Interpretament*) and attributively.[67] The various possibilities for the interpretation of *σῶμα* are reviewed. An Aramaic equivalent for it is highly improbable, particularly on account of the un-Aramaic *τὸ ὑπὲρ ὑμῶν*. Käsemann concludes that *σῶμα* ought not to be translated 'I' (Bultmann), but 'body', and the following *τὸ ὑπὲρ ὑμῶν* specifies that this body is the 'body of Jesus given over to death for us' (29 f./129 f.).[68] Thus, the words over the bread relate to the death of Jesus. The disparity between the two sets of words is, therefore, of theological and historical significance.

[67] However, the *τὸ ὑπὲρ ὑμῶν* in the words over the bread can also be regarded as an interpretative gloss.

[68] Käsemann does not defend his assumption that the meaning of the anthropological term *σῶμα* should determine the meaning of the eucharistic *σῶμα Χριστοῦ* (see also the next note).

However, Käsemann goes on to argue that, in Paul, the words over the bread also relate to participation in the exalted lord. Here he appeals to two 'presuppositions' of Pauline thought. Firstly, the anthropological term σῶμα indicates the possibility of communication, and, because Christ is the 'bodily' resurrected one,[69] there exists the potentiality and the actuality of communication with Christians.

For what he [Christ] now is, he is precisely not as a person in the sense of individuality, but in orientation to us and for us, just as he acted 'for us' as the incarnate and bodily dying one. The resurrected one continues what the incarnate and crucified one did. He exists 'bodily' for us, he gives us 'bodily' participation in himself. Thus he who is now exalted can, in the Lord's supper, continually give us that which in his death he gave us once and for all: τὸ σῶμά μου τὸ ὑπὲρ ὑμῶν (32 f./133, ET modified)

Thus, the disparity between the two words of institution does not allow a separation of the cross and resurrection: the exalted lord is the one who was crucified (ibid.).

Secondly, while it is the corporeality of the resurrected one which makes possible his self-giving (*Selbsthingabe*) in the sacrament, the reality of the sacrament is otherwise always described by Paul as the imparting of the spirit. Thus, to put it pointedly (*zugespitzt*), one would expect Paul's version of the bread word to read 'This is my spirit', and in fact, put pointedly, this is Paul's view (33/134). For Christ's corporeality is σῶμα πνευματικὸν as he himself is πνευματικὴ πέτρα and τὸ πνεῦμα. Σῶμα Χριστοῦ and πνεῦμα Χριστοῦ are, therefore, in certain respects, interchangeable for Paul. In 1 Cor. 12 the community only becomes Christ's body (*Christusleib*) through Christ's spirit (*Christusgeist*) which works in it, and in Rom. 8: 9 Christians have Christ's spirit as those who have been sacramentally incorporated into Christ's body.[70] 'The Apostle is maintaining against every possible magical, metaphysical or mystical misinterpretation that it is the *Kyrios* himself in his

[69] Güttgemanns notes Käsemann's criticisms of an individualistic understanding of the resurrection while opposing his emphasis on the *bodily* resurrection of Christ. Käsemann's views on the anthropological term σῶμα should not be transferred to the interpretation of Paul's eschatology and christology which should be interpreted in temporal terms (Güttgemanns 1966: 260 f.).

[70] This reference to incorporation into the body of Christ presupposes that this motif lies behind Rom. 8: 9; it is not in the text.

self-manifestation who is dealing with us, and in such a way as to lay hold on our will, lay claim to our obedience and set himself over us indeed as our Lord'[71] (33/134, ET modified).

Thus, to sum up, for Käsemann, the sacrament of the Lord's supper issues in the epiphany of the crucified *and* exalted Christ.[72] While the tradition of the history-of-religions school saw the meal primarily as a cultic affair, for Käsemann it has a much wider significance. In it Christians are claimed for concrete bodily obedience in the body of Christ. In this way Christ proves himself as *cosmocrator*, who grasps the world into his lordship in the bodies of Christians, and with his body constitutes the new world (34/135).[73] Käsemann concludes: 'Paul's doctrine of the Lord's supper is thus part of his christology and only if we treat it strictly as such can we fully appreciate its special concern and its particular character [*Eigenart*; ET: 'originality']' (ibid.).

This section of Käsemann's essay is poorly organized and somewhat confusing. The subject under discussion changes constantly, and, more seriously, while Käsemann argues that there is a discrepancy between the words over the bread and those over the cup (where the former refer to the crucified lord alone, the latter to the crucified and exalted lord), in fact he finds the same double reference in the words over the bread ('this is my body', 'this is my spirit'). This last conclusion is in line with his view that Paul never separates the death and resurrection (33/133). The complexity of this section is due, to a certain degree, to the series of equations which are built up in the course of his three discussions of the Pauline Lord's supper. The new covenant is the form of God's kingdom introduced by Christ, or the lordship of Christ, or the body of Christ. The eucharistic *σῶμα Χριστοῦ* is also the spirit, or the lordship of Christ. From this series of equations Käsemann

[71] The next sentence should read 'It is all the more essential to notice [ET: 'to establish']', and the following one is also wrongly translated: 'The Apostle's clear intention here is to lay stress on the element of the reality of the self-imparting of Christ'.

[72] This is Käsemann's final answer to the stock question whether the meal gives participation in the death of Christ or in the exalted Christ. Up to this point (and even in the essay of 1947/8, 16 f./114) he tends to hold the latter with Heitmüller, but his final position is that the two aspects are not to be separated.

[73] Käsemann's point is not that in his own body Christ inaugurates the new world (ET) but that Christ's body *is* the new world.

concludes that it is the lord himself who is encountered in the sacrament. This approach gives his interpretation its cohesion, but it has to be asked whether Paul's language is so fluid that each of these motifs can be used in place of the others.

APOSTLESHIP IN 2 CORINTHIANS 10–13

In 1942 Käsemann published a long essay on 2 Corinthians 10–13[74] whose main concern is the historical reconstruction of the views of Paul's opponents and of Paul's response to them. Käsemann's approach is to identify the opponents' catch-phrases, now embedded in these chapters, and to reconstruct their views from them ('Legitimität' 476, 498 f.). Following Lütgert and Reitzenstein on the pneumatic, enthusiastic, character of Corinthian Christianity,[75] Käsemann corrects the former by arguing that, in contrast to 1 Corinthians, Paul is now confronted with a form of Jewish Christianity (483 f.). However, the opponents are not the 'primitive apostles' (*Urapostel*) themselves, who are to be equated with the *ὑπερλίαν ἀπόστολοι* of 11: 5 and 12: 11, but a circle of Jewish Christians who stand next to them, and who attempt to advance their Judaizing programme under the name of the 'primitive apostles' (492).

The conflict concerns apostleship. Paul is accused of lacking the signs of an apostle (12: 12), pre-eminently the ability to work miracles. Thus, the opponents' main point is that 'he is no genuine pneumatic' (477). Paul's *μέτρον τοῦ κανόνος* and his *δοκιμή* are questionable (13: 3, 6), because, unlike their

[74] 'Die Legitimität des Apostels: Eine Untersuchung zu II Korinther 10–13'.

[75] Reitzenstein 1910/1927, 336 f. Lütgert's work is particularly important: Paul's opponents in 1 Cor. were hyper-Paulinists, pneumatics, gnostics who believed in the 'other Jesus', spirit, and gospel of 2 Cor. 11: 4, and who radicalized the notion of freedom. 'They are libertarian pneumatics. They believe themselves to be going in the same direction as Paul but to be going beyond him. To them he is a weakling who has remained halfway along the way. He is not a real pneumatic—without the spirit, power, courage, confidence, certainty of victory, and assurance which characterizes the pneumatic. He is not consistent in exercising his freedom but hide-bound and fearful, both in his relationship to God, and in relation to the community and the world. They, on the other hand, act with boldness and impudence in all three directions. They fear neither God, nor any person, nor any sin . . . They stand in the same relationship to him as the enthusiasts to Luther' (1908: 86).

own, his apostolic existence does not go back, via the Jerusalem church, to the historical Jesus. Thus, as Baur[76] saw, the question of 'legitimacy' was raised (495). Further, Paul is accused of sarkic behaviour (10: 2), and, specifically, of unreliability (1: 13, 17), calculated craftiness (12: 16), and coldness towards the Corinthians (11: 11). Nor can it be ruled out that, although he has supposedly rejected financial support from them, in fact, he has been compensating himself secretly and has had the profit motive uppermost all the time (7: 2, 12: 17 f.). Finally, he is primarily concerned with his own person whether in 'boasting' (10: 13, 15), recommendation (7: 2; 12: 17 f.), self-defence (12: 19), or even in proclamation (4: 5). Thus, in the light of the catchwords *εξέστημεν* (*ἐξίστημι*, to be out of one's senses; 5: 13) and *πανοῦργος* (crafty, sly; 12: 16; 477 f., 495), he can be depicted as virtually not responsible for his own actions. On the basis of this reconstruction Käsemann concludes that the opponents in 2 Cor. 10–13 are pneumatics, but, *contra* Lütgert and Reitzenstein who regarded them as gnostics (483 f.), pneumatics on Jewish soil, on account of their interest in tradition and legitimacy (491, 496).

While historical reconstruction is the main theme of this essay, it is also of wider Pauline and theological interest. Firstly, Käsemann argues that the concepts 'God' and 'apostle' cannot be objectified and understood neutrally (506) but only through the 'mind of Christ' (1 Cor. 2: 16). The apostle speaks as a pneumatic, his standards are not 'earthly-objectifiable' (*irdisch-vorfindlich*) but 'heavenly' (*himmlisch*; 504–6). Here Käsemann moves between historical and theological levels: the designations 'heavenly' and 'pneumatic' and the opposition earthly–heavenly are historical and descriptive, while the term 'objectifiable' introduces a note of theological evaluation.[77] The latter is also present in the demand for a standard for an apostle which human beings can have power

[76] Baur 1845: 289.

[77] Because, for Käsemann, 'apostleship' is a genuinely theological concept, there can be no direct knowledge of it, nor is it a 'given entity'. To regard it as such would be tantamount to 'works'. For Bultmann's critique of objectified language about God, see Bultmann 1925*b*: 58–61; 1933*d*: 313 f. Building on Johnson 1974, Thiselton 1980 deals at length with the philosophical and theological background to the idea of 'objectification' (for a summary, see 210–12).

over and scrutinize (*ein verfüg- und kontrolierbarer Maßstab*). Thus, Käsemann finds a correspondence between controversies in primitive Christianity and the debate between dialectical theology and other modern (but, especially, liberal) theologies. This concern is intertwined with the use of a model of Protestant criticism of Catholic ecclesiology which goes back to the Reformation. Käsemann argues that the opponents are promoting an ecclesiology based on a 'principle of tradition' or of 'legitimation' (*Traditionsprinzip*, *Legitimationsprinzip*; 496, 498). Thus, while the catch-phrase 'early catholicism' (*Frühkatholizismus*) does not yet appear,[78] Käsemann is clearly concerned with this question here; his interpretation is already being formed by the contrast between Paul and early catholicism.

A second major argument concerns apostleship directly. The starting-point is the view that 'apostle' and 'gospel' are correlates (494). Consequently, an attack on Paul's apostleship is an attack on, or perversion of, the gospel (*εὐαγγέλιον ἕτερον*, 2 Cor. 11: 4). Further, Paul appropriates the reproachful catchword *ἀσθένεια* for his christologically orientated theology. His *ἀσθένεια* is connected with the sufferings of Christ (1: 5; 499) and is the place of revelation of the divine *δύναμις* on earth.[79] If grace means the power demonstrated in the apostles as the bearers of Christ (12: 7 f.; Rom. 1: 5; Gal. 2: 9), then weakness is its manner of revelation, its medium and necessary correlate (500). Finally, Käsemann makes the christological connection explicit in commenting on 13: 4, which he regards as the decisive, if overlooked, verse:

> Weakness is the sphere of the crucified one, God's power the sphere of the exalted Christ. And as God's power is simultaneously the basis of the resurrection of Christ, and the power which reaches its peak in this resurrection, so weakness is the root [*Wurzelboden*] of the cross, and the cross the deepest unfolding of this weakness. (501)

The determining role of christology, understood in the light of the cross, in Käsemann's interpretation of Paul is beginning to emerge here.

[78] The first use of this catchword is *ThLZ* 73 (1948), 666. Cf. 'Probleme' 141–4, 167 f.; *EVB* i. 239 n. 1/236 n. 1.

[79] Following, among others, Stählin 1933: 491.

If Christ is the prototype[80] for the apostle, there are also implications for the community in the present time. As the resurrected one, Christ has been removed from the sphere of weakness but the community has not; it still awaits its life to be revealed at the parousia. Its life in the present is in the demonstration of love, and any attempt to anticipate the future is satanic deception. This point then becomes another part of Paul's critique of enthusiastic Christianity: 'For the weakness of the sphere of the cross of Jesus is for the moment the sole reality of belonging to Christ, the *σχῆμα* of Christian and apostolic existence *per se*' (503).

For Paul, the *μέτρον τοῦ κανόνος* of an apostle does not relate to a link with the historical Jesus, but is simply a matter of dependence on the lord. The mind of Christ has taken possession of him. Here again a christological perspective determines Paul's view: the apostle is under the power of his lord, and this issues in both freedom and limitation. In particular, Christ's lordship is asserted in the Corinthian context against the rule of the arbitrary (*die Willkür*; 505), the characteristic mark of enthusiasm.

Paul's anti-enthusiastic stance is dwelt on at length in the exegesis of 2 Cor. 12: 2–10. Käsemann emphasizes the uniqueness of this passage (512) and the way that Paul distances himself from his ecstatic experience (513). The passage does not deal with Christian existence *per se*, nor with a revelation of God or Christ (513, 514), nor the one Christian mystery, salvation in Christ. It refers to *μυστήρια*, eschatological secrets, about which Paul cannot or may not speak. Because his translation to heavenly places did not concern the Logos (*sic*), and because he was out of the body and the *νοῦς* was not affected (515), the entire episode is to be relegated to the events of his private life which did not affect his understanding of his office as an apostle (517).[81] Thus, the anti-

[80] The idea that Christ is the prototype (and not merely an example to be imitated) which Käsemann emphasizes later, is present here, even if the term 'prototype' (*Urbild*, *Prototyp*) is not.

[81] While Käsemann's view of Paul is influenced by Reitzenstein's research into the hellenistic mystery religions, a fundamental difference between their interpretations can be seen at this point. Reitzenstein equates *πνεῦμα* and *νοῦς* (1910/1927: 338), whereas Käsemann makes *νοῦς* (along with eschatology and the doctrine of charisma) the basis of Paul's critique of enthusiasm. For Käsemann, Paul is an anti-enthusiastic pneumatic.

enthusiastic thrust of Paul's understanding of Christian existence is emphasized in this essay (cf. 'Wunder IV: Im NT', *RGG*, 3rd edn., 6 (1963), 1835–7). Käsemann sums up in a final paragraph which draws the consequences of his interpretation for his own theological tradition:

> The true sign of an apostle is not the individual mighty works, nor ecstatic experiences, but the continuity of service in the community, carried out in *ὑπομονή* and *ἀσθένεια* and marked by *σωφρονεῖν* and *ἀγάπη*. In the church it is only the charisma which has true *ἐξουσία*. This certainly divides gospel ministry[82] from all enthusiasm, and sets an unmistakable boundary over against both enthusiasm and traditionalism. (520 f.)

The essay of 1942 contains several themes of great importance for Käsemann's interpretation of Paul's theology. Firstly, there is the criticism, started in *Leib und Leib Christi*, of 'objectifiable' standards for apostleship. This criticism is now combined with an attack on the idea that the authority of the gospel can be legitimated by a chain of tradition. Secondly, the point that it is Christ alone, and not his earthly disciples, who has left the sphere of weakness provides a criterion for the criticism of enthusiastic Christianity. Putting these two points together, Käsemann can argue that the gospel is involved in a battle on two fronts, enthusiasm and traditionalism.[83] However, it is noticeable that this point appears for the first time in the conclusion of the essay and not, as later, from the first as a key to the interpretation of Paul's theology. Equally important for the future is the determining role which christology plays in the understanding of other aspects of Paul's theology, here apostleship and the church. Christ's lordship is connected with both his exaltation and the cross; these two aspects must be held together. Consequently, Paul urges the cross against the Corinthians who have focused only on the exalted lord.

[82] 'Das evangelische Amt' could also be translated 'the Protestant ministry (or, ministerial office)', but here Käsemann has the 'ministry determined by the gospel' primarily in mind.

[83] Elsewhere in this early period he argues that the gospel has only two enemies, 'pharisaism and gnosis' (*VF* 3 (1946/7), 191 f.; 'Entmythologisierung', 6) or 'enthusiasm and nomism' (*VF* 5 (1951/2), 217, where it is said for the first time that this 'critical function' is the centre of Paul's theology). Cf. Bultmann, who argues that Paul made the knowledge given in faith explicit on the two fronts of Judaism and gnosticism (1929*b*: 207), and Luther.

These arguments point forward to Käsemann's later work. After 1960 all the Pauline themes discussed are related to a central complex of christology understood in the light of the cross and the doctrine of justification, and this theological pattern is defended as essential for an understanding of the Christian faith. In 1942, apostleship is interpreted in the light of Paul's christology; however, this argument is part of the interpretation of Paul's theology (level 2). Only in the last sentence of the essay is it made explicit that this understanding of the gospel has contemporary theological significance (level 3).

CHRIST AS *COSMOCRATOR* IN PHILIPPIANS 2: 5–11

Käsemann's study of Phil. 2: 5–11,[84] one of his longest and most influential essays,[85] proceeds by way of detailed debate with the history of interpretation in twentieth-century German Protestant exegesis to a new interpretation in which the hymn is read against a hellenistic-gnostic history-of-religions background. With Barth, Käsemann emphatically rejects the ethical view of this passage which appeals to the paraenetic context of 2: 6–11 and sees Christ as a model of humility and self-denial for the Christian life.[86] In this view the *ἐν Χριστῷ* of v. 5 is understood to refer to the pre-existent Christ or the Jesus of history. Käsemann polemicizes against 'ethical idealism' (and its key word, 'attitude', *Gesinnung*) as the

[84] 'Kritische Analyse von Phil. 2, 5–11' (1950; ET 1968). The omission of this essay from *ENTT*, presumably on the grounds of length, was short-sighted.

[85] Martin's monograph of 1967 (now to be supplemented by his commentary of 1976) describes Käsemann's essay as 'the most weighty and important contribution made to the study of Philippians ii. 5–11 in the post-Lohmeyer period' (1967: 90). Käsemann repays the compliment in his brief but approbatory review of Martin's monograph. His only criticism is that Martin continues the apparently ineradicable use of the category of 'poetry' in New Testament studies, a category with false associations in this context (*ThLZ* 93 (1968), 665 f.).

[86] Christ is not an example for the ethical life, and *φρονεῖν* in v. 5 does not refer to 'attitude' but to orientation. *'Εν Χριστῷ* means 'in the sphere of Christ' (Barth 1928: 53). But Käsemann criticizes Barth for translating *μορφή* as *Erkennbarkeit* (recognizability, visibility), thereby reintroducing the old dogmatic two-natures approach into the discussion. Barth fails to see the myth around which the hymn is structured and instead finds in it the paradox of Christ who is both God and human being, and precisely in his humility (*EVB* i. 58/51 f.).

sponsor of this reading. While this view flourished in the nineteenth century, it continues to exert influence on the expositions of Lohmeyer (*EVB* i. 55/49 f.), Dibelius (61/55), and Michaelis (62 f./56 f.).[87] He also criticizes interpretations which continue the older dogmatic tradition and see a two-nature christology as the central point of the passage (58/51, 71/65).

In the exegesis of this passage Käsemann starts from three fundamental points made by Lohmeyer. Phil. 2: 6–11 is a pre-Pauline hymn[88] which is to be interpreted, at least initially, in isolation from its immediate paraenetic context (52/46). Secondly, the hymn is structured around a myth in which the destiny of a divine being on his way through the stages of pre-existence,[89] incarnation, and exaltation is portrayed (54/48). Thirdly, the hymn does not concern the believing individual, nor even the Christian congregation, but a 'world-wide revelation event' (55/49). To these points Käsemann adds two further arguments: the hymn is deeply influenced by primitive Christian eschatology and is to be read against a hellenistic and gnostic background.

As noted above, the hypothesis of a pre-Pauline hymn leads, in the first instance, to an interpretation which is independent of its context in Phil. 2, and in particular of its use in paraenesis. The ethical interpretation cannot account for the second stanza of the hymn, which on this view has to be regarded as an excursus or a digression (59 f./52 f.). This point has been taken into account in all subsequent exegesis, even that of E. Larsson who has attempted to revive the ethical view, though not in a convincing way.[90]

[87] Lohmeyer 1928*a*, Dibelius 1923/1937, Michaelis 1935 ad loc.

[88] Käsemann agrees with Lohmeyer (1928*b*: 96), and with Bultmann in his review of Lohmeyer (1930*b*: 777), that the hymn is made up of six triplets (or of two stanzas of three triplets each), and that *θανάτου δὲ σταυροῦ* in v. 8 is a Pauline addition (*EVB* i. 82/75). The alternative view, arranging the hymn into six couplets, was first put forward by Jeremias (1953). For a recent restatement of the case for Pauline authorship, see Hawthorne 1983 and 1987.

[89] With others, Dunn rejects the view that the hymn speaks of Christ's pre-existence; rather, it is part of the Adam christology of early Christianity (1980: 114–21, with extensive bibliography on recent discussion).

[90] Larsson argues that, like Christ, Christians will be glorified as a reward for their obedience (1962). In reply Martin points out that 'there is nothing in the text which hints at the Church's glorification with her Lord', however common this theme may be elsewhere in the New Testament (1967: 88).

The hymn is concerned with the way of the redeemer in descent (*Erniedrigung*)[91] and exaltation (*Erhöhung*) and not with the mind or attitude of the redeemer, far less of the redeemed. Through the scheme of a myth, it tells of the salvation event in an objective way (58/52, 72/66, 80/74); through its eschatology, its speaks of the salvation of the cosmos (78/71). Even the phrases ἑαυτὸν ἐκένωσεν (v. 7), ἐταπείνωσεν ἑαυτὸν, and γενόμενος ὑπήκοος (v. 8), which have provided support for the ethical theory, do not refer to the attitude of the redeemer but to stages in the myth of redemption. What is important in v. 8, for example, is the objective state of affairs, the 'having descended', and the fact that he was obedient (77/70 f.).

The use of the category of myth is also important for the criticism of the traditional christological view of the passage. The hymn does not satisfactorily answer dogmatic questions because its concern is to set forth a series of occurrences as part of a unified event. Thus, Käsemann argues, 'he emptied himself, took the form of a slave, appeared as an entity like a human being, one could see that he had become human. The concern here is not for the identity of a person in different phases but the continuity of a miraculous event' (76/my translation, cf. ET 70). For the same reasons it is illegitimate to abstract ἑαυτὸν ἐκένωσεν from the sequence in order to build up a kenosis doctrine (72/66).

As already mentioned, Käsemann argues that the hymn is to be interpreted against a hellenistic and gnostic background. For the purpose of analysis it is important to distinguish between his appeal to the gnostic primal-man redeemer myth and to the hellenistic world-view which is said to be reflected in the hymn.[92] With regard to the gnostic myth Käsemann makes four points. The descent/humiliation scheme (where the obedience of the one who has descended is critical) is common to this passage and the 'obedient human being' christology of Rom. 5 and Heb. 5: 8; all these passages presuppose the primal-man myth. Indeed, by portraying the

[91] Käsemann avoids the connotation of personal humility—which is almost inevitably suggested by the English 'humiliation'—by speaking both of *Erniedrigung* and *Niedrigwerden* (descending, becoming lowly).

[92] Georgi cautions against merging the epithets 'gnostic' and 'hellenistic' (1964: 263 f.).

redeemer as the counter-image (*Gegenbild*) of the fallen primal man, the myth itself offered the possibility of the Pauline modification which sees the descending one as the obedient one. The next step was to identify the primal man with the Adam of scripture and, thus, the contrast between the disobedient Adam and the obedient Christ was arrived at and became a central theologoumenon (79 f./73). Secondly, 1 Tim. 3: 16 and Heb. 1: 3 f. are said to present Christian variations of the same myth in the context of the heavenly enthronement motif (83/76). Thirdly, the phrase ἴσα θεῷ (v. 6) is used in Corp. Herm. 1. 13 f. of the primal man (69/63). Lastly, a point of difference between the myth and the hymn is emphasized. While both regard the coming of the redeemer as the beginning of the end of the world, the hymn does not follow the myth in speaking of the apotheosis of humanity by absorption into the deity. In the Christian variation of the myth the world does not come to itself but to its lord (93/86).[93]

Käsemann then gives an account of the hellenistic world-view. In comparison with classical times, the chaos, which had stood on the boundaries of the ordered world, has broken into the cosmos and transformed it into a battleground (*Kampfplatz*). Everything is now included in the conflict of the powers. The world is no longer formed by the logos but stands under ἀνάγκη, and, consequently, salvation consists of freedom from ἀνάγκη (66/59, 81/74). The terminology of the hymn is to be explained against this background. *Μορφή* is not 'form' in contrast to 'content' but has come to mean 'being' (*Wesen*), which in turn is the bearer of a particular energy (*Energie*). In magic texts and the Hermetica *μορφή* means 'mode of being in a particular orientation', existence orientated to a particular divine being or power (66–8/60 f.). The word *δουλεία* means slavery to *εἱμαρμένη*, matter, the stars, and the powers, and therefore the *μορφὴν δούλου* of v. 7 refers to Christ's subjection to the powers (73/67).[94] *Ὁμοίωμα* (v. 7)

[93] The gnostic interpretation has been rejected by most scholars (e.g. Georgi 1964: 263 f.; Martin 1967: 92). It has been re-presented, with modifications, by Wengst (1972: 154) and Schenke (1973: 205 ff.)

[94] Hofius objects that in hellenistic texts the name of the subjugating master is always given, and argues (with Jeremias 1953) that vv. 7*b* and 7*c* belong to different couplets and are therefore not to be taken as parallel (1976: 62).

is to be understood in the context of the hellenistic εἰκών teaching where it means either 'duplicate', or refers to a correlation or analogy with the original form. While it is used in the former sense in Rom. 5: 14, 6: 5, in 8: 3 it is introduced to show a final difference despite other similarities. In the same way, in Phil. 2, Christ is in human likeness but is distinguished from humanity by his obedience (74–6/68 f.). Thus, the hellenistic world-view determines the hymn's understanding of existence (humanity under 'destiny' or the powers) and its view of the nature of salvation (freedom from the powers through the redeemer who has become enslaved to the powers).

In the second stanza Käsemann emphasizes the portrayal of the enthronement of Christ which culminates in the conferral of the name and acclamation by the powers. Here he is particularly indebted to Peterson's interpretation of *ἐξομολογεῖσθαι*. Peterson argued that this word originally refers to the acclamatory shout of the crowd on the appearance of an emperor or other dignitary. This acclamation has legal significance in that, under certain circumstances, it was regarded as legal acknowledgement of title and dignity. In the papyri the word means 'to recognize something as lawful'. Secondly, acclamation was thought of as inspired and is related to *ἐνθουσιασμός*, the response to a divine epiphany.[95] In the light of this, Käsemann understands the acclamation of the powers in response to the conferral of the new name as their public and irrevocable recognition of Christ as lord. It is 'an act of holy law, a binding obligation to be carried out in dutiful response to a divine epiphany' (87/80). In the acclamation and the conferral of the name there is a transfer of power (*Machtübertragung*) from the powers to Christ. He is now *pantocrator*, or, as Käsemann says more frequently, *cosmocrator*. The powers were the 'bearers of destiny' (*Schicksalsträger*) for humankind but now the world has been freed from demons, and Christ is the one with whom the world has to do (85/78,

[95] Peterson (1926: 320) cites the example of Eusebius' account of the election of Bishop Fabian following the descent of the dove on the otherwise unfavoured candidate: 'whereupon the whole people, as if moved by one divine inspiration, with eagerness and with one soul cried out "worthy," and without more ado took him and placed him on the episcopal throne' (Ecclesiastical History 6. 29. 4; ET: Lawlor and Oulton 1927: ii. 83).

88/81). 'He [Christ] determines the destiny of the universe and of each individual being. He is this destiny as *deus revelatus*, as criterion and κριτής of all history' (85/78). At this point Käsemann has moved from historical reconstruction to contemporary theological statement.

If the ancient world longed for freedom from destiny, the Christian message not only offered such freedom in Christ, but, uniquely, saw the free person as being put under a new lordship, the lordship of Christ (94/86 f.). Instead of the promise of apotheosis, the gospel offers the possibility of true human existence in which human striving for self-transcendence is under constant criticism. Here Käsemann finds a connection with the doctrine of justification. Finally, because human beings are set free from one lordship and placed under another, this change can be called a 'change (or exchange) of lordship' (*Herrschaftswechsel*, 94/86). This idea, which is rooted in Käsemann's reconstruction of the hellenistic world-view, comes to have considerable theological importance for him.

Käsemann builds an interpretation on the basis of these technical discussions. In line with Lohmeyer's analysis, he focuses on the two movements of descent and exaltation: 'The one who is like God became a slave and obedient; the one who became [ET: 'is'] obedient in his earthly enslavement becomes the *kyrios*' (79/73). It is the revelation of the obedient one on earth that is the true eschatological event (ibid.).[96] This is why the turn in the course of events depicted in the hymn, marked by διό in v. 9, follows γενόμενος ὑπήκοος in v. 8. The theme of obedience is maintained in the second stanza where the cosmic scope of the eschatological event is brought to the fore: 'The divine action at the enthronement of Christ emphasizes that the activity of him who became obedient on earth affects the whole world and is the [ET: 'a'] salvation event, that such obedience was more than the ethical deed of an individual, i.e., it was revelation' (84/my translation, cf. ET 77). Thus, the relationship between Christ and the believer is not to be understood as that of a model (*Vorbild*) to be imitated, as in the idealistic tradition; rather, Christ is

[96] 'Das eigentliche eschatologische Ereignis' (*EVB* i. 79): not 'an eschatological event' (Martin 1967: 90).

the archetype or prototype (*Urbild*).[97] With this designation Käsemann emphasizes Christ's lordship over believers.

The other pole of this christology of the obedient one is exaltation to the position of *cosmocrator*. Käsemann's use of this title is significant for his view of Paul's theology as a whole and merits a separate investigation.

Excursus: cosmocrator

The word *κοσμοκράτωρ*[98] does not occur in the Christ hymn of Phil. 2; indeed, as a title (or in the singular), it does not occur at all in early Christian literature.[99] The only occurrence in the New Testament is in the plural form in Eph. 6: 12, where Christians are said to be fighting, not against 'flesh and blood', 'but against the principalities, against the powers, against the world rulers of this present darkness [*πρὸς τοὺς κοσμοκράτορας τοῦ σκότου τούτου*], against the spiritual hosts of wickedness in the heavenly places' (RSV). Here, as the parallel phrases indicate, the word refers to the evil powers which rule the present order.

The word has its background in ancient astrology where it meant a planet which was believed to exercise influence on human affairs. As such the planets were regarded as 'bearers of destiny'.[100] The word took on the meaning 'ruler of the world' and became synonymous with *παντοκράτωρ*.[101] In the third century BC, under the influence of oriental religions, the emperor was regarded as the representative of God on earth and thus was elevated to the dignity of *κοσμοκράτωρ*. After the single occurrence in Ephesians, the use of the singular form became important in the second century AD. For Marcion the *κοσμοκράτωρ* was the evil god of the Old Testament. In Valentinian gnosticism the title was used for the devil in

[97] Cf. Barth 1922: 154. However, in the later Romans commentary, Käsemann concedes that in Phil. 2: 5 ff. (and Rom. 15: 1–6) Christ is both model and prototype (*Römer* 369/381 f.).

[98] To my knowledge the only detailed discussion of this word is to be found in Cumont 1919: 313–28; cf. also Reitzenstein 1904: 77, n. 1; Dibelius 1909: 164; Peterson 1926: 173 n. 1, 238, 318; Schlier 1930: 11 n. 1; Michaelis 1938: 913 f.

[99] Bauer 1979: 445*b*.

[100] Peterson 1926: 259 n. 2, 262 f., 326 f.

[101] On this word, see Hommel 1953/4. It occurs in Revelation and once in Paul, in 2 Cor. 6: 18, in a quotation from the LXX, where it is common but is always used of God (Bauer 1979: 608 f.).

person, as formed by the demiurge and the spirit of evil, who dominates the sub-lunar world of humanity.[102]

On the basis of this review, it appears that *κοσμοκράτωρ* as a title is not attested in early Christian literature, and, in general, is never an honorific title for the saviour figure, with the exception of the usage of the emperor which is not relevant here. Given this background it is highly surprising that Käsemann took up the term and has championed it as a christological title.[103]

Käsemann never discusses the background and history of the title at any length. Some clues to how he understands it can be gleaned from his occasional comments. He connects it with the world saviour of Virgil's Fourth Eclogue. 'The heathen myth of the divine child who seizes the lordship of the world at his enthronement and who with the subjection of the powers effects an eschatological peace which surpasses the *pax Romana* is transferred to Christ' (*ZThK* 56 (1959), 370). In particular he argues that the title summarizes the hymns of the enthusiastic primitive Christian community. Thus, he contrasts the lack of christological content in the argument of Rom. 13: 1–7 with the hymns which:

> proclaimed that the lordship of Christ had already broken in on the world and the cosmic powers had been brought into subjection. But these hymns originated in the enthusiastic religious life of the community and to this extent it is no accident that they base their message on the myth of the world saviour figure familiar to us from Vergil's *Fourth Eclogue.* (*EVB* ii. 213/206)

However, Käsemann's appeal to Virgil to illuminate the primitive Christian hymns is not very convincing. The Fourth Eclogue speaks primarily of a figure who restores the world, not a 'world ruler'. Equally, the hymns do not refer to the birth of a child who is the saviour. While there was some

[102] Cumont 1919: 318, 322–4, 327.

[103] *ThLZ* 73 (1948), 668; *VF* 4 (1949/50), 215 f.; *EVB* i. 279; *Gnomon*, 21 (1949), 345; 'Probleme' 148; *EVB* i. 34/135, 85/78 (ET: 'cosmic ruler'); cf. 88/81 (*pantocrator*); 93/86 (ET: 'ruler of the cosmos'), 95/87, 113/68, 117/72 f.; *ZThK* 56 (1959), 359, 370; *EVB* ii. 23/14, 212/205 (the ET is incorrect here: not 'thus refraining from ascribing to Jesus the title of Cosmocrator', but 'thus not yet ascribing to Jesus the title of Cosmocrator'), 213/206; cf. 187/174 (*Weltenherr*); 'Versöhnung' 51/54, 52/56, 53/57; *PP* 43/22, 52/27, 100/55, 142/81, 199/114, 235/136; *Römer* 11/14, 134/143, 149/157, 171/179, 220/229, 226/234, 234/242, 243/251, 282/292, 297/306, 360/372.

interest in the Fourth Eclogue among German New Testament scholars in the early part of this century, their concern was with parallels to the infancy narratives and not the primitive Christian hymns.[104]

If, from a historical point of view, it is difficult to see why Käsemann adopted the title *cosmocrator*, it becomes necessary to suggest a reason in terms of the history of research. The term κύριος is always associated in this tradition of exegesis with the work of Bousset in which it is the title of the lord who is worshipped by the community in the cult. Käsemann accepts this view and even argues that in Phil. 2: 11 the title is employed in a way which is atypical for Paul because it means lord of the world and not lord of the cult (*EVB* i. 84 f./77 f.). With Bultmann,[105] he argues that Lohmeyer's work on Phil. 2: 11 must lead to a modification of Bousset's hypothesis on the origin of the κύριος title, because it shows that the pre-Pauline community, under the influence of the LXX, gave the title a content which stands out above the level of analogy with the cult heroes (85/78).

Given that Bousset had tied the meaning of κύριος to the lord worshipped by the community in the cult, it can be suggested that, wishing to emphasize that Christ is the lord of the world, Käsemann launched the title *cosmocrator*, without reference to its historical roots, in the sense of its literal translation, 'world ruler'. Käsemann's case is that the title reflects the *substance* of Paul's theology: as *kyrios* of the body of Christ,[106] Christ is the lord of the new aeon, and the Stoic τὰ πάντα formula is used of him (1 Cor. 8: 6; *EVB* i. 85/78). Further, it is the *cosmocrator* title which allows Käsemann to make one of the key connections in his interpretation of Paul: as *world* ruler, Christ claims our bodies as the piece of the *world* (*das Stück Welt*) which belongs to him (*EVB* i. 279; cf. 111/65; *EVB* ii. 23/14; *PP* 199/115; *Römer* 169/178).

After 1960 Käsemann emphasizes that Christ is not simply the *cosmocrator*, but the designated or future *cosmocrator*: his rule

[104] See Lietzmann 1909 and especially Norden 1924: 116–28. Norden argues for a parallel in the 'exaltation and enthronement to world rulership' between the Fourth Eclogue and Luke 1: 32, and for setting 1 Tim. 3: 16 in this circle of thought. There is no discussion of primitive Christian hymns, apart from the briefest mention of 1 Tim. 3: 16 just noted. See also the mention of the Fourth Eclogue in Bornkamm 1950: 17 f.

[105] Bultmann 1930*b*: 780.

[106] On this formulation, see p. 114 below.

is still contested and is not yet complete (*EVB* ii. 213/206; *PP* 43/22, 100/55, 142/81, 199/114; *Römer* 134/143, 220/229, 243/251). This modification reflects his view of Paul's eschatology: Christ is not yet the lord of the world, and he has not yet given up the kingdom to God (1 Cor. 15: 28). On the contemporary theological front, he continues to use the *cosmocrator* title to express the point that Christ is not merely the lord of the believing individual, nor the god of the cult (*PP* 133/75).

However, even with this modification, Käsemann's use of *cosmocrator* cannot be justified. The use of the transliteration gives the impression that he is referring to historical texts which contain the word *κοσμοκράτωρ*: the very rarity of the word, in both ancient and modern religious texts, leads to that assumption. But, as has been seen, Käsemann's use of the title is contrary to its meanings in antiquity (with the exception of its use of the emperor which plays no role here). Nor can this usage be justified in the name of theological interpretation: while it is legitimate to go beyond the statements of a text in order to express its meaning, here Käsemann's view is not related to the meaning of the word in antiquity. His view can be expressed very simply—if not with the same rhetorical flourish—in the statement that Christ is the lord of the world.

With regard to the exegesis of Phil. 2: 11 itself, Käsemann follows the views of Kögel, Peterson, Lohmeyer, and Bultmann.[107] As he says: 'With full justification Lohmeyer has untiringly emphasized that Jesus is here proclaimed as Lord of the world and not of the community' (*EVB* i. 85/78).

In the final section of the essay Käsemann raises two further questions: the relation of the hymn to its setting in Phil. 2, or at least to the *ἐν Χριστῷ* of v. 5, and the problem of the appropriation of the mythical nature of the hymn in modern times, which will not be dealt with here. Surprisingly the question of tradition and Pauline interpretation is not raised clearly in this essay.[108] The subject is broached in two

[107] Käsemann's view of the passage ran along the same lines before he adopted the *cosmocrator* title: Christ is king of the worlds and ruler (*Weltenkönig*, *Herrscher*; *Gottesvolk* (1939), 69/114). Kögel argued that 'Christ is king of the world [*König der Welt*] to whom all and everything belongs' (1908: 24); cf. Peterson 1926, 237, 262; Bultmann 1930*b*: 780.

[108] This question is clearly faced in his study of Rom. 3: 24–6 of the same period.

ways. Firstly, it is argued that the *cosmocrator* idea, which Käsemann finds in the hymn, expresses a concern of Paul's theology. Thus, he postulates an important point of contact between the hymn and Paul's theology without substantiating it in detail.

A second, more important, point comes in Käsemann's criticism of Lohmeyer's interpretation. The latter recognized that the hymn does not speak of the response of the individual (or the congregation), and felt constrained to leave the salvation event 'between heaven and earth'. This is theologically inadmissible because in this view the salvation event is not proclaimed as *justificatio impii* (56/50). Thus, Käsemann criticizes Lohmeyer for an interpretation which does not square with what Käsemann believes is the heart of Paul's gospel.[109] He believes that this doctrine is expressed in the christology of the hymn, here summed up with reference to the *ἐν Χριστῷ* of v. 5. In this verse *ἐν Χριστῷ* means that:

> at the turn of the aeons, God became human in order to dissuade humanity from wishing to become like God. In the incarnation a *ταπεινοῦν ἑαυτὸν* occurred, and *ταπεινοφροσύνη* is now the law of the new aeon where salvation reveals itself on the cross. The *cosmocrator* is the one who places people where they can truly become human, namely in obedience. (94/my translation, cf. ET 87)

This understanding of Christianity which sees christology and justification as two aspects of one central doctrinal complex is an explicit theme of Käsemann's later interpretation of Paul's theology.

Be that as it may, this view of the relationship of the hymn to its context cannot be maintained. While *ταπεινοφροσύνη* is mentioned in 2: 3, it should not be singled out from a catalogue of qualities as 'the law of the new aeon'. Similarly, the theme of obedience is picked up by Paul in 2: 12, though again this theme should not be isolated from the rest of the passage. The reference to the *justificatio impii* (and the related idea of human beings becoming truly human) is at a greater remove from the text, and Käsemann cannot be said to have made the case that this theme should be brought in here. Käsemann also brings other extraneous, if Pauline, themes to

[109] That the *justificatio impii* is the heart of the gospel is not defended here.

bear on the understanding of the hymn, particularly the idea of Christ as judge. Commenting on the hymn he says that Christ judges the world by the criterion of obedience (90/83). But while the theme of obedience is present in the hymn, it is the obedience of the redeemer figure which is mentioned, not obedience as the criterion of judgement. Finally, it is not enough to relate the hymn to the *ἐν Χριστῷ* formula; it has to be related to v. 5 as a whole, and to the argument of Phil. 1–2.

The fact that Käsemann makes comments on several levels—the history-of-religions background of the hymn, the pre-Pauline hymn, the place of the hymn in Paul's theology, the nature of Paul's theology in general, the contemporary significance of his view of Paul's theology—without always distinguishing clearly between the various levels, has caused problems for the critics who have debated with him. K. Wengst argues against Käsemann's focus on obedience, making the valid point that no one stage of the redeemer's way is to be isolated and emphasized.[110] But in fact this point is respected in Käsemann's literary-critical observations in which the hymn is seen as a continuous drama; however, at the same time he goes on to abstract the descent/exaltation theme (based on the two stanzas), and finally the message of *justificatio impii*. Wengst's criticism fails to come to terms with the several levels of Käsemann's interpretation,[111] but it is not difficult to see how this problem arises. Thus, in addition to well-known doubts about the hypothesis of a gnostic background for the hymn, there are serious problems in Käsemann's interpretation of this passage in the area of tradition and interpretation.

The main contribution of this essay to the theme of lordship is in the title *cosmocrator*. Christ is lord of the world, not merely of the community or cult or individual, and correspondingly, and in line with Paul's eschatology, salvation is cosmic in scope. At the same time these ideas are related to the doctrine of justification—it is the *cosmocrator* who places human beings

[110] Wengst 1972: 149 n. 24.

[111] Martin's summaries of Käsemann's views are accurate as far as they go, but he omits the Pauline and theological level (christology-justification), and consequently repeats the conclusion of the hymn (confession and acclamation) as if it were Käsemann's view of Paul's interpretation of the hymn (1967: 76). For Käsemann, confession and acclamation are parts of the myth which Paul interpreted theologically.

where they can become truly human—and thus again it is implied that Paul's theology has an underlying unity. Finally, while the connection between Paul's christology and his doctrine of justification is present in this essay, it is again the case that in this earlier period the significance of this point for contemporary theology is not emphasized.

CHARISMA: 'THE PROJECTION OF THE DOCTRINE OF JUSTIFICATION INTO THE AREA OF ECCLESIOLOGY'

The final topic in this earlier period is given its fullest treatment in the essay 'Amt und Gemeinde im Neuen Testament' (1960).[112] Despite its title, a very large proportion of this essay is devoted to a discussion of Paul's understanding of the nature of ministry. It breaks new ground in Käsemann's interpretation of Paul in that here, to a far greater extent than in the discussion of Phil. 2: 5–11, the centrality of the doctrine of justification is important for the argument. The essay thus forms a bridge between Käsemann's pre-1950 and post-1960 work. Curiously the date of the essay also spans the same period. The essay goes back to a lecture given in 1949 but was only published in 1960 (*EVB* i. 109 n. 1/63 n. 1), an unusual delay, especially when the importance of the essay is considered.[113] In fact Käsemann was hoping to convert the lecture into a monograph but this project was never completed and the format of a long essay was chosen.[114]

In its section on Paul the essay advances four arguments. Paul's understanding of charisma originated in, and is to be understood as, a critique of the ecclesiology of the Corinthian

[112] ET: 'Ministry and Community in the New Testament'. *Leib* 179–83 contains a conventional discussion of charisma (though a charisma is already seen as 'a particularisation of χάρις'; cf. 'Frau' 28). Käsemann's characteristic view also appears in 'Legitimität' 518–20, and later in *VF* 4 (1949/50), 197–200; *Gnomon* 21 (1949), 346; 'Gemeinde' 3 f.; 'Geist' 1273–6.

[113] The essay was reprinted in the *Wege der Forschung* volume, *Das kirchliche Amt im Neuen Testament* (Kertelge 1977).

[114] This information was provided in a letter from Prof. Käsemann of 2 May 1985: 'My charisma essay appeared so late because I had been carrying the manuscript of a book around with me since 1947 and had found no time to revise it. Finally I decided to convert it into a long essay which was then published in my first volume of essays. In all important details it was already sketched out in wartime and committed to paper in 1947' (my translation).

enthusiasts. Secondly, a charisma is the mode of the *cosmocrator*'s claim on the world. Thirdly, the doctrine of charisma is the projection of the doctrine of justification into the area of ecclesiology, and, fourthly, it is the basis of Paul's ethics. Thus, the essay covers a very large area and a fuller account of Käsemann's understanding of Paul's ecclesiology and ethics will be held over to Chapter 5. Here the main concern will be with the contribution of this topic to the lordship of Christ construct and its place in Käsemann's view of Paul's theology.

Käsemann notes the absence in the New Testament of a true equivalent for our present-day technical concept of ministerial office (*Amt*). However, in the Pauline and post-Pauline communities the charisma concept describes theologically, in an exact and comprehensible way, the being and task of all church ministries (*Dienste*) and functions (109/64). The importance of this concept can be gauged from the certainty that Paul was the first to use the word technically and theologically. This suggests to Käsemann that it records a view of ministry which is critical of other views within primitive Christianity. Thus, there is a historical and theological problem to be tackled (110/64).

Käsemann's starting-point is Rom. 6: 23: 'The charisma of God is eternal life in Christ Jesus our Lord.' There are only charismata because there is this one charisma to which all the others relate. They only exist where the gift of eternal life appears in the eschatologically established lordship of Christ. Thus 'gift of grace' is a misleading translation of charisma because it does not show that the gift is inseparable from the power of grace (*Gnadenmacht*) which confers it. A charisma is the manifestation and concretion of grace (110 f./64 f.; cf. 'Legitimität' 514).

In support of the view that there is only one gift, the lord himself, in a variety of manifestations and concretions, the following exegetical points are briefly made (*EVB* i. 110 f./65):

1. *Χάρισμα* is interchangeable with *χάρις*, *δωρεά*, and *δώρημα* in Rom. 5: 15 f.
2. The *χαρίσματα* are described as *ἐνεργήματα* in 1 Cor. 12: 6, 11 in which the *φανέρωσις τοῦ πνεύματος* of v. 7 results.

3. The spirit is our present participation in eternal life—but we can only possess the spirit as people who are under his claim and are thereby called to service. Thus, in 1 Cor. 12: 4 ff. the *χαρίσματα* alternate with the *διακονίαι*.
4. The *χαρίσματα* and the *κλῆσις τοῦ θεοῦ* are connected or interchangeable in Rom. 11: 29 and 1 Cor. 7: 7, 17 f.

Käsemann sums up and argues that the charisma concept relates the individual to the lordship of Christ:

For Paul, to have a charisma means to participate for that very reason in life, in grace, in the Spirit, because a charisma is the specific part which the individual has in the lordship and glory of Christ; and this specific part which the individual has in the Lord shows itself in a specific service and a specific vocation. For there is no divine gift which does not bring with it a task, there is no grace which does not move to action. Service is not merely the consequence but the manifestation [ET: 'outward form'] and the realization of grace . . . First of all the lordship of Christ brings me into subjection and then through my act of submission there shines the glory of him whose purpose is to bring all the world into subjection and who in me has taken possession of one single fragment of this world which is his by right [*eines Stückes der ihm gehörigen Welt*]. (110 f./65)

In addition to the use of the title *cosmocrator* to denote the lord who claims his world through individuals, Käsemann speaks of the cosmic scope of Christ's lordship in the more conventional theological language of ubiquity and omnipotence. This has its exegetical basis in the interpretation of Eph. 4: 1–16: 'Christ himself, who not without reason strode through the depths of the earth and through heaven, as *cosmocrator* grasps the world in the fullness of the charismata—that is with the attack of grace. His body as the sphere of his ubiquity is simultaneously the instrument of his omnipotence' ('Epheserbrief' 518; cf. *EVB* i. 113 f./68).

The key place of charisma in the lordship construct is now beginning to emerge. The charismata relate the individual to Christ's lordship and in so doing they set the believer's whole life under that lordship. Conversely, it is through the charismata that Christ makes his claim on the world: the charismatic is the 'piece of world' claimed by Christ.

This last point is greatly strengthened because Käsemann believes that the charisma concept refers not only to a narrow list of 'gifts', and certainly not exclusively to the supernatural gifts which were so highly prized by the Corinthians. It also extends to conditions, or states of life: the circumcised and uncircumcised, marriage and virginity, slave and free, male and female. This list is not exhaustive: 'Paul bases the prescriptions of the so-called "household code" firmly on the idea of charisma and in so doing mirrors the scope and the riches of him who fills all in all, that is, who reveals himself as the Cosmocrator in and over the multiplicity of these charismata which penetrate so deeply into the secularity of the world' (115 f./71). Thus, any state can be a charisma if a person recognizes God's call and command in it. In this way Christ reaches out for the whole world and no area is to be labelled 'secular' and left untouched. 'The field of the Church's operation must be the world in its totality, for nothing less can be the field of Christ the Cosmocrator' (117/72).

The charisma concept is related to Paul's gospel in another way: it grew out of his critique of the theology of the Corinthian enthusiasts. They celebrated the powers of miracle and ecstasy, the πνευματικά. The fact that Paul only uses this term when dealing with the Corinthians leads Käsemann to argue that he is using a term borrowed from them. However, Paul replaces it with his own term, χάρισμα, because for him what validates the work of the spirit is not the *fascinosum* of the preternatural but the edification of the church (112/66). In addition Paul uses the catch-phrases of popular philosophy in his critique, measuring heavenly revelations and powers by the standard of what is 'useful', i.e., what edifies the community (112/67). Paul's theology is radical and critical: 'Its critical power lies in the Gospel itself which shatters the autonomy and the self-justification of the pious, even of the spiritually gifted. Heaven comes to earth when grace creates obedience and responsibility, and is alone understood as the foundation of service' (113/67; second sentence retranslated).

Paul's doctrine of charisma is, thus, the projection of his christology (118 f./74) or of the doctrine of justification into the area of ecclesiology (119/75 f.). The *gift* and the *claim* of the lord must be held together. If the dialectic of gift and claim is not maintained, the way is open for the self-appointed leadership of the undisciplined and for the chaos which is the result of religious gifts in competition (119/75):

The doctrine of charisma is for him [Paul] the concrete expression of the doctrine of the new obedience, just because it is at the same time the doctrine of the *justificatio impii*. God gives life to the dead and, through the invasion of grace, sets up his kingdom . . . God creates among the rebels that *pax Christi*, which is at once the subjection, the reconciliation and the new order of the cosmos. That the godless become obedient and charismatics is the eschatological miracle, the activity of God's deity [*Gottheit Gottes*], the triumph of grace over the world of wrath. (ibid., ET modified)

Here, for the first time, the eschatological, cosmic, individual, and ecclesiological aspects of justification are presented together in a unified interpretation.

Käsemann is quick to draw far reaching consequences for the understanding of Paul's theology from his discussion of charisma (ibid.):

1. Paul did not make a fundamental distinction between justification and sanctification, as he did not understand the former as purely declaratory.
2. Justification by faith is firmly bound to baptism so that it is not permissible to drive a wedge between a juridical and a sacramental side of Paul's thought.[115]
3. Faith is understood constitutively as the 'new obedience'. Thus, there is no tension between faith and ethics.
4. As noted above, justification is a 'cosmic' event and cannot be interpreted purely individualistically (119/76).

Käsemann makes several very important points here which will be elaborated at much greater length in the post-1960 period. Point (1) takes up a dogmatic problem which arose in Protestant theology concerning the relationship of the beginning of the Christian life to its continuation. By arguing that sanctification is lived justification, Käsemann is concerned to

[115] Cf. Käsemann's brief comment that Paul's doctrine of baptism makes concrete and unfolds the *justificatio impii* which enables him to unify 'salvation historical-eschatological', ethical, and apparently mystical statements (*VF* 5 (1951/2), 211).

rule out the idea that while the beginning of the new life is the result of God's grace, its continuation depends on human effort. At the same time, the attempt to replace the idea of sanctification with 'lived justification' reveals an anti-Catholic slant in the argument. Conversely, the point that justification is not just a gift but has to be lived, meets the accusation of 'cheap grace' (*GPM* 7 (1953), 145): 'For grace seizes the whole person with all his powers and makes him responsible . . . They [the charismata] are the specific participation of the individual Christian in grace and, at the same time, the service of Christianity' (ibid.). Point (2), in which key themes from Paul's juridical and participatory lines of thought are brought together, is the basic insight which enables Käsemann to reject the cleft in Paul's theology postulated by the dominant German interpretation of the late nineteenth century. Point (3) again rejects the notion of a separation between the beginning and the continuation of the Christian life, here in the sphere of ethics. These points are of particular importance because they prepare the ground for incorporating the doctrine of justification (and thus the juridical element in Paul's theology) into the lordship of Christ construct; up to this point it has been made up primarily of participatory themes (spirit, sacrament, etc.).

The fundamental argument that underlies all these points is the intrinsic connection between the gift and the giver.[116] The gift of justification is always accompanied by the claim of the giver on the life of the recipient, and hence has direct implications in the areas of sanctification and ethics. Or again, a person has a charisma on account of baptism, but the very nature of this charisma is a liberation from the sinful desires of envy and greed. The charisma is a gift from God, and so cannot be construed as human 'achievement' (*EVB* i. 120/76). In this way—which depends on tracing an inner logic in Paul's thought, rather than on the exegesis of particular texts—Käsemann can say that Paul ties justification to baptism. Thus, even in the pre-1950 period, the lordship of Christ construct, which originated in interpretations of participatory

[116] For the theological background to this theme, see p. 44 above.

themes, is extended to other strands of Paul's theology and the unity of his thought is defended.

1933–50: LORDSHIP, COHERENCE, THEOLOGICAL INTERPRETATION

The main lines of Käsemann's interpretation of Paul from his dissertation up to 1950 have now been outlined. There remains the task of drawing together the threads of his work in this period, enquiring further into his understanding of the unity of Paul's thought, and studying his view of the task of theological interpretation. The natural starting-point for this enquiry is the special case of *Leib und Leib Christi*.

The Catholic Paul in Leib und Leib Christi *and its significance for Käsemann's later work*

It is beyond the scope of this study to comment on the particular exegetical arguments of *Leib und Leib Christi*[117] but the view of Paul's theology which it puts forward is of importance for Käsemann's later work.[118] In recent years Käsemann has rightly been regarded as a staunch supporter of a Lutheran interpretation of Paul in which justification by faith is the central doctrine.[119] However, if it is asked which

[117] Contemporary reviews made two main historical criticisms. Firstly, they criticized Käsemann's constant use of the aeon concept without an adequate account of this idea (Wikenhauser 1934: 271; Michaelis speaks of 'aeon psychosis', 1933: 389). Secondly, they deplore the failure to discuss the meaning of σῶμα in the LXX (Schneider 1934: 348; Michaelis 1933: 387). In addition, Schneider notes another problem: if the authentic Pauline letters are also influenced by gnosticism, then they are extraordinarily close to the deutero-Pauline letters (which Käsemann argues on other grounds) and the latter should be regarded as authentic (350).

[118] Scroggs finds several themes in *Leib* which will become important for Käsemann's later work: the influence of the Old Testament (a person being defined in terms of relationship); the use of the gnostic aeon conceptuality against an immanent, psychologizing individualism; the indissoluble relationship between a person and his world; the location of the individual, not in the church but in Christ—but see pp. 108 f. below; and the theme of no salvation apart from a continuing relationship with Christ (Scroggs 1985: 260 f.). Harrisville implies that Käsemann spoke of Paul's apocalyptic christology in *Leib* (1985: 257), which is not correct. In this early work the catchword 'eschatology' does not point *inter alia* to the cosmic perspective of Paul's theology but to its existential significance.

[119] e.g., Sanders 1977: 435 f., Beker 1980: 14.

part of Paul's theology is regarded as central in the dissertation and, secondly, how the relationship between Christ and the church is understood, a very different view emerges. These two questions are dealt with together in the conclusion: 'The centre of Pauline proclamation is the "in Christ". *It is to be maintained, as in the deutero-Paulines, that this "in Christ" is interpreted as "being in the church"* . . . The church is the meaning and *telos* of both the Pauline christology and his anthropology' (*Leib* 183, Käsemann's emphasis). Thus 'in Christ' is the centre of Paul's proclamation. Elsewhere in *Leib und Leib Christi* it is said that the centre of Paul's doctrine is in the close connection between sacrament and church (161), or the concept of spirit,[120] which in turn is dominated by the idea of the sacrament (127 f.). There is no conflict between these views because these themes are interconnected. The sacrament (baptism or the Lord's supper) is the basis of the activities of the spirit and of 'being in Christ' (161). To sum up, it is clear that in his dissertation Käsemann regarded the participatory themes as the centre of Paul's theology.[121] As he also argues that Paul's proclamation is eschatological through and through, his view (at least in summary form) is similar to Schweitzer's, and indeed he quotes him with approval in his final summing up: the 'manifestation of the pre-existent church' is the centre of Pauline 'mysticism'.[122]

This non-Lutheran interpretation of Paul is confirmed by Käsemann's discussion of the relation of sacrament to preaching. By reversing a Lutheran dictum he clearly intends to be critical of an orthodox Lutheran view: 'Thus preaching is effective because the sacrament has been effective. For primitive Christianity it is not that the sacrament is *verbum visibile* but rather the reverse: for Paul preaching is *sacramentum audibile*' (181). While Käsemann issues a caution against

[120] Cf. Lohmeyer's view on the centrality of the spirit, though as a metaphysical reality (1929*a*: 181).

[121] This was noted by A. Oepke: 'Since E. Wissmann (1926) . . . and Albert Schweitzer (1930)—and also Ernst Käsemann, *Leib und Leib Christi* (1933)—it is, as it were, agreed that it was Christ-mysticism which Paul "truly meant"' (Oepke 1954: 364).

[122] *Leib* 183, citing Schweitzer 1930: 116. For a comparison of the understanding of the church in Schweitzer and Käsemann's *Leib*, see n. 27 above. On Käsemann's view of eschatology in this period, see n. 118 above and p. 125 below.

pressing this distinction too hard (ibid.), the direction of the argument is clear.

Käsemann is also rightly associated with the view that in Paul christology determines ecclesiology (and not vice versa), that the church is always subordinate to Christ.[123] But, as has been seen, in the dissertation it is the church which is the meaning and *telos* of Pauline christology, and this is confirmed by Käsemann's more detailed statement:[124] '*Just as the church is the concretion of the Christ who is identical with her, so it cannot be loosed from Christ.* She is never his "representative"; Christians only remain the church in Christ and his *pneuma*' (185, Käsemann's emphasis). This statement is ambiguous but Käsemann starts from the identity of the church and Christ,[125] and even the order church–Christ is significant. The second part of the statement, with its rejection of a Catholic view of the church as Christ's representative or 'vicar' (*Stellvertreterin*), runs against the exegetical arguments of the dissertation, and is to be regarded as an expression of Lutheran theological conviction which receives no exegetical support.[126] Thus, on these two important issues, the centre of Paul's theology and the relationship between Christ and the church, Käsemann's views in *Leib und Leib Christi* are in stark contrast with his later views[127] and present a view of Paul with a strongly Catholic orientation.[128]

[123] The change in Käsemann's theological perspective is not noted by Häring who stresses the continuity between the views of *Leib* and the essay of 1969 on the body of Christ (Häring 1972: 294 f.).

[124] Cf. the arguments that the Christian is dependent on the church (*Leib* 178) and the phrase 'the order of salvation of the church' (177, 183).

[125] By contrast Lohmeyer understood the church in terms of a relationship with the spirit of identity *and* opposition: the spirit is the community *and* stands over it (1929*a*: 182).

[126] Thus, Güttgemanns, from within the Lutheran tradition, can correctly object that in the dissertation Käsemann dissolves Christ into the church or identifies the two (Güttgemanns 1966: 252 n. 32, 269 f.). However, he fails to notice the ambiguity of Käsemann's statement.

[127] In later publications Käsemann is scathing about his dissertation, saying that it was overambitious in the material it covered (*KK* i. 8); that he too had learned something in the last twenty-five years on the subject of the gnostic background to the body of Christ (though he is not more specific than this in 1956); and that he would no longer agree with Schlier theologically, i.e., with the Catholic interpretation of Paul (*ThLZ* 81 (1956), 585). Thus, as Käsemann says, the 'primacy of christology' was an insight which was only won, and formulated sharply, later than his dissertation. In general he regards his first work as being determined by the approach

This account of Käsemann's view of Paul's theology in the dissertation needs one very important qualification. As noted above, at one point Paul's participatory language is interpreted in the light of his juridical language: the existential meaning of the spirit draws on the doctrine of justification. Thus, while the doctrinal shape of Käsemann's interpretation in *Leib und Leib Christi* is not Lutheran, the typically Lutheran concern for the doctrine of justification is present.

Within five years Käsemann moved away from the view that the participatory themes are the centre of Paul's theology, arguing instead that justification is the centre of Pauline and New Testament proclamation ('Abendmahl' (1937) 90, 93). However, the approach of his dissertation continues to be of the highest importance. His interest in the participatory themes continues, especially in the period up to 1950. More significantly, the solution to the problem of the supposed lack of cohesion in Pauline thought which is implied in *Leib und Leib Christi* is taken much further in the later essays of this first period. Paul's theology is not regarded as comprising two or three disparate lines of thought, nor is there a simple preference for one element over the others; the correct approach is to use the different lines of thought to interpret one another. Käsemann's interpretation proceeds on the assumption that there is an underlying unity in Paul's thought which is uncovered by this approach.

This attempt to uncover the unity of Paul's thought can also be related to Käsemann's attempt to resolve the conflict between the two main views of Paul which he inherited. By interpreting the theme of the spirit in the light of the doctrine

and outlook of his first teacher Peterson (*KK* i. 8 f., 241). However, it was written under Bultmann and Käsemann only spent one term at Bonn before moving to Marburg. In fact its themes were of contemporary theological interest: Heitmüller had called Paul the father, not of the Reformation, but of catholicism (Heitmüller 1917: 21) and the doctrine of the church was being rediscovered in contemporary Lutheranism (*Freiheit* 173/91).

[128] The doctrinal significance of Käsemann's views was noted by some reviewers. As a Catholic, Thieme hailed *Leib* as an epoch-making study because it means no less than the collapse of the Protestant focus on individual salvation in Pauline studies (Thieme 1935: 46; cf. Jampen 1937; Schaefer 1938: 69). As a Protestant, Heidler objects that the church cannot be the concretion of the Christ who is identical with her because this is against Reformation tradition and because in Ephesians Christ is the head of the church. The gnostic-hellenistic context cannot be regarded as decisive for biblical theology (1934: 559).

of justification, and vice versa, he can uphold the Lutheran view of Paul, which was revitalized by the theological developments of the 1920s, while taking up many of the insights of the dominant critical interpretation of the late nineteenth century which found the centre of Paul's religion in the participatory themes.

A concern for the underlying unity of Paul's theology has been seen in the interpretation of most of the themes in this period: the Lord's supper, apostleship, the Christ hymn of Phil. 2, and, especially, the charisma theme. One further example—another aspect of the interpretation of the Lord's supper—merits discussion here. Käsemann takes up the challenge of Heitmüller's claim that there is a fundamental incongruence between sacrament and faith in Paul.[129] In his essay of 1937, Käsemann notes that the word 'faith' is completely lacking from the Lord's supper passages, and that it is here that the history-of-religions influences are at their strongest. The formulation of this argument is precisely that of Heitmüller but Käsemann draws a different conclusion. 'Naturally this does not mean that the Pauline doctrine of the Lord's supper stands outside his central proclamation of faith and justification' ('Abendmahl' 90). This is supported by the argument that the *sola fide* theme can be detected as the theological impulse behind the argument in 1 Cor. 10: the sacrament does not guarantee salvation. Pleading lack of space for a full discussion of the relationship of sacrament and faith, Käsemann concludes: 'Only the following is now plain that a clear harmony of these two lines in Paul is not to be expected, nor did it take place' (ibid.). This is confirmed by the development within the church which quickly reached the position of Ignatius' designation of the eucharist as a φάρμακον ἀθανασίας (ibid.). Thus, in 1937 Käsemann emphasizes Paul's influence on the development of sacramentalism within the church, while at the same time noting that he is critical of this tendency. In addition Käsemann judges that the sacramental and juridical sides of his theology cannot be fully squared. Here he is still within the tradition of

[129] Heitmüller 1903: 36; 1917: 21. Bultmann highlighted this as a problem for research (1929*a*: 321).

the history-of-religions school, though he has begun to close the gap between the two sides of Paul's thought.

In the essay of 1947/8 he argues for a much closer integration of the sacraments with Paul's 'central concerns'. The body of Christ is the new order of salvation, the sphere of Christ's lordship, into which people are incorporated by baptism and the eucharistic 'body of Christ'. At the same time, participants in the supper are confronted with the lord as saviour and judge—because the Lord's supper is determined by Paul's christology or his doctrine of justification. By this tortuous route, the problem of the relationship of the sacraments and faith is solved and the coherence of Paul's theology upheld. However, it is noticeable that it is solved, not by exegesis of the relevant Pauline texts, but by bringing together and reflecting on Pauline themes abstracted from the text. Nevertheless, the question of the coherence of Paul's theology is a theme of Käsemann's dissertation and early essays, and remains on the agenda for his later work on Paul.

Finally, it is by no means only Käsemann's dissertation which has Catholic emphases in its interpretation of Paul. This tendency continues even when he puts forward distinctively Protestant themes. Thus, when he argues that the Pauline Lord's supper is determined by his christology and doctrine of justification, he none the less maintains that the words of institution imply the notion of real presence,[130] while distancing himself from the doctrinal developments associated with this term (*EVB* i. 28/128). Equally, baptism *and the Lord's supper* incorporate participants into the body of Christ. As with the taking up of participatory themes in a view of Paul's theology in which justification is central, so Käsemann takes up Catholic themes within a Protestant view of the apostle's thought.

The origins of the lordship construct

As has now been seen, the lordship of Christ is the underlying theme of Käsemann's interpretation of Paul in this early period. This theme is a construct and it will be useful to

[130] Notwithstanding Luther's continued adherence to the doctrine of the real presence, this is not a Protestant theme.

review the various influences and exegetical hypotheses which contribute to it.

1. Bousset's study, *Kyrios Christos* is foundational for the tradition of interpretation in which Käsemann studied and began his career as an exegete. For Bousset '*Kyrios Christos* is Jesus of Nazareth in essence as the Lord of the community, venerated in the cultus.'[131] (In addition it is argued that in Paul κύριος and πνεῦμα are virtually interchangeable, a point which Käsemann builds on.) Without doubt it is because of this study that Käsemann limits his discussion of κύριος to modifications of Bousset's hypotheses, and never investigates the title in detail in this period.[132] It can also be suggested that this surprising omission is due to the point that Käsemann's interest in the lordship of Christ is not directly related to the title itself but to lordship as the underlying theme of Paul's theology.[133]

2. Lohmeyer's work on the primitive Christian hymn in Phil. 2: 6 ff. provides a second aspect which Käsemann takes up directly in his essay of 1950: Christ is not merely lord of the community or cult or the individual; he is lord of the world, or, as Käsemann says, *cosmocrator*.

3. Peterson's work on ἐξομολογεῖσθαι contributes the quasi-legal and enthusiastic aspects of the lordship construct: to acclaim the lord is the necessary and binding consequence of the divine epiphany in the community. Confession marks the boundary between the old age and the new.

4. This last point is then combined with Käsemann's reconstruction of the hellenistic world-view and the notion of the 'exchange of lordship'. Human beings are not free agents who can determine their own destinies by the exercise of choice; rather, they are under the influence of the powers, and their actions merely ratify or reject the lordship under which they live. However, in the acclamation of the new name conferred on Christ, there is a transfer of power; a 'change (or

131 Bousset 1913/1921, 11.

132 Käsemann's first systematic discussion of the title occurs in his last exegetical work (*Römer* 11 f./13–15).

133 Cf. Sauter's comment on Käsemann's use of 'apocalyptic' which, instead of being simply a historical form of thought, is also a means of depicting obligatory theologoumena (*ein . . . Darstellungsmittel für theologische Verbindlichkeiten*; Sauter 1976: 84).

exchange) of lordship' (*Herrschaftswechsel*) takes place. Thus, Christ's lordship is a sphere of power in opposition to the lordship exercised by the powers of this age. (At this point, the world-views of hellenism and Jewish eschatology coincide.)

5. Käsemann's own work on the gnostic background to Paul's anthropology and ecclesiology introduces the crucial aeon conceptuality which is then used to interpret a large number of Pauline concepts. The aeon is a spatial[134] and dynamic concept, a sphere of power into which people are incorporated. It is supraindividual and constitutes a 'world' which determines those who are within it. (At this point it comes close to the hellenistic world-view which sees reality as conflicting spheres of power, as noted above.) It is the notion of a sphere of power, drawn from history-of-religions work, which provides the conceptuality with which Käsemann expounds the theme of lordship. This conceptuality continues to be determinative after Käsemann has discarded the direct focus on particular concepts and the hypothesis of gnostic influence on Paul.

6. Paul's fundamental anthropological insight is summed up in the term *σῶμα*: as *σῶμα* human beings are 'claimed humanity', under the lordship of God or sin.

7. An apostle is determined by the gospel and therefore the lord. From him the apostle receives both freedom and destiny. This dialectic is characteristic of life under Christ's lordship.

8. In the Lord's supper it is the lord himself who is present—as gift and claim, as saviour and judge. *Κοινωνία* means to have fallen under the power of a lord. The eucharistic *σῶμα Χριστοῦ* incorporates participants into the ecclesiological *σῶμα Χριστοῦ*, and thus into Christ's lordship.

9. The individual has a share in the lordship of Christ through the charismata; at the same time, the gifts claim their recipients for the service of Christ's lordship. Consequently, a gift is not a human 'achievement' and, thus, Paul's doctrine of

[134] Following Deissmann's local interpretation of *ἐν Χριστῷ* in 1892, there was a considerable vogue for spatial conceptuality in New Testament studies. See, e.g., O. Schmitz's understanding of *ἐν Χριστῷ* which can be compared at many points with Käsemann's view of the body of Christ: 'For Paul the "in Christ" means the sphere of salvation [*Heilsbereich*] which is given with the event of salvation, in which he knows he has been directly set, along with all those who belong to Christ' (Schmitz 1924: 244; quoted in Neugebauer 1961: 24).

charisma is the projection of the doctrine of justification into the area of ecclesiology. Along with the existential interpretation of spirit (pp 60 f. above), this introduces the doctrine of justification into the lordship construct, which up to this point has been based primarily on Paul's participatory language.

These are the principal aspects of the lordship construct in Käsemann's interpretation of Paul in the pre-1950 period. However, these points are not just a list of unconnected themes; the theme of lordship functions in Käsemann's work as a theologoumenon in its own right. Connections are made between the various aspects of the construct which are not defended exegetically. Thus, Käsemann speaks of the '*kyrios* of the body of Christ', a combination of aspects (1) and (8), or of the '*cosmocrator* who sets man in the place where he can become fully human' ((2) and (9)), or again of 'a member of his lordship' ((1) and (8) again). In strict exegetical terms these are mixed (Pauline) metaphors.

Changes in Käsemann's understanding of the task of theological interpretation

From his dissertation onwards Käsemann is committed to the theological interpretation of the New Testament and not merely to historical interpretation in a narrow sense. However, there are changes in some aspects of the way he approaches this task in this first period. In *Leib und Leib Christi* he takes up Bultmann's programme: Paul's 'concepts' (and these range from the theme of the spirit to individual words such as ἀνάμνησις) and the myths he utilizes are interpreted existentially. To take an example from the latter: while Paul's understanding of the body of Christ is based on the gnostic primal-man myth, unlike Colossians and Ephesians, he does not take over the metaphysical conceptuality of the gnostic myth but interprets it existentially. It is the combination of the acknowledgement of the presence of mythical material in Paul and the demand for existential interpretation of it which is characteristic for this programme of theological interpretation. With respect to the Pauline concepts, Käsemann takes up Bultmann's understanding of 'concept analysis' (*Begriffsanalyse*) to elucidate Paul's theology: 'How else, other than in concepts are theological ideas given and how can they be understood other than in the work of concept analysis?'[135] Thus, for Käsemann, concepts are always mirror images of an 'understanding of the world' or of a self-understanding ('Abendmahl' 77).

However, the concepts also play a role in the historical and theological task of reconstructing Paul's theology. To change the metaphor, they are building blocks which are used to make a greater edifice. Käsemann is not only interested in the meaning of the individual concepts as derived through the methods of historical criticism (level 1), but in the way they relate to each other within Paul's theology (level 2). Finally, he also continually has an eye for the doctrinal implications of the resulting Pauline theology for contemporary theology (level 3).

In this earlier period the move from level 1 to level 2 interpretation is often signalled by the use of transliterations. Thus, while *kaine diatheke* appears to be a simple transliteration of καινὴ διαθήκη, in Käsemann's use of it, it refers, firstly, to a linguistic and historical (level 1) interpretation in which, following Behm and Lohmeyer, he understands the phrase to mean 'the new order of salvation'. Secondly, the transliteration refers to a more complex interpretation in which it is related to other concepts in his own view of Paul's theology (level 2). Here *kaine diatheke* is identical with the world-wide body of Christ, into which people are incorporated by baptism and the Lord's supper. (The implication for contemporary theology is that God's relationship to humanity is to be thought of in terms of the theologoumenon of the world-wide lordship of Christ.) In this interpretation a series of concepts are related to one another; in fact they are used to interpret one another, and in this way a particular view of Paul's theology is built up. Another important example is the use of *cosmocrator*, though, as has been seen above, this transliteration never refers to κοσμοκράτωρ in a historical text but to Käsemann's view of the content of Paul's theology.

However, the possibility of confusion over the status of these transliterations cannot be overlooked. They appear to

135 So Bultmann, replying to Deissmann's rejection of 'concept analysis' (1926*c*: 274).

relate directly to words in the Pauline text, understood as a historical text (level 1), but in fact this is far from the case. There is also the danger that supposedly Pauline concepts take on a life of their own within the hermeneutical scheme of the interpreter, as has already been seen with the lordship theme. More precisely, the danger is that level 2 interpretations which depend on the approach, the starting-point, and a prior series of exegetical conclusions of the interpreter are mistaken for level 1 linguistic or historical work.[136]

The dangers of Käsemann's approach can be illustrated from the example of his use of 'to incorporate' and 'to make a member' (*einleiben*, *eingliedern*) in interpreting the place of the Lord's supper in Paul's thought. Commenting on 1 Cor. 10: 17, he argues that the bread 'which we take in bodily [*einverleiben*], incorporates [*einverleiben*] us simultaneously into the body of Christ' ('Abendmahl' 80; cf. the similar statement using *eingliedern*, 81). This argument, which is important to Käsemann's lordship construct, and which he has often repeated, gives the impression that 'to incorporate' and 'to make a member' refer directly to cognates of *σῶμα* or *μέλος* in the Pauline text and thus that participants in the eucharist are *thereby* made members of the church. But Paul does not have terminology based on either of these words which speaks of the transfer[137] of people from outside the church into the church, either in 1 Cor. 10: 17 or elsewhere. Käsemann's use of Pauline language gives a spuriously Pauline air to a significant part of his interpretation of the apostle's thought which in fact depends on a highly problematic interpretation (see n. 50 above) of just one verse.

After his dissertation Käsemann exchanges the somewhat rigid focus on concepts and myths for the genre of the essay which discusses a particular Pauline subject. However, the multi-layered approach to interpretation continues. It is particularly interesting to note the coincidence of certain history-of-religions categories and hypotheses, and Käsemann's

[136] Of course, not even the 'simplest' linguistic or historical work is free of hypotheses but it is important to be aware of the different sets of presuppositions which operate in levels 1 and 2.

[137] On 'transfer terminology' in Paul, see Sanders 1977: 463–72.

theological vocabulary. The spirit is said to take possession of us and claim us as his own (*EVB* i. 19 f./118). Here a description of the activity of the spirit in early Christianity is simultaneously pressed into service to commend a particular theology to Käsemann's twentieth-century readers (with the characteristic use of 'us'). Or again, the idea of 'change (or exchange) of lordship' is, at the historical level, a description of the event of salvation within the hellenistic world-view and presupposes the thoroughly mythological notion of a 'transfer of power' from the cosmic powers to Christ (87/80). However, this idea comes to take on theological significance for Käsemann, particularly in his critique of the individualistic tendency of Bultmann's interpretation of Paul. Another prominent example, which has already been discussed, is Käsemann's use of *cosmocrator*. In the latter two examples, historical hypotheses have been put to theological use; in the first, a theological dialectic (gift–claim) has been given historical grounding.

Finally, Käsemann increasingly focuses on the question of the doctrinal shape of Paul's theology in this period. In *Leib und Leib Christi* he pursues the question of the appropriate conceptuality for the interpretation of Paul's theology, and the actual, theological and existential, interpretation of Paul's concepts, though he does also comment on the question of the centre of Paul's theology: In the essay of 1942 on apostleship, historical questions are to the fore, and he finds it sufficient to argue that the nature of apostleship is determined by the gospel, and to conclude with a comment on the gospel's 'war on two fronts'. However, by the late 1940s, the centrality and determining position of the doctrine of justification (understood as an aspect of Paul's christology) begin to be evident in the interpretation of the Lord's supper and the charisma concept. Thus, Käsemann's work becomes more concerned with the doctrinal shape of Paul's theology—and particularly with a characteristically Lutheran view. At the same time there are the first signs that Käsemann's doctrinal concerns (especially with respect to what he will later call the primacy of christology) are beginning to dictate the questions which are to be put to the text. In short, in the pre-1950 period Käsemann's historical work is increasingly motivated, not only by a concern for theological interpretation in a wide sense, but by specific doctrinal commitments. As will now be seen, this tendency is even more marked in the post-1960 period.

3

The Apocalyptic Character of Paul's Theology

Before the apocalyptic character of Käsemann's interpretation of Paul can be examined it is necessary to deal with some introductory issues concerning the nature of Käsemann's Pauline publications after 1960, his change of mind on a fundamental history-of-religions question, and his understanding of the terms, 'eschatology' and 'apocalyptic'.

INTRODUCTORY QUESTIONS

Käsemann's work on Paul after 1960

In the post-1960 period Käsemann published a considerable Pauline corpus comprising fifteen essays, which are either solely concerned with Paul or contain substantive discussions of Pauline theology, and the crown of his life's work, the commentary on Romans.[1] Some of the essays were published together in *Paulinische Perspektiven* but, as the title indicates, this does not constitute a comprehensive account of Paul's theology. However, Käsemann's view of Paul's theology as a whole can be studied from these publications for several reasons.

Firstly, as the use of the word 'perspectives' indicates,[2] the majority of essays in *Paulinische Perspektiven* are concerned with the 'shape' or structure of Paul's theology. While not every topos of Paul's religion and theology is discussed or set in its place within a system, the overall shape of Käsemann's view of Paul and the place of the most important elements within it are clearly described. These post-1960 studies, read in the

[1] The count of fifteen essays includes two published in 1959. In addition there are two chapters on Pauline subjects in the final edition of *Der Ruf der Freiheit*, some work on deutero-Pauline themes, and book reviews. Regrettably the copy of Käsemann's NT theology lectures to which I have had access is not complete and the section on Paul is missing.

[2] Cf. Morgan 1973: 54.

light of the programmatic essay 'Gottesgerechtigkeit bei Paulus' (1961), leave the reader in no doubt as to the main lines of his interpretation. Further, while Käsemann's work on Paul in the pre-1950 period starts from individual motifs or themes (body, apostleship, charisma, etc.), some of the post-1960 essays start from questions of structure (for example, the relationship of justification and salvation history), and all deal with the question of structure overtly.

Secondly, Käsemann's approach to interpretation leads him inexorably to wider theological issues and thus to questions about Paul's theology as a whole. Thus, his discussions of δικαιοσύνη θεοῦ or of Rom. 8: 26 f. are not concerned merely with exegetical or historical questions but also deal with the consequences of his exegetical observations for his view of Paul's theology. In this second period Käsemann often goes further and discusses the contemporary theological significance of his views directly; indeed, in this later period he never tackles a problem without these wider questions in mind.

Thirdly, the Romans commentary, while following the convention of a running commentary on the epistle, is in reality an interpretation of Pauline theology from the starting-point of Romans. Exegetical questions are treated in more detail and more evenly than in the essays, as a commentary demands, but there is no fundamental change in approach. This is reflected in Käsemann's modification of the conventional form of the commentary. Exegetical, historical, and history-of-religions discussions are introduced as and when they are felt to be necessary but this material is not separated from wider theological comment. Introduction, formal excursuses, and indices are dispensed with, and even the convention of arranging the discussion around verse divisions is dropped.[3]

[3] Käsemann retains the conventions of giving a translation of the text and providing bibliographies. In dispensing with an introduction he is following Bultmann's John (1941*a*). Reviewing Bultmann's book, Käsemann acknowledged that this omission might be regretted but gave the rationale that it promotes 'confrontation with the text itself' and encourages an assessment of 'the results' on that basis (*VF* 3 (1946/7), 183). Cf. his comment in the preface to his own Romans commentary: 'The impatient, who are concerned only about results or practical application, should leave their hands off exegesis. They are of no value for it, nor, when rightly done, is exegesis of any value for them' (*Römer* p. iv/p. vii).

This undoubtedly makes the commentary very difficult to use, and even difficult to read,[4] but the aim is to subordinate all to the central task of wrestling with the theological content of the letter and with Paul's theology. However, whatever problems this approach brings with it,[5] it does allow Käsemann's post-1960 work on Paul to be read as a unified interpretation of the apostle's theology.

Fourthly, Käsemann's understanding of the nature and purpose[6] of Romans is pertinent here (*Römer* 387–91/402–6). Käsemann looks back to F. C. Baur as the one who broke the old dogmatic approach and broached the question of the historical situation of the letter. However, Romans cannot be regarded simply as an introduction to Paul's beliefs for the unknown Roman church. Paul certainly also addresses the concrete question of the relationship of Jewish and Gentile Christians. The two most important factors which allow the purpose of the letter to be determined are that the apostle is seeking the support of the Roman church in his dealings with the Jerusalem church, and that he wishes to use Rome as a springboard for his mission to Spain. It is particularly the former which leads him to present his 'central message' (390/404) in the letter. His aim is to win over the Jewish Christian minority at Rome,[7] in order to get rearguard protection in his relationships with Jerusalem. The letter is to be read as a report giving a formal account (*Rechenschaftsbericht*, 376/390) of

[4] This is due to Käsemann's compressed style and the abrupt switches from historical to theological considerations, from a philological detail or a history-of-religions question to a fundamental insight of Pauline or Christian theology. Giblin speaks pertinently of the need for an exegesis of the commentary simultaneously with an exegesis of Paul (1975: 119).

[5] This approach has been criticized for its adverse effects on Käsemann's historical discussions. Harrington points out that Käsemann cites texts from all over the ancient world merely as parallels and without discussion of questions of dependence or influence, or even date, citing the liberal use of the post-Pauline 2 Baruch (1974: 586). Fitzmyer overstates the case when he complains that it ought to have been made clear that Käsemann comments on the text with the concern of a systematician (1974: 747). Again: 'The danger of this approach is that it will almost by necessity defer "purely" historical problems to the category of "Hilfswissenschaft"' (Betz 1975: 143). On a slightly different tack, Riches criticizes Käsemann for neglecting other history-of-religions material in favour of apocalyptic sources (1976: 558).

[6] On this much discussed subject, see especially the collection of essays in Donfried 1977.

[7] The ET should be corrected to 'Even as a minority, however, they played a not inconsiderable role [ET: 'no very big part'], (405).

his proclamation, which reflects his earlier experiences and insights. While it offers a summary of Paul's theology, it does so from a particular, limiting perspective, and should not be read as a 'doctrinal tractate' (ET: 'teaching tractate'; ibid.). Thus, Käsemann's view is that Romans is a summary of Paul's theology addressed to a particular historical situation. This point furthers the possibility of giving an account of his view of Paul's theology as a whole from his post-1960 work.

The history-of-religions question: from a gnostic to an apocalyptic Paul

The most important change between Käsemann's view of Paul in his pre-1950 and post-1960 publications is in the question of the history-of-religions background against which Paul's theology is interpreted. Broadly speaking, in the first period the hellenistic and gnostic background is regarded as the dominant history-of-religions influence, although an eschatological perspective is always present; in the second period the dominant influence is the 'apocalyptic'[8] background to Paul's theology.[9] (The meaning of this last statement will be an important topic in itself in this chapter. This is partly due to the problem of the meaning of the terms eschatology and apocalyptic.)

The first indication of the change in Käsemann's view is to be found in a letter to Bultmann, dated 18 April 1949.[10] Responding to a number of issues raised by Bultmann's *Das Urchristentum im Rahmen der antiken Religionen* of the same year, Käsemann writes of his increasing distance from Peterson's and Schlier's interpretations of Romans, and pays tribute to

[8] The word 'apocalyptic' was introduced into biblical studies in 1820 by K. I. Nitzsch and was taken up by F. Lücke (1820/1852) who contributed the first comprehensive study of the phenomenon (Schmidt 1969: 98 n. 3). The meaning of the term and its use in scholarship has become a matter of debate, particularly in the period since the revival of interest in the subject in the 1960s (among many discussions, see Koch 1970, Hanson 1975, Collins 1979, Glasson 1981, Hellholm 1983). As the current state of affairs is one of competing and overlapping approaches, the present study will limit itself to analysis and criticism of Käsemann's understanding of the phenomenon.

[9] Cf. Schille on this change (1975: 73, 79).

[10] While only four letters from Käsemann are preserved in the Bultmann Nachlaß (11 Jan. 1941; 18 Apr. 1949; 10 Dec. 1964; Apr. 1965), this one sheds a great deal of light on the direction of Käsemann's thought in the late 1940s.

Schlatter. He then reports on his own lectures on Romans: 'With zeal I am championing the thesis that one can only understand the Pauline doctrine of justification against the background of Jewish apocalyptic and that in it one must see an adaptation of the cosmological views of this apocalyptic. The interpretation of the Reformation did not see that and therefore deviated considerably from Paul.'[11] Käsemann continues by telling his former teacher of his polemic against Bultmann's view of myth: in the New Testament, myth is always in the service of eschatology, indeed of an apocalyptic eschatology. New Testament apocalyptic is concerned with God's divinity (*Gottheit Gottes*, a phrase which Käsemann associates with Schlatter), his seizure of power, and with the theme of the fourth beatitude, hungering and thirsting after righteousness. As such it is to be contrasted with Jewish apocalyptic which is dominated by the themes of retribution in favour of the pious, or expectation of the time of the salvation. Equally, Käsemann contrasts this New Testament apocalyptic—in which 'God comes to his right on this earth'—with Bultmann's focus on the new understanding of existence, and calls the former the theme which unites the New Testament writings in all their diversity. Bultmann would no doubt call this message 'mythical' but the message of the New Testament stands and falls with this 'mythical message'.[12]

[11] 'Mit Eifer verfechte ich die These, daß man die paulinische Rechtfertigungslehre nur auf dem Hintergrund der jüdischen Apokalyptik verstehen könne und in ihr eine Abwandlung der kosmologischen Anschauungen dieser Apokalyptik zu sehen habe. Die reformatorische Auslegung hat das nicht gesehen und kommt deshalb doch zu erheblichen Abweichungen von Pls.'

[12] 'Von der Apokalyptik her habe ich übrigens im vorigen Semester auch fleißig gegen Sie polemisiert, ob freilich mit Verstand, weiss ich noch nicht. Meine These: Im N.T. steht der Mythos durchweg im Dienste der Eschatologie, und zwar einer apokalyptischen Eschatologie. Wenn man diese Apokalyptik des N.T. auf ihr eigentliches Thema hin befragt, erhält man die Antwort, es gehe ihr um die Gottheit Gottes, mit Schlatter zu sprechen, um seine Machtergreifung, also um das Thema der 4. Seligpreisung. Dieses Thema scheint mir nun von dem der paulinischen Rechtfertigungslehre nicht verschieden zu sein, sich dagegen doch erheblich von der Thematik der sonstigen Apokalyptik zu unterscheiden, bei der doch die Vergeltung im Interesse der Frommen dominiert bezw. die Erwartung der Heilszeit. An diesem Punkte setzt nun meine Kritik an Ihnen ein. Daß Gott zu seinem Rechte auf dieser Erde kommt, ist doch noch etwas anderes, als was Sie neues Seinsverständnis nennen, und ist, wie mir scheint, das Thema, welches die nt.lichen Schriften in all ihrer Verschiendenheit merkwürdig eint. Sie können diese Botschaft wohl nur mythisch nennen. Aber

This letter of 1949 outlines many of the themes which Käsemann treated in detail in his publications on Paul, beginning in the early 1960s. However, it does not throw much light on his understanding of the history-of-religions question in detail, and particularly on the relative importance of gnostic and apocalyptic thought for the understanding of the New Testament. (Käsemann's essays on the gnostic background of hymns embedded in Philippians and Colossians appeared as late as 1949 and 1950.) This question begins to be resolved in his responses to the newly discovered Dead Sea Scrolls in the 1950s.[13] In his first response to the Scrolls (1952) Käsemann claimed that they confirmed the hypothesis of the existence of a pre-Christian gnosticism,[14] although the redeemer myth, which otherwise is the heart of the gnostic system, was not taken over by the community at Qumran. The Scrolls offer close parallels to the 'eschatological–ethical dualism' and the 'apocalyptic eschatology' of primitive Christianity ('Probleme' 139 f.). Käsemann dropped the first point in 1957 when he merely cautions against the contemporary rush to abandon the pre-Christian gnosticism hypothesis. Against this trend he argues that 'the enthusiasm of the Corinthians is to be classified as a Christian variety of a mythological gnosis' (*EVB* ii. 28/20). Gnosticism was a possibility as soon as Christianity moved out of a Palestinian Jewish context[15] and into hellenistic circles (ibid.). However, by the 1970s Käsemann specifically criticizes Reitzenstein's 'redeemed redeemer' hypothesis,[16] and declines to comment on the general question of

mit dieser mythischen Botschaft steht und fällt die Botschaft überhaupt, wie ich meine.'

[13] While Käsemann was at Göttingen (1951–9) there was a project on the Qumran texts (Arbeitsgemeinschaft über die neueren Palästinatexte), although his name only appears in connection with this group in the lecture list for the summer semester of 1956.

[14] Thus, he aligns himself with the view of his Göttingen colleague, K. G. Kuhn, that the Scrolls show a 'preformation of gnosis' (1950*a*, 1950*b*).

[15] In 1952 Käsemann had claimed that it was now clear that at least a form of gnosticism was a possibility on Palestinian Jewish soil ('Probleme' 139).

[16] In *VF* 10 (1963/5) Käsemann distances himself in general from his own 'first work' (*Leib*) on the grounds that he had sought the key to NT interpretation in 'hellenistic-gnostic' sources (85). More specifically, in the 1970s he followed Colpe and Schenke's criticism of Reitzenstein and Bousset (*NTS* 19 (1972/3), 238; *Römer* 136/144; cf. *KK* i. 17). Colpe showed that Reitzenstein's redeemed redeemer is a modern construction from various gnostic and Iranian texts which cannot be found in

the history of gnosticism (*Römer* 137/146). The hypothesis of a pre-Christian, gnostic myth centred on the redeemed redeemer (though not the more general appeal to hellenistic influence) plays no further role in Käsemann's work.[17]

Eschatology and apocalyptic

Having traced the changes in Käsemann's view of the history-of-religions question, there remains the introductory task of examining Käsemann's understanding of the terms eschatology and apocalyptic. In *Leib und Leib Christi* he had maintained the importance of eschatology[18] for the interpretation of Paul's theology. He understood the concept 'spirit' from an eschatological point of view, emphasizing, with Bultmann, its existential significance.[19] Other themes which are later called 'apocalyptic' are also present (the Adam/Christ christology and the new creation; *Leib* 184). However, the cosmic scope of

any single text or gnostic system. Colpe himself did not entirely reject Reitzenstein's arguments, arguing that the matter (*Sachverhalt*) but not the concept (*Begriff*) of the redeemed redeemer is to be found in the sources. Secondly, while Reitzenstein concentrated on the identical ontological structure of the redeemer and the redeemed, the myths themselves emphasize the difference between the two, and thus the redeemed redeemer should be given its gnostic name, the 'foreign man' (*der fremde Mann*; Colpe 1961: 171, 175, 186). Schenke shows the methodological errors committed by Bousset and Reitzenstein and concludes that the Manichaean congregations arrived at their views not from Iranian or Indian models, but by speculation on the divine man motif in Gen. 1–2. He agrees with Colpe that the combination of myths resulting in Reitzenstein's redeemed redeemer did not take place until the third century AD. The later Manichaean views are dependent on the NT and not vice versa. Further, the texts which Käsemann cited in *Leib* as evidence for the giant body of the redeemer all refer to the aeon concept and have nothing to do with the God-man (Schenke 1962, especially 155). Rudolf has recently resurrected Reitzenstein's view (in modified form) in his textbook on gnosis (1977: 121; cf. 1971, 12).

[17] See p. 239 below for possible grounds for confusion on this point, and p. 246 below for Käsemann's continued use of a conceptuality derived from the study of gnosticism.

[18] Kümmel gives an overview of the history of research into eschatology, and points to the expansion of meaning of this term in the post-1918 period (1982).

[19] Thus, Kümmel can rightly maintain that *Leib*, despite its emphasis on gnostic influence, presents an eschatological view of Paul, and is, therefore, part of the re-examination of the view of Paul which followed the publication of Schweitzer's *Die Mystik des Apostels Paulus* (Kümmel 1970: 97). However, on this second point, Käsemann's dissertation must be regarded as a parallel development to Schweitzer's book as its main lines had been set before the latter appeared.

Paul's theology is attributed, not to apocalyptic, but to the gnostic aeon concept.

In the period up to the end of the war Käsemann also makes use of themes which he would later call 'apocalyptic' in contemporary theological debate. One of the roots of his interest in these themes was the German experience under the Third Reich. Although he only refers to this in print in the 1960s and after, his use of the motifs of the two, antithetical, aeons and their respective powers or lords can be seen in an unpublished address of 1945:

> Life is a clash between cosmic powers, as one might, perhaps, say today. The Bible says more simply and perhaps also more adequately, conflict between God and Satan. The spheres of power overlap in battle, they alter and separate anew in each new generation. The earth is the battlefield, human being the true object of the struggle, in which, however, nature in its entirety is also dragged in. And, in any case, the cross of Christ is the place at which the division of the spirits and powers constantly comes into view. ('Zusammenbruch' 10)[20]

This passage indicates that one of the roots of Käsemann's interest in eschatology, and, more specifically, its demonology, is the need to find a language to speak about the power of evil at a suprapersonal level.

The importance of eschatology is also emphasized in Käsemann's early essays: the Lord's supper is determined by eschatological beliefs, and the Christ hymn of Phil. 2 proclaims 'the eschatological event'. More important, however, is Käsemann's conviction concerning primitive Christianity as a whole (1950):

> even apart from Revelation, there is an overwhelming abundance of statements in the New Testament that emphasize the cosmic dimension of the work of salvation. This is due to the fact that the ancient Christian kerygma is eschatologically determined and

[20] 'Leben ist Aufeinanderprallen kosmischer Kräfte, wie man es heute vielleicht formulieren wird. Die Bibel sagt einfacher und vielleicht auch adäquater: Auseinandersetzung Gottes und des Satans. Die Machtsphären überlagern sich im Kampf, verschieben und scheiden sich mit jeder neuen Generation neu. Die Erde ist Schlachtfeld, der Mensch eigentliches Objekt des Ringens, in das aber auch die gesamte Natur hineingerissen wird. Und jedenfalls ist das Kreuz Christi der Ort, an dem die Scheidung der Geister und Mächte unablässig neu in Erscheinung tritt.'

describes no eschatological events which would not affect the entire world. (*EVB* i. 78/71)

Thus, for Käsemann, the first major point concerning the nature of primitive Christian eschatology is that it expresses a hope for the world, and not just for the individual (cf. *EVB* i. 146 f./182). Here he is guided by one of the fundamental points made in P. Volz's standard work on Jewish eschatology (1934). In the preface Volz states:

In the following, eschatology is understood as the doctrine of the last things where, as unified acts or events, they concern the community, people or world. The eschatology of the individual is a contradiction in terms. The individual is to be considered only as a part of the whole which is involved in the eschatological acts and conditions.[21]

It is important, however, to note that Käsemann's view of *apocalyptic* is derived from Volz's view of *eschatology*. From the 1960s on, Käsemann often expresses his conviction concerning the cosmic scope of early Christian apocalyptic by adopting Ps. 24: 1 in the form of a question, thereby connecting it with the theme of lordship: 'Apocalyptic . . . is the disquieting question which not only moves the apostle [Paul] but apparently faces every Christian, a question bound up with his task and his existence: to whom does the earth belong?' (*PP* 48/24 f., ET modified; cf. *EVB* ii. 129/135; *Römer* 169/178)

Despite Käsemann's theme of the cosmic orientation of eschatological thought, in 1950 he is still in agreement with Bultmann's view of the importance of present eschatology. New Testament eschatology, on account of its theme of the presence of salvation, is to be differentiated from Jewish apocalyptic. The latter held out the hope of future salvation to be brought by the messiah; by contrast the church adopted the hellenistic myths in order to express 'a present salvation exclusively related to Christ' (*EVB* i. 92/85).

Käsemann's public debate with Bultmann does not begin until 1957 but the outline of it is clear in his essay on 2 Peter of 1952 in which he gives a sketch of Paul's theology in order to

[21] Volz 1934: 3. Käsemann specifically recommends Volz's book in his NT theology lectures: 'On the Jewish religion and apocalyptic, P. Volz, *Die Eschatologie der jüdischen Gemeinde*, 1934, is still the most informative' ('Theologie' 34).

use it as a foil for the criticism of the theology of 2 Peter (see pp. 10f. above). He argues that, in Paul's theology, eschatology is integrated with the doctrine of christology, his central doctrine of justification, and his doctrine of God (145–7/181–3):

It is unthinkable for Paul that the God who brings that which is into existence out of nothing, who effects the *justificatio impii*, the obedience of the children of Adam, the *resurrectio mortuorum*, should be faced with an endless fight against sin and death as the powers sovereign over this world; that he should not finally overcome all his enemies and reign as unquestioned Lord of his creation. A God so limited would not be really God . . . Pauline eschatology . . . centres round the question whether God is indeed God and when he will fully assert himself as such. It proclaims the sovereignty [*Herrschaft*] of God in the doctrine of justification: equally, it proclaims the sovereignty of God in its apocalyptic. (146/182)

Here the points of the letter of 1949 are made for the first time in print and Käsemann's second major point becomes clear: Paul's eschatology expresses a particular theology in which the leading ideas of God's sovereignty or lordship and the doctrine of justification are brought together. From this basis Käsemann criticizes the 'anthropologically [ET: 'manward'] orientated eschatology' of 2 Peter.

In his review of New Testament studies of 1957 Käsemann makes the same points, now specifically in criticism of Bultmann's interpretation of Paul. Bultmann interprets Paul's theology by focusing on his anthropological terms and thus on the individual. For Käsemann, Paul's anthropology merely has the specific function of expressing 'the reality and radical nature of Christ's seizure of power as the Cosmocrator' (*EVB* ii. 23/14). The two aspects mentioned so far (cosmic orientation, lordship) are brought together in criticism of the anthropological orientation of Bultmann's interpretation:

Apocalyptic is therefore not less meaningful in his [Paul's] theology than anthropology. It proclaims that the apostle was very deeply moved by the quest of the Johannine apocalypse for the revelation of the godhead of God [*Gottheit Gottes*], and his doctrine of justification revolves around the rightful claim which God will make good on his own created world. (24/15)

This last passage demonstrates Käsemann's characteristic use of the term 'apocalyptic'. However, it is important to bear in mind that before 1952 he emphasized the cosmic orientation of primitive Christian hope using the term 'eschatology', and that this term is superseded by, and used alongside, the term 'apocalyptic' once the term 'eschatology' has become a matter of debate. (In addition it was seen that Käsemann's understanding of apocalyptic is indebted to Volz's view of eschatology.) Just as Käsemann probably adopted the term *cosmocrator* because of the dominance of Bousset's interpretation of *κύριος* (p. 96 above), so he adopts the term 'apocalyptic' because of the dominance of Bultmann's view of 'eschatology'.

Käsemann's third major point is that imminent expectation of the end is the characteristic mark of New Testament eschatology or apocalyptic. This theme is mentioned briefly in the essay of 1952 on 2 Peter (*EVB* i. 156/194) but in the key essays of the early 1960s it is said to be the defining mark of apocalyptic.[22] Within the development of Käsemann's views this is the last of the three themes to emerge.

To sum up: Käsemann's adoption of the term 'apocalyptic' is to be understood as a convenient shorthand for his understanding of primitive Christian eschatology, the main points being its cosmic scope, its expression of a theology focused on the hope of God coming into his right on earth (with the consequent defeat of the powers of evil), and the theme of an imminent future expectation. 'Apocalyptic' becomes a label for an interpretation of Paul's theology which is focused, not on anthropology, but on Christ's lordship and God's final triumph, and as such is a deliberate demarcation of Käsemann's own position over against Bultmann.

[22] When pressed by Ebeling (1961: 230 f.) to define the term 'apocalyptic', Käsemann comments: 'Since eschatology and the doctrine of history became almost identical in Germany, we have been embarrassed by no longer having any specific term for the particular kind of eschatology which attempts to talk about *Endgeschichte* [ET: 'ultimate history']' (*EVB* ii. 105 n. 1/109 n. 1). This is a rather general criticism but Käsemann's point is clear: for him 'apocalyptic' refers to imminent expectation of the end (ibid.) and 'eschatology' no longer denotes that. His view of the relationship of the two terms is summarized in extremely general terms in his NT theology lectures: 'Eschatology is the doctrine of the end of the world and of history, brought in by God's activity. Apocalyptic is a particular form within eschatology understood in this way' ('Theologie' 39). Unfortunately he does not elucidate this distinction further.

As was seen above, in the early 1960s Käsemann employed the theme of apocalyptic as the key for his reconstruction of the history of primitive Christianity. In addition to the major points regarding the nature of apocalyptic just outlined, within this historical reconstruction Käsemann identifies particular apocalyptic features, some of which have already been noted. These include, as the primary feature, imminent expectation of the parousia (*EVB* ii. 104 n. 1/109 n. 1); an orientation to the world and not to the individual, within which a human being is understood as a 'piece of world' (23/14); the two-aeons motif (*PP* 119/67); the correspondence of primal time (*Urzeit*) and end-time (*Endzeit*; *EVB* ii. 94/96); a belief in the transvaluation of all values at the end (97/99); the 'eschatological law' of the correspondence of deed and recompense (*jus talionis*, 97/98); and a form of community rule within primitive Christianity in which eschatological judgement impinges on the present through the words of prophet-leaders (79/78), resulting in blessing or curse (71 f./69). In addition, apocalyptic is credited with making historical thinking possible within primitive Christianity: within the apocalyptic world-view, history has a definite beginning and end, a course with a clear direction which could therefore be divided into epochs. More specifically it understood history as a 'parallel, even if antithetically ordered, course of salvation history [*Heilsgeschichte*] and the history of disaster' (*Unheilsgeschichte*, 95/96). However, Käsemann does not give a systematic account of apocalyptic, nor does he discuss its history. These points constitute little more than a list of features with the two key ideas of the imminent expectation of the end and a view of the world determined by the concept of the two, antithetical, aeons.

It has now been seen that Käsemann's understanding of apocalyptic is made up of a combination of theological and historical arguments, supplemented by piecemeal observations on characteristic apocalyptic features. Given this state of affairs, it is not surprising that his views have been strongly criticized. Kümmel does not get to the root of the problem when he suggests that the term 'apocalyptic' should be replaced with 'historical eschatology' or 'universal eschatology'.[23] More pertinently Moule criticizes the fluidity of the terms and the tendency for theological meanings to predominate: 'Misleading also, at least for English readers, is the use of "eschatological" and even "apocalyptic" in such wide senses as to threaten to debase linguistic currency. "Eschatological" seems to denote almost anything that is of God, as opposed to evolutionary, rational, or humanly self-assured.'[24] Benoit makes a fundamental point when he criticizes Käsemann's simple equation of apocalyptic and eschatology.[25] Further, Käsemann's 'apocalyptic' has no clear relationship to the content or the world of the apocalypses. Given these general criticisms it is apparent that it is necessary to scrutinize Käsemann's use of these terms constantly. In particular, the dual and often overlapping use of 'apocalyptic' as a historical term (cosmically orientated eschatology with a strong expectation of an imminent end) and as a designation of a particular type of theology (centred on the God who comes to claim his right on earth) has to be borne in mind.

ESCHATOLOGY AND THEOLOGY: THE STRUCTURE OF PAUL'S THOUGHT

The doctrine of eschatology is of fundamental significance for dialectical theology. It is not regarded as one doctrine among others, the conventional last subject of dogmatics; rather, the entirety of Christian belief is eschatological through and through. For Käsemann, the total proclamation of Paul (and of the New Testament) is eschatologically determined (*EVB* ii. 205/196; *PP* 18/6 f.). The interpretation of Paul's eschatology

[23] Kümmel 1974: 485.

[24] Moule 1981: 501. Cf. the criticism that Käsemann uses 'apocalyptic' as a totally unqualified noun (Rollins 1970, 459). For further criticisms, see p. 175 below.

[25] 1977: 304. Rowland has recently argued that apocalyptic is to be understood as a way of apprehending the divine will and that eschatology refers to the Jewish hopes for the future, a subject which can, but need not be discussed in apocalypses (1982: 48). In the light of this attack on the tendency to regard eschatology as the centre of apocalyptic thought (or to see the two as synonymous), it is interesting to note that Volz's understanding of apocalyptic does not centre on eschatology but more broadly on the divine secrets in space and time (1934: 5). It is only within this framework that he argued that the eschatological material dominates the apocalypses.

is not a matter of discussing the details of the explicitly eschatological passages in the epistles, but of reflecting on fundamental points concerning the structure of Paul's theology. However, as an exegete, Käsemann does have particular views on Paul's eschatology and the wider issues concerning the structure of Paul's thought are best approached through these views.

The antithetical correspondence of primal time and end-time

In *Schöpfung und Chaos in Urzeit und Endzeit* (1895), H. Gunkel argued that primitive Christian eschatology regarded the end-time (*Endzeit*) as a restoration of the primal time (*Urzeit*).[26] Gunkel prefaced his work with the saying from Epistle of Barnabas 6: 13: *ἰδού, ποιῶ τὰ ἔσχατα ὡς τὰ πρῶτα*. While he was concerned with the interpretation of Gen. 1 and Rev. 15, P. Volz adduced evidence for the theory from Jewish literature.[27] In turn, Käsemann argues that Paul's eschatology is based on this motif, citing two passages in particular, Rom. 4: 17b and 5: 12–21. In general, primitive Christianity believed that the new aeon had succeeded the old and, secondly, that the new confronts the old spatially (*Römer* 119/126). Paul presupposes the apocalyptic two-aeon motif but modifies it. He did not, however, adopt the historicizing schema (ET: 'historical schema') of two successive aeons. The end-time has already begun and issues in the presence of life (*Römer* 133/142) but the old aeon has not simply vanished; the old aeon radiates temptation in the midst of the new.[28] In the present time there is no clear temporal or spatial separation between the two aeons (*Römer* 125 f./134). Finally, it is not the return to the golden age of the primal time which is characteristic of

[26] Cf. Gunkel's general comment on the eschatological reinterpretation of myths: 'what the poets tell of the primal time the prophets understand as pictures of the events of the end-time' (Gunkel 1913: 628 f.). Barth makes some use of this idea (1922: 219, 231).

[27] Volz gives a more complex view: there were two golden ages in Jewish belief, paradise and the age of Moses, and the blessedness of the end-time can be seen as a return to either period (Volz 1934: 359) Cf. Bultmann 1950: 370–5; Jervell 1960: 284–92, who argues that Paul uses the motif very sparingly; Schwantes 1963; Schrage 1964: 129. H. Stegemann proposes to interpret Jesus' eschatology on the basis of the motif (1982: 13 n. 54).

[28] Cf. Schrage 1964: 126.

Paul's thought but the antithetical correspondence of primal time and end-time (*Römer* 134/142, 138/146, 144/153). This is particularly connected with the two 'bearers of destiny', Adam and Christ. The long digression in Rom. 5: 13 ff., where Paul hesitates before completing the comparison begun in v. 12,[29] is caused by the 'apocalyptic antithesis of primal time and end-time' (134/142): the 'reign of Christ [*regnum Christi*][30] confronts the reign of sin and death initiated by Adam' (ibid.).

Käsemann regards 4: 17*b* as significant for Paul's theology as a whole (116/122 f., with further reference to 1 Cor. 1: 28; *PP* 172 f./98 f.). Paul is said to relate two traditional formulae ('God who raises the dead'[31] and *creatio ex nihilo*) according to the primal time/end-time principle (*Römer* 116/123). (However, the mass of history-of-religions comment and theological exposition in the commentary at this point is not matched by similar attention to the meaning of the Pauline text.) One of the reasons why Käsemann regards this as a key verse is because it demonstrates the unity of the divine action: there is a correspondence between God's first act of creation and his salvation-creating act (*PP* 124/70, 133/75).[32] Paul's eschatology does not merely offer information about the end but is rooted in his doctrine of God.

However, there are substantial arguments against Käsemann's interpretation of Rom. 4: 17*b*. In this verse Paul employs the predicates in the order: end-time activity (who gives life to the dead), primal time activity (calls into existence the things that do not exist). Secondly, there is no evidence that the relationship between the end-time and the primal time (whether they are said to be similar or antithetical) is of importance here (though cf. 2 Cor. 4: 6 which Käsemann does not bring into the discussion). The two predicates are used in

[29] On the theological significance of Paul's anacolutha, see Bornkamm 1952*b*; on Rom. 5: 12–21, 80–90.

[30] In the Romans commentary Käsemann sometimes uses the Latin *regnum Christi* when he wishes to talk about the lordship of Christ (*Römer* 95/101, 123/131, 133/142, etc.; cf. also *regnum Dei*, *PP* 77/42, 84/46, *Römer* 177/185, and *regnum Adae* 172/180). There does not appear to be any material reason for his choice of this phrase or its German equivalents. The ET does not distinguish between them.

[31] N. M. Watson (1983) takes up this motif as a summary of Paul's theology.

[32] The reference to the last day is omitted by the ET which should read: 'Since creation and until the last day, God has acted no differently . . .'.

parallel, in a transferred sense, of the present, saving activity of God. The original protological and eschatological contexts of the predicates play no role in Paul's argument. By contrast, the history-of-religions background of these predicates weighs more heavily with Käsemann than Paul's use of them.

Käsemann's claim that this theme is 'constitutive' for Paul's theology[33] rests precariously on very few verses. His attempt to demonstrate his case is limited to Rom. 4: 17*b*, 5: 12 ff.; his other references to the theme are either imposed on other topics (e.g., anthropology, *PP* 15/5; Paul's theology in general, 177/101), or occur in discussions of his theory of typology which again is based on Rom. 5, and where there is a tendency for the 'primal time' to expand to the whole Old Testament (cf. the phrase the 'previous time' (*Vorzeit*), *Römer* 7/9). Käsemann can find some other passages to parallel Rom. 4: 17*b*, but this is in respect of the *creatio ex nihilo* theme (2 Cor. 3: 5 f., 4: 7 ff., 12: 9, 13: 4; 1 Cor. 1: 26 f.; *PP* 15–61/91 f., *Römer* 116/123), and not the primal time/end-time theme. Thus, it would seem that Käsemann's only case for the importance of the primal time/end-time scheme is 5: 12 ff., though he might also have appealed to 2 Cor. 4: 6.

Eschatology and the structure of Paul's theology

Bultmann interprets Paul's eschatology (and that of the New Testament) as a form of realized eschatology:

> The salvation-occurrence is the *eschatological occurrence* which puts to [an] end the old aeon. Though Paul still expects the end of the old world to come as a cosmic drama that will unfold with the imminent parousia, that can only be the completion and confirmation of the eschatological occurrence that has now already begun.[34]

As such Paul's position can be contrasted very neatly with Jewish beliefs: 'what for the Jews is a *matter of hope* is for Paul a *present reality*—or, better, is also a present reality'.[35] Eschato-

[33] Lewandowski notes that Rom. 4: 17 is the source of Käsemann's most frequently repeated images of God which emphasize his sovereign power (1974: 224).

[34] Bultmann 1951: 306; this point goes back to his demand for theological criticism (*Sachkritik*) in the interpretation of 1 Cor. 15. Paul is speaking of a closing scene of history but this is outside his legitimate concern and intention (Bultmann 1926*b*: 81, 86; Kümmel 1984: 180).

[35] Bultmann 1951: 279.

logical righteousness is already present, although the other signs of eschatological salvation are not (Rom. 5: 1–11). Life is a thing of the future which determines the present.[36] Consequently, the subject of hope is not given a section of its own in Bultmann's arrangement of Paul's theology; it is discussed under 'The Structure of Faith'.[37] Hope is 'the freedom for the future and the openness toward it which the man of faith has because he has turned over his anxiety about himself and his future to God in obedience'.[38] Paul has lifted the eschatological event out of the dimension of the cosmic and into the existential: '*the salvation-occurrence is nowhere present except in the proclaiming, accosting, demanding, and promising word of preaching.*'[39] In summary, Bultmann finds the theological significance of Paul's future eschatology in the eschatological salvation already present, focused on the individual believer.

Even in the post-1960 period Käsemann accepts some of Bultmann's fundamental points. Most importantly he agrees that eschatological salvation is already present before the parousia (e.g., *EVB* ii. 183/170, 190/178), and he can therefore give qualified assent to the catch-phrase 'realized eschatology' (190/178). Secondly, Paul is not concerned primarily with an apocalyptic timetable (though he does have his own apocalyptic scheme, *PP* 47 f./24). Thirdly, the presence of eschatological salvation is brought about by the preached word (e.g., *Römer* 161/169). These fundamental agreements need to be noted before Käsemann's debate with Bultmann can be discussed.

Käsemann's main point is that the emphasis in Paul is not on realized but on future eschatology. The framework of his theology is 'apocalyptic'; the dominant eschatological motif is the imminent expectation of the end. It is only within this framework that realized eschatology has its limited place. Thus, one can speak of Paul's 'double eschatology' (*EVB* ii. 183/170), or, preferably, of the dialectic of present and future eschatology (193/181; *Römer* 112/119): 'The apostle's present eschatology cannot be taken out of its context of future eschatology . . . Even as a Christian, Paul remained an

36 Ibid. 347, cf. 279.
37 Ibid. 31–22. Cf. also the section on 'freedom from death' (345–52).
38 Ibid. 320.
39 Ibid. 302, Bultmann's emphasis; cf. 307.

apocalyptist' (*EVB* ii. 193/181, ET modified). However, the poles of the dialectic are not of equal importance: present eschatology is set within the context of future eschatology, thus reversing Bultmann's emphasis. Käsemann does not devote an essay to this theme. Rather, having made his programmatic statements in the essays 'Neutestamentliche Fragen von heute' and 'Gottesgerechtigkeit bei Paulus', he reads Romans as a whole in this light.

There is little exegetical debate with Bultmann on Paul's future eschatology because, as has been seen, Bultmann acknowledged that the imminent parousia was important to Paul. Käsemann underlines the importance of this future expectation by speaking of Paul's 'apocalyptic self-understanding'. The most important difference between the two scholars is on a point of historical reconstruction. Käsemann argues, with others,[40] that the Qumran documents now provide evidence of an apocalyptic Jewish sect whose beliefs contained elements of realized eschatology. Paul's belief in eschatological salvation in the present is not—*contra* Bultmann—the distinctive feature of his eschatology; rather, on this point, Paul stands within one stream of Jewish apocalyptic thought (*EVB* ii. 190/178; *Römer* 23/25).

At the level of contemporary theological statement, Käsemann argues against Bultmann that Paul's eschatology cannot be interpreted adequately in anthropological terms. Of the phrase 'realized eschatology' he says: 'One may speak of realized eschatology only very dialectically and even then not exclusively in the anthropological category of "futurity" (*contra* Bultmann's basic thesis in *History and Eschatology*[41])' (*Römer* 112/119). The referent of Paul's eschatology is not anthropology but his doctrine of God; its concern is God's final triumph. Käsemann here appeals to his understanding of Paul's doctrine of justification in an important passage which has already been quoted in part:

> [Paul's] doctrine of justification, standing though it undoubtedly does under the sign of his present[42] eschatology, cannot be

[40] e.g., Kuhn 1966.

[41] Bultmann 1957.

[42] The ET omits the reference to 'present' eschatology and thus obscures the allusion to Bultmann's interpretation. It also omits the 'only' in 'it is not only a question'. Again Schrage follows Käsemann here (1964: 127, 147).

understood at all without his apocalyptic in which it is not only a question of reward or completion but, according to 1 Cor. 15.28, a question of God's becoming all in all . . . Apocalyptic is therefore not less meaningful in his theology than anthropology. It proclaims that the apostle was very deeply moved by the quest of the Johannine apocalypse for the revelation of the godhead of God, and his doctrine of justification revolves around the rightful claim which God will make good on his own created world. (*EVB* ii. 24/15)

This point becomes a criticism of the fundamental structure of Bultmann's interpretation. For Bultmann, Paul's theology is not a speculative system but deals with 'God as He is significant for man'. His presupposition runs: 'Every assertion about God is simultaneously an assertion about man and vice versa. For this reason and in this sense Paul's theology is, at the same time, anthropology.'[43] The same insight is applied to christology and soteriology: 'Thus, every assertion about Christ is also an assertion about man and vice versa; and Paul's christology is simultaneously soteriology.'[44] Bultmann then indicates how he is going to treat Paul's theology in practice: 'Therefore, Paul's theology can best be treated as his doctrine of man: first, of man prior to the revelation of faith, and second, of man under faith, for in this way the anthropological and soteriological orientation of Paul's theology is brought out.'[45] This last quotation reveals that Bultmann's initial analysis, which is fully reciprocal (theology–anthropology, christology–soteriology), is not to be carried through in the execution of his programme. His judgement that 'Paul's theology can best be treated as his doctrine of man' is not given support in this preliminary discussion. Theoretically the converse ought to be equally true. It is at this point that Käsemann takes issue.[46] He agrees that 'Paul neither talks about God and Christ nor about the world and man in isolation' (*PP* 9/1), but argues that Bultmann fails to take up the 'and vice versa' of his programme.[47] There is an 'irreversible descent' towards anthropology (27/12). Käsemann then outlines his approach: 'If the dialectic of "and vice versa"

[43] Bultmann 1951: 191.

[44] Ibid. Cf. Bultmann 1933a, 277 and his quotation from Melanchthon.

[45] Bultmann 1951: 191.

[46] So also Güttgemanns 1966: 210.

[47] Käsemann therefore emphatically disagrees with H. Conzelmann's explicit rejection of the 'and vice versa' (1967: 159, cited on *PP* 27 f./12).

is seriously meant, neither theology nor anthropology can "properly" [*sachgemäß*, materially] be conceded priority. Yet it might be possible to develop the connection of the two in the light of Pauline Christology, thus avoiding the danger both of a Christian metaphysic and of a Christian humanism' (ibid.). As was seen repeatedly in Käsemann's work before 1950, he here again seeks a unifying interpretation. Instead of opting for one pole of the theology–anthropology dialectic, he seeks to integrate both poles under the theme of christology, a christology summed up in the 'Christ must reign' motif drawn from 1 Cor. 15: 25 ff. (*δεῖ γὰρ αὐτὸν βασιλεύειν . . .*). Elsewhere Käsemann makes the general judgement that 'right theology' is christocentric (*Freiheit* 259/155), and he summarizes his programme in the catch-phrase 'the primacy of christology'.[48] At the same time he repeatedly stresses the theme of God's action, particularly in the apocalyptic motif of the God who claims his right on this earth. Thus, Käsemann makes a twofold 'correction' to Bultmann's theology: he emphasizes the 'theology' pole of the theology–anthropology dialectic, and he interprets both theology and anthropology in the light of the lordship of Christ.

Käsemann's fundamental disagreement with Bultmann on the interpretation of Paul's theology arises from a different view of Pauline eschatology. As was noticed above, this debate over the contemporary theological relevance of Paul's eschatology does not lead to extensive exegetical debate on this theme because Bultmann and Käsemann agree on Paul's belief in the imminent parousia. Nevertheless, it is curious that 1 Cor. 15: 25 ff., the passage which contains the 'Christ must reign' motif, is never given detailed exegetical treatment by Käsemann.[49] The twofold 'correction' of Bultmann's interpretation is worked out in the rest of Käsemann's interpretation of Paul.

[48] Presumably Käsemann has borrowed this unusual phrase from Iwand whose essay 'Vom Primat der Christologie' argues this case for the content and shape of dogmatics, contrasting the views of Harnack with those of Calvin and Barth (Iwand 1956).

[49] The nearest he comes to this is in his discussion of the relationship of 1 Cor. 15: 3–5 (understood as pre-Pauline catechetical tradition) to vv. 20–8 (understood as Pauline interpretation; 'Konsequente Traditionsgeschichte?' *ZThK* 62 (1965), 141).

PAUL'S APOCALYPTIC SELF-UNDERSTANDING

One of the most important pieces of evidence that Käsemann presents for his apocalyptic reading of Paul is his interpretation of the apostle's self-understanding. As has been seen, Käsemann does not believe that 'the Pauline dialectic of present and future eschatology' primarily concerns his anthropology. 'Consciously, and under a sense of apocalyptic pressure, Paul conceived his task to be the world mission of the church' (*EVB* ii. 193/181; ET: 'the universalization of the Church's mission'). As the apostle to the Gentiles he is the precursor of the parousia,[50] along the lines of Mark 13: 10 (125/131; *Römer* 286/296, 302 f./312 f., 297/307). The most important passages for Käsemann's view are Rom. 10: 14–21, 11: 13–15, and 15: 16–23.

In demonstrating Israel's guilt in **10: 14–21**, Paul argues that Israel is at fault because, although the gospel has gone out by means of the Christian mission (vv. 14 f., *Römer* 285/294), the message has not been accepted by all (v. 16*a*). Verses 18 and 19 then rob Israel of all basis for excuse. Ps. 18: 5 LXX is quoted in v. 18 to prove the world-wide dimension of Christian preaching, to which Israel has failed to respond. Paul's 'apocalyptic self-understanding' is clear from the way that he applies the eschatological interpretation of scripture to his own work (286/296).[51]

In **11: 13–15**, Paul argues that Jewish unbelief itself has a part in God's plan: the Gentile mission arises out of it. It is Paul's specific calling to be the apostle to the Gentiles (v. 13). His task is nothing less than bringing in the full number of the Gentiles in order to provoke the Jews to faith:

> Paul is not content to be merely an apostle to the Gentile world. He has obviously learned from Deut 32: 21 that God will convert his people by provoking it to jealousy of Gentile-Christians. Christ, reigning as *cosmocrator* over the nations and confessed by them, will

[50] Käsemann is here following G. Sass's understanding of Paul's apostleship: the preachers of the gospel are the messengers before the breaking-in of God's royal lordship which will be damnation or rescue for the whole of the world (Sass 1939: 29).

[51] So also Barrett 1957: 205; Schlier 1977: 318; Cranfield 1979: 537; Wilckens 1980: 230.

be to the Jews the sign of the end that has dawned and of the promises that have been fulfilled. (297/306)

Thus, the apostle is an instrument in the conversion of Israel (ibid.) and understands himself to be the precursor of the parousia (297/307). Further, the passage as a whole is marked by an apocalyptic perspective. In v. 11*b* the idea that the trespass of the Jews will lead to the salvation of the Gentiles is influenced by the apocalyptic idea that the first will be last and the last first (294/304). Verse 15 contains a reversal of the Jewish apocalyptic hope that the Gentiles will come in to Zion at the end (297/307).

The theme of reversal is employed again by Paul in 11: 25–32 (302 f./312 f.), though here it may be combined with a tradition which speaks of the attack of the Gentiles on Jerusalem.[52] More important is the belief, well-attested in Jewish sources, that the restitution and the conversion of the people belong together (ibid., with references). As a prophet, Paul takes up Jewish and Christian traditions and reshapes them in line with his apocalyptic expectation and self-understanding (303/313).

The most important passage for Käsemann's view of Paul's self-understanding is **15: 16–21, 23**. The self-designation *λειτουργὸν Χριστοῦ Ἰησοῦ εἰς τὰ ἔθνη* (v. 16) is understood as 'priest of the Messiah Jesus to the whole of the Gentile world' (378/392). Paul's role has cosmic breadth. The phrase *ἡ προσφορὰ τῶν ἐθνῶν* (v. 16) does not refer to the Gentiles' self-offering which the apostle brings about, but to the Gentile world which itself is the offering (epexegetical genitive). This notion is said to be fully apocalyptic and corresponds to 11: 11 ff. (379/393). Käsemann continues:

> In the last resort his [Paul's] metaphor of the priest of the Messiah is interchangeable with that of the cosmic conqueror (cf. 2 Cor 10: 4 ff.). On both occasions the subject is [ET: 'Either way the reference is to'] the singular mandate and worldwide function of the apostle to the Gentiles who places the ungodly at the feet of his Lord and sets them in his triumphant procession. (Ibid.)

[52] Käsemann refers to Rev. 11: 13 and Rom. 11: 1–3, and the interpretation of Müller (1964: 42).

Verse 19*b* is particularly revealing of Paul's self-understanding. *Πεπληρωκέναι τὸ εὐαγγέλιον* is to be explained in the light of the indication of area: the gospel 'fashions an earthly sphere of validity for the lordship of Christ' (380/394). *Κύκλῳ* is a dative of place used adverbially and does not mean widening circles around Jerusalem but the wide arc between two specified points:

The apostle is not thinking of individual churches but, in accordance with his apocalyptic approach, of peoples and lands. The eastern part of the empire is defined by Jerusalem on the one hand as the salvation-historical center of the world and the starting point of the gospel, and by the end of the Via Aegnatia on the other hand . . . Even if it is assumed that Paul himself is content to establish symbolic centers from which Christianity will develop independently, the statement is an enormous exaggeration when measured by geographical reality. (380/395)

Again the underlying assumption is that the apostolic mission is preparatory for the imminent parousia[53] and Paul finds his activity prefigured in scripture (v. 21; 381/395). Finally, v. 23 can hardly be historically correct and is psychologically impossible apart from Paul's apocalyptic conception of his work (382 f./397).

In these arguments Käsemann uses the term 'apocalyptic' in two different ways. Firstly, in a history-of-religions sense, Paul's apostolic activity is determined by his belief in the imminence of the parousia and the reversal of the tradition of the Gentile pilgrimage to Zion. 'The mission of the apostle is a colossal detour to the salvation of Israel, whereby the first become last' (*EVB* ii. 244/241). Secondly, apocalyptic takes on its popular, derogatory sense when Käsemann speaks of Paul's 'apocalyptic dreams' (*Römer* 300/310) or of a possessed man pursuing an impossible dream (*EVB* ii. 244/241). However, this is not left as a remnant of liberal scorn, but is taken up and reflected on theologically. Since apocalyptic (or eschatology) binds together justification and salvation history

[53] So also Cullmann 1936 and Schoeps 1959: 229. Michel (1955/1979: 460) does not regard the passage as a problem, while Cranfield (1979: 762) gives a non-eschatological interpretation. Knox 1964 and Munck 1954: 49 ff. seek a middle position. Jülicher (1908/1917: 328) emphasizes the scope of Paul's 'exaggeration' (quoted in Munck 1954: 53).

in the unity of divine action, Paul's theological system will fall apart without it: 'Paul has left us a theological conception [*Konzept*; ET: 'concept', which is better reserved for *Begriff*] which cannot be maintained as a unity but whose parts, even when they have fallen apart, have again and again had an impact on world history' (287/296). For Käsemann, Paul's apocalyptic language guards the cosmic scope of Christian hope and the constant need to speak of God's final triumph. This has the corollary that the role of the church and the presence of salvation are relativized in the light of the future hope, as will now be seen.

APOCALYPTIC AND THE ATTACK ON ENTHUSIASM

Paul's anti-enthusiastic theology in Corinth and in the Letter to the Romans

In the pre-1950 period Käsemann depicted Paul's theology as a critical response to enthusiastic Christianity. The main features of this enthusiasm, which Käsemann finds within the New Testament,[54] can be summarized as follows:

1. Viewed theologically, following Luther, enthusiasm is the attempt of Christians to deny that, in this life, they continue to live within the tension created by the overlap of the two realms of fallen creation and redemption in Christ (n. 65 to ch. 1 above).

2. In history-of-religions terms, enthusiasm is characterized by the direct operation of a transcendent spirit in an individual or community.[55] It manifests itself in the response

[54] Käsemann's most detailed and systematic treatment of this subject is in his NT theology lectures, in which he gives an outline of the history of the NT period around the concept of enthusiasm (cf. the similar surveys around the concepts 'apocalyptic', summarized in ch. 1 above, and 'freedom' in *Freiheit*). Above all Käsemann appeals to the evidence of the underlying theological tendency which led to the various troubles reflected in 1 Cor. (*EVB* ii. 121/125 f.; cf. *Freiheit* 81–7/61–4) and the tradition of the primitive Christian hymns (Eph. 2: 5 f., 5: 14; Col. 2: 12 f.; *EVB* ii. 120/125). In citing the evidence of pre-Pauline tradition embedded in post-Pauline epistles, Käsemann is following Bultmann (e.g., 1951: 140–3). Wedderburn argues that the Col. and Eph. passages are deliberate revisions of Paul's earlier statements, not the re-emergence of earlier traditions (1983: 346).

[55] Krodel 1965.

to a divine epiphany (Peterson), for example, on account of a miracle (*RGG* (3rd edn.) 2, 1835).

3. Within primitive Christian circles, the fundamental feature of enthusiasm is the belief that salvation in its fullness has already arrived, the resurrection has already occurred. Following baptism, which conveys the totality of salvation, Christian life is the temporal representation of heavenly or angelic being. Believers already participate in Christ's resurrection and enthronement. Removed from the old aeon and its powers, they are freed from social convention and earthly authority (following Lütgert, see n. 75 to ch. 2 above; *EVB* ii. 125/131). Christians are removed from the sphere of earthly weakness and of the body. The Lord's supper is celebrated as an eschatological banquet and Christianity understood as a mystery religion (*EVB* ii. 120/125). The ecstatic and the supernatural characterize the life of the congregation.

Before 1950 Käsemann's view of Paul's criticism of enthusiastic Christianity was based on a number of major themes: christology (it is Christ alone, not Christians, who has left the earthly sphere), eschatology (the resurrection has not dawned yet, Christians are still *in via*), the doctrine of ministry (charisma as gift, demand, and limit), anthropology (the Christian as *σῶμα* and as having a *νοῦς*). The same programme of interpretation is now continued—with renewed vigour—and extended, under the slogan of 'apocalyptic' (*EVB* ii. 126/132).[56] Käsemann's fundamental point still concerns the separation of Christ and Christians with regard to the resurrection. The believer does not yet participate in the resurrection and thus the Christian life in its entirety is under the 'eschatological reservation'.[57] Paul's doctrine of resurrection is primarily concerned with christology ('Christ must reign', 127/133) and not with the experience of Christians. To these points are added the use Paul makes of 'apocalyptic' in combating the illusion of the enthusiast, particularly by emphasizing the Christian's solidarity with the created order.

[56] Cf. Schrage 1964: 136 f., 150 f.

[57] Barth emphasizes the dialectic of 'having/being' and 'not having/being' under the eschatological reservation: 'No anticipation of the fundamentally future, other worldly, eternal, other than by faith' (1922: 130).

Käsemann then outlines the historical and theological implications of his view of Paul. The apostle should not be regarded merely as a particularly important representative of the hellenistic church (with Baur, Bousset, and Bultmann, 125/131); rather, he reintroduced Jewish apocalyptic into the church in the service of his anti-enthusiastic theology. This is not a backward step—as it would have to be regarded on the premisses of Bultmann and the liberal tradition—but a permanent contribution to Christian theology:

Present eschatology by itself, and not comprehended within a future eschatology—that would be for the Christian nothing but the hubris [ET: 'pure glorying'] of the flesh, such as enthusiasm has certainly sufficiently demonstrated in every epoch. It would be illusion and not reality. It is precisely the apocalyptic of the apostle which renders to reality its due and resists pious illusion. The Christian Church possesses the reality of sonship only in the freedom of those under assault [*Anfechtung*]—the freedom which points forward to the resurrection of the dead as the completion of the *regnum Christi*. (130/136 f.; ET modified)

Here Käsemann sets out his programme and continues the theological rehabilitation of the term 'apocalyptic'.

Two elements in this programme call for elucidation: illusion and reality, and 'Anfechtung'. Against liberal interpretation it is stated that apocalyptic is not illusory (cf. 122 n. 16/127 n. 20); in fact it combats the illusion of the enthusiast and respects reality—the reality of Christian incompleteness before the end. (With regard to Rom. 8, Käsemann also emphasizes the reality of the Christian's continuing solidarity with enslaved creation.) Secondly, Christian existence is characterized, not by a removal from the present aeon, but by the freedom of those under assault (*die Freiheit der Angefochtenen*) in the midst of the present aeon. The idea of *Anfechtung* is very important to Käsemann.[58] It does not

[58] Käsemann mentioned the theme twice in *Leib* (using the word *Versuchlichkeit*, 133, 181, but in an eschatological context) and it has figured prominently ever since: *VF* 3 (1946/7), 194; 5 (1951/2), 208; 7 (1956), 152; 'Vaterunser' 6; *EVB* ii. 184/171, 188/176, 193/181; *PP* 11/2, 12/3, 16/5, 32/15, 70/38, 82/45, 104/57 f., 120 f./67 f., 148/84, 158/90, 162/92, 167/95, 215 ff./124 ff., cf. 148/83; *Römer* 86/92, 87/93, 89/95, 103/109, 104/110, 117/123, 148/156, 153/161, 167/175, 168/176, 172/180, 174/182, 181/189, 216/225, 218/226, 229/237, 231/239, 232/240, 234/242, 364/377; see also Käsemann's use of related ideas: temptation (*Versuchung*, 103/110), endangering

primarily mean temptation in a moral sense (*Versuchung*), though this is included, but the eschatological assault or attack. Christians are still assaulted or assailed by the powers of the present evil aeon. It is enthusiasm to deny this, or to live as if Christians have been removed from this conflict.

Käsemann gives these points exegetical support in the course of his Romans commentary. This is significant in itself as enthusiasm has normally been regarded primarily as a Corinthian problem.[59] However, for Käsemann, the gospel always arouses the double reaction of nomism and enthusiasm.[60] Thus, if he is to make his case that Romans is a summary of Paul's theology, it is incumbent on him to demonstrate the importance of enthusiasm for this letter. He does this particularly in the interpretation of parts of chapters 5, 6, and 8.

The 'humanization of humanity' (Romans 5: 1–11)

Käsemann does not accept the division of Romans, common within Protestant exegesis, in which the first eight chapters of the letter are divided into two sections dealing with justification (chs. 1–5) and sanctification (chs. 6–8). Paul's thesis—that the new age has come and that righteousness is already present—has been presented and proved in chapters 1–4. He now turns to the task of showing that the signs of the new age, freedom from sin and death (to which Paul adds, freedom from the law), are present (150/158 f., 237 f./246).[61] Thus, Rom. 5: 1–11 is either an introduction to the section comprising chapters 5–8, which corresponds to the conclusion in 8: 31–9, or a prelude to the following pericope, with motifs which anticipate chapters 7 and 8. These views are not necessarily exclusive possibilities (124/132).

(*Gefährdung*, 125/134, 221/229), distress (*Bedrängnis*, 127/136), hardships (*Drangsale*, 131/139), suffering (*Leiden*, 132/141). On this theme, cf. Barth (1922: 132) who quotes Luther: 'No one ought to deceive themselves: if he wishes to be unassailed, he is no Christian, but a Turk and enemy of Christ.'

[59] Note, e.g., the scope of the studies of Lütgert (1908; though cf. 1909) and Winter (1975).

[60] See pp. 28 f. above and *EVB* ii. 18/9, 126/131 f., 231/226, 236/232; *PP* 22/9, 32/15, 71/38, 120/67, 131/73; *Römer* 167/175; cf. the similar phrase 'Judaism and Pneumaticism', 389/403.

[61] Following Bultmann 1959: 143 f.

Throughout his exegesis of the first part of Rom. 5, Käsemann argues that the theme is still the justification of the ungodly. In vv. 3–5 the hope of God's triumph can only be maintained if sufferings can be understood as the sphere in which grace seeks to manifest itself (cf. 2 Cor. 12: 9; 126/134). This reflects Paul's theology of the cross and can be described as the 'humanization of humanity' (*die Menschwerdung des Menschen*: more precisely, 'the becoming human of the human being'; 126/135). This catch-phrase[62] certainly does not refer to humanization in a cultural sense but to the theology of justification in which God is revealed to be God (as the one who alone creates salvation) and a human being becomes human (by giving up the attempt at self-justification and accepting the status of a creature dependent on God's grace). Human beings become human by living out the doctrine of justification. (The converse of this doctrine is the human being's constant attempt to achieve deification; *PP* 231/134.) Paul continues in v. 5 by referring to the pouring out of the spirit which saves the event of justification from 'historicization', i.e., from becoming a one-off event in the past. In vv. 6–8, although the argument is not clear, Paul seeks to show how inconceivable the divine action in the death of Jesus is, and does so under the motif of the justification of the ungodly. This theme continues in 5: 17 but in such a way that the eschatological abundance of grace becomes evident (*Römer* 148/156 f.).

Within this view of chapter 5, v. 1 states that, under the lordship of Christ, strife with God ends, and there is peace and unhindered access to the place of the *praesentia Dei* (v. 2*a*). Verse 2*b* introduces the note of future hope, and it is now stated, in paradoxical antithesis to 3: 27, that there is a *καύχησις* proper to the creature:

> If as Paul sees it existence is defined by its lord, the basic understanding of existence comes to expression in boasting. In this a person tells to whom he belongs. In his fallen state he boasts of himself and the powers . . . According to 3: 23 ff. the Lord of whom we can and should boast is the one who with the gift of righteousness restores mankind's lost image. (125/133)

[62] *EVB* ii. 191 f./180, 196/186, 225/219; *PP* 75 n. 10/40 n. 10 (quoting Schlatter 1929, 12), 163/93; *Römer* 48/52, 52/56 f., 126/135, 258/268, 277/287, 307/317.

Paul does not say that the δόξα, the image lost by Adam, has already been transferred to Christians, because, before the end, like resurrection, δόξα is primarily a christological predicate. With the exception of the divergent tradition in 1 Cor. 11: 7, it is given to the Christian 'only apocalyptically' (*nur in apokalyptischer Sicht*; perhaps with the meaning 'at the end'; ibid., cf. *PP* 20 f./8; *Römer* 89/95, 225/233, 237/245). In the present time, 'there is faith only face to face with the threat of the powers still dominant on earth, i.e., under temporal assault' (125/134). The earth is the battleground of the two aeons: 'Assailed faith and the vanquishing of the powers mark the place where Christian boasting paradoxically proclaims that peace and freedom are already granted [ET: 'secured'] even in the midst of ongoing conflict' (126/134).

This theme is continued in vv. 3–5 where the voice of Christian experience is heard. Suffering is not just a means of divine instruction but reflects the shadow of the cross in which alone God's eschatological power intends to work. The Jewish tradition underlying these verses describes how solid character arises; Paul's concern is for the end-time miracle of the 'humanization of humanity':

> Apocalyptic is anthropologically deepened and made concrete, so that the text corresponds antithetically to 1: 24 ff. If the creature falls step by step under the wrath of God, he does not climb up again to heaven after justification, as enthusiasts think. But in the earthly state and its difficulties he proves [*bewähren*] his calling [*Berufung*] to give honour to God. (126 f./135)

In this highly compressed passage Käsemann draws conclusions on the basis of a contrast between 5: 3–5 and 1: 24 ff. 'Apocalyptic' presumably refers to the hope of future glory (2*b*, 5*a*), the restoration of the divine image. It is 'anthropologically deepened' in the sense that the cosmic statements of 3: 19 f., 29 f. are now related to the life of the individual. 'Antithetic' refers to the antithetical correspondence of the time of wrath and of grace. In the present time Christians prove or confirm (*bewähren*)[63] their calling and acknowledge

[63] Käsemann's repeated use of *bewähren* expresses his understanding of the connection between, on the one hand, the doctrine of justification and, on the other, Christian life and ethics: Christians are not called to do 'works' which might be held

their lord. Thus, while Paul proclaims the presence of peace, and access to the divine presence, the dialectic of present and future eschatology makes him speak of these realities only in the context of the conflict of the two aeons. Before the end there is no final resolution of this conflict in the experience of the Christian. Hence this section of the commentary can be given the title 'Paradoxical[64] standing in the presence of God'.

Baptism in the light of the eschatological reservation (Romans 6: 1–11)

Just as Rom. 5 is said to continue with the same theme as the preceding chapters, so Käsemann argues for a close connection between Rom. 5 and 6. The universal realization of eschatological life (ch. 5) is made intelligible in everyday life, the community, and the individual (ch. 6). Christians are to confirm in their personal lives the change of aeons which has taken place (151/159). The justification of the ungodly is again the theme of the chapter and what is normally called sanctification is to be understood as lived justification (ibid.).

Käsemann's starting-point for exegesis is the history-of-religions (ET: 'historical', 152/160) study of the sacraments and specifically the enthusiasts' belief that baptism has already set them in an angelic state (153/161). Baptism results in translation out of the sleep of sin and into the world of the resurrection. It is participation in the death and resurrection of Christ, or his glory (8: 29), incorporation into the destiny of the cultic god, Christ (154/162).[65]

Paul stands within this tradition, though not uncritically. Käsemann argues that he combines it with a second theme, the close connection between baptism (ch. 6) and the new Adam theme (5: 11–21, 6: 6). The baptized are withdrawn from the power of sin and integrated into the new Adam (6: 2;

to earn salvation; nor, however, are they to remain inactive. By service and discipleship, they authenticate, verify, prove, or confirm that they have been transferred to a new lordship.

[64] This note is struck by Bultmann (1959: 146, 150) and Barth ('believing in the midst of an unredeemed world'; 1922: 132). Characteristically Schlatter portrays the dialectic in christological and theological terms: Christ has come and is coming, God's righteousness is both a possession and a goal (1935: 175).

[65] In the Romans commentary Käsemann responds to the objections raised by Wagner (1962) to this reconstruction of the enthusiasts' view of baptism.

2 Cor. 1: 21; Gal. 3: 27—though Käsemann does not substantiate his claim that the new Adam motif is present in these verses; 157/165). As such, baptism results in incorporation into the body of Christ (154/162, 155/163) and is 'ultimately a matter of participation in the *regnum Christi*' (157/165, ET modified). The notion of incorporation into the fate of the cultic god does not fade away because of Paul's eschatological perspective. He uses the *σὺν Χριστῷ* motif to give precision to his concept of Christ as a 'bearer of destiny'. Baptism is not merely an event at the beginning of the Christian life but brings the believer under the continuing power of Christ:

> In baptism the new world initiated by Christ seizes the life of the individual Christian too, in such a way that the earthly path of the exalted Lord is to be traversed again in this life and Christ thus becomes the destiny of our existence. Baptism is the projection of the change of aeons into our personal existence, which for its part becomes a constant *reditus ad baptismum* to the extent that here dying with Christ establishes life with him and the dialectic of the two constitutes the signature of being in Christ. (155/163, ET modified)

The event of baptism and life continually determined by the change of aeons must not be separated.

The specifically anti-enthusiastic thrust of the passage becomes explicit in vv. 3 ff. Verse 3*b* is regarded as traditional, the past tenses pointing to a past and unique event, the death of Christ (158/165). While the non-Palestinian pre-Pauline community and the enthusiasts focused on participation in the destiny of the son and hence on his death and resurrection (158/166), Paul's eschatology leads him to a much more cautious statement. He differentiates between the already risen lord and believers:[66] 'As in 2 Cor 13: 4 the power of the resurrection which is in fact at work in them asserts itself initially by setting them contrariwise [*sub contrario*] under the shadow of the cross and makes this in a special way the mark of the new life' (ibid.). Instead of speaking about the resurrection of believers, Paul uses the verb *περιπατεῖν*, indicating that the present is the time of discipleship, not of

[66] Cf. Bornkamm who makes the same point but without claiming that the passage is 'anti-enthusiastic' in orientation (1939: 76–8). For an extensive bibliography on this interpretation of 6: 3 f., see Wedderburn 1983: 338 n. 3.

resurrection, which is a hope for the future. At the same time, vv. 12–23 show that the *nova oboedientia* is an anticipation of the resurrection, the sign of the present reality of its power (159/167, 169/177 on 6: 12; cf. 216/224 on 8: 11 and 339/352 on 13: 11 f.)

The idea of eschatological reservation is also important in vv. 5–7 where Paul restates his case: the future in v. 5*b* is eschatological and not logical, and here Paul modifies the tradition by laying stress on the cross (161/169). In vv. 8–10[67] the future hope is repeated (v. 8), and exclusively christological statements are again made (vv. 9, 10; 162/170). In this way the distinction between Christ and his followers is underlined: 'The salvation event which has been established "with Christ" is to be grasped by the Christian as binding on himself, and while it is not to be repeated it is to be verified in discipleship. He who has died to the power of sin can exist on earth only for God unless he denies his Lord' (163/171). The relationship between Christ and the believer can be correctly understood only if the eschatological reservation is taken into account. The Catholic model of mystical union is inappropriate because it merges Christ and the believer. Rather: 'His [Paul's] concern is that we take the place occupied by the earthly Jesus and thus declare the lordship of the exalted One' (161/169). Before the parousia the baptized remain under the eschatological reservation and verify the power of grace in their discipleship.

Assailed faith and the future hope for the world (Romans 8)

Käsemann regards Rom. 8 as a whole as anti-enthusiastic in orientation. The basis of Paul's criticism in vv. 1–11 is not, as it will be later in the same chapter, the eschatological reservation, but the christological determination of the spirit:

> The Pauline doctrine of the Spirit is constitutively shaped by the fact that the apostle, so far as we can see, is the first to relate it indissolubly to christology. In the Spirit the exalted Lord manifests his presence and lordship on earth. Conversely the absolute criterion

[67] The first two sentences of the second new paragraph on p. 170 of the ET should read: 'In the third argument in vv. 8–10 the point of emphasis shifts. The new life as the theme of the next section [i.e., v. 12 f.] is envisioned . . .'

of the divine Spirit is that he sets the community and its members in the discipleship of the Crucified, in the mutual service established thereby, and in the assault of grace on the world and the sphere of corporeality. The difference from enthusiasm is that the Spirit is to be tested in terms of christology, and christology is not set under the shadow of ecclesiology. (205/213)

Again, commenting on 8: 3 f., the same basic point can be made of the spirit and the doctrine of justification:

The Spirit—by pointing us back to the cross of Christ as the place of salvation and thus continually actualizing justification—sets us unceasingly in the sphere of the Crucified, and is the earthly presence of the exalted Lord. If the motif of union is to be used at all, it must be precisely understood as incorporation into the lordship of the Crucified.[68] (212/219, ET modified)

Given this fundamental point, the doctrine of the spirit can be mobilized against nomism and enthusiasm (ibid.). However, an eschatological and a christological critique of enthusiasm are, of course, far from mutually exclusive in Käsemann's mind and he finds a reference to the former in 8: 11. Here again there is a distinction between Christ and the believer on the basis of the eschatological reservation: for the present, *nova oboedientia* is the anticipation of the future glory (216/224). The same pattern is again apparent in 8: 17 where Paul speaks of the coming glory only to link this theme immediately with present suffering.

However, it is in 8: 18–30 that the various threads of Paul's anti-enthusiastic theology come together (222/231). Verses 18 and 28 set out the future hope but the main part of the passage (vv. 19–27, introduced by 17*c*) argues, against the enthusiasts, that glory is paradoxically linked to vulnerability, and that the community and each member are set under the cross. Genuine Christian faith is assailed faith. Against the enthusiasts' appeal to present eschatology, Paul makes use of Jewish apocalyptic (223/232). Käsemann draws attention to the belief in the imminent parousia reflected in v. 18: *ὁ νῦν καιρός* is the moment of destiny which precedes the future glory, the

[68] This last phrase (*die Herrschaft des Gekreuzigten*, also 161/170), a precise summary of Käsemann's interpretation of Paul and of his own theology, is used by Ehler (1986) as the title of his study of Käsemann's understanding of the centre of scripture.

time of the messianic woes (224/232). However, the usual apocalyptic scenario is omitted and Paul concentrates on the motif of freedom (225/233 f.) which materially coincides with glory: 'Eschatological glory is perfected freedom and this in turn is the content of the eschatological glorification of the children of God. This is pressed to the point where it represents the true revelation of the parousia' (225 f./234). This 'reduction', the viewing of the parousia from an anthropological perspective, is unusual, particularly in comparison with 1 Cor. 15: 24 ff. (ibid.). Nevertheless, the cosmic perspective of the passage must not be lost sight of:

> By allowing Christians to suffer with Christ, the Spirit brings about the transforming of the old creation into an expectancy of glorification and an initial participation in this . . . He [Paul] was concerned to show, however, that within the world, in remarkable connection with ecstatic events during Christian worship, and *sub contrario* [ET: 'by contrast' (!)] in the community which suffers with Christ, eschatological freedom as salvation for all creation appears in outline . . . This is not to be regarded as mere exhortation after the manner of Calvin. For all the mythical form of expression the concern here is with the centre of the Pauline message [ET corrected]. This is what necessarily makes him a world missionary. In these verses the justification of the ungodly appears in a new cosmological variation as salvation for the fallen and groaning world. (226/234 f., ET modified)

Here the strands of future expectation, cosmic orientation, and the doctrine of justification come together.

Käsemann is at pains to stress that the mythical elements in the passage do not preclude its continuing theological significance. The world-view of the Enlightenment can no longer be the yardstick of modernity, and the apocalyptic outlook comes close to the profound alienation of the contemporary world (226/235; *PP* 25/11). Here Käsemann picks up a theme in which he finds an important convergence between, on the one hand, Paul's eschatology and demonology and, on the other, contemporary alienation with its sense of the world (and not just individuals) gripped by destructive forces. For Paul the world, apart from Christ, is ruled by demonic forces; Christians are not yet delivered from their powers, they continue to be assailed, but they look for the reality of the kingdom when the demonic world is conquered and complete freedom is established. This theme runs through Käsemann's earlier and later work ('Abendmahl' 67, 81; *EVB* i. 73/67, 88/81; *PP* 15 f./5 f., 46/23, 84/46; *Römer* 38/42). Finally, in contrast to common misconceptions about apocalyptic, Paul's future expectation does not lead to contempt for the world or resignation, nor does he lose himself in illusions about the future; rather, he keeps reality firmly in view (commenting on *ἀποκαραδοκία*, 8: 19, *Römer* 227/235).

However, 'assailed faith' is not the final word, despite the anti-enthusiastic thrust of the passage; Paul also looks forward to God's complete victory over the forces of the cosmos. *Contra* Bultmann, this is a concrete hope: 'For him [Paul] the resurrection of the dead was no mere symbol of openness to the future but the end of earthly pain' (229/238). However, before the parousia, the church continues in solidarity with unredeemed creation, even in its worship (see below).

The chapter and this section of the epistle are brought to a conclusion in 8: 31–9. The anti-enthusiastic note is maintained even in this highly formalized section, the theme being 'dying in the discipleship of the Crucified' (v. 36; 241/250). The apocalyptic world-view alone can 'preserve us from the usual edifying interpretation' of v. 37 and in its place state that only the death of Christ and his intercession can protect the Christian against the powers (ibid.). It describes reality as a universe detached from God, impenetrable, limiting people on every side (vv. 38–39*a*); it hears in this reality the cry of an enslaved creation, and understands the cry as the messianic woes (243/251):

> In Paul apocalyptic does not lead to enthusiasm but to an experience of the world which is ruled by horror. It is against this background that the confession of the predestined cosmocrator Christ, of *libertas christiana*—as an anticipation of the resurrection and the joy of conquerors—gains definition. Even when inferno threatens on all sides, the Christian is stigmatized by the lord who is present for him, and is set in *παρρησία*. (243/my translation, cf. ET 251)

By trusting in the love of Christ despite all appearances, assailed faith refuses to let its discipleship be hindered and thus represents both the earthly lordship of the truth of 'that which can be known about God' (1: 18 ff.), and the eschatological future (*Römer* 243/251). In conclusion, 'God's righteousness reveals itself in the midst of its enemies and creates a new world in the old aeon' (243/252). Thus, 8: 31–9 provides a summary of the chapter and of Paul's theology (ibid.).

From these sections of Romans, Käsemann attempts to show not only how all-pervading Paul's 'apocalyptic' is, but also how it intermeshes with his central concerns, the doctrine of justification and his christology. Paul deploys these themes together in his critique of enthusiasm. Thus, it has proved impossible to discuss eschatology in an isolated way, and if one did so, the results would be artificial. For Käsemann, Paul's apocalyptic perspective influences all other aspects of his theology, and particularly the central themes of the doctrine of God and of justification, as will be seen in Chapter 4 below.

PAUL'S ANTHROPOLOGY IN APOCALYPTIC PERSPECTIVE

Given the prominence which Bultmann gives to Paul's anthropology, its central position in his interpretation of Paul, and Käsemann's own extensive work on this subject, it is hardly surprising that this is a major area of debate between the two scholars.[69] Two questions predominate. The first, which has already been discussed, concerns the shape of Paul's theology: apocalyptic, not anthropology, determines the main lines of the apostle's theology. Secondly, Käsemann deals with the narrower question of anthropology itself.[70]

[69] Käsemann's main discussions are to be found in *EVB* ii. 22–4/13–15, 'Zur paulinischen Anthropologie' (*PP* 9–60/1–31), and, on *σῶμα*, *Römer* 168 f./176 f. However, *PP* and *Römer* never lose sight of the theme of anthropology for long.

[70] The essay on Paul's anthropology is unusually wide-ranging in its concerns, even by Käsemann's standards. It discusses the history of interpretation of this theme, the *Zeitgeist* as it affects questions of interpretation, the need for a critique of the idealistic heritage, the question of the structure of Paul's theology, the place of anthropology within that theology, and, only then, Paul's anthropology itself.

Käsemann's essay of 1969 on Paul's anthropology is highly instructive for his approach to the subject because it debates with Bultmann directly.[71] It will, therefore, be profitable to follow its main arguments and to supplement it from Käsemann's other work on this theme. It is highly significant that, instead of concentrating on the anthropological terms themselves, as Bultmann did, Käsemann attempts to put the subject in a wider Pauline context. A human being is not considered essentially as an individual or in relationship with him- or herself, but in relationship with others and with his or her lord. As a member of the body of Christ, the Christian is the 'irreplaceable representative of his Lord' (*unvertretbarer Platzhalter seines Herrn*, *PP* 11/2). This difference of starting-point has profound implications for the interpretation of Paul's anthropology and ecclesiology. Secondly, because of Paul's concern for the word of God which addresses—or, more sharply, lays down a challenge (*Provokation*) to—humanity, a human being is essentially 'a challengeable and a continually challenged being' (*ein provozierbares und ständig provoziertes Wesen*; 15/5, *Römer* 102/108). Here Käsemann is in agreement with Bultmann (*PP* 14/4), but he wishes to make this insight part of the structure of Paul's anthropology. 'Challenge' does not end with conversion, for salvation is not simply a state but an 'endless path', characterized by forgetting what lies behind and straining forward to what lies ahead (Phil. 3: 13; *PP* 16/5). Thus, Käsemann sets Paul's anthropology within the context of the doctrine of the word and his eschatology.

Käsemann takes up debate with Bultmann on three main points. Lying behind all three is the charge that, despite his efforts to the contrary, Bultmann is still a prisoner to the idealist tradition. Firstly, Bultmann presupposes that Paul shares the notion of continuity of existence. Secondly, he enquires after the historicity of existence which, in turn, focuses on the individual. Thirdly, the notion of self-understanding leads Bultmann to think of a human being as a 'spiritual being'.

[71] Bultmann's approach to Paul through his anthropological terms appeared first in his dictionary article 'Paulus' (1930*a*) and was expanded in *Theologie des Neuen Testaments* (1951).

Käsemann can start his discussion on a point of agreement: 'The basic insight of Bultmann's interpretation was that the apostle's anthropological termini do not, as in the Greek world, characterize the component parts of the human organism' they apply to existence as a whole,[72] while taking account of its varying orientation and capacity in any given case' (19/7; cf. 37/18, 41/20 f.). Be that as it may, the approach from the historicity of existence ought not to lead to the conclusion that Paul shared the idealist notion of the continuity of existence:[73] 'In places where we would speak of development, the idea of miracle takes hold in Paul, the miracle which bridges the gap between different things' (20/8). This is true of baptism, the statement of Gal. 2: 20, and Paul's use of the divine image idea, which for him does not remain after the fall, which Christ alone has and is, and which, before the parousia, Christians receive only by faith. Further, Paul regards salvation history as being divided into epochs, and his understanding of the resurrection shows that for him discontinuity is the mark of existence and history. God alone is the source of continuity and this manifests itself in miracle (21/8 f.). While Paul does speak of a 'self', he also speaks of it dying (Rom. 7: 9, 22; *PP* 23/10). In fact, Paul's understanding of existence is fundamentally marked by hiatus—between the worlds of creation and fall, between the lordships of sin, Christ, and the resurrection reality (44/22). This series of 'worlds' implies criticism of the twofold scheme ('human being outside of faith' and 'human being in faith') around which Bultmann organizes his Pauline theology. Käsemann does not wish to reinstate an actual scheme of salvation history; rather, he uses these Pauline themes to assert the discontinuity of existence,[74] and the multiplicity of competing 'worlds' (53/28).

Secondly, Bultmann's narrowing down of the question of history to the meaning of the historicity (ET: 'historical nature') of existence has led him inevitably to say that Paul's theology is orientated to the individual (24/10). Käsemann agrees that this approach has been fruitful, and that Paul,

[72] For exegetical discussion of this fundamental point, see Jewett 1971 and Gundry 1976.

[73] So Bultmann 1951: 198.

[74] Cf. Schrage 1964: 152.

unlike the rest of the New Testament, does bring the individual into prominence, particularly in the doctrine of justification (10/2). However, this is not the end of the matter. Käsemann challenges the dominance in theological circles (under the guise of what he believes is an outdated understanding of modernity) of individualistic models in anthropology:

> Contemporary theology is still having to pay for the fact that it is still a victim of the heritage or curse of idealism to a greater degree than it cares to admit. It could have learned as much from Marxism as it did from Kierkegaard and would then have been unable to go on assigning the absolutely decisive role to the individual. (25/11)

Just as Käsemann's reaction to an approach which focuses on the individual is not one of outright rejection, so his reaction to Bultmann's interpretation is carefully differentiated.[75] Thus, summarizing Bultmann, he says that the authentic human being is the one who has given up his or her securities and is called back to creatureliness; that 'detachment from the world' (*Entweltlichung*) does not mean spiritualization and pious introspection but 'characterizes the believer as being no longer determined by what is at hand in this world but as being eschatologically liberated for his future' (29/13, cf. 200 f./115). Käsemann can go as far as saying that these slogans do pick up elements of the biblical proclamation. However, they are open to misunderstanding, and his fundamental objection is that they define the human being constitutively as a spiritual being (*geistiges Wesen*; 29 f./13 f.). The form of Käsemann's rejection of the individualistic tendency of Bultmann's approach becomes clear only after this third point has been considered.

If human beings are to be regarded as spiritual beings it is surprising that Paul speaks so little of 'soul' or 'spirit' (in the anthropological sense). In fact he speaks of the latter only once in a sense which implies a direct relationship with the divine spirit (1 Cor. 2: 11; *PP* 30/14). This is an exceptional case as normally Paul emphasizes the need for divine

[75] His reaction to Conzelmann, who in his view has dissolved the theology–anthropology dialectic into anthropology alone, is correspondingly more critical (27/12). Many of Käsemann's stronger statements are not aimed directly at Bultmann but against an individualizing or spiritualizing tendency in modern interpretation.

revelation, not natural human capability (33/15). Again, human beings possess reason, but this only enables them to adjust or control possibilities which present themselves to them. Reason does not give a human being the truth about him- or herself (35/17). Similarly, 'conscience' only indicates that the human being is subject to transcendent demands. Rom. 2: 15 f. pictures a human being as standing 'in the shadow of the last judgment; that is to say, he is always standing before a tribunal whose seat of justice is not yet clearly occupied', confronted by a mysterious 'opponent'.[76] These points show that a human being cannot be understood as an individual fundamentally separated from the rest of the world (36/17).[77] This insight leads to the repeated assertions that anthropology cannot be reduced to the sum of recurrent anthropological (i.e., individual) decisions (*Römer* 42/46, cf. 156/60, 165/173, 166/174; *PP* 117/65).

Käsemann then turns to *σῶμα*, the interpretation of which is the key to Bultmann's understanding of Paul. In comparison with his work of 1933 and even 1947/8, there is a new emphasis on corporeality (*Leiblichkeit*). Paul often uses *σῶμα* and *σάρξ* as parallel terms implying that corporeality is of decisive importance for him. Rom. 12: 1 and 1 Cor. 6: 12 f., 20 emphasize the offering of the body, and Paul speaks of the resurrection of the body. Indeed, the notion of corporeality is fundamental to his theology:

> The coherence of Pauline soteriology is destroyed once we modify in the slightest degree the fact that for Paul all God's ways with his creation begin and end in corporeality.[78] For him there is no divine act which is not directed towards this or which does not desire so to manifest itself. This fundamental interest displays itself again in the fact that Paul ascribes to corporeality not only anthropological but also eucharistic, ecclesiological and even Christological relevance:

[76] The ET ('counterpart') is misleading as Käsemann does not intend to imply a relationship of equals, nor any reciprocity. The judge is 'the one who stands over against' humanity (*das Gegenüber*). Cf. the more clearly christological use of this title in the discussion of Paul's ecclesiology (p. 247 below).

[77] Cf. Käsemann's autobiographical comment (n. 143 to ch. 1 above).

[78] Käsemann made this point briefly in 1947/8. On F. C. Oetinger's (1702–82) dictum (*Leiblichkeit ist das Ende der Wege Gottes*), see Schweizer 1964*b* and for a further study under this title, Bauer 1971. Unusually, Käsemann himself points to the tradition in which he stands: Barth 1922: 425; Schlatter 1935: 332; Althaus 1959: 112 (*EVB* ii. 200 n. 7/191 n. 7).

the exalted Lord manifests himself on earth in the physical [*leiblich*] food through which we can participate in him and which binds together the members of the church in his body. (38/18 f.; cf. 'Leiblichkeit' 9)

By contrast, Bultmann's interpretation of *σῶμα* seeks to minimize the importance of corporeality (*PP* 38 f./19). This tendency is carried over ('under Heidegger's influence', 39/19)[79] into his hermeneutics so that human reality is primarily conceived of as 'possibility'. If ontology is important for Paul at all (42/21), at the most he sees possibility as a 'form of appearance' (*Erscheinungsform*) of reality, and he assigns to the body the realities of creatureliness, the fall, redemption, and the resurrection of the dead. Thus, Käsemann wants to interpret *σῶμα* ontically (as an entity in its actual relations with other entities), and not, with Bultmann, ontologically (as a being with regard to its range of possibilities).[80] As such, the body is never 'neutral in itself'[81] but always 'qualified' (40/20), always in the mode of belonging or participation (43/21). Käsemann does, however, offer a statement of his position in ontological terms: 'corporeality is the nature of man in his need to participate in creatureliness and in his capacity for communication in the widest sense, that is to say, in his

[79] To my knowledge, this is, astonishingly, the only mention of Heidegger in Käsemann's work, reflecting his aversion to the philosopher whose conceptuality was taken up by Bultmann. As the present discussion shows he is deeply suspicious of the categories of 'authenticity' and 'possibility'. Nevertheless, he does not depart from this philosophical tradition. As Hübner demonstrates, both Bultmann and Käsemann's interpretations of Paul are within the limits of Heidegger's concept of 'being-in-the-world' (*In-der-Welt-sein*), but Käsemann's interpretation is a theological specification of Heidegger's formal analysis. Käsemann's decision to give primacy to the apocalyptic (i.e., cosmic) horizon, does not exclude him from making existential statements. 'Above all it must be recognised that paradoxically it is precisely the starting-point in the universal horizon (understood theologically) which . . . shows that a fundamental insight of Heidegger's understanding of existence is confirmed, namely that perception [*Erkennen*] is a form of being of "being-in-the-world" [*eine Seinsart des In-der-Welt-seins*], and that therefore perception and understanding of the world [*Welterkennen und Weltverstehen*] cannot be separated from the perceiving and understanding subject.' (Hübner 1974/5: 486; Prof. Hübner informs me that Käsemann agrees with his analysis on all important points.) Cf. Käsemann's statement when accused of 'existentialism': 'To me existential interpretation is inalienable—and indeed in line with the Reformation [*und reformatorisch!*]—however much its use and limits are a matter of controversy between Bultmann and me' ('Erwiderung' 595).

[80] On this distinction in Heidegger, see Macquarrie 1955: 30.

[81] *Contra* Conzelmann 1967: 173 f. (*PP* 40/20).

relationship to a world with which he is confronted on each several occasion' (ibid.; cf. *Römer* 168/176). Ontically this means that 'man is always himself in his particular world; his being is open towards all sides and is always set in a structure of solidarity' (*PP* 44/22). This keeps open the possibility of interpreting σῶμα as a term which denotes the whole human being. Despite his intention to understand the anthropological terms as denoting the whole person in a particular perspective, Bultmann fails to do this in practice because for him the body is the instrument of our acts, and therefore cannot be a term for the whole human being. Against his stated intention, Bultmann has reintroduced subject–object language (41/20 f.; *Römer* 168/176). Finally, while 'spirit' and 'conscience' can speak of a human being in relationship to him- or herself, as 'body' a human being stands in a sphere which can by no means be summed up under the individual aspect (*PP* 42/21). Human beings are always themselves within their own particular worlds (44/22).

Käsemann continues by giving examples from Paul's letters which indicate the importance of corporeality. He cites the questions of parents and children (1 Cor. 7: 14), the fate of the dead (1 Thess. 4: 13 ff.), vicarious baptism (1 Cor. 15: 29), union with a prostitute (1 Cor. 6: 15), the nakedness of the transitional state (2 Cor. 5: 2 ff.), the handing over of the body of the incestuous man (1 Cor. 5: 5), and Paul's being caught up in the body (2 Cor. 12: 2). These examples demonstrate the futility of narrowing down 'creatureliness' to the individual, and of separating the 'authentic person' from nature, society, history, and creation in general (45 f./22 f.).

By contrast, in Paul, 'human being' and 'world' are not separated, nor is the human being to be related solely to one 'world':

> since Adam man has wandered through many worlds, as he does in his personal life—worlds divided by the frontiers of fall, law, promise, gospel, and resurrection or judgment. . . . Man is a mutable being whose possibilities range from the human animal through those set in fixed hierarchies—the barbarian and the Greek, the Gentile and the Jew—to the member of Christ's lordship and the perfected. To put it in dangerously epigrammatic form [*um es recht gefährlich zuzuspitzen*], man is all this as projection of a world which is

distinguished from other simultaneously-existing or successive worlds, without there being any all-transcending harmony, as in the Middle Stoa. The world is not neutral ground; it is a battle-field, and everyone is a combatant [*Parteigänger*]. (45/23, second sentence retranslated; cf. *Römer* 168/176)

Simultaneously, Paul sees human beings as standing under the sphere of power of either Adam or Christ. As such, a human being is not the subject of his or her history, but its object and projection (*Römer* 139/147), or at the most the exponent of the power which rules him or her (ET: 'it'; 142/150). Thus, anthropology and cosmology are intrinsically linked:

Anthropology must then *eo ipso* be cosmology just as certainly as, conversely, [with Bultmann] the cosmos is primarily viewed by Paul under an anthropological aspect, because the destiny of the world is in fact decided in the human sphere. But neither the exegetical nor the theological findings allow what the apostle calls the universe to be reduced to the human world alone. (*PP* 46/23, ET modified)

Just as Käsemann wishes to restore the tension of the theology–anthropology dialectic, and reverse the emphasis within it, he does the same for the cosmology–anthropology dialectic,[82] a point which he does not tire of emphasizing in the Romans commentary (*Römer* 30/33, 82 f./87, 87/92, 125/133, 126 f./135, 132 f./141, 142/150). Again the two poles of the dialectic are not equal: anthropology is crystallized cosmology (48/52, *PP* 56/29, cf. *Römer* 77/82, 151/159, 286/296).

Above all it is Paul's demonology and associated metaphysical dualism which rules out the idea of regarding human beings in an individualistic way. Since the fall humanity is not free but enslaved to the power of demonic forces from which it can only be rescued by an eschatological *creatio ex nihilo*. Here Paul is firmly within the apocalyptic tradition (*PP* 46 f./23 f.). Käsemann does not reject the demand to demythologize but the standard of interpretation must not be that of private self-understanding (48 f./25). The antithesis of spirit and flesh

[82] Cf. Barrett's conclusion, commenting on Rom. 1: 18 ff., 5: 12–21, Phil. 2: 6 f., that 'along with the existential interpretation of Paul there must be a cosmological (apocalyptic-mythical) interpretation' (1962: 21).

indicates that Paul uses the same words to describe individual existence and a universal power. This indicates the right lines for interpretation: 'The terms used in Pauline anthropology all undoubtedly refer to the whole man in the varying bearings and capacities of his existence; but they do not apply to what we call the individual at all. Here existence is always fundamentally conceived from the angle of the world to which one belongs' (51/26).

Käsemann's view of Paul's anthropology is particularly clear in his debate with Bultmann over the interpretation of Rom. 5: 12. Bultmann had argued that 5: 12*a–c* speaks of destiny but is pre-Pauline tradition which is interpreted by Paul in v. 12*d*. By adding *ἐφ' ᾧ πάντες ἥμαρτον*, Paul speaks of the human being's concrete decision and responsibility: 'sin came into the world through sinning'.[83] Paul makes use of the gnostic primal-man myth to express the point that the two epochs of mankind are determined by their originators, but he corrects the myth by adding 'because all sinned', and complements it with a salvation-historical consideration by his reference to the law.[84] Thus, Paul interprets the myth existentially.[85]

Käsemann rejects the view that Paul cites a piece of tradition (*Vorlage*, ET: 'model') here; rather, he stands in a solid Jewish tradition which juxtaposes destiny and guilt (*Römer* 140/148, with references). In v. 12*a–c* Paul does not speak of personal sin and natural death but of the powers of sin and death. Correspondingly, the spheres of Adam and Christ, of death and life, are spoken of in a thoroughly mythological way as alternative, exclusive, ultimate, and of global breadth (*Römer* 139/147). Within this tradition Paul radicalizes the idea of guilt (v. 12*d*) by positing the actualization of the power of sin in concrete sinning, and goes on to reaffirm the notion of destiny in vv. 13 f. (141/149). Thus, *contra* Bultmann and all those who cause cosmology to evaporate into individual anthropology, Paul speaks of the

[83] Bultmann 1938*a*: 15; quotation: 1951: 251; also 1959: 152.

[84] Bultmann 1959: 154.

[85] Bultmann is followed by Fuchs 1949, Bornkamm 1952*b*, Brandenburger 1962. Jüngel argues that Paul is concerned, not with the individual act, but with the history of humanity and that the law is indispensable to the Adam/Christ scheme (1963: 154 n. 32).

ruling powers which entangle all people individually, and which everywhere determine reality as fate (142/150). The conclusion for anthropology is that: 'The person is not seen primarily as the subject of his history; he is its object and projection. He is in the grip of forces which seize his existence and determine his will and responsibility at least to the extent that he cannot choose freely but can only grasp what is already there' (142/150).

Finally, Käsemann expresses his interpretation of Paul's anthropology in terms of lordship, and connects it with the idea with which he began, the human being as a representative:

> As created being, man does not only belong to his respective, already existing world but also with it to a given lord. Man's reality is to belong to a lord[86] . . . man is the creature who, radically and representatively for all others, commits himself [ET: 'submits'] to his Lord, becoming the instrument which manifests his power and his universal claim. (54/28; cf. *Römer* 168/176)

This definition of existence not only stresses the notion of 'belonging to a lord', as opposed to the human being as a divided self, but of human beings as being able only to react to realities (worlds or lordships) which are already present. Because this is the case, the change of existence (*Existenzwandel*) which is spoken of by existentialist interpretation is in reality a 'change (or exchange) of lordship' (*Herrschaftswechsel*; *PP* 55/29; *Römer* 39/43; cf. 'Versöhnung' 52/55, 54/58 f.; *Römer* 171/179, 272/282, 351/363). Human beings are always under a lord. They cannot escape from the power of sin to an independent state. As a Christian a human being exchanges this lordship for the lordship of Christ.

Käsemann's position can be summed up with reference to the three points of debate with Bultmann. Discontinuity, not continuity, is characteristic of human existence, where miracle (divine action) bridges the gaps of history and human experience. Secondly, while Paul is foremost in the New Testament in the development of the idea of the individual, paradoxically his anthropology is not focused on this idea, but on the sphere of lordship. Thirdly, a human being is not to be thought of as an essentially 'spiritual being' but in terms of

[86] The ET omits the preceding 1½ sentences.

corporeality, in his or her solidarity with the created order, and in his or her ability to communicate and to be challenged.

If anthropology is not Paul's central concern, nor the theme around which his theology is to be organized (*Römer* 286/296), its place within his theology has to be determined afresh. For Käsemann, 'anthropology is only the spearhead of Pauline theology, not its central subject or its goal. Rather, in it, precisely as in ecclesiology, christology projects itself on earth. The struggle for the world-wide lordship of Christ takes place in the mission and verification[87] of the community and its members' (*PP* 217/my translation, cf. ET 126; see also *EVB* ii. 192/181, *Römer* 207/215). For Käsemann, Paul understands a human being as a part of creation in which the lordship of Christ is authenticated or denied.

It is characteristic of the post-1960 period that Käsemann debates with Bultmann's views directly and that the argument is explicitly exegetical *and* theological. Thus, it is equally important for him to show that Paul is deeply influenced by apocalyptic ideas and that this tradition has as much to say to the contemporary theological scene as the philosophical traditions of Kierkegaard and Heidegger.

ADAM AND CHRIST: CHRISTOLOGY IN APOCALYPTIC PERSPECTIVE

Adam and Christ in Romans 5: 12–21

Käsemann believes that Paul's christology finds its deepest expression in the doctrine of justification (ch. 4 below) in conjunction with the Adam and Christ theme, particularly as it appears in Rom. 5: 12–21. In this passage three of Käsemann's apocalyptic principles are prominent:

1. The Adam and Christ theme reflects Paul's modification of the two-aeons motif. Before the parousia there is no temporal or spatial separation of the conflicting aeons: 'the reign of Christ confronts the reign of sin and death initiated by Adam' (*Römer* 133/142).

[87] The ET renders *Bewährung* with 'preservation' (*Bewahrung*) and gives *insofern* (in this respect) an incorrect temporal meaning ('Thus far').

2. The cosmic scope of Paul's theology is evident in the Adam and Christ theme:

> Common to all these passages [Rom. 5: 12 f.; 11: 32; 1 Cor. 15: 22] is that all-powerful grace is unthinkable without eschatological universalism and that cosmology overshadows anthropology as its projection . . . The intention of the apostle is to present the universality of the reign of Christ in antithesis to the world of Adam. New creation is proclaimed and this points to the end when, as 1 Cor 15: 28 puts it, God will be all in all. (149/157)

3. The idea of antithetical correspondence is used by Paul to argue that the end-time figure, Christ, corresponds to, but is far greater than, the primal time figure, Adam. Here Käsemann builds on the repeated *πολλῷ μᾶλλον* of Rom. 5: 15, 17 (144/152).

In addition, a further apocalyptic feature is Paul's use of typology (*PP* 167–75/95–100),[88] a particular way of understanding the past and of relating it to the present. It sees the figure or event in the past as historical; the future reference of the original event is brought to light only by subsequent eschatological understanding (*Römer* 120/127). Typology does not make use of any random historical event but works within the primal time/end-time framework (119/126). Further, it relates the present to the event or person in a particular way: 'What is stressed is not the element of example but that which is pregnant with destiny [*das Schicksalsträchtige*], which transcends individual existence and determines the world as a whole' (120/127). The idea of destiny is particularly important for Käsemann's understanding of the Adam and Christ theme, and will be discussed further below.

Given these apocalyptic elements in the christology and typology of Rom. 5: 12–21, it is surprising that Käsemann does not argue for an apocalyptic history-of-religions background for the Adam/Christ theme.[89] He comes to no final conclusion on this point but believes that the background of the theme can be localized (134/142). Barth's theological solution, in which the *anthropos* is humanity,[90] is rejected, as is

[88] Cf. Bultmann 1950.

[89] For a summary of the recent discussion of this problem, see Kim 1981: 162–93.

[90] Barth 1952*a*.

Käsemann's own previous view of gnostic influence. Further, the *anthropos* is not a combination of the primal man and the son of man, nor of the servant and the son of man (136/145). The idea of corporate personality has been vastly overworked, but, if it is subordinated to the apocalyptic antithesis of primal time and end-time, it contributes the idea that the fate of the descendants is settled in the forefather (134/142 f.). This cannot be the sole derivation because Paul's main interest is in the contrast between the two figures who alone inaugurate the worlds of salvation and perdition (*Heil/Unheil*; 134/143), and because, theologically, this would weaken the lordship of Christ in favour of union with him.

Paul's antithesis between the protoplast and the messiah,[91] based on the common denomination of *anthropos*, is said to go back to pre-Pauline tradition, as can be seen from the variations in Paul's use of the theme in Rom. 5 and 1 Cor. 15, and in its further use in Col. 3: 9 f., Eph. 2: 15, 5: 25 ff. The basic motif is the *eikon* of Gen. 1: 27 (135/144). From the primal-man tradition Paul has only taken the name *anthropos*. This has been combined with the figure of wisdom, the mediator of creation, who, in turn, was identified with the Torah, with the *logos* in hellenistic Judaism, and with the *anthropos* in Philo (137/145). The history-of-religions situation can be summarized thus: 'Hellenistic Judaism passed on to primitive Christianity both the idea of the mediator of creation and also the title of this mediator as Logos and Anthropos. Christianity accepted this complex because in this way it could characterize the pre-existent Christ as the inaugurator of a new humanity' (137/146). Finally, Paul combined this tradition with the apocalyptic two-aeons motif so that the two Adams could be contrasted, and the second Adam portrayed as infinitely greater (138/146).

Käsemann does not, therefore, argue that the Adam/Christ theme is apocalyptic in origin; rather, Paul took over an early Christian tradition which has its roots in the idea of corporate personality and in the wisdom tradition, and modified it by

[91] The use of 'messiah' here is surprising as Käsemann has not mentioned this area of Jewish thought. He is thinking of Paul's messianic interpretation of Ps. 110: 1 and 8: 6 in 1 Cor. 15: 25, 27, where the messiah is probably (omitted by the ET) characterized as the eschatological Adam (*Römer* 135/144).

setting it within his theology with its dominant apocalyptic themes. If anything Käsemann minimizes the parallels between the Adam and Christ theme and the Adam figure of the apocalypses and Qumran (e.g., 137/145). This is a surprising position, and his view can only be called 'apocalyptic' in the sense that the primal-man motif is said to be modified by Paul's apocalyptic theology (cf. pp. 238 ff. below on the history-of-religions background of the body of Christ).

Destiny and bearer of destiny

The ideas of 'destiny' (*Schicksal*) and 'bearer of destiny' (*Schicksalsträger*)[92] have been touched on several times in this discussion, but the precise status of these terms needs to be ascertained. Käsemann uses them at different levels in the process of interpretation. The term 'bearer of destiny' is first used in 1950 in a history-of-religions discussion of the powers of the old aeon (p. 92 above), a sense which is continued in the Romans commentary. On both sides of the eschatological divide there is a power (or powers) which determines all within that sphere. The thought is eschatological but also relates to the hellenistic view of the world as being the battleground of competing powers.

In 1959 Käsemann published an article on Paul's apostleship in 1 Cor. 9: 14–18 which focuses on the word *ἀνάγκη* (fate, compulsion). The word has its background, if only formally, in the impersonal force of blind ill-omen or chance (Greek, *ἀνάγκη*; Latin, *fatum*; *EVB* ii. 234/230), but Paul's use of it goes back to Old Testament prophetic models (234/229). In the presence of the divine epiphany the prophet experiences an ineluctable destiny. Käsemann argues that Paul gives the idea a theological interpretation so that it comes to mean 'the power of the divine will which radically and successfully challenges man and makes its servant its instrument' (235/230).

The idea of destiny is employed again in the discussion of baptism and the *σὺν Χριστῷ* motif. Alongside the eschatological meaning of the hope of being 'with Christ' at the parousia, this

[92] *EVB* ii. 192/180; *PP* 173/98, where the ET should read 'Adam [ET: 'Moses'!] in Rom. 5.12 ff.'; *Römer* 134/143, 138/146, 144/153, 147/155, 151/159, 155/163.

motif has a cultic *Sitz im Leben* and denotes the conforming of the destiny of the believer to that of the god. In baptism, understood as a mystery event, the devotee is incorporated into the destiny of the cult god, Christ (*Römer* 154/162). Paul incorporates this into his own theology by linking the *σὺν Χριστῷ* theme of Rom. 6: 7 ff. with the idea of Christ as a 'bearer of destiny' in 5: 12–21 (ibid.). Further, *σὺν Χριστῷ*, along with *ἐν Χριστῷ*, is used by Paul to give precision to his concept of Christ as a bearer of destiny. Christ is the power which determines the life of the Christian, but, at the same time, Christians have to follow the earthly path of the exalted lord (155/163). Here the 'bearer of destiny' motif functions as an underlying theme of Paul's theology.

In the discussion of Rom. 5: 12–21 itself, the 'bearer of destiny' idea is not treated as a history-of-religions category, nor as a true theological idea. It is an 'aid' which 'indicates the lines along which the theologoumenon of Christ's lordship should be made more precise' (135/143). Käsemann here takes up and extends Schlatter's interpretation of the Adam/Christ theme in Rom. 5: 12–21.[93]

On the basis of this interpretation of Rom. 5: 12–21, Käsemann argues that the 'bearer of destiny' theme helps to answer a fundamental question concerning the 'shape' of Paul's theology. The question concerns the relative importance of the idea of corporate personality, with its related theme of union with Christ (ideas which Käsemann associates with a Catholic interpretation of Paul), and Paul's christology, with its emphasis on the dignity of the *kyrios* (which Käsemann associates with a Protestant view of Paul). The 'bearer of destiny' theme indicates that the latter is the dominant mode of thought in Paul (135/143). Thus, with regard to Rom. 5: 12–21, Käsemann regards the 'bearer of

[93] 'Through the one who determines the behaviour and destiny [*das Geschick*] of all, Paul explains what he says when he calls Jesus the Christ, the lord' (Schlatter 1935: 185). Thus, both Schlatter and Käsemann regard the passage as significant for Paul's concept of Christ's lordship in general. Barth uses the idea of destiny only of the world of Adam (1922: 155, 157 f.), although sin and death, and righteousness and life, do 'comprehend and characterize' the worlds of Adam and Christ respectively (154). He is primarily concerned with the divine predestination to election and rejection, themes which lie behind Käsemann's use of the 'destiny' motif and which Käsemann interprets existentially (human beings are determined by the sphere of lordship in which they stand).

destiny' theme as a Pauline theme, but one of permanent theological relevance. Primarily, it allows Käsemann to articulate the theme of the lordship of Christ, and, secondarily, to criticize the tendency, within contemporary theology, to focus on the individual.[94]

Thus, Käsemann uses the idea of a 'bearer of destiny' in a variety of ways. At one level he offers a variety of history-of-religions observations on his theme (the powers which rule on each side of the eschatological divide, the idea of blind fate in antiquity, the prophetic sense of calling, and the solidarity between the devotee and the god established in the cult). Secondly, the concept is a theme or an 'aid' within Paul's theology. Thirdly, as was found with a number of history-of-religions concepts in Käsemann's work before 1950, the concept of destiny is adopted for contemporary theological use.

Finally, Käsemann does not wish to portray Christian life as an 'ineluctable fate'. To this end he distinguishes between 'destiny' (*Schicksal*) and 'fate' or 'disaster' (*Verhängnis*), where the former is the formal category for the power which a lord exercises over those under his lordship, and the latter is specifically the lordship of sin or death.[95] Thus, while a human being is never removed from a lordship, and is never more than an instrument of one power or another, Christ breaks the universal fate (*Verhängnis*) which has determined humanity and sets the believer in the place of assailed faith, which is not an irrevocable destiny (*Schicksal*, *Römer* 148/156; cf. 151/159).

To sum up: Käsemann's use of the 'bearer of destiny' theme is important for his understanding of two areas of Paul's theology. It again makes clear his view of Paul's anthropology: a human being is not to be considered as an individual, free agent but as determined by one or other bearer of destiny. Secondly, the 'bearer of destiny' theme ties anthropology specifically to christology, and more particularly to the theme of Christ as ruler (*Herrscher*), which is constitutive for Paul's

[94] See the criticism of theologians and exegetes who shy away from the concept of destiny (*EVB* ii. 232/228; *Römer* 134/143).

[95] The ET of the Romans commentary is erratic: e.g., it translates *Verhängnis* as 'destiny' (56), and then correctly as 'doom' on the next page.

christology (135/143). Here the theme of the primacy of christology is beginning to emerge.

'APOCALYTPIC': LORDSHIP, THEOLOGICAL INTERPRETATION, CRITICISM

The present chapter has not covered all aspects of Käsemann's apocalyptic interpretation of Paul; as he regards Paul's theology as being influenced throughout by apocalyptic themes, the subject will necessarily reappear in the rest of this study. (In particular, the apocalyptic character of Paul's doctrine of justification, with some connected themes, has been held over to the next chapter.) Nevertheless, the main lines of his interpretation have been outlined and they allow the conclusion that Käsemann has carried through the programme of reading Paul's theology in an apocalyptic perspective very thoroughly.

In Käsemann's pre-1950 work it was possible to isolate nine basic elements which contributed to the lordship of Christ construct. Several new elements have been noted in this chapter, and, by implication, some of the old points have been revised:

1. Paul's modification of the two-aeons motif contributes the idea that Christ's lordship, while it is already present in an anticipatory way on earth, is subject to the attacks of the old aeon until the parousia. Thus, to be a Christian is to be under a new lordship but still to be under attack (the *Anfechtung* theme).

2. The cosmic scope of salvation and the claim of God's (or Christ's) lordship on the world are no longer based on the gnostic aeon concept and redeemer figure, but on the nature of primitive Christian apocalyptic. This theme will be expanded when the doctrine of justification in its cosmic orientation is considered.

3. Two important themes are developed with regard to Paul's eschatology. The distinctive shape of Paul's eschatology is summed up in the phrase 'the antithetical correspondence of primal time and end-time'. The lordships of Adam and Christ are related *antithetically*, while the *correspondence* between God's

activity in the primal time (the God who creates *ex nihilo*) and the end-time (the God who raises the dead) points to the unity of divine action. Secondly, despite the proclamation of present salvation, Paul's future eschatology sets all under the eschatological reservation. The new aeon has begun but the present order is still caught up in the conflict between the two aeons. God's final triumph is the subject of Christian hope, not a present reality. Further, the theme of eschatological reservation allows the lordship theme to be extended to the whole range of human and church activity in the period before the parousia. In this period the lordship of Christ is to be 'verified' or 'confirmed' in the lives of Christians and in the church, as will be seen in Chapter 5.

4. In the area of anthropology, Käsemann continues to speak of human beings as under a lord: a human being is the representative or exponent of his or her world and of its lord. Exegetical support for this conclusion is no longer sought in a history-of-religions model (the gnostic aeon) but as a conclusion from observations on the way Paul speaks about human beings (as capable of communication with others and of being confronted by God). While the move to start with Pauline usage is to be welcomed, it has to be noticed that the primary exegetical argument for the spatial and dynamic understanding of the lordship construct has been withdrawn with the end of the theory of gnostic influence.

5. The ideas of 'destiny' and 'bearer of destiny' now move into the foreground in Käsemann's understanding of lordship. In this way the lordship of Christ construct is given a further christological connection. Christ and Adam determine their respective spheres or worlds. In turn, human beings are both determined by and, in their action, 'confirm' (or deny) one or other lord.

As in the pre-1950 period, Käsemann continues to interpret Paul's theology with the aid of the concept of a sphere of lordship. However, in comparison with the earlier period, there are two major changes. Käsemann is no longer dealing predominantly with Paul's participatory language. Instead he claims that the whole of Paul's theology is 'apocalyptic' in orientation. This means that his choice of conceptuality will have to prove itself to be appropriate over a much wider range of themes. Secondly, Paul's theology is now read against a different history-of-religions background. The gnostic background (with its spatial conceptuality modelled on the aeon) ought no longer to be a factor, though the hellenistic world-view (in which reality is understood as comprising a series of competing and overlapping worlds) continues to play a subsidiary role. Käsemann never discusses the effect of these major changes for his fundamental concept of lordship as a sphere of power. By implication his conceptuality is now based primarily on the Adam/Christ theme of Rom. 5: 12–21: as bearers of destiny, Adam and Christ each exercise power over their own sphere. (As was seen in ch. 2, the lordship construct is in fact built up with reference to a variety of Pauline themes.) However, while the appropriateness of the lordship concept for the Adam/Christ theme in Rom. 5: 12–21 may be granted, its extension to other Pauline themes[96] has to be kept under scrutiny.

Käsemann's understanding of the task of theological interpretation, as evidenced by the current topic, can be stated very simply because of his concentration on the debate with Bultmann. Agreeing with Bultmann that Paul's theology is to be understood within the theology–anthropology and cosmology–anthropology dialectics, Käsemann moves the emphasis from the second pole, where Bultmann had put it, to the first.[97] An apocalyptic interpretation rules out an anthropological reduction of Paul's (and Christian) theology and

[96] Theissen notes that Käsemann puts the 'symbolism' of exchange of power (*Machtwechsel*) at the centre of Paul's theology and interprets the justification theme from this centre (see ch. 4 below). He regards this as a great service to Pauline studies because (1) it represents the 'discovery' of a neglected theme of Paul's theology which does influence his theology as a whole—though, *pace* Käsemann, it is not itself the centre of Paul's thought—and (2) it pushes back existentialist interpretation which does not do justice to Paul's cosmic and mythological statements (1974*b*, 285 n. 6). However, Theissen argues that Rom. 6: 15–23 is the only Pauline passage which speaks of a change from one dependency to another (and is, therefore, the main proof-text for this interpretation) and Paul immediately goes on to disown this line of thought (ἀνθρώπινον λέγω, v. 19). 'The point is not the change of lord while the structure of dominance remains, but the restructuring of the dominance-relationships through the salvation event' (286). Curiously, Käsemann does not lay great stress on Rom. 6: 15 f.; in fact, he does not mention the 'exchange of lordship' theme here. For better or for worse, his system does not need a key text because he is working with a construct.

[97] Cf. Becker 1970: 596.

demands that the emphasis be laid on the cosmological and theological poles of Paul's thought. Thus, while Käsemann agrees with Bultmann on a dialectical interpretation of Paul, by moving the emphasis from one pole to the other, he arrives at a different view of Paul. Secondly, Käsemann pleads for the theological importance of Paul's 'apocalyptic', particularly in the fight against enthusiasm, one of the two fronts which the gospel has to face. Here Käsemann is in agreement with Bultmann,[98] although he raises this theme to the centre of his interpretation.

Throughout this chapter it has been clear that Käsemann's interest in 'apocalyptic' is motivated primarily by contemporary theological concerns.[99] Within the context of Lutheranism,[100] Käsemann's adoption of 'apocalyptic' as a theological term is undoubtedly deliberately provocative (cf. *EVB* ii. 193 n. 9/181 n. 9). It is an attempt to open out new perspectives for contemporary Protestant theology on the basis of the interpretation of pre-Pauline and Pauline theologies.

The main points which Käsemann brings to bear on contemporary theological debate are, firstly, that interpretation of Paul must speak of God (in relation to human beings), not just of human beings (in relation to God). Secondly, Christian theology, in line with its apocalyptic beginnings, should be orientated, not to the individual, but to the world. Thirdly, the idea of the final revelation of God's lordship is of permanent significance to Christian theology. Fourthly, apocalyptic eschatology is anti-enthusiastic in character. On the one hand, it guards against the pietist's (or the Catholic's)

[98] Bultmann 1964*b*: 480.

[99] *Contra* J. C. Beker, who, astonishingly, criticizes Käsemann for being a prize example of the failure to use apocalyptic as a 'relevant possibility for the church today': 'His assertion that apocalyptic is the mother of Christian theology is not followed by a hermeneutical transfer of apocalyptic to the present—something he engages in eagerly when treating topics such as justification by faith' (1982: 63). Beker believes that both the cosmic-universal and temporal concerns of apocalyptic (the hope of the concrete occurrence of God's final incursion into history which is to be expected in time) are theologically relevant (116 f.). J. Becker (1970: 594) and Klein (1973: 242) note Käsemann's contemporary theological concerns, acknowledging that his theological emphases fell on eager ears, although they disagree with him, both theologically and on the interpretation of Paul.

[100] This is commented on by Ebeling who quotes Luther on the lack of clear witness to Christ in Revelation ('it befits apostolic office to speak of Christ and his acts plainly and without symbol or vision'; Ebeling 1961: 51, n. 6).

retreat into an inner, 'spiritual' life or a specifically Christian sphere, and summons the Christian to his or her continuing solidarity with enslaved creation.[101] On the other hand, future expectation curbs the innate tendency towards enthusiasm of an exclusively present eschatology. The new aeon issues in the possession of Christian freedom in the midst of the eschatological assault, which in turn points forward to the completion of the *regnum Christi*. Fifthly, Paul's eschatological dualism with its attendant demonology offers an appropriate language with which to talk about the continuing power of evil in the world, a power which cannot be adequately spoken of with exclusive reference to individuals. These last points are tied in with Käsemann's understanding of human being as 'body'. In bodily obedience the Christian, as a 'piece of *world*', gives him- or herself over to Christ and thus acknowledges Christ as *cosmo*crator. By this action the final future—the untrammelled reign of Christ—is anticipated. Christian hope is more than openness to the future (Bultmann), and cannot be reduced to the belief that all hours in history are one and the same last hour (Althaus).[102] Thus, the term 'apocalyptic' has the task of carrying a great number of Käsemann's theological concerns[103] behind which stand the figures of Barth and Schlatter. This conclusion is strengthened by the point that the term 'apocalyptic' was adopted for the purpose of criticizing Bultmann's interpretation and theology which focused on the term 'eschatology'. G. Sauter's judgement that in Käsemann's work 'apocalyptic' is a construct by means of which obligatory theologoumena are depicted (as opposed to the label for a particular historical form of thought)[104] is borne out by this study.

[101] Klein points to the internal contradiction involved in the claim that apocalyptic is orientated to the world: although apocalyptic appears to be able to convey the social responsibility of theology and the church, at the same time Paul's social conservatism is put down to his expectation of an imminent end (1973: 242).

[102] Althaus 1922/1957: 272, cited in *EVB* ii. 106, n. 2/109 n. 2.

[103] Thus, what worries Käsemann about existential interpretation (or, better, Bultmann's version of it) is not only 'a concern for the *significance* of history against the "dehistoricizing" of eschatology' (Sandifer 1979: 2 f.; his emphasis), but the whole cluster of issues outlined here.

[104] Sauter 1976: 84, followed by Wright 1982: 14; Ehler 1986: 297. Sauter notes the parallel between Bultmann's use of gnosis and Käsemann's use of apocalyptic: neither are close to the texts to which they appeal; nevertheless, the concept they employ acts as a context for interpretation.

Sauter also notes that Käsemann's view of the contemporary theological role of apocalyptic is complex. On the one hand, the apocalyptic elements of Paul's theology (for example, his apocalyptic self-understanding and expectation of an imminent end) create a critical distance to all Christian modernism. On the other hand, apocalyptic makes a positive contribution to contemporary theology and, as has been seen, Käsemann works hard to rehabilitate the term for contemporary theology. 'Apocalyptic' helps to heal the division between history (*Historie*) and theology because it concentrates the problem of history (*Geschichte*) on the turn of the ages brought about in Christ, while at the same time not falling into an enthusiastic lack of history;[105] it made historical thinking possible within primitive Christianity; it is rooted in Paul's doctrine of God; and it allows Paul to resist enthusiastic illusion and render reality its due. To summarize, it is the early Christian and Pauline *modification* of apocalyptic which Käsemann regards as having continuing theological significance. Käsemann's use of apocalyptic is motivated by theological concerns and his interpretation seeks to solve theological problems—while also claiming to be based on sound historical foundations.

Undoubtedly the greatest weakness in this part of Käsemann's work is the failure to keep the historical and theological meanings of 'apocalyptic' sufficiently distinct. Indeed there are places where it is difficult to know what Käsemann intends by the term. Secondly, at the historical level, apocalyptic becomes virtually synonymous with eschatology, with the result that the particular characteristics of the apocalypses (from which the term 'apocalyptic' should be derived) are overlooked. (It ought to be noted again that Volz did make this distinction, and that Käsemann's view of apocalyptic takes up a point from Volz's view of eschatology.) Furthermore, Käsemann's approach allows him to bypass certain features of apocalyptic thought. Thus, among other points, Wright argues that the apocalypses, far from being orientated to the world, proclaim that God will condemn the world and save Israel. This central feature of apocalyptic thought is, in historical terms, non-negotiable, but

[105] Sauter 1976: 85.

Käsemann demythologizes it for the purpose of criticizing Bultmann's views. In fact 'apocalyptic' plays the same role in Käsemann's theology as 'hellenism' did in an earlier generation: it shows how Paul's theology transformed a Jewish-Christian message into a gospel for the world.[106] Thus, while Käsemann's essays of the early 1960s helped to reawaken historical interest in the subject of apocalyptic,[107] by the time the Romans commentary was published its understanding of apocalyptic thought was already outdated.

[106] Wright 1982: 14. See also n. 104.

[107] In addition to the work of his own students (Stuhlmacher 1965 and 1968, Schrage 1964, Müller 1964) in terms of Pauline studies, Baumgarten 1975, Froitzheim 1979, Beker 1980, Schade 1981, de Boer 1988 should be noted.

4

God's Righteousness and the Justification of the Ungodly

For Käsemann, standing in the tradition of Luther and Barth, the doctrine of justification is 'the truth of the Christian faith *per se*' (*Römer* 105/111, ET modified; cf. *EVB* ii. 181 f./168; *PP* 131/74). For him this doctrine is the centre of the New Testament proclamation (*PP* 114/64), of Paul's theology,[1] and of Romans (*EVB* ii. 181 f./168; *Römer* 86/92, cf. 105/111; also *EVB* ii. 22/14, *PP* 68/36, 74/40, 84/46, 131/74, 135/76, 141/80). On these points Käsemann is in agreement with Bultmann,[2] and this is also the case with the further point that the doctrine of justification is Paul's true christology. However, this large area of initial agreement quickly becomes the background to a wide-ranging debate over the interpretation of these themes. The starting-point for considering this part of Käsemann's work is his understanding of the place of the law in Paul's theology.

THE LAW, PIETY, AND THE JEW

Käsemann's understanding of the law

In the sphere of the old aeon, and even when they are not under the law, human beings are nevertheless pointed to their lord and to their own creatureliness. They are aware existentially, and not by deduction, of their dependence on their creator and of their limitation by their lord (*Römer* 38/41 f., commenting on Rom. 1: 19 f.). Through the fall creatureliness is not lost but it is perverted. It continues to be the basis of the accountability of the Gentile. Reverence, thankfulness, a lack of arrogance, and responsibility are

[1] For his earlier view, see pp. 106 ff. above.

[2] e.g., Bultmann 1933*a*: 278 f.

required (47/51, commenting on *δικαίωμα τοῦ θεοῦ*, 1: 32). But for Paul a human being's continuing creatureliness has no value in itself. It only serves as the basis on which judgement is passed on all humanity. In fact, while the fundamental possibility of the creature–creator relationship has not passed away: 'man in his historical reality constantly assaults God's omnipotence, because in flight or aggression he tries to escape his own creatureliness' (39/43). Human beings have fallen victim to 'illusion', which can take either Jewish or Gentile forms. Paul's argument is basically orientated to the Jew, whose history (42/46) and reality (50/54) are exemplary for all, and who is portrayed as the representative of the 'pious' person (80/85, 82/87).[3] It is from this perspective that Käsemann interprets the law in Paul.

With Bultmann,[4] Käsemann maintains that Paul never distinguishes between ritual and ethical law. Rather, Paul thinks concretely about the Torah (57/62, 82/87, 113/119). Nevertheless, his view is not limited in scope to Israel but reaches out to the world: 'the Gentiles also experience the transcendent claim of the divine will and thus become, not *the* law or *a* law, but law to themselves' (59 f./64, commenting on 2: 14). Thus, the negative side of Paul's theology is universal in scope.

The law, as the mark of the old aeon, is contrasted with the key themes of the new aeon, the gospel (*PP* 119/67; *Römer* 20 f./23),[5] God's righteousness (112/118), the promise (ibid.), faith (*EVB* ii. 192/180), and the obedience of faith (*Römer* 88/94). But if the law is part of the old order, it is not entirely negative but is seen in terms of a dialectic. On the one hand, it is God's gift and the expression of his will, a witness to salvation (*Römer* 88/93 f.), and the record of the divine claim on humanity (21/23). On the other hand, the law actually only reaches people in the 'religious perversion' of a summons to achievement (87 f./92 f.).[6] Thus, 'the *nomos* interpreted and practised by the Jew' is the object of Paul's polemic (83/88). It

[3] This is mentioned but not emphasized by Bultmann (1930*a*: 157).

[4] Bultmann 1951: 260 f.

[5] Cf. Bultmann 1940: 60.

[6] While Bultmann interpreted the human attempt to fulfil the law in terms of a struggle for recognition (1940: 43), Käsemann replaces this general anthropological category with a specifically religious category.

is only when this has come to an end, that the law in its character as summons to the righteousness of faith can be perceived (99/105). The same dialectic can be put in terms of the recipient of the law: the Jew is the recipient of revelation and the typical representative of human piety directed to achievement (83/88). When only the negative side of the law is in view, Paul speaks of 'letter' in antithesis to 'the Spirit' (71/76).

According to Käsemann, the law as it is in fact experienced leads human beings into two fundamentally wrong ways. Firstly, it leads to the piety of achievement (ET: 'human piety directed to performance', 83/88) via the demand for 'works' (88/94) which allow human beings to trust in their own achievement and to deny God's lordship over them. Thus, the righteousness of works is in fact a 'more powerful form of godlessness' (*potenzierte Gottlosigkeit*; ET: 'a higher form of godlessness'). Secondly, the law leads to reliance on God's gifts, especially on the possession of the Torah, instead of on the creator alone (57/61 f.).[7] In this second case God's gifts to Israel are taken by the pious Jew as a 'privilege' which conveys immunity from judgement. The gift of the law is isolated from its demand, the call to obedience. Thus, 'an appeal to the fathers is even more characteristic of the will of the flesh than the idol worship of the heathen' (*EVB* ii. 191/179). In summary, the law does not justify but leads to sin (*Römer* 82/87)—because it leads human beings into piety.

The law is to be understood as a power[8] which creates the sphere of piety and works. It is also a power in the salvation historical sense that it divides Jews from Gentiles (*PP* 45/23). Whereas for Bultmann human beings fall under the power of the law because they seek to live out of themselves, for Käsemann the law is a power which exercises lordship over human beings. This characteristic emphasis on the human being as under a power is complemented by an understanding of the individual under the law: 'the law in fact throws a person back upon himself and therefore into the existing world

[7] Cf. Luther 1515/16: 159 and Bultmann 1951: 264.

[8] Not passively as in the ET ('the greatest of snares'; *PP* 82/44) but actively as an 'entangling power' (129/72); nor as a power which was part of salvation history (ET), but a power in or over salvation history.

of anxiety [*die Sorge*] about oneself, self-confidence and unceasing self-assurance'[9] (*Römer* 96/102; cf. 97/103).

Finally, the key role of the law in Käsemann's interpretation of Paul's theology needs to be noted. The law is the 'radical spearhead' of the doctrine of justification (*PP* 128/72, cf. *Römer* 96/102, 178/186, 202/210) because it makes plain that the very attempt of humanity to be justified by works or through the privilege of the possession of the law is the true measure of its flight from creatureliness. By these means human beings attempt to bring God into dependence on them and to rob him of his power. Käsemann generalizes this in order to make its continuing theological validity clearer:[10] 'Our task is to ask: what does the Jewish nomism against which Paul fought really represent? And our answer must be: it represents the community of pious [ET: 'good'] people which turns God's promises into their own privileges and God's commandments into the instruments of self-sanctification' (*PP* 127 f./72).

Käsemann drives home his interpretation by the use of a number of catchwords and phrases which have already been introduced into the discussion:

1. The catchwords relating to the concept of 'piety' (*die Frömmigkeit, fromm*) are used in the two ways in which the law is said to mislead, neither of which refers, in the first instance, to the common meaning of religious devotion. Primarily they refer to a reliance on the possession of God's gifts, especially the Torah, as a guarantee against God's judgement. In this case the law is no longer understood as a gift but as a possession (*PP* 129/72; *Römer* 57/61 f.). Equally the law is abused if its character as gift is separated from the claim which it makes (*Römer* 51/55). Further, reliance on the law as a means of avoiding judgement leads to the pious fencing themselves off in a sacred enclosure, in contrast to Jesus who went to the ungodly and to Paul who proclaims the justification of the ungodly (*PP* 130/73). From here it is a

[9] Although this language is highly reminiscent of Bultmann, in fact, he specifically denies that Paul argues against the law on the grounds that it leads to despair (1932*a*: 175).

[10] Käsemann specifically criticizes those who limit the discussion of piety and justification to the exegetical level (*PP* 127 f./71 f.).

short step to Käsemann's criticism of the sectarian tendencies of modern pietism (*PP* 130 f./73). Secondly, piety can also refer to the righteousness of works (cf. 'legal piety', *Gesetzesfrömmigkeit*, 72/77). In this respect various Jewish groups or writers are labelled 'pious' (Pharisees and rabbis, *Römer* 64/68 f., Philo, 106/112, Ben Sira, 119/125, and Qumran, 82/87)[11] and are used as foils for the interpretation of Paul.[12] The concept of piety is used extensively by Käsemann in his contemporary theological statements: 'The Nazarene has suffered most from the pious and has been kept at bay most powerfully by Christianity.'[13]

2. The concept of 'religion' (*Religion*, *Religiosität*, *homo religiosus*, *der fromme Mensch*) is used primarily in the sense championed by Barth[14] as a synonym of piety (e.g., *EVB* ii. 191/179, *PP* 75/40, *Römer* 80/85, 81/86). Occasionally 'religion' is used in a theologically neutral sense (e.g., 'authentic religiosity', *Römer* 31/34, cf. 65/69).

3. 'Achievement' (*die Leistung*) is the human effort or work on which is staked the claim for justification before God[15] (e.g., *EVB* ii. 188/175; *PP* 129/72; *Römer* 84/89; cf. also 'the piety of achievement', *die Leistungsfrömmigkeit*, 83/88, and 'the principle of achievement', *Leistungsprinzip*, *Römer* 96/102).

4. 'Boasting' (*der Selbstruhm*; ET: 'self-boasting'!) denotes, with Bultmann,[16] a living out of and for oneself (96/102). It is neutral in itself, and is right or wrong solely according to its object, God or the flesh. While Käsemann agrees with

[11] Willi-Plein takes Käsemann to task for his liberal use of the slogan *antijüdaistisch*, particularly on account of Käsemann's frequent use of parallels from Qumran. 'Christian exegesis is always in danger of contrasting the Jewish "pious work" with the Pauline miracle of grace, even though in the Jewish sources the pious work is also a consequence and sign of the end-time grace' (1975: 41).

[12] For Käsemann the only parallel to Paul in Judaism with regard to criticism of justification by the righteousness of works is the 'heretical' viewpoint of 4 Ezra 8: 31–6 (*Römer* 24/26 f.).

[13] 'Das Thema des Neuen Testaments', *1845–1970 Almanach: 125 Jahre Chr. Kaiser Verlag München* (Munich, 1970), 83; cf. the essay, 'Das Evangelium und die Frommen', in H. J. Schütz (ed.), *Wir werden lachen—die Bibel: Überraschungen mit dem Buch* (Berlin, 1975), 125–34; ET 1982.

[14] Barth 1922 *passim*; e.g., 164 or the heading to Rom. 7: 14–25: 'the reality of religion'. Cf. Luther 1515/16: 68 f. Wright notes that Käsemann attempts to give this theology an exegetical basis in the interpretation of Paul (1982: 11).

[15] Luther 1515/16: 101, 119.

[16] Bultmann 1938*b*: 1951, 242, 243, 264, 267, 281, 300, 304, 315.

Bultmann that its fundamental character is trust (65/69 f.), he modifies this in line with his emphasis on lordship: boasting tells a person 'to whom he belongs' (125/133). However, the major difference at this point between Bultmann and Käsemann is in the relative significance they give to the themes of boasting and piety: for Bultmann the former is central, for Käsemann the latter. Käsemann again shifts the emphasis from the general anthropological level to a specifically religious expression of it by arguing that it is by 'religion' that human beings distort their status as creatures (65/70).

5. 'Illusion' is the general term which Käsemann uses for the attempt human beings make to transcend themselves (e.g., *PP* 75/40), the attempt to win salvation by one's own efforts. It is any state which attacks the creator's lordship by forgetting one's creatureliness (*Römer* 54/58). Its Jewish form is through the abuse of the law; its Gentile form through the attempt to transcend creatureliness. Against this Paul sets the judge who always comes upon the scene in conflict with human illusion (54/58, commenting on 2: 6 f. and 1: 22 f.). However, like all these terms, 'illusion' is very elastic in its meaning, and can be used, for example, against theologies judged not to be christologically orientated (ibid.).

Romans 1: 18–3: 20 as a test case of Käsemann's view of the law

Käsemann's major attempt to establish exegetically the importance of the theme of piety for the interpretation of Paul comes in his Romans commentary. For reasons of space it is not possible to discuss all the relevant passages.[17] Particular attention will be paid to his interpretation of 1: 18–3: 20 because of the fundamental place it has in Käsemann's view of the argument of Romans, which in turn is understood as a summary of Paul's theology. In order to demonstrate that Paul proclaims the justification of the *ungodly*, Käsemann first

[17] Käsemann's interpretation of one key passage not discussed here (Rom. 9: 30 ff.) has been criticized by Sanders on the grounds that, with many others, Käsemann illegitimately connects christology and the renunciation of self-striving, reading Paul's christological objections to Judaism as objections to a supposed Jewish self-righteousness. Further, Käsemann individualizes and generalizes Paul's attack on Judaism so that the righteousness which comes from the law comes to mean 'self-righteousness' (Sanders 1983: 154–7).

argues that Paul's negative case in 1: 18–3: 20 is an attack on the Jew as the representative of *religious* humanity: 'In the first part [1: 18–32] the spotlight falls on the Gentile world, but the total emphasis [in 1: 18–3: 20] increasingly involves criticism of religious humanity, specifically represented by Judaism' (30/33).

In the light of the current debate about the understanding of the law in Judaism,[18] two specific questions have to be put to Käsemann's interpretation of this section of the letter. Is the concept of piety the most appropriate category for interpretation? Is it the case that the Jew as a representative of this piety increasingly stands for all humanity in this section?

1. The concept of piety does not arise in **Rom. 1: 18–32** because the issue is the human (and, specifically, the Gentile) attempt to escape creatureliness (*Römer* 47/51).

2. For Käsemann the main point of **2: 1–11** is that the criterion of judgement for all, Jew or Gentile, is works (*Römer* 50/54). Paul rejects the view of Wis. 15: 1 ff.[19] where God's judgement against Gentile idolatry and vice is contrasted with his mercy towards Israel. Thus, the passage contains criticism of piety in the sense of a misappropriation of God's promises. There is no hint of legalistic piety; in fact, Paul's main concern

[18] Although the Lutheran interpretation of the law in Paul (and specifically the view that the law is not the way of salvation because it leads to the sins of legalism and false security) had not gone unchallenged in recent New Testament studies (e.g., from within Lutheranism by K. Stendahl—the law is the custodian of the Jews until the coming of Christ (1963)—and U. Wilckens—the law is not the way of salvation because in fact human beings have sinned (1969)), the debate about the law in Paul has been reopened in a fundamental way by Sanders 1977 and 1983. Sanders shows, firstly, how the Lutheran stereotype of Paul's understanding of the law persisted in the face of historical study of Judaism, and, secondly, by means of a comprehensive survey of Palestinian Jewish literature in the period 200 BC to AD 200, that Judaism was not an inherently legalistic religion. (Only 4 Ezra provides evidence for the view that the Jew has to earn salvation by doing the works of the law—and even here the covenant precedes obedience, though, as obedience has to be perfect, any failure will lead to condemnation.) Jewish religion is, rather, 'covenantal nomism': first God's grace is shown in the giving of the covenant and the law; then Israel keeps within the covenant by doing the works of the law. Thus, the legalistic religion against which Paul is supposed to have polemicized simply did not exist. Cf. also Räisänen 1978, 1980, and 1983; Dunn 1983; Watson 1986; and for commentaries on Romans from this perspective, Dunn 1988*a* and 1988*b*; Ziesler 1989. For a recent defence of the Lutheran interpretation, see Hübner 1979/80 and 1978/1982.

[19] On the use of this tradition, cf. Barrett 1957: 44; Cranfield 1975: 138; Schlier 1977: 68; and Sanders 1983: 128.

is that those who claim that they have moral perception are sinning (v. 3).

Secondly, the demand for *μετάνοια* in 2: 4 is explained as a reminder to the pious person that God's long-suffering cannot be divorced from the demand for repentance. But Käsemann is only able to interpret *μετάνοια* in terms of piety by subsuming it under the theme of *πίστις*. He notes that *μετάνοια* is used relatively rarely by Paul, and suggests that this is because it was replaced by *πίστις* in missionary preaching in order to accentuate the constant demand inherent in faith. It is then said that repentance as an integral element of faith calls for submission to God (51/55). The problem with this interpretation is that the theme of faith is not present here and Paul chose not to reinterpret[20] the traditional *μετάνοια*, the call to turn from sin as the appropriate response to God's long-suffering.

3. To the section **2: 12–16** Käsemann gives the heading 'The Possession of the Torah is no Privilege'. The possession of the law is relativized by Paul through the introduction of the question of the Gentiles who, without the law, 'do the things of the law' (v. 14). Mere possession of the Torah is of no avail and, seen retrospectively, 'apparently inviolable privileges end, illusions are unmasked, and the coming judgement is thus intimated' (63/68). The second part of this section (vv. 14–16) makes the point that 'the Gentile, like the Jew, can understand the proclamation of the last judgement and the criteria which will apply in it' (ibid.). Here again the idea of piety is only present (i.e., is criticized by Paul) in the sense of false confidence in God's gifts.

4. In **2: 17–24** Paul's attack on the Jews turns to the discrepancy between their claims (vv. 17–20) and their practice (vv. 21–3). The Jew who judges others, himself transgresses the law (67/71). Thus, neither of the aspects of piety are present, though Käsemann does introduce the idea in the discussion of *καυχᾶσθαι* (cf. vv. 17, 23; 65/69 f.). This is said to be a key word in Paul's theology which differentiates between true and false religion. However, it is noticeable that Käsemann does not claim that it plays a part in this passage.

[20] Cf. Sanders 1983, 127 ff. on the lack of Pauline redaction of this hellenistic Jewish passage.

Here Paul does not attack the Jew for boasting but for not keeping the law (vv. 21–3). Even the contrast in v. 23 between the Jewish boasting or glorying in the law is not an attack on boasting as such but on the lack of a corresponding keeping of the law (v. 23*b* and v. 24). Thus, the introduction of the point about true and false religion is irrelevant to the interpretation of the passage.

5. In order to throw light on the question of circumcision in **2: 25–29** Käsemann appeals to his earlier work on Paul's criticism of the 'enthusiastic' understanding of baptism in 1 Cor. 10: 1–11. Even before chapter 6 the sacramental problem is raised in the question of whether circumcision operates *ex opere operato*, delivering human beings from judgement (68/72; cf. *PP* 240–51/140–6). In attacking this view Paul is again rejecting a false sense of trust in God's gifts. The reference to an 'enthusiastic' misunderstanding of the idea of sacrament indicates how elastic the catch-phrases can become: 'enthusiasm' here overlaps with 'piety'. Again, Käsemann does not emphasize Paul's concern for doing the law (doing the law contrasted with transgressing the law, v. 25; keeping the precepts of the law, v. 26; keeping the law, v. 27), a concern which militates against the view that the piety of works is Paul's target.

Käsemann further states that 2: 26 indicates that the uncircumcised, on the basis of their obedience, will be placed on the same footing as the 'Jewish pious' in the judgement (*Römer* 68/73, ET modified). However, the theme of piety is not relevant here: the Gentile and the Jew, irrespective of circumcision are to be judged on the criterion of keeping the just requirements of the law (v. 26). Thus, while it is correct that Jew and Gentile are on the same footing before the judgement, this is not because the piety of the Jew is representative for all, but because both will be judged according to works. In fact, piety, either as the righteousness of works or as wrongly claimed privilege, plays no part in v. 26. Paul is concerned with judgement according to works, not the righteousness of works.[21]

[21] Sanders criticizes Käsemann's interpretation of Rom. 2 because while Käsemann resists harmonization of Paul's views here with his views elsewhere up to v. 26–i.e., he assumes for the moment that human beings can achieve salvation by

6. Because the perspective is said to change in **3: 1–8** from Israel to the whole world Käsemann continues his argument under the catchword 'illusion'. The special case of Israel, alluded to in the theme of God's faithfulness to the covenant, is used by Paul to exemplify God's dealings with the whole world. Käsemann sees v. 7 as an objection of the pious to the justification of the ungodly (79/84). However, it is difficult to agree with the views that the pious would accept the premisses of the question (my falsehood, a sinner) or that the idea of the justification of the ungodly is present. Käsemann finds the latter because of the mention of 'God's righteousness' in v. 5, which he understands in contrast to the righteousness of works. However, the meaning of God's judicial rectitude or fidelity[22] is to be preferred here because of the parallels with God's faithfulness and truth. However, the main criticism must be that Käsemann loses sight of the thrust of the passage, the assertion of God's fidelity and truth. Paul rejects the questions of vv. 3, 5, and 7 because to accept them would be to admit unacceptable consequences for his view of God. Käsemann makes this point but it is then submerged under the supposedly connected question of the justification of the ungodly. That God triumphs over the ungodly is the implication of v. 4, but *contra* Käsemann and Stuhlmacher,[23] the passage is focused on a more limited question than the supposed introduction of the theme of justification in its cosmic width.

7. Käsemann finds confirmation that the Jew as representative of the *homo religiosus* is Paul's 'real opponent' in 3: 19 f., which sums up **3: 9–20** and states the goal of this part of the epistle (82/87). Indeed these verses, with their movement from the Jew to the indictment of the whole world, are undoubtedly Käsemann's strongest argument for the view that the Jew is the representative of all.[24] However, it is more

doing the works of the law—the argument is said to change to the question of Gentile obedience in v. 27 and again to that of Christian experience in v. 29. For Sanders the statement about the Gentiles is not hypothetical and a double change in viewpoint is unlikely (1983: 126 f.).

[22] Sanders 1977: 491.

[23] Cf. Stuhlmacher 1965: 86, whose accent on God's fidelity to the covenant is to be accepted but not his fusion of this with the theme of God's justifying act.

likely that having indicted the Jews and the Gentiles separately,[25] Paul now sums up. Paul maintains the distinction between the Jews and the Gentiles in the qualification of *πάντας ὑφ' ἁμαρτίαν εἶναι* with *'Ιουδαίους τε καὶ ''Ελληνας* (3: 9). Käsemann does not bring this out and thus his interpretation fails to emphasize the main point of these first three chapters, that the Gentiles are equally the target of the Christian mission (1: 16*c*, 18; 2: 12; 3: 9, 22*b*–24, 29 f.). Secondly, it is not in any case the 'piety' of the Jews which would make them representative of all humankind, but their actual transgressions of the law, as the *florilegium* of vv. 10–18 emphasizes.

The phrase *ἔργα νόμου* occurs for the first time in 3: 20 and Käsemann interprets it as a Pauline catch-phrase for the works which a human being does in order to be able to make a claim against God. They are the ground of 'boasting'. The result of these works is in fact the spread of sin and the need for the new beginning which Christ brings (84 f./89 f.). Thus, for Käsemann, Paul sums up with a reference to piety in the sense of the righteousness of works. However, this interpretation cannot be maintained. Firstly, even on Käsemann's account, Paul has not mentioned piety in the sense of the righteousness of works up to this point, and thus it is implausible that he makes it the climax of an argument which goes back to 1: 18.[26] Secondly, the immediate context speaks of the Jews' transgression of the law and not of their attempt to win salvation by doing works of the law. Thirdly, the *περισσόν* of the Jew which has been under debate is not the righteousness of works but the kindness, forbearance, and patience of God (2: 4), the gift of the law which revealed God's will (2: 17 f.), circumcision (2: 25 f.), and scripture (3: 2). This again makes it improbable that Paul now refers to the righteousness of works. The most likely interpretation is that

[24] Cf. Barrett 1957: 70; Cranfield 1975: 196.

[25] Black 1973: 64.

[26] To meet this problem Schlier (1977: 100–2) and Barrett (1957, 70) regard 3: 19 as an anticipation of Paul's view of the law as yet undeveloped. In favour of this is the anticipation of 7: 7 f. in 3: 20*b*. However, this is not of much help to Käsemann's much stronger form of the argument, that 1: 18–3: 20 is substantively Paul's case that the Jew is the representative of pious humanity.

Paul is reaffirming that no one will be justified by works of the law because all have sinned.[27]

It has been shown that the idea of piety in the sense of the righteousness of works does not play any role in 1: 18–3: 20.[28] In its second important sense (a false trust in God's gifts, particularly the possession of the Torah), it does play an important role in Paul's argument, especially in 2: 1–11, 12–16, 25–9, and 3: 1–8—though not to the extent that Käsemann claims for it in the last two passages, and not at all in 2: 17–24 and 3: 9–20. Further, the Jew is certainly not regarded as the representative of religious humanity; on the contrary the transgressions of the law by the Jews are emphasized. Thus, the use of piety as the major category for the interpretation of 1: 18–3: 20 cannot be accepted. The sense of the righteousness of works does not play a role, and without it the sense of a false confidence in the possession of God's gifts ought to be seen in a new light. If the primary issue is the 'advantage' of the Jews, the theme of the whole is not the problems which arise out of the law but the question of the relative standing of Jews and Gentiles in the light of the revelation of the gospel.[29] Paul's answer to this question is that all are on the same level because all have sinned. The catchword 'piety' is misleading because it draws attention away from this and because it inevitably recalls Käsemann's criticisms of modern pietism. Finally, the criticism that Käsemann speaks abstractly of the Jew as a type of 'religious humanity' and not of the Jews as a historical entity[30] is fully borne out by the above discussion.

GOD'S RIGHTEOUSNESS

Käsemann's understanding of the doctrine of justification in Paul is discussed primarily with reference to the phrase 'God's

[27] Wilckens 1969, especially 84; Cranfield 1975: 197 f.; Sanders 1977: 486 n. 44; Räisänen 1980: 69.

[28] Even if the anticipation hypothesis (n. 26) is accepted, this in itself rules out any significant role for piety as the righteousness of works in this part of Romans.

[29] So also Ince 1987.

[30] 'It is very important . . . that when Paul speaks about the Jews, he really speaks about Jews, and not simply fantasy Jews who stand as a prime example of a timeless legalism' (Stendahl 1963: 36 f.). Also Wright 1980: 83 and Sanders 1983: 157.

righteousness' (δικαιοσύνη θεοῦ). The publication of his essay of 1961[31] on this subject reawakened interest in this area of Pauline thought,[32] and his interpretation of this phrase is a key to understanding his interpretation of Romans. His views led to considerable debate, particularly in the German-speaking world, which will be noted in the following discussion.

As with the theme of 'apocalyptic', Käsemann's principal debating partner is Bultmann. For the latter 'God's righteousness' means 'the righteousness from God which is conferred upon him [man] as a gift of God's free grace alone'.[33] It is to be interpreted against the background of the Jewish doctrine of righteousness. By God's grace human beings are 'righteoused',[34] i.e., they receive a favourable verdict in the divine judgement. As Jewish piety became increasingly determined by eschatology, righteous status becomes the verdict to be received from God's eschatological judgement.[35] Up to this point Paul is in agreement with Jewish teaching but because of Paul's different eschatological belief, what for the Jews was a matter of hope is for Paul 'also a present reality'. Secondly, the condition of God's acquitting judgement is, for Paul, 'without works of the law' and 'by, or from, faith', and not, as in Judaism (so Bultmann), the doing of the works of the law. Righteousness is not won by human effort but is 'sheer gift'.[36] In fact it is only when human beings cease to wish to establish themselves before God that they can receive God's gift, and thus it is precisely to transgressors to whom it is available. Paul's teaching on justification is, therefore, a 'polemical doctrine'. To recapitulate, Paul speaks of *God's* righteousness,

[31] *Contra* Sandifer whose chronology is wildly inaccurate when he claims that 'the dispute over the interpretation of the righteousness of God in Paul had significant ramifications for Käsemann in relation to the Nazis' (1979: 153).

[32] For the history of interpretation, see Stuhlmacher 1965, Brauch in Sanders 1977: 523–42, and, more briefly, Hultgren 1985: 13–18.

[33] Bultmann 1951: 285; 'The δικαιοσύνη θεοῦ is rather the righteousness conferred by God on the individual, that is, which is conferred in the eschatological judgement which has already been presented in Christ' (1936*b*: 9).

[34] Sanders puts forward good reasons for this neologism, which allows words from the δικ- group to be recognizably cognate in English translation (1983: 13, n. 18). In addition to the reasons he gives, it is also noticeable that this device enables him to dispense with 'justification' vocabulary, thereby creating a linguistic separation from Lutheran views.

[35] Bultmann 1951: 271–3.

[36] Ibid. 281.

because its foundation is God's grace; it is 'God-given, God-adjudicated righteousness'.[37] Consequently, in the technical debate about the type of genitive which occurs in δικαιοσύνη θεοῦ, Bultmann argues for a genitive of author. At a theological level, he interprets the phrase in terms of the new self-understanding which is offered to a human being: 'If man's death has its cause in the fact that man in his striving to live out of his own resources loses his self, life arises out of surrendering one's self to God, thereby gaining one's self.'[38] Thus, for Bultmann, 'God's righteousness' is understood in terms of Paul's soteriological anthropology and with reference to the individual.

'God's righteousness' as a fixed formula stemming from Jewish 'apocalyptic'

Käsemann's starting-point for interpretation is the hypothesis that the phrase δικαιοσύνη θεοῦ was not coined by Paul, but is a fixed formula (*feste Formel*; ET: 'ready-made formulation'),[39] or technical term, going back via Qumran[40] and other Jewish writings to Deut. 33: 21 (*EVB* ii. 185/172), or, reflecting the influence of the dissertation of his pupil, Stuhlmacher,[41] a fixed formula stemming from Jewish 'apocalyptic' (*Römer* 27/30). As a fixed formula its history is to be investigated separately from the concept of righteousness in general (*EVB* ii. 185/172). It is used independently in the New Testament (Matt. 6: 33;[42] Jas. 1: 20),[43] in T. Dan. 6: 10, 1 QS 10: 25, 11: 12, and in the inscriptions on the standards for the holy war in 1 QM 4: 6. Käsemann does not accept the much longer list suggested by Stuhlmacher[44] and concedes that 'the Jewish

[37] Bultmann 1951: 285.

[38] Ibid. 270.

[39] The theory of a fixed formula goes back at least to Oepke 1953: 261. Cf. Brauch in Sanders 1977: 527.

[40] On the relationship between Qumran and Paul on the topic of justification as a whole, cf. Schulz 1959. However, the objection of Becker that righteousness as a forensic term does not occur at Qumran should be noted (1964: 251 f.).

[41] Stuhlmacher 1965.

[42] While the τοῦ θεοῦ should probably be read, thus giving a reference to δικαιοσύνη θεοῦ, if it is not read, as in ℵ, αὐτοῦ would then refer back to ὁ πατὴρ ὑμῶν (Metzger 1971: 18 f.).

[43] Cf. also 2 Pet. 1: 1.

[44] Stuhlmacher 1965: 154 ff.

references to it are not overwhelming' (*Römer* 27/29). He concludes, without discussion of these passages, that 'the formulation which Paul has taken over speaks primarily of God's saving activity, which is present in his gift as a precipitate without being completely dissolved into it' (*EVB* ii. 185/172). Thus, Käsemann's argument is that the power–gift dialectic, from which he will interpret δικαιοσύνη θεοῦ in Paul, comes from the Jewish apocalyptic technical term 'God's righteousness'. He also argues that Pauline usage points to the existence of such a term. Paul does not just speak of justification, but of God's righteousness. His antithesis of one's own righteousness and God's righteousness, and the personification of God's righteousness, are easier to explain on the hypothesis of an existing formula (*Römer* 27/29).

Käsemann also seeks support from history-of-religions considerations for his view that righteousness is to be regarded as power. T. Dan. 6: 10 is evidence that 'in Judaism God's righteousness has a field of radiation and a place of manifestation' (25/28).

The hypothesis that 'God's righteousness' is a fixed formula in Jewish apocalyptic tradition has not fared well in the ensuing debate. Bultmann objected that for a word or phrase to be called a fixed formula it must have a clearly fixed meaning which relates to a special situation or event, and this is not the case with this phrase in Old Testament or Jewish texts, but only in Paul.[45] This criticism is not cogent in itself in that the criteria for a fixed formula cannot be tied to meaning but only to form-critical considerations. A far more penetrating critique is given by Güttgemanns who subjects Käsemann and Stuhlmacher's[46] views to stricter linguistic analysis. Käsemann is justified in isolating δικαιοσύνη θεοῦ as a fixed formula for examination but this hypothesis must be applied strictly, with the passages which do not contain the formula being excluded. In the Old Testament and Jewish tradition this leaves only Deut. 33: 21, T. Dan. 6: 10, 1 QS 10: 25, 11:

[45] Bultmann 1964*a*: 474. On the break between OT/Jewish and Pauline usage, cf. Watson 1970: 36; Ziesler 1972: 170 and 186, and Wilckens 1978: 211.

[46] After the appearance of Stuhlmacher's dissertation there is a tendency to conflate his views with Käsemann's, even though they are by no means identical.

12, 1 QM 4: 6, and possibly 1 En. 71: 14 as examples.[47] Secondly, a genuine technical term does not vary but this is not true of *δικαιοσύνη θεοῦ* in Paul. It is broken up by *γάρ* (Rom. 1: 17) and *δὲ* (Rom. 3: 22); an article can be added to *θεοῦ* (Rom. 10: 3 twice); and it can be modified to *τὴν ἐκ θεοῦ δικαιοσύνην* in opposition to *δικαιοσύνην τὴν ἐκ νόμου* (Phil. 3: 9).[48] Thus, strictly, only Rom. 3: 21 and 2 Cor. 5: 21 count, and, therefore, there can be no talk of a technical term. Given this situation, the correct procedure is to study *δικαιοσύνη θεοῦ* within the *δικαιο-* word-field and to give priority to the word-field as a whole over this particular formulation.[49] In the light of these criticisms it is clear that *δικαιοσύνη θεοῦ* cannot be regarded as a fixed formula stemming from Jewish apocalyptic tradition.[50] While these criticisms are fatal for

[47] Güttgemanns 1971: 77 f. This criticism ought to be aimed at Stuhlmacher's longer list. Lohse notes that Käsemann cannot find enough examples to justify the talk about a technical term. Deut. 33: 21 is the only occurrence in the OT but Paul never refers to this verse, while the LXX translates it in quite a different way. Further, Qumran is not simply to be allocated to 'apocalyptic' and its usage taken as typical of a unified apocalyptic use of language. Its use of the righteousness of God theme is varied, as is Paul's use of *δικαιοσύνη θεοῦ, δίκαιος*, and *δικαιόω* (Lohse 1973*a*: 213 f., 216, 222). Sanders finds no examples of the righteousness of God used as a technical term for God's saving power (1977: 494). In Paul, God's righteousness is both the power and action of God which are manifest in wrath and grace, and his rightness and fidelity to what he intended, without there being any need to beat these into one meaning (491). For Wright's view, that the righteousness of God in Jewish literature is not a technical term but a live metaphor with a variety of connotations (1980: 64), see n. 50. Soards rejects Käsemann's appeal to T. Dan 6: 10, noting that the *β* version of the text, now preferred, reads 'the righteousness of the law of God', not 'the righteousness of God (*α*), and that in any case the verse refers to a norm of appropriate human behaviour, not God's power (1987).

[48] Cf. Wright 1980: 82.

[49] Güttgemanns 1971: 80 f.; also Wright 1980: 65. The last point was made first by Gäumann (1967: 138 n. 17) who also objects that there are far too few occurrences of *δικαιοσύνη θεοῦ* in Paul (and that its meaning varies) to speak of a formula (157). Zeller points out that the tradition uses *δικαιοσύνη θεοῦ* and *δικαιοσύνη* together. Adopting Güttgemanns's methodology he argues that Paul uses the word group in two ways: (1) in the context of the message of justification where the noun, verb, and adverb are determined by *ἐκ πίστεως* and in opposition to *ἐξ ἔργων νόμου* and (2) in traditional contexts, e.g., baptism (1973: 163–78, esp. 171). By contrast Ziesler argues that the verb is essentially relational or forensic, while the noun and the adjective describe behaviour within a relationship (1972: 212).

[50] More recently Berger has argued that *δικαιοσύνη θεοῦ* means God's demanding and reacting holiness which has its OT background in the theme of judgement and not of righteousness (Berger 1977). Wright also stresses the OT background of righteousness. The fundamental point is that God is the righteous judge. This is called into question by the disasters which befall Israel, but God is vindicated

Stuhlmacher's version of the hypothesis, they are not so damaging to Käsemann's interpretation as his real interest lies in Paul's use of the theme.

Paul's understanding of 'God's righteousness'

Käsemann affirms that the interpretation of 'God's righteousness' which speaks of 'gift' can find strong support in the texts and is theologically fundamental: 'It is beyond dispute that the general tenor of the Pauline utterances on this subject, like that of the Reformation tradition which determines our attitude, tells in favour of the objective genitive' (*EVB* ii. 182/169). Thus, 'God's righteousness' means the righteousness which is acceptable in God's eyes and is bestowed by him. Phil. 3: 9 sets a righteousness from God over against Paul's own righteousness (ibid.).[51] This passage is regarded as 'normative' and the 'key passage' (*Römer* 22 f./25 f.).[52] Rom. 2: 13 indicates that a human being's status 'before God' is

because he is right to punish his erring people and he remains true to his fundamental intentions in the covenant and will save those whom he will. The present is the time when God restrains his judgement to allow people to repent, or be hardened. The righteousness of God's people is their right standing in the metaphorical lawcourt where God will find in their favour because of his covenant. This right standing includes ethical righteousness, but depends on the covenant (1980: 57 and 64; cf. also Wright 1978). Hultgren collects some important texts from the LXX, mainly from Pss., Isa., and Jer., and argues that it is an expected messiah figure who manifests God's (eschatological) righteousness (1985: 22). However, he does not draw attention to the significant point that Ps. 97: 2 and Isa. 51: 5–6 LXX contain the theme of the revelation to the nations/the Gentiles, a point which is central to the argument of Romans and which has rarely been brought into the debate about God's righteousness. This theme is touched on in a general way by Williams who interprets the phrase in terms of 'God's faithfulness to his promises to Abraham, promises which focus upon the eschatological gathering of all nations in the people of God' (1980: 270).

[51] The 'gift' interpretation of Phil. 3: 9 f. is minimized only by Stuhlmacher and Müller, and in both cases unconvincingly. Stuhlmacher finds the motif of divine creation in the phrase *τοῦ γνῶναι αὐτόν*, which seems unlikely in this context, and thus sees 'the righteousness from God' as the individuation of God's faithfulness to creation which is salvation-creating righteousness. However, Stuhlmacher does acknowledge the element of 'gift' here (1965: 100 f.). Müller relativizes the importance of Phil. 3: 9 by pointing to its context: here Paul is speaking only of his personal destiny and this leads to the contrast of the two types of righteousness (1964: 73).

[52] Given Käsemann's final conclusion that 'God's righteousness' is to be understood within the gift–power dialectic, this judgement is premature and unconsciously reflects Lutheran doctrinal convictions.

characterized by δικαιοῦσθαι and cognates. Further, the fundamental either/or of the righteousness of faith and the righteousness of works is only comprehensible from this perspective and in this context the accent will naturally fall on the gift aspect. The righteousness of faith is a gift, as the explicit δωρεὰ τῆς δικαιοσύνης of Rom. 5: 17 makes clear (*EVB* ii. 182/169, 185/172 f.). Rom. 3: 22 is another statement that righteousness is a gift which comes to human beings by faith (*Römer* 88/94, cf. 24/26, 26/28, 77/82, 117/123). This adherence to the fundamental point of Lutheran interpretation has often been overlooked by commentators, beginning with Bultmann.[53]

However, it is not sufficient to speak of God's righteousness only as a gift. The gift is not passively received but is effective in and through Christians and 2 Cor. 9: 9 f. and Phil. 1: 11 name its fruit (*EVB* ii. 183/170).[54] Further, if righteousness is a gift which has been received, it is also still a matter of hope (ἐλπίς δικαιοσύνης, Gal. 5: 5).[55] The dialectic of present and future eschatology is projected on to the very condition of being a Christian (183/170), and is expressed in the technical formula λογίζεσθαι εἰς δικαιοσύνην (Rom. 4, Gal. 3: 6).[56] Righteousness 'is only to be had on earth as a pledged gift, always subject to attack, always to be authenticated in

[53] Although Bultmann goes on to mention the gift–power dialectic, he gives this no weight in his summary of Käsemann's view: 'He [Käsemann] thinks that the genitive θεοῦ is a subjective genitive and that δικαιοσύνη θεοῦ is not the righteousness given to the believer but "God's saving activity" or God's "salvation-creating power"' (Bultmann 1964*a*: 470). Ziesler (1972: 11), Plutta-Messerschmidt (1973: 6), Cranfield (1975: 96), and Wright (1980: 56, but cf. 83) take Käsemann's position to be the subjective genitive on its own. Cf. correctly, Klein (1967: 2), Kertelge (1967: 12), Dinkler (in Bultmann 1967: xix–xx), and Güttgemanns (1971: 64 f.).

[54] Käsemann does not expand on these statements, and against his assumption that 'righteousness' in 2 Cor. 9: 9 f. (where Ps. 111: 9 is quoted) refers to justification is the possibility that it has a moral sense here (Barrett 1973: 238). Again Phil. 1: 11 is open to a variety of interpretations. The phrase 'fruit (or fruits) of righteousness' means either 'the fruit which consists of being rightly related to God' (Collange 1973: 50) or, with Käsemann, the ethical results of that right relation. Given the context of a formal thanksgiving and the Pauline abbreviation διὰ Ἰησοῦ Χριστοῦ a final decision is difficult (cf. Martin 1976: 70).

[55] Cf. Burton 1920: 278; Schlier 1949/1971: 168; Mussner 1974: 350, and Betz 1979: 262. This is contested by Klein who argues for the 'hope whose base is the already received righteousness' (1967: 4).

[56] But the promise which Paul speaks of here is not that salvation will only be complete at the parousia, but the promise of Gen. 18: 18, 33: 17 f.

practice—a matter of promise and expectation' (ibid.). The goal has not yet been reached (Phil. 3: 12). Finally, the 'gift' interpretation is inadequate because 'the divine righteousness possesses us before we grasp it, and we retain it only as long as it holds us fast' (183/170). In support of this Käsemann appeals to Rom. 5: 6–10, but it is a very loose appeal ('we can formulate it in terms of Rom. 5: 6–10'), and with reason. These verses can only substantiate the first part of Käsemann's point: the initiative lies with God and not with the weak or ungodly. They do not substantiate the second half ('we retain it only as it holds us fast'), and this is important because it is this second half which provides the link to Käsemann's next argument, that the gift itself has the character of power.

Apart this weakness in Käsemann's argument, it is noticeable that, despite his methodological commitment to the technical term *δικαιοσύνη θεοῦ*, most of his evidence concerns 'righteousness' in general, and not the fixed formula. Nevertheless, he has shown that righteousness cannot be regarded simply as a 'gift'. It also has to be borne in mind that the formats of an essay and a commentary do not allow for a full discussion of the evidence.

Secondly, Käsemann reviews the possibility that 'God's righteousness' should be regarded as a subjective genitive, the righteousness which is God's salvation-creating power (*heilsetzende Macht*, additional note to *EVB* ii. 181/168, 193/181; *heilschaffende Macht*, *PP* 137/77).[57] Paul speaks not merely of the righteousness bestowed on us, but emphatically of God's righteousness (*EVB* ii. 182/169) which appears in personified form as power in Rom. 1: 17 and 10: 3 ff. (ibid.; *Römer* 27/29, cf. 271 f./281). Because of this it can be identified with Christ (1 Cor. 1: 30) and in 2 Cor. 5: 21 it describes the reality of the redeemed community. In Rom. 3: 5, 25 f.[58] it is 'undisputedly'[59] a subjective genitive which speaks of God's activity and nature. Further, there are parallels in Paul to 'God's

[57] For God as 'powerful action' (*Machtaktion*), cf. von Soden 1931: 362, 365. 'God's righteousness' was understood as a subjective genitive in the earlier part of the century; see Müller 1905: 87–110, Schrenk 1935: 206 f.

[58] Although Käsemann here says 3: 25 f., in fact his view is that 'God's righteousness' is to be understood as a subjective genitive in v. 25 and in the true Pauline sense of genitive of author in v. 26 (*EVB* i. 96 and 100).

[59] This is now disputed by Plutta-Messerschmidt (1973: 9 f.).

righteousness' as his power in the phrases about his δύναμις, glory, love, peace, and wrath,[60] which equally can be used in personified form (*EVB* ii. 185/173; *Römer* 25/28, 89/95). In addition, Paul speaks of the power of righteousness in other contexts, for example, the βασιλεύειν of grace through righteousness (Rom. 5: 21); the 'weapons' of righteousness (Rom. 6: 13 and 2 Cor. 6: 7); and the δουλεία (Rom. 6: 18) and the διακονία of righteousness (2 Cor. 3: 9; *EVB* ii. 186/173). Paul sets the whole Christian life under the sign of submission to righteousness in Rom. 6: 13 ff. and he even identifies δικαιοσύνη and θεός by placing them in parallel in 6: 18 and 22 (*Römer* 25/28). This is summed up in the 'characteristic expression' in Rom. 10: 3: 'become obedient[61] to God's righteousness' (*EVB* ii. 186/ 173). This is said to be characteristic of Paul because power becomes gift when it takes possession of us (ibid.).

However, 'God's righteousness' is not to be taken one-sidedly as a subjective genitive. It is not a property of the divine nature as in Greek theology; the phrase speaks of the self-revealing God of the Old Testament and Jewish tradition, not of the self-subsistent God of the Greeks (*EVB* ii. 186 f./ 174). Nor is it 'saving action' or 'salvation' as then Paul could have spoken of ἀγάπη θεοῦ; his choice of δικαιοσύνη θεοῦ indicates his concern with the motif of covenant faithfulness (189/177). Finally, the element of a gift which is granted to faith and the forensic and apocalyptic (i.e., cosmic) horizons of 'God's righteousness' should not be neglected (*Römer* 25/ 27).

Following this review of 'God's righteousness' as an objective genitive and as a subjective genitive, Käsemann returns to his conclusion from the historical background: the correct starting-point is summed up in the catch-phrase, 'the power character of the gift' (*der Machtcharakter der Gabe*, *EVB* ii. 183/170; cf. 186/174 cited below, 189/176; *Römer* 54/58; and the phrase, 'power–gift structure', 26/29). His fundamental

[60] Cf. Luther 1515/16: 68, 116 and Barth 1922: p. xvii. Fitzmyer objects that the equation of God's glory, power, and righteousness is not evident in Rom. 6: 4 and 2 Cor. 13: 4 (1974: 746).

[61] The ET (*NTQT* 173) translates 'submit to' which is a more accurate translation of Rom. 10: 3, but not of Käsemann's *gehorsam werden*.

point is that, in Paul's view, 'gift' and 'power', far from being mutually antithetical, are indissolubly connected:[62]

> the gift which is being bestowed here is never at any time separable from its Giver. It partakes of the character of power, in so far as God himself enters the arena [*auf den Plan tritt*] in it and remains in the arena with it. Thus address, obligation and service are indissolubly bound up with the gift. When God enters the arena we ourselves still experience his lordship in his gifts; indeed it is his gifts which are the very means by which he subordinates us to his lordship and makes us responsible beings. (*EVB* ii. 186/174, ET modified)

Thus, when Käsemann speaks of power in this context he means God's power, and then God himself, so that 'gift–Giver' can replace 'gift–power'.[63] The gift–Giver theme allows him to emphasize God's action and presence in the act and gift of justification. His characteristic phrase, *auf den Plan treten* ('to arrive or come on to the scene, to enter the arena'),[64] is elucidated in the course of his debate with Bultmann.

[62] Lietzmann spoke of an iridescent or enigmatic (*schillernd*) double meaning of *δικαιοσύνη θεοῦ*—the divine behaviour and the righteousness conferred on human beings—(1906/1933: 95), a view which is discussed but rejected by Oepke (1953: 358, 363).

[63] Cf. Luther: 'For when we acknowledge his [God's] words as righteous, he gives himself to us, and because of this gift, he recognises us as righteous, i.e., he justifies us' (1515/16: 78). At this point Käsemann's fundamental indebtedness to Schlatter's interpretation of God's righteousness becomes clear. However, Schlatter does not have a single definition which Käsemann takes over. He subordinates the theme to the *εὐαγγέλιον θεοῦ* of Rom. 1: 1, cf. v. 16, so that the reception of the message is the reception of the deliverer (1935: 10). God's righteousness is his own righteousness, as his power and wrath are his own, which is found *ἐν αὐτῷ*, that is *ἐν τῷ εὐαγγελίῳ* (Rom. 1: 17; 1935: 36). The message is not the acquisition or possession of human beings but conveys an activity of God to them, which reveals to them what God is doing for them and is making of them. God's power grasps them through the word. But this righteousness is not one quality among others: 'In every statement about God Paul thinks about the creator who wishes, works, reveals himself and brings man into the relationship which he desires. That his activity creates right, and orders his relationship to man in such a way that all evil is excluded from him by the power of his glorious will is based in the deity of God (*Gottheit Gottes*)' (ibid.). Käsemann takes up the gift–Giver idea, the emphasis on God's activity, the effectiveness of God's righteousness, the right of the creator theme, and the theological basis in the nature of God (*Gottheit Gottes*), but not the derivation via the *ἐν αὐτῷ* of 1: 17. On Schlatter's view, cf. Dantine 1966: 70. For Barth's influence on Käsemann at this point, see n. 77 below. Michel took the opportunity of reviewing Müller's monograph of 1964 to point to his own indebtedness to Schlatter (God as creator) and his own debate with Bultmann which anticipated Käsemann's views and made use of rabbinic and apocalyptic sources (Michel 1966).

[64] Cf. of God, *PP* 76/41, 257/150; *Römer* 26/29, 88/94, 117/123, 271/281; of God as judge, *Römer* 52/56, 54/58; of Christ, 102/108.

This debate focuses on the translation of Rom. 1: 16b (δύναμις γὰρ θεοῦ ἐστιν εἰς σωτηρίαν) which, with considerable ingenuity, Bultmann rendered 'the "possibility" of salvation is the gospel'. Bultmann's soteriological and anthropological orientation is particularly clear here. He argues that Käsemann understands δύναμις one-sidedly as power (*Macht*), whereas it should be translated as *Kraft*, which Bultmann connects with 'ability' (*können*) and thus 'possibility'.[65] Käsemann's reply is equally revealing of his own theological and exegetical position:

> Characteristically Bultmann chooses the translation which substitutes for the motif of the God who acts and creates and who prevails in the gospel the different motif of an anthropological given . . . But for me everything depends on the gospel being the manifestation of this God in which he himself enters the arena in his lordship and prevailing power. (*in welcher er selber herrschend und sich durchsetzend auf den Plan tritt*, *EVB* ii. 185 n. 4/173 n. 4, ET modified)

Here again Käsemann's reinstates the 'theology' pole of the 'theology–anthropology' dialectic. Secondly, he derives Paul's doctrine of God (creator, lord, judge) from his understanding of the doctrine of justification. Thirdly, the 'apocalyptic' perspective is again apparent. The God who prevails (*sich durchsetzen*) is the one who overcomes the powers of the old aeon, and the rebellious world. Käsemann concludes by connecting the doctrine of justification with the 'Christ must triumph' motif; indeed he states that 'Paul's doctrine of justification is simply a precise theological variation of the primitive Christian proclamation of the kingdom of God as eschatological salvation'[66] (*Römer* 26/29)

Käsemann, therefore, holds a middle position (*PP* 137 n. 27/76 n. 27) which takes up both 'gift' and 'power'. He wishes to emphasize God's saving activity and presence in the attack of grace on the world,[67] but not apart from the gift of

[65] Bultmann 1964*a*: 473, n. 6.

[66] This connection between the kingdom of God as the centre of Jesus' proclamation and God's righteousness as the centre of Paul's theology—on the grounds of a shared eschatological outlook—was made by Bultmann (1929*c*: 232) and developed by Jüngel (1962; see also Käsemann's review of Jüngel, *ThLZ* 90 (1965), 184–7). Käsemann acknowledges that there are points of contact between his views and those of Jüngel (187).

[67] In an unpublished address of the 1980s Käsemann takes this theme further in a

justification. Thus, he speaks of the gift *in which* God's presence and lordship are experienced. Consequently, in the technical debate he opts for the genitive of author in which the soteriological sense of the phrase is the dominating one (*PP* 136 f./77).

Käsemann then argues that the gift–power dialectic is present in a wide range of themes in Paul's theology: the power of God in 2 Cor. 12: 9 f. and 13: 3 f. is a gift at work in the Christian; the spirit effects the resurrection of the dead and is ἐν ἡμῖν; Christ both gives himself for us and dwells in the believer; χάρις is primarily the power of grace but in its individuation as χάρισμα it is bestowed on the Christian; the ἀγάπη of God is the power from which nothing can separate us (Rom. 8: 39) and the gift poured into our hearts (Rom. 5: 5). The gospel appears in 1 Cor. 9: 19 as ἀνάγκη controlling the apostle, in 2 Cor 2: 14 ff. as the power of life or death, and as δύναμις θεοῦ in Rom. 1: 16; yet in the kerygma we become partakers of it and Paul can speak of 'his' gospel. Finally, the eucharistic body of Christ incorporates the Christian into the ecclesiological body of Christ (*EVB* ii. 187/174 f.; *Römer* 26/28; p. 73 above). Käsemann concludes: 'The key to this whole Pauline viewpoint is that power is always seeking to realize itself in action and must indeed do so. It does this with the greatest effect when it no longer remains external to us and, as the apostle says, makes us its members' (*EVB* ii. 187/175).

Käsemann's thesis concerning the power character of the gift is itself directly related to his concern to do theology by the interpretation of Paul. He argues that the power–gift dialectic is the solution to the long-standing theological debate on whether justification is declaratory or effectual,[68] and to the related question of the relationship of justification and sanctification. In Paul there is a dialectic between 'declare righteous' and 'make righteous', and justification and

social and political direction: 'Our God must intervene in a partisan way for his lost and godless creatures if we are to be helped, and we must emulate him if the earth is not to remain an inferno.' (*Unser Gott muss parteiisch für seine verlorenen und gottlosen Geschöpfe eintreten, wenn uns geholfen werden soll, und wir müssen es ihm nachtun, wenn die Erde nicht überall ein Inferno bleiben soll.*; 'Gottesgerechtigkeit bei Paulus', unpublished lecture, 2.) 'The earth is the lord's must be worked out politically' (8).

[68] For the state of the question, see Ziesler 1972: 1–7, who begins his study from this problem.

sanctification are not to be separated either theologically or chronologically (the ET omits 'theologically [*sachlich*] or chronologically'). The lordship of Christ, which is the content of God's righteousness, can only be received as *promissio*, and it is only the *nova oboedientia* which proves that the *promissio* is heard and appropriated (*EVB* ii. 189/176 f.). The key to this is the creative, effective power of the word (ibid.; *Römer* 106 f./112 f.):

Faith is recognised to be righteous because, in a way that is past human comprehension, it allows God to act on it instead of wanting to be and to achieve [ET: 'to do'] something in itself and thereby seeking a ground for boasting. It lets itself be placed by the word in the possibility of *facultas standi extra se coram deo per Christum*. (*Römer* 107 f./113, ET modified)

Here the centrality of the doctrine of justification for Käsemann's view of Paul (and of Christian theology) is clear.

Käsemann has found some following for the thesis that Paul's theology is marked by a gift–power dialectic,[69] even when it is denied that this is the correct way to interpret 'God's righteousness'.[70] On the other hand, there have been more attempts to resolve the tension in his dialectical interpretation, in one direction or the other.[71]

Käsemann explicates the nature of the power which comes in the gift[72] by taking up the theme of God's faithfulness. It is

[69] Wilckens agrees in principle and reformulates Käsemann's argument in line with his own emphasis on 'covenant-righteousness' (1978: 211). Cf. Kertelge 1967: 81 and 108.

[70] Bultmann 1964*a*: 472: the 'power character of the gift' is correct to the extent that the gift should become a power in the believer.

[71] Müller comes closest to absolutizing the 'power' interpretation, describing the structure of God's righteousness as the 'eschatological realization of God's right over his creation'. He is closely followed by Stuhlmacher, for whom God's righteousness is the creative, liberating right of the creator on and over his creation, which spans the aeons. It is located in challenge, realizes itself today as the word, and is personified in Christ. Brauch misses some of these elements in his report (in Sanders 1977: 531 f.). Sanders protests against the attempt to beat all the elements of Paul's use of God's righteousness into one meaning (ibid. 491). At the other end of the spectrum are Lührmann (1965: 144), Klein (1967: 11), Conzelmann (1968: 398), Bornkamm (1969: 147 f.), Thyen (1970: 165, 168), and Koch (1971: 151) who absolutize the 'gift' aspect. There is a marked tendency among those who argue for the latter case to acknowledge the subjective genitive in Rom. 3: 5 and 25 but to argue that these verses are not important for the interpretation of Paul's view because they are traditional.

[72] Plutta-Messerschmidt's extended analysis of the views of Bultmann and Käsemann is fatally distorted by the adoption of the wrong starting-point: the

the power of the creator who exercises his right (*Recht*) over creation as its lord (*Römer* 32/35, 52/56, 87/93, 117/123). Paul has taken up the idea of covenant faithfulness (*Bundestreue*) from the tradition and universalized it, or transferred it to creation (*Schöpfungstreue*, 'faithfulness to creation'). Käsemann does not claim that this is the content of Paul's message but that it is the theological framework of his thought. The interconnection of justification, the creation theme, and salvation history cannot be read directly out of the text which only hints at it (*Römer* 89/95, commenting on 3: 23). This reconstruction of the theological framework of Paul's thought allows Käsemann to sum up by saying that 'God's righteousness' in Paul is 'God's lordship over the world which reveals itself eschatologically in Jesus' (*EVB* ii. 192/180, ET modified; cf. *PP* 133/75) or, from a different angle, that Paul's 'teaching about justification gives a clear definition of what the apostle understands by the lordship of Christ' (*PP* 136/76 f.).

It is a curious feature of Käsemann's interpretation of 'God's righteousness' that although he pays a great deal of attention to the historical background of the theme and to the nature of Paul's theology in general, he does not treat the actual occurrences of the theme in Paul's letters in any detail. Thus, he has only two comments on **δικαιοσύνη θεοῦ** in 1: 17 in the Romans commentary, despite the thinly disguised excursus on the phrase (*Römer* 22–7/24–30): it is here proclaimed as the righteousness of faith (21/23), and the context of this verse indicates that power and gift are not true antitheses in Paul's eyes (26/28). Of course, Käsemann can refer to the work of Stuhlmacher, but, as has been seen, their views are not identical, and in particular Käsemann has an obligation to demonstrate the gift–power structure with respect to the occurrences of **δικαιοσύνη θεοῦ**. In fact he argues the case that this structure is central to Paul's theology (or at least to the themes listed on p. 199 above) and posits that this is also the case for **δικαιοσύνη θεοῦ** in general, while isolating either one

criterion for the doctrine of justification is the word and deed respectively. She fails to take account of the gift–power dialectic, and imports the idea that the effectiveness of justification leads to the corollary that God's deed is set alongside a human deed. Thus, the Christian deed again becomes the criterion of the reality of faith (1973: 5–8). This is a travesty of the way Käsemann relates justification and ethics, as will be seen below.

or other element for the various occurrences of the theme. Thus, *δικαιοσύνη θεοῦ* is a gift from God in Phil. 3: 9, God's faithfulness to the covenant and then to creation in Rom. 3: 5 and 25, is personified in 1: 17[73] and 1 Cor. 1: 30, and is the manifestation of the community in 2 Cor. 5: 21. It is only with Rom. 10: 3 ff. that Käsemann argues that God's righteousness is to be understood as a power to which one is to be subject and a gift which takes possession of us and enters into us. Even here the appeal is, once again, via a particular interpretation of Paul's theology, on this occasion through a discussion of the nature of power in Paul.[74] This means that Käsemann's interpretation depends on a general view of Paul's theology, but that the validity of this overview for its central motif, *δικαιοσύνη θεοῦ*, has not been demonstrated exegetically. Secondly, Käsemann looks for support for his hypothesis to the historical background of this theme, which draws the accusation that the history-of-religions background is more important than Paul's usage.[75]

In addition, as was seen with Käsemann's pre-1950 work, his use of Pauline language can take on a life of its own. Thus, Wright can object that God's lordship over the world is not his righteousness but his kingdom (and the two are not identical), and that the gift and power that create salvation is the spirit, not God's righteousness (on the relationship between God's righteousness and the spirit in Käsemann's view of Paul, see p. 208 below). Käsemann uses a Pauline phrase for different (Pauline) concepts.[76]

[73] This is the only example where the gift–power theme is at all clear (and was Schlatter's starting-point): God's righteousness is revealed in the gospel which is the power of God to salvation and simultaneously salvation to all who believe. If it is by faith, it is a gift. However, Schlatter is right to see that the overarching concept here is not God's righteousness but the gospel.

[74] In 10: 3 Paul contrasts *τὴν τοῦ θεοῦ δικαιοσύνην* and the Jews' righteousness. He speaks of them 'not submitting' to this righteousness but this refers not to the 'power' of that righteousness but to their failure to convert to the righteousness which is by faith (and which Paul polemically calls 'God's righteousness'). The word *ὑποτάσσω* does not refer to the *nova oboedientia* as Käsemann appears to claim (*Röme.* 271 f./280 f.).

[75] Conzelmann 1966*a*: 180; Klein 1967: 4; Koch 1971: 153–5; Güttgemann 1971: 75.

[76] Wright 1982: 15.

'God's righteousness' as his claim on the world

Käsemann's view that God's righteousness is his right or claim (*Recht*)[77] on the world is supported by the more general point that Paul has modified the Jewish-Christian idea of God's 'faithfulness to the covenant' (*Bundestreue*) to the comprehensive notion of his 'faithfulness to creation' (*Schöpfungstreue*).[78] Thus, while God has remained faithful, the particularism of Judaism has been overcome. On this point Käsemann appeals to interpretations of Rom. 1: 23*b*, 3: 3–5, and 3: 24–6.

By applying Jer. 2: 11 to the Gentiles in **Rom. 1: 23*b*** Paul extends what had been restricted to the people of God to the whole human race: 'for Paul the history of Israel documented in Scripture has exemplary significance for the world. He thus breaks the framework of a mere covenant history and establishes the eschatological interpretation which is expressly demanded in 1 Cor. 10: 11' (*Römer* 42/46). The story of the worship of the golden calf is taken up in criticism of Gentile idolatry and understood fundamentally as a fall from creatureliness. However, while a standard previously understood to be applicable to the Jews is extended here, there is no reason to connect this with the idea of faithfulness to creation as the text is concerned with the sinfulness of all. Further, there is no indication that the use of Jer. 2: 11 in v. 23*b* is to be emphasized and isolated from the passage as a whole.

Rom. 3: 3–5 is the most important message for Käsemann's view as the theme of God's faithfulness to the covenant is said to be taken up explicitly by Paul here and is related to God's righteousness. The starting-point is the question whether

[77] Käsemann here takes up two ideas from Barth: God's faithfulness is part of his 'self-justification' (*Gottes Selbstrechtfertigung*), and, secondly, the eschatological self-revelation of God's lordship in Christ is related to the 'right' with which he claims back his world (Dantine 1966: 88). Whereas the former concern for the doctrine of God is Barth's central concern, the latter, with its connection with the doctrines of creation and justification, is more important for Käsemann. Thus, while Käsemann affirms the 'arrival' and presence of God in the event of justification over against Bultmann, he does not reflect on the doctrine of God as such.

[78] Ehler claims that, for Käseman, God is first of all the creator (1986: 287); this is a potentially misleading statement in that, for Käsemann, God is the creator who claims back his creation in the act of justification (as Ehler says, 289; e.g., *Römer* 129/138). Ehler also incorrectly speaks of the 'love' of the creator (1986: 289), where Käsemann speaks of the creator's 'right' or faithfulness.

Israel's unfaithfulness means that she has lost her significance in salvation history (Rom. 3: 1; *Römer* 77/81). This is not the case, because of the promises and of God's faithfulness. But it is not simply that God has remained faithful to the covenant: 'In a most remarkable way the problem is extended to every human being and to God's trial with the whole world. This makes sense only if the faithfulness of God to Israel is a special instance of his faithfulness to all creation' (77/81 f.). Thus, salvation means the victory of God over the world contending with him (v. 4*b*). The metaphor here is a legal one: God wins the legal trial with the world (*Prozeß*, cf. *Streit*, *Auseinandersetzung*; *Römer* 76 f./81 f., 80/84, 89/95, 148/156).[79] Israel is no longer mentioned but is included in this statement. The answer to the initial question is that 'the promises given to Israel are fulfilled in no other way than elsewhere and everywhere' (77/82). Verse 4 is not a rhetorical digression but 'the key to the [ET: 'a'] solution of the problem [of God's faithfulness and Israel's unfaithfulness] and beyond that of Paul's message of justification, which applies equally to Jews and Gentiles and which gives the epistle its unity' (ibid.).

In this interpretation *πᾶς ἄνθρωπος* in v. 4 is understood to refer, literally and with intention, to all people. However, in context, this is unlikely. Paul does not appear to have left the problem of the Jews, which he has been discussing since at least 2: 12. Käsemann does not discuss the possibility that these verses are directed to the Jews alone.[80] The mere presence of *πᾶς ἄνθρωπος* does not necessarily indicate a break: rather the choice of Ps. 115: 2 LXX is probably due to the apposite way it complements Paul's own statement (*γινέσθω δὲ ὁ θεὸς ἀληθής*). The point is not that Paul consciously widens the scope of the covenant to all, but that God's truthfulness is upheld even though this means that all people are consigned to the judgement of v. 4*a*.

A further problem with Käsemann's interpretation is that it necessitates taking 3: 1–4 as speaking of the problem of Israel; only then can be said that Paul *extends* his critique to all people. However, there is a break in the argument between vv. 2 and

[79] This motif is particularly emphasized by Müller (1964) and goes back to Luther (1515/16: 68).

[80] So Cranfield 1975: 136 ff. ('Jewish man is no exception'); Hall 1983.

3. In v. 2 Paul begins to answer the question raised in v. 1, but, by the use of 'entrusted' (ἐπιστεύθησαν) in his answer, he triggers off a new question concerning faithfulness (πίστις). The question of the advantage of the Jews is put in abeyance, and the issue is now whether the unfaithfulness (ἀπιστία) of Israel has not nullified God's faithfulness (πίστις). From v. 3 to v. 8 the primary concern is not the problem of Israel but whether Paul's beliefs do not have unacceptable implications for his doctrine of God. Käsemann's interpretation, while acknowledging this last point, emphasizes the secondary element in the argument (the sinfulness of Israel, and then of all people).[81] Thus, the passage is much more limited in scope than Käsemann claims. It does not raise in a preliminary way the doctrine of the justification of the ungodly, nor does it give the key to the problem of Israel.

The theme of the extension of God's faithfulness from the sphere of the covenant to that of the world is dealt with again in Käsemann's article on **Rom. 3: 24–6** of 1950/1.[82] This article is primarily concerned with the hypothesis that vv. 24–26*a*[83] are a fragment of pre-Pauline tradition which Paul has interpreted by the addition of v. 26*bc*. In 1933 Käsemann commented more generally that 3: 25 and 5: 9 were clearly traditional (*Leib* 176 n. 6). Bultmann first made the suggestion that 3: 24–6 is a traditional fragment[84] on the grounds that the specifically Pauline phrases (δωρεὰν τῇ αὐτοῦ χάριτι and διὰ πίστεως) can be identified and, when removed, leave a traditional fragment, the theology of which is pre-Pauline (ἱλαστήριον is found only here in Paul; αἷμα and not σταυρός is used to speak of Christ's death; the divine δικαιοσύνη here demands expiation). Käsemann adds the following points:

1. The sentence structure begun in v. 23 is not continued in v. 24, the emphasized πάντες of v. 23 being left without a counterpart (*EVB* i. 96; *Römer* 89/95).

2. In addition to the words noted above, πάρεσις, προγεγονότα ἁμαρτήματα, προτίθεσθαι in the sense of 'to demonstrate,

[81] Cf. Cranfield 1975: 136 ff., Hall 1983, and Wilckens 1978: 161–3 on the chain of thought.

[82] 'Zum Verständnis von Römer 3, 24–26', *EVB* i. 96–100.

[83] When Käsemann refers to v. 26*a*, he means as far as πρὸς τὴν ἔνδειξιν κτλ.

[84] Bultmann 1936: 12; 1951: 46.

show openly', and ἀπολύτρωσις as the designation of an already effected redemption, are, at the least, not characteristic of Paul (*EVB* i. 96).

3. The 'overladen style' of these verses, with their prepositional connectives, is reminiscent of the deutero-Pauline epistles and originates in the hymnic tradition of the Near East (ibid.).[85]

4. The decisive point is the 'curious fact of the formal parallelism and the material digression of v. 25*b* and v. 26*a*' (98). The salvation event is proclaimed by both but from different points of view. Following Jülicher,[86] there is a conflict with regard to God's attitude to the past between 1: 18–3: 20 which speaks of God's wrath and v. 25*b*–26*a* which speaks of God's forbearance (ἀνοχή) and 'remission of sentence', and, therefore, forgiveness (πάρεσις).[87] Further, v. 25*b* does not simply describe God's action in the past in contrast to the present as in v. 26*a*; v. 25 describes the change of aeons (*EVB* i. 99; *Römer* 92/98, 94/100).

5. The theology of v. 25*b*, with its joining together of righteousness, forgiveness, and patience, is Jewish-Christian. 'Righteousness' means faithfulness to the covenant and is therefore almost synonymous with goodness and mercy (*EVB* i. 98, *Römer* 93/99 f.). The central idea is the renewed covenant. The ἱλαστήριον, the means of atonement, breaks the complex of infringements of covenant duty (*EVB* i. 99). However, for Paul 'God's righteousness' did not mean the restoration of the old covenant but the founding of a new covenant which is antithetical to the old. The salvation event is not a final dealing with old sins but the justification of the ungodly and the obedience of faith (100). To the Jewish-Christian *sola gratia*, Paul adds *sola fide*, both in v. 26*b* and in the disruptive[88] insertion of διὰ πίστεως in v. 25*a*. Verse 26*b* is a liturgical conclusion, formulated by Paul, which reflects the parallel clauses in vv. 25*b* and 26*a*, along the lines of the traditional 'who is alive' and 'who makes alive'.[89]

[85] Käsemann refers to Percy 1946: 191, 213.

[86] Jülicher 1908/1917: 18.

[87] So Lietzmann 1906/1933: 51; cf. Kümmel 1952: 157.

[88] Ljungman objects that Käsemann does not substantiate this point (1964: 46 n. 1).

[89] Käsemann's proposal of pre-Pauline tradition in Rom. 3: 24–26*a* has met with widespread approval (Jeremias 1949: 197–9 and Kümmel 1952: 164 had already

Thus, while the Jewish-Christian tradition regards Jesus' death as leading to the renewal of the covenant, Paul no longer speaks of the people of God but of individuals, and, therefore, universally (ibid.). Indirectly this means that God's 'covenant faithfulness' has become 'faithfulness to creation' (*Römer* 95/101).

However, Kertelge has argued decisively against this view: Paul's concern is not with 'faithfulness to creation', but with all sinners: 'It [God's righteousness] proves its eschatological, creative powerfulness precisely in declaring the sinner righteous—and indeed, out of grace.'[90] The abbreviated argument that Paul speaks of individuals and therefore universalistically builds a very large conclusion on very little evidence. These key passages do not confirm the idea of faithfulness to creation as an important motif in Paul's theology.[91] The theme is rather to be understood as part of Käsemann's rejection of Bultmann's exclusive orientation to the individual.

followed Bultmann). Käsemann's arguments have been accepted by, among others, Schulz 1959: 178; Hunter 1961: 120–2; Wegenast 1962: 76–9; Müller 1964: 110 f.; Stuhlmacher 1965: 88–91, but see below; Schille 1965: 60; Schweizer 1966: 255; Reumann 1966: 432–52; Zeller 1968: 51–75 (though he wants to include v. 26 as a whole); Pluta 1969: 43 (who regards διὰ πίστεως as pre-Pauline); Lührmann 1970: 437; Thyen 1970: 163 f.; and Ziesler 1972: 170. The hypothesis has been modified by Lohse to extend only to vv. 25–26*a* on the grounds that ἐν Χριστῷ Ἰησοῦ in v. 24 cannot be regarded as traditional but is characteristically Pauline, and v. 25 begins with the relative pronoun ὅν, which is typical for the beginning of traditional material (1955/1963: 149–54; followed by Conzelmann 1968: 38 f.; Schrage 1969: 77; Koch 1971: 157; Delling 1972: 12 f. who takes v. 25*a* alone as pre-Pauline; Stuhlmacher, who now takes this view in his review of recent interpretation of this passage, 1975: 315–33, and Meyer 1983). Wright suggests that the hypothesis is unnecessary here, even though he argues that 1: 2–4 could be such a fragment (1980: 55, 74). Fitzer 1966: 161–83 and Talbert 1966: 287–96 argue for a post-Pauline interpolation consisting of v. 25*b* and vv. 25 f. respectively. Finally, Kuss 1957/1963: 161; Lyonnet 1957; Cambier 1967: 73 f.; Young 1974: 23–32, Cranfield 1975: 200 n. 1, and Schlier 1977: 107 n. 8 have rejected the suggestion of pre-Pauline tradition here. However, there has been no full discussion of Käsemann's case by these scholars. Young considers the *hapax legomena* in detail but not Käsemann's other and more important points.

[90] Kertelge 1967: 108.

[91] Apart from being taken up by his pupils Müller and Stuhlmacher, Käsemann's hypothesis has not been well received (Güttgemanns 1967: 83 f.; Kertelge 1967: 70; Klein 1976: 751; Lohse 1973*a*: 224; Wilckens 1978: 204 f.; Zeller 1973: 184 n. 213). Wright criticizes an overemphasis on the idea of God the creator (1980: 83).

'God's righteousness' as the centre of Käsemann's interpretation of Paul's theology

As Käsemann regards the doctrine of justification as the centre of Paul's theology and concentrates his discussion of this doctrine on the motif of 'God's righteousness', his interpretation of this motif is naturally critical to his understanding of Paul's theology as a whole. As has been seen, this theme is interpreted with the aid of the gift–power dialectic which Käsemann believes is characteristic of Paul's theology.[92] However, the gift–power (gift–Giver) theme is not new in Käsemann's work; rather, as Chapter 2 showed, it is a key to Käsemann's pre-1950 work on the participatory themes of Paul's theology. The spirit is understood by Paul as the sacramental gift which conveys participation in the Giver; the eucharistic 'body' issues in the presence of the lord as saviour or judge; a charisma is a gift which is realized in service, it is the means by which Christ grasps the 'piece of world' which the Christian is. Further, Käsemann had begun the process of interpreting the various categories of Paul's thought in the light of each in the pre-1950 period. He now takes a second major step by using the gift–power conceptuality to interpret the motif of 'God's righteousness' and, thus, the doctrine of justification. In this way the juridical doctrine of justification is interpreted by means of a conceptuality first applied to the study of Paul's participatory themes.

This procedure has three very important consequences. Firstly, it continues the process of overcoming the divisions within Paul's theology which were posited by late nineteenth- and early twentieth-century exegesis, thereby providing the key to Käsemann's unified view of Paul's theology. Käsemann makes this point explicitly when discussing the tensions between 'gift' and 'power' in the interpretation of God's righteousness: 'our particular problem is to identify the unified centre [*einheitliche Mitte*] from which he [Paul] managed to combine present and future eschatology, "declare righteous" and "make righteous", gift and service, freedom and

[92] Maurer notes that the dialectic of Christ as gift of grace and as sphere of power is the *cantus firmus* of the Romans commentary (1974: 193).

obedience, forensic, sacramental and ethical approaches' (*EVB* ii. 184/171 f., ET modified).[93]

This list of themes for which Käsemann posits the 'unified centre' of the power character of the gift contains (1) the dialectically related pairs through which Käsemann interprets Paul's theology (present and future eschatology, gift and service, freedom and obedience), (2) a problem of interpretation which has particular doctrinal significance for the traditions of the Reformation (declare righteous, make righteous), and (3) the conceptual divisions in Paul's thought posited by historical-critical exegesis (forensic, sacramental, and ethical approaches). Thus, even in his programmatic statement, Käsemann combines and interrelates exegetical and theological questions. Further, he explicitly raises the question of the continuing theological relevance of understanding and maintaining this Pauline dialectic: 'Only after we have answered this question [of the unified centre of Paul's theology] with the necessary clarity can we say whether it is possible and necessary for us to pursue this same dialectic in our day' (*EVB* i. 184/172, ET modified). In addition, at the same time as addressing problems within his own doctrinal tradition, Käsemann's view of 'God's righteousness' is also of ecumenical significance because he rejects the 'either–or' of traditional Protestant and Catholic interpretation.[94] Thus, he accommodates both justification and sanctification, 'declare righteous' and 'make righteous'.

Secondly, Käsemann relates the gift–power dialectic to Paul's war on two fronts against legalism and enthusiasm (cf. p. 145 above). In summary, the gift aspect confronts the legalism which thinks that it can earn salvation; the power aspect, expressed in the claim of the gospel, confronts enthusiasm in its security that salvation has already been experienced in full and has been guaranteed for the future.

Thirdly, Käsemann's decision to interpret God's righteousness by means of the conceptuality first applied to the

[93] Although Käsemann does not provide a full statement of this goal in the Romans commentary, the programme remains the same and the individual dialectical pairs are discussed (sacrament and ethics, 164/172, 174/183; sacrament and justification, 174/182; sacrament and faith, 350/362; and juridico-ethical and sacramental, dogmatic and hortatory lines of thought, 388/402).

[94] Watson 1983: 385.

understanding of Paul's participatory themes enables him to carry over his earlier work on these themes into his post-1960 work which centres on the juridical themes, especially justification. If, in *Leib und Leib Christi*, Käsemann's view of Paul was centred on *ἐν Χριστῷ* and other participatory themes, but these were interpreted, at least in one place, in the light of the doctrine of justification, in the post-1960 work, the centre is the doctrine of justification, interpreted in the light of the participation themes and of Paul's 'apocalyptic'. By this means Käsemann can affirm both the Lutheran tradition on the centrality of justification and what he has learnt from the history-of-religions school (and Catholic interpretation) on the importance of spirit and sacrament in Paul. This is a very unusual approach, and has not been widely or fully understood.[95] Finally, the practice of allowing the various sides of Paul's theology to interpret each other is the fundamental reason for the phenomenon of the fluidity of the terms which Käsemann uses in his interpretation. If 'apocalyptic' and justification, or justification and participation, and so on, mutually interpret each other, the resultant picture gains in overall cohesiveness but the various terms and themes merge into each other. This procedure gives Käsemann's interpretation its quality as a piece of sustained, coherent, systematic thought; at the same time, the danger of imposing a theological construct on Pauline texts and phrases becomes correspondingly greater. In the case of interpreting the phrase *δικαιοσύνη θεοῦ*, it has been seen that Käsemann's views are not strongly supported by his exegesis.

[95] Riches writes perceptively (but without noting the key role of the participatory themes) that what Käsemann 'does is to open up the problems of the relation between Pauline eschatology on the one hand and ethics and justification on the other, by a re-examination of the notion of justification' (1976: 561). Sanders sees the problem: 'Käsemann takes "the justification of the ungodly" to be the core of "righteousness by faith", he then defines "the justification of the ungodly" as being given in the presence and lordship of Christ—and these are cosmic. I find myself essentially in agreement that Paul's participationist and cosmic language should define the righteousness by faith terminology, and not vice versa—if this is what Käsemann means. But then one wonders why the phrase "righteousness by faith" is taken to indicate the key concept in Paul's soteriology. Is it any more than agreement with Lutheran tradition?' (1977: 438 n. 41) The solution to this conundrum lies in Käsemann's practice of interpreting the themes in the light of each other, or, put biographically, in the relationship between his earlier and later work.

THE JUSTIFICATION OF THE UNGODLY AND THE RIGHTEOUSNESS OF FAITH

As has been seen, the basic contrast which Käsemann finds in Paul's theology is between the righteousness of works and the righteousness of faith. Paul's doctrine of justification is a 'polemical doctrine' (*Kampfeslehre*) because it is a rejection of the Jewish doctrine of justification through works of the law. Here Käsemann is in full agreement with Bultmann[96] and his criticism of Wrede and Schweitzer. The latter were correct to see that Paul's doctrine of justification was formed in a polemical situation but they drew the wrong conclusions that its polemical nature was of importance only in its specific historical context,[97] or that it is a secondary element which cannot be derived from Paul's central concerns[98] (*PP* 125 f./70 f., *Römer* 96/102, 116/123). On the contrary, Paul's theology is polemical at its very centre, and this ought to be carried over into the interpretation of Paul today (ibid.).[99]

Paul's theology is polemical at a fundamental level because it attacks the *homo religiosus* (pp. 181 f. above). Here again Paul is interpreting and deepening a pre-Pauline view. Two pre-Pauline fragments, Rom. 3: 24–26a and 4: 25 (*Römer* 121 f./128 f.), speak of the justification of the sinner (93/99, or of the

[96] Bultmann 1924*a*: 198 n. 11 and 1933*a*: 278 f. For Käsemann's debate with Stendahl, see pp. 222 ff. below.

[97] The doctrine of justification 'is Paul's polemical doctrine which is only understandable from his debate with Judaism and Jewish Christianity and only intended for this purpose'. To this extent, it is certainly historically important and characteristic of Paul (Wrede 1904: 67).

[98] The doctrine of freedom from the law was not developed out of Paul's central concern, the 'mystical' doctrine of redemption through the being-in-Christ, and is therefore a 'subsidiary crater, which formed within the rim of the main crater' (Schweitzer 1930: 224 f.). Cf. more recently Strecker 1976, and his pupil Schnelle 1982.

[99] This view leads Käsemann to protest in the strongest terms against interpretations of Paul which reduce him to a non-controversial figure within the history of the NT period (rev. of F. Amiot, *Die Theologie des Heiligen Paulus* (1962), *ThLZ* 90 (1965), 355) or to a figure who remains a prisoner of Rome and of academic industry (rev. of *Studiorum Paulinorum Congressus Internationalis Catholicus* (1963), *ThLZ* 91 (1966), 186). Cf. also the frequent, strident, bibliographical asides in the Romans commentary. On the polemical character of Käsemann's view of Paul, see Jewett 1980 and Haufe 1971.

ungodly,[100] 122/129). Paul radicalizes the tradition by breaking the limitations of a covenant theology: he specifically proclaims the justification of those who have no 'merit' or 'achievement'. These are the 'ungodly', a term which is used by Käsemann in this particular sense and which has nothing to do with an absence of religion or impiety in a conventional sense: 'It is the predicate of the [ET: 'a'] person who has to do radically with his Creator and who learns that he must be created anew in grace. He has nothing to which to appeal and will produce nothing that might prejudice God's creative act. He is the man who has no ground of boasting before God' (106/112). Käsemann sums up his view of this theme, its significance for Paul's theology, and his opposition to certain trends in interpretation in the following important passage which introduces his discussion of 3: 27–31:

> Paul's proclamation of justification is in fact a polemical doctrine.[101] We are not to weaken this element . . . It is the inalienable spearhead of justification because it attacks the *homo religiosus* and only in so doing preserves the sense of the *justificatio impiorum*. Otherwise the Christian message of grace will become a form of religion[102] and Paul's doctrine of justification will be reduced, as happens throughout modern exposition, to a proclamation of salvation which speaks profoundly of the love of God and therefore does not set the pious person before his Judge, no matter how much it talks about future judgement. Grace is simultaneously judgement because it fundamentally sets man, even in his factual piety [ET: 'even a religious person'], in the place of the godless. This is the criterion of Paul's theology and the consequence of his christology. (96/102, ET modified)

The two most important verses for this interpretation are 3: 28 and 4: 5b. The former is regarded as a doctrinal statement (*λογιζόμεθα γὰρ*, ibid.), and the interpretation turns on the view that *χωρὶς ἔργων νόμου* means without the attempt at

[100] It is not absolutely clear at this point whether Käsemann is discussing 4: 25 as tradition or as taken up by Paul. 'Sinner' would certainly be more appropriate as an interpretation of the tradition as it speaks of Christ being given up *διὰ τὰ παραπτώματα ἡμῶν*.

[101] Not 'Paul's doctrine of justification is in fact a militant one' (ET), which makes the doctrine of justification both the subject and predicate of the next sentence but one.

[102] Käsemann here takes up Lutheran and Barthian themes: *redigi ad nihilum*; the coincidence of grace and judgement; and the criticism of 'religion'.

self-justification by doing works of the law. This view is improbable because the works concerned are 'covenant works'[103] and in v. 29 Paul continues by specifically rejecting the idea that the Jews are in a privileged position. Again, as in 1: 18–3: 20, Paul is concerned with the notion of the Jews' supposed privilege and not with the righteousness of works.

In 4: 5*b* Paul speaks explicitly of the God who justifies the ungodly (cf. also 5: 6). This phrase is based on liturgical predications of God and, therefore, gives a basic characterization of divine action (*Römer* 105/111). However, while Paul contrasts faith and works here, the point of the contrast is not the striving for achievement or the attempt at self-justification as opposed to the free gift of faith. Paul is concerned to show that righteousness by faith is a gift to all who believe (with particular reference to the key example of Abraham), and the point of 4: 4 f. is to underline its character as gift, not to indicate the nature of the righteousness of works.[104] Nor is the reference to the 'godless' or 'impious' to be taken in Käsemann's 'positive' sense (a human being with no ground of boasting before God), despite the parallel between 'not working' and faith/'being righteoused'. As Abraham's sin is not in view, Wilckens's suggestion that Paul refers to Abraham as 'the one who has in fact sinned' is ruled out.[105] It is more likely that 'the one who believes in him who righteouses the ungodly' does not refer specifically to Abraham but to sinners in general, and that as such it anticipates the next verses in which Paul quotes Ps. 32: 1 with its references to sinfulness.[106] Schlier's conclusion is certainly correct: the theme of the justification of the ungodly is more important to Käsemann than to Paul.[107]

Käsemann's essay on 'God's righteousness' was criticized on the grounds that it made the concept of faith redundant.[108]

[103] On works as covenant works, and circumcision as the 'badge' of belonging to the Jewish religion, see Dunn 1983: 107–10.

[104] Cf. Sanders 1983: 34 f.

[105] Wilckens 1978: 263.

[106] Sanday and Headlam 1895/1902: 101. For the ungodly as those who have sinned, cf. Wilckens 1969: 94 f., and 104 f.

[107] Schlier 1977: 125 n. 16.

[108] Conzelmann states that the theme of faith scarcely appears in the essay, and not at all in connection with righteousness (1966*a*: 180). In fact the theme of faith does appear (*EVB* ii. 183/170, 189/177, 190/178, 192/180) though not in the summarizing statements (God's righteousness is his lordship over the world which

Consequently, he is careful to emphasize the importance of faith in the Romans commentary (e.g., in 3: 25, 26*c*; *Römer* 95/101; and the use of 'the righteousness of faith' in the headings to the sections 3: 21–4: 25 and 5: 1–8: 39). Phil. 3: 9 is said to be the key passage for Paul's doctrine of justification in which God's righteousness is directly defined as 'righteousness from God' and is a gift. With reference to Rom. 3: 22 he says: 'Whatever else God's eschatological righteousness may be, at any rate it is a gift that comes to a man *διὰ πίστεως*' (88/94). Here it needs to be reiterated that Käsemann does not wish to replace the idea of gift with that of power but to speak of the power character of the gift, which is received by faith.[109] Although God's righteousness claims the world, it does so through the faith of the individual who is a 'piece' of that world. Thus, while Käsemann's summarizing statements are perhaps misleading (see n. 108 above) because they do not emphasize or even mention faith, his interpretation has never excluded the notion of faith. This is true even of the essay of 1961 which was intentionally critical of the tradition which tended to speak exclusively of the gift of God's righteousness and, therefore, of faith.

reveals itself eschatologically in Jesus; 192/180; cf. *Römer* 26/29). Koch objects that although Käsemann himself pointed out earlier that *διὰ πίστεως* was added by Paul to the traditional fragment in 3: 25, this is omitted in the 1961 essay (1971: 151 f.). Gäumann criticizes Käsemann at the theological level when he draws a parallel between Käsemann's emphasis on God's power and the *iustitia* of God in which Luther could find no salvation. Käsemann disregards faith, and his use of 'instrument of grace', *nova oboedientia*, and *promissio* is dangerously close to *humilitas* (1967: 147 n. 115). Käsemann replied that these points 'no longer reflect my interpretation but nightmares for which I have neither an explanation nor an answer' (*PP* 138/77). Bornkamm's criticism is more temperate and has some grounding in the historical-critical level of the debate: it is not what Paul shares with apocalyptic that is significant but what is new in Paul, namely, the co-ordination of God's righteousness and faith. Käsemann's view puts the emphasis in the wrong place (1969: 147).

[109] Thus, Jüngel is correct to comment in general that Käsemann's interpretation ought not to be judged by the standards of the research which it precipitated (presumably Müller 1964 and Stuhlmacher 1965) because the latter has probably removed itself further from Käsemann's position than Käsemann wished to remove himself from Bultmann (1968: 77 n. 31).

JUSTIFICATION AS THE SPECIFICALLY PAULINE UNDERSTANDING OF CHRISTOLOGY

Käsemann's interpretation of God's righteousness, and thus of the doctrine of justification, as it has been depicted so far, has been, in a sense, preparatory to his central conviction that the doctrine of justification is the specifically Pauline understanding of christology (*Römer* 21/24). Here he takes up one of Bultmann's formulations and interprets it in line with his own view of Paul's theology.[110] Bultmann interprets this view from within his anthropologically orientated theology: 'Paul's teaching of justification is, it could be said, his real christology, for "to know Christ is to know the benefits he confers" (. . . Melanchthon). The teaching of justification demonstrates forcibly that christology does not consist in speculation on the nature of Christ; that christology is the proclamation of the event of Christ's coming, and that an understanding of the event requires not speculation but self-examination, radical consideration of the nature of one's own new existence.'[111] Käsemann takes up the criticism of a speculative christology but replaces the focus on the new self-understanding of the individual with the themes of the justification of the ungodly, the lordship of Christ, and the double-fronted attack on legalism and enthusiasm.

Käsemann's starting-point is an explicitly theological[112] theme, the theology of the cross in the tradition of Luther: *crux sola est nostra theologia* (*PP* 64/34). Although Käsemann does not make the point in detail, Luther himself argued for a close connection between Paul's soteriology and his christology:

[110] Lührmann is correct to point out that the idea that justification is Paul's true christology is open to many interpretations, and indeed has produced a variety of interpretations within the Bultmann school. In addition to the views of Bultmann and Käsemann, he notes that Conzelmann interprets it in terms of a dialectical anthropology. For Lührmann himself the distinctive mark of Paul's contribution was in removing faith from its orientation to the law in Judaism and making christology the key for credal confession and experience (Lührmann 1976: 351, 363).

[111] Bultmann 1933*a*: 279.

[112] The translation of *sachlich* with 'factual' in the ET of *PP* is particularly misleading ('With this varying approach the theological [ET: 'factual'] emphasis has changed as well.' 62/33; cf. 151/86, 167/95, 'practical' 242/141; 'facts' for *Sache*, 189 f./109, and 'dialectical treatment of the facts' for *Sachdialektik*, 117/65 f.). The translation 'substantially' (158/90) is much better, as it points to the theological subject-matter.

Wherefore they that do deny the divinity of Christ, do lose all Christianity and become altogether Gentiles and Turks. We must learn therefore diligently the article of justification (as I often admonish you). For all the other articles of our faith are comprehended in it: and if that remain sound, then are all the rest sound. *Wherefore when we teach that men are justified by Christ, that Christ is the conqueror of sin, death and the everlasting curse, we witness therewithal that he is by nature God.*[113]

For Käsemann it is the *particula exclusiva*, the insistence on 'through Christ alone, by faith alone' (*allein durch Christus, allein aus Glauben*), which has to be urged against approaches to Paul and Christianity which concentrate on 'philosophy', 'psychology' (i.e., the emphases of German idealism) or 'the history-of-religions' (i.e., merely historical work; 62/33). In particular it is M. Kähler's formulations which Käsemann takes up. The cross is the 'basis' and 'standard' of christology: 'Without the cross no christology, and in christology no single feature which cannot find its justification in the cross.'[114] From this starting-point Käsemann argues that traditional soteriological and christological statements are interpreted by Paul in terms of his doctrine of the justification of the ungodly, and that the content of God's righteousness is the lordship of Christ. While Käsemann's primary debating partner is again Bultmann, he defends his view against a wide variety of theologies.[115]

Käsemann's first point is that the Pauline and deutero-Pauline letters speak technically (the ET omits 'technically') of the cross and the crucified one, rather than merely of his death or his blood.[116] This is particularly clear in the insertion

[113] Luther 1535: 274 (my emphasis), commenting on Gal. 3: 13.

[114] Kähler 1911: 13, cited on *PP* 64/34; cf. Kähler's title: *Das Kreuz: Grund und Maß für die Christologie*.

[115] Thus, as has been seen, justification is not 'past polemics' (Wrede), nor a 'subsidiary crater' (Schweitzer). Further, it is not (1) merely the consequence but the content of the gospel (E. Molland), (2) the shadow of salvation history, (3) the specific application and explanation of eschatology (H. Ridderbos). The theme of Romans is not merely christology (G. Friedrich; *Römer* 21/24), and Paul's message cannot be understood primarily with reference to reconciliation, sacrifice, or as a theology of the facts of redemption.

[116] For this antithesis in Paul, see p. 205 above. However, this does not hold for the deutero-Pauline letters which do speak of Christ's blood (Col. 1: 20, which Käsemann regards as an insertion into a pre-Christian hymn, *EVB* i. 37/152; Eph. 1: 7, 2: 13).

of θανάτου δὲ σταυροῦ into the pre-Pauline hymn in Phil. 2: 8 (ch. 2 n. 88 above; *PP* 67/36).

Another aspect comes to light in Gal. 2: 19, 21, and 3: 13, where Paul interprets Jesus' death as that of a human being under a divine curse which sets him outside of the covenant and negates the way of the law: 'This was evidently important for the apostle and had the deepest possible influence on his understanding of Jesus' death. For Paul, that death incontestably contained the inherent conflict which is a central characteristic of his theology, with its irreconcilable opposition of law and gospel' (68/36). Considering the importance that Käsemann attaches to these verses, it is astonishing that he does not expound at least 3: 13 in more detail,[117] even if this interpretation is well established within this exegetical tradition.[118] Käsemann goes on to combine this theme with that of the Christ who dies in a state of godlessness, outside the area of God's presence (*Gottesferne*; 68 f./36 f.), thus introducing a further nuance to the idea of the 'ungodly'. He acknowledges that this goes beyond the Pauline text to Hebrews and contemporary restatement (ibid.).

As has been seen, Paul's theology of the cross is targeted not only on legalism but also on enthusiasm. Käsemann now employs this argument against modern pietism (*PP* 71 f./38 f.). Paul's theology of the cross divides the world into the two camps of legalism and enthusiasm: 'Everything depends on whether Christian devotion [*Frömmigkeit*], in Kähler's words, finds its foundation and its criterion in the cross right down to everyday life' (72/39).

Käsemann's second major argument is that Paul takes over traditional soteriological and christological material and interprets it in terms of his doctrine of justification. In this way the doctrine of justification is won from the cross, and, conversely, justification is his interpretation of the cross (77/42; the ET is not clear here). The oldest example of one basic motif is 'Christ died for our sins' (1 Cor. 15: 3, with variations

[117] Käsemann does not even distinguish between the direct christological/soteriological theme of 3: 13, and the use of the same theme as a description of Paul's experience, which in turn is a paradigm of Christian experience, in 2: 19 and 21.

[118] e.g., Bultmann 1951: 297; Betz comes to the same conclusion but stresses the numerous problems in this passage and verse (1979: 151).

in Rom. 4: 25, 8: 32; Gal. 1: 4, 2: 20; 2 Cor. 5: 14 f.)[119] In this tradition, love is understood as the 'manifestation of existence for others, displayed in concrete form and with special emphasis on the act of dying' (73/39). However, a more typically Pauline idea is the motif of Christ's dying for the ungodly and sinners (Rom. 5: 6), for Christian brethren (14: 15), and for all (2 Cor. 5: 14). Here 'for us' means both 'for our advantage' and 'in our stead', and emphasizes that we cannot achieve salvation by ourselves. Salvation is a gift (Rom. 3: 24, 5: 6 ff.), an act of the God who is and remains the one who gives life to the dead and calls into existence the things that do not exist (Rom. 4: 17*b*).

At this point Paul's own theology has been reached (74/40). He has taken up traditional statements but has given them new depth by asking 'who God really is and who man really is'. The cross reveals that the 'true God' is the creator who works from nothing, who, since creation, always raises the dead. Correspondingly, with regard to soteriology, the 'true human being' is the sinner who is fundamentally unable to help him- or herself (ibid.); and with regard to christology, the 'true human being' is the one who is intolerable to the 'pious' [ET: 'good'] and can only die for them (130/73; cf. *Römer* 129/138, 203/211, 258/268, 277/287, 307/317). In line with Lutheran tradition, Käsemann interprets the Chalcedonian summary from the perspective of the doctrine of justification, and thus 'christology' does not in the first instance refer to the technical debate about the person of Christ but to the theology of the cross.

Secondly, Käsemann argues that Paul is a true interpreter of Jesus: Paul's gospel of the justification of the ungodly corresponds to the Jesus who disturbed the 'pious' and associated with the religious outcasts (*PP* 130/73; *Römer* 307/317 with particular reference to Mark 2: 17). This understanding of God and of Jesus Christ, which Käsemann finds in the ministry of Jesus and the theology of Paul, is the centre of his understanding of the New Testament and of Christian faith.

With regard to the interpretation of Paul, it has to be

[119] Käsemann does not speak of 'divine sacrifice' (ET) in these passages, but of Christ as 'given up by God' (*Hingabe durch Gott*). As will be seen, he intends to minimize the notion of sacrifice in Paul.

objected that Käsemann's elevation of Rom. 4: 17*b* and suppression of the traditional motifs contained within Paul's letters is arbitrary. 'Christ died for our sins' cannot be translated without remainder into 'human beings are unable to win salvation for themselves'. Important themes of Paul's theology are being interpreted away (on the insufficient grounds that they are traditional) because they are not theologically congenial to Käsemann. Nor can all Paul's soteriological themes be finally reduced to the doctrine of justification. Rather, it is necessary to come to terms with the variety of ways in which Paul speaks of the death of Jesus.[120]

In the Romans commentary Käsemann supports his argument that the doctrine of justification is Paul's true christology by examining the relationship of christological statements to the doctrine of justification in the structure of Romans itself. (Implicitly this is a further argument that Romans is a summary of Paul's theology; see pp. 120–2 above.) The content of the gospel is initially stated by the quoting of a christological traditional fragment in 1: 3–4.[121] It is then called present σωτηρία in 1: 16 and is interpreted 'constitutively'[122] by the theme of the righteousness of faith in the same verse (*Römer* 21/23 f.). Conversely, in 3: 24–6 Paul gives the righteousness of faith a christological basis and connection (89/95). Thus, *contra* Bultmann, Paul's statement

[120] This variety is set out in Theissen 1974*b*. Stuhlmacher objects that Käsemann fails to bring together Jesus' expiatory sacrifice and resurrection, and justification (1973: 23).

[121] Käsemann puts forward the following reasons for this hypothesis. (1) These verses are composed with particular care (antithetical parallelism, the use of the participle, and the Semitic placing of the verb first). (2) Both κατά phrases are pre-Pauline because, in Paul, the flesh/spirit contrast is anthropological, and not, as here, christological. *Περὶ τοῦ υἱοῦ αὐτοῦ* is probably a Pauline anticipation of the traditional *υἱὸς θεοῦ*. *'Εν δυνάμει* is typical of the christological hymn. *Πνεῦμα ἁγιωσύνης* is unexpected, as is the instrumental role of the spirit in the enthronement of Christ as son of God. (3) The christology (the motif of the messianic king, his enthronement, the function of the spirit) is very early and possibly Palestinian (*Römer* 8–11/10–13). The hypothesis of a traditional fragment here has been very widely accepted. Thus, for example, Cranfield, who rejects this hypothesis for 3: 24–6, accepts it here (1975: 57). Wright argues that it could be pre-Pauline, but that Paul endorsed every word of it (1980: 55).

[122] Käsemann's *konstitutiv* does not just mean 'existentially' (Moule 1981: 501), though there is an existential element in the claim of the gospel on the life of the believer; it is related to Käsemann's concern for the substance of the gospel which determines all other parts of Paul's theology. It this way *konstitutiv* borders on *sachlich*.

about justification is 'on no account to be rendered anthropologically independent by a doctrine of faith' (ibid.). (At this critical point the ET renders *Glaubenslehre* as 'a religious doctrine', which makes Käsemann's already cryptic reference to Bultmann's theology disappear.) Justification is and remains applied christology and only thus remains gospel (89 f./96). Further, in 4: 25 christological tradition is interpreted in terms of justification. This argument from the structure of Romans is much stronger than Käsemann's view of Paul's interpretation of the traditional soteriological motifs: faith, which is mentioned repeatedly in 1: 16 f. and 3: 21–6, cannot be separated from its christological object which is spoken of in 1: 3 f. and 3: 21–6.

Finally, Käsemann argues against some other important modern approaches to Paul's soteriology, discussing views which emphasize the themes of sacrifice, vicarious death, redemption, and reconciliation, and the question of the relationship of Christ's death and resurrection. With regard to the first four themes, he again argues that Paul takes up these motifs from the tradition, does not assign great importance to them, but uses them to proclaim the doctrine of the justification of the ungodly. The notion of sacrifice occurs in traditional statements (Rom. 3: 25; 1 Cor. 5: 7, 10: 18 ff.) or where the christological overtones are not dominant (Rom. 12: 1; 15: 16; Phil. 2: 17; *PP* 78 f./42 f.). It is only the idea of representation (*Stellvertretung*; ET: 'vicariousness') which is christologically important. Gal. 3: 13 and 2 Cor. 5: 21 give no support for theories of vicariously borne punishment as they are concerned with the deep ignominy of the incarnation which brought salvation without our aid (79/43).

The idea of reconciliation is present, but cultic notions are to be minimized. Reconciliation, a subject to which Käsemann devoted a short study,[123] means the ending of enmity between the world and God, and starts with individuals and the church. Again Paul subordinates this motif to that of

[123] 'Erwägungen zum Stichwort "Versöhnungslehre im Neuen Testament"', in E. Dinkler (ed.), *Zeit und Geschichte* (Tübingen, 1964), 47–59; ET in J. M. Robinson (ed.), *The Future of our Religious Past* (London, 1971), 4–64. This paper was first given at an ecumenical consultation of NT scholars in Montreal in 1963, and was then published in the Festschrift for Bultmann's eightieth birthday.

justification (80/43 f.; 'Versöhnung' 49/52, 57/63). Thus, in Rom. 5:9–11, Paul introduces the theme to 'heighten to the greatest possible degree the concept of the *justificatio impiorum*, namely, by the assertion of the *justificatio inimicorum*' ('Versöhnung' 49/52; cf. *Römer* 130/138). The most important passage, 2 Cor. 5: 19–21, is a liturgical fragment.[124] Käsemann concludes that these verses were of less importance to Paul than to the tradition, that they remain soteriologically orientated, and that they do not make a contribution to christology itself ('Versöhnung' 53/57, 56 f./61). His approach is to minimize Paul's cultic imagery by arguing that it is transposed into eschatological statements. The eschatological is not a mere variant of the cultic, it is the shattering of it (54/58; cf. below on Rom. 12: 1 f.). There is a strong anti-Catholic slant in Käsemann's arguments here.[125]

With regard to the relationship between cross and resurrection, Käsemann argues passionately against theologies, ancient and modern, which centre on the resurrection, and which, by so doing, in his view, bypass the cross. The argument here is almost entirely theological. The prototype for these theologies is that of the opponents at Corinth who believed that they had already experienced the resurrection. For Käsemann, the resurrection is not itself the centre of Paul's (and of Christian) theology:[126] the slogan 'through cross to crown' does not

[124] Käsemann makes the following points. The style is marked by hymnic solemnity, participial predicates, a transitional ὡς, and a ὅτι-recitative introducing a quotation. The theology is not Pauline. The idea of God not reckoning sins is reminiscent of the hymnic fragment in Rom. 3: 25. The ὑπὲρ Χριστοῦ in v. 20*ab* is said to refer to the continuing work of the earthly Jesus which the exalted Christ is not capable of doing, and the Pauline 'in Christ' is replaced by 'for Christ'. (However, this point depends on an unacceptable separation of v. 20 from v. 19 with its typically Pauline ἐν Χριστῷ which is to be taken instrumentally.) In addition, Käsemann argues that there is a tension between the reconciliation of Christians in v. 18 and of the world in vv. 19 f. Paul is not given to reflecting on the sinlessness of Christ (v. 21) elsewhere. The verses are Jewish Christian in milieu, certainly contain traditional motifs, and are probably a hymnic fragment ('Versöhnung' 49 f./52 f.).

[125] Käsemann's cavalier treatment of the theme of reconciliation in Paul provoked a strong response from those to whom this theme is more theologically congenial and who could point out that, as Paul himself edited the pre-Pauline fragments he chose to quote in Rom. and 2 Cor., the theme must have a greater importance for Paul than Käsemann allows (Goppelt 1968, Fitzmyer 1975, Marshall 1978, Stuhlmacher 1979, Martin 1981: 71–9).

[126] Although Käsemann is critical of a general tendency in modern pietistic theology here, he has W. Künneth's *Theologie der Auferstehung* (1933/1951) particularly in his sights.

reckon with the points that the cross is 'the signature of the risen one', and that the name of the crucified one is inalienable (*PP* 102/56). At the same time, the cross is not to be relativized by being included within a chain of events (pre-existence, incarnation, exaltation, second coming), as in fact happens in the 'theology of the facts of redemption'. This approach not only denies that the cross alone is the real, or even the sole, theme of Paul's (and Christian) theology[127] (85/47), it also breaks the connection between the cross and the word.[128] 'The cross helps no one who does not hear the word of the cross and ground his faith on that' (91/50). Further, this approach distracts from the heart of Christianity and what is distinctive about it. This is to be found in the proclamation 'Jesus is lord' which in turn requires further definition: 'the sign [ET: 'token'] which distinguishes his [Christ's] lordship from the lordship of other religious founders is undoubtedly the cross and the cross alone. If theology is to make unique and unmistakable assertions about Jesus, everything it says must be related to the cross' (98/54). Paul's gospel circles around the attempt to bring out the saving significance of his cross: 'It is a theology of the Word because it is only through the word of the cross that Jesus' death remains present, remains grace, remains promise and obligation [ET: 'covenant']; and it is the work of the one who is risen to let this Word manifest itself in preaching, in the sacraments and in the Christian life' (106/59). Here the resurrection is an aspect of the theology of the cross, and not vice versa. Christ's lordship is the lordship of the crucified one who continues to be present in the word, the sacraments, and discipleship.

JUSTIFICATION AND SALVATION HISTORY

In 1963 K. Stendahl published his now celebrated article 'The Apostle Paul and the Introspective Conscience of the West', in

[127] With the claim that the cross is the sole theme of Paul's theology, provocation spills over into exaggeration; cf. 'the central and in a sense the only theme of Christian theology' (*PP* 87/48).

[128] *Contra* Künneth, who argues that 'the facts alone have a fateful and destiny-determining quality.' (Künneth 1966: 38, quoted in *PP* 91 n. 31/50 n. 31) Künneth's view also reintroduces objectified language about God into theology.

which he argues that Paul's view of the law is not determined by his failure to keep it in practice and hence a bad conscience. Rather, Paul is concerned with the place of the Gentiles in the church and in God's plan, and with the area of the relationships between Jews and Gentiles, Jewish Christians and Gentile Christians.[129] Käsemann responded in 1969,[130] arguing that for him the issue here is the fundamental question for the interpretation of Paul: is justification or salvation history the centre of Paul's theology (*PP* 119/66; cf. *Römer* 245/255)? It is fundamental because, if the latter is correct, this amounts to a denial of the Reformation interpretation of Paul and finally of the Reformation itself (*PP* 125/70). The interpretation of scripture via the concept of salvation history strengthens the authority of the church:

> To put it bluntly: with salvation history one is always on the safe side. For it allows us to think in terms of a development which, in spite of many false starts and many needful corrections, leads to growing understanding and ultimately to the goal which the church has before it, a goal whose outline is already to be traced in the church itself. (112/62 f.; cf. 'the security of a guaranteed salvation history', *VF* 4 (1949/50), 207)

Thus, for Käsemann, an interpretation of Paul which centres on salvation history is immediately suspect. He associates such a view with, on the one hand, the ('idealistic') notion of an immanent development within history, and, on the other, with a ('Catholic') theory of church history. Consequently, any real debate with Stendahl is excluded from the outset because Käsemann does not take up Stendahl's concerns.[131]

In addition there are other factors lying under the surface of this debate. Käsemann believes that the Reformation heritage

[129] Stendahl 1963: 84.

[130] 'Rechtfertigung und Heilsgeschichte im Römerbrief' (*PP* 108–39/60–78).

[131] Stendahl responded by showing that Käsemann had not understood his position: he did not argue that the doctrine of justification grew out of the struggle with the Judaistic interpretation of the law but that it defends the rights of Gentiles to be full members of the church; nor that it was a polemical doctrine but that it is apologetic. Käsemann forces Stendahl into the dichotomy of justification or salvation history as the central category for the interpretation of Paul, whereas for Stendahl the alternatives are whether the doctrine of justification answers the question about the place of the Gentiles in the Pauline mission and church (Stendahl) or the question of how I can find a gracious God (the Western tradition, going back to Augustine and Luther; Stendahl 1976*b*: 130–3). Cf. Stendahl 1976*a*.

is in danger because it is misunderstood legalistically in the English-speaking world, is eyed with suspicion because of its twentieth-century alliance with existential approaches which seem to end in individualism (a reference to Bultmann, cf. *EVB* ii. 24/15), and because the ecumenical spirit of the age emphasizes what unites and not what divides (*PP* 115/64). To compound the problem, salvation history also manifested itself in a secularized and politicized form in the ideology of the National Socialists under Hitler (114 f./64; cf. *EVB* ii. 210/202 f.). These points indicate that behind the exegetical debate over the place of salvation history in Paul's theology lie a variety of contemporary, theological, ecclesiological, and even socio-political factors. Käsemann's position is set out in outline in the essay of 1969 with an eye to the contemporary theological scene (cf. the radio talk of 1961, 'Paulus und Israel', *EVB* ii. 194–7/182–7) and given more detailed exegetical treatment in the Romans commentary.

Käsemann's argument again concentrates on Romans. It is one of the most important features of his approach to the epistle that he attempts to integrate chapters 9–11 as a whole into his interpretation (and not just 10: 5 ff. on the 'word', as is often the case with Lutheran interpretation of Paul). He states that the history of interpretation shows that the failure of the Reformation to integrate these chapters into the interpretation of Romans led to F. C. Baur's solution of regarding chapters 9–11 as the centre of the epistle, and to Wrede and Schweitzer's view that justification is not the centre of Paul's theology (*Römer* 243 f./253). In summary, Käsemann takes a middle line between those who, following Bultmann, regard salvation history as theologically unimportant,[132] and those who regard it as the dominating theme of Paul's theology[133] (*PP* 76 n. 27). Salvation history is the horizon of Paul's theology but it must be subordinated to the doctrine of justification and be understood in the light of his 'apocalyptic'. 'God's righteousness' is the centre of salvation history which,

[132] e.g., Klein 1963 and 1964. On this trend in scholarship, cf. Morgan 1975: 70, and Achtemeier's comment: Käsemann rescues the concept of salvation history which had been consigned to the dump by one section of German scholarship (1976: 191).

[133] Munck (1954 and 1956), Cullmann (1946/1962 and 1965), and Wilckens (1961, 1964, 1978, 1980, 1982).

in turn, is the world-wide dimension of 'God's righteousness'. Given the centrality of the doctrine of justification, the two themes are not alternatives but have an indissoluble material relation. It is within this framework that the problem of Israel must be discussed (*Römer* 246 f./256).

The key verse for Käsemann's interpretation is Rom. 11: 32 (*EVB* ii. 191/179). 11: 25 ff. is not to be dismissed as purely speculative; if this were the case, it could have followed the introduction to this part of Romans (9: 1–5) immediately. In fact Paul has organized this section of the epistle with great care. He demonstrates the validity and provisional goal of the divine election of Israel (9: 6–29) and Israel's guilt and fall (9: 30–10: 21) before he comes to speak of the mystery of salvation history (11: 1–36). This section of the letter concludes with a hymn of praise (11: 33–6) which corresponds to the introduction (*Römer* 247/257, 288/298, 293/303, especially 304 f./314 f., 308/318). 11: 28–32 is marked by dialectic and unusually careful construction, which show how important this section is for Paul (304/314, with Barrett).[134] In summary, the nature of the justification of the ungodly as the *redigi ad nihilum* is set forth with reference to the 'pious' who are represented by Israel. In v. 32 the fundamental divine law of all history, the dialectic of judgement and mercy, is proclaimed (306/316).[135] The transition from universal judgement (1: 18–3: 20) to universal grace (3: 21 ff.) is repeated in chapters 9–11, and in this verse.

Käsemann's case is that, correctly understood, the theme of salvation history is determined by the doctrine of justification. It is not only the first five or eight chapters of Romans that deal with this doctrine; rather 'the whole epistle stands under the sign that no person is justified by works and that even the pious do not enter the kingdom of God on the basis of piety. What is generally called salvation history usually serves only to rob Paul's basic principle of its severity and to obscure the doctrine of justification . . .' (307/317). The justification of the

[134] Barrett 1957: 224.

[135] Käsemann is here following Barth: 11: 32 is the 'grim unsettling axiom' which is the key and sum of the epistle to the Romans (1922: 407, where Barth adds 'and not only of Romans!'—i.e., of the Christian faith *per se*). Käsemann also notes his agreement with Barrett 1957: 227, and Stuhlmacher 1971: 558, 567 f.).

ungodly, with its dual themes of judgement and new creation, is the only hope both of the world in general and also of Israel (*EVB* ii. 197[136]/187). Paul views both each individual and world history from the standpoint of the doctrine of justification (*Römer* 307/317). Finally, it is only 'apocalyptic' which offers the history-of-religions possibility of extending the doctrine of justification beyond the individual to the salvation historical problem of Israel (ibid.).

The line of argument here is noteworthy. Käsemann proceeds from a theological conviction (that the doctrine of justification determines salvation history, and not vice versa) to a particular problem in Pauline theology (the place of the Jews in the divine plan), and to a history-of-religions argument (only 'apocalyptic' allows justification to be construed in a non-individualistic way). This is particularly surprising given that the problem of Israel is the concrete case on which the theological theme of salvation history is based; at the same time, he decides the history-of-religions question on the basis of this theological conviction.

If the doctrine of justification determines salvation history, then this has particular consequences for the nature of salvation history itself. Firstly, it cannot be conceived of in terms of an 'immanent continuity', a process of development in history.[137] Salvation history is created by God's word which meets with faith and denial (*Glaube*, *Unglaube*), and, consequently, salvation history is always accompanied by its opposite (*Heilsgeschichte*, *Unheilsgeschichte*;[138] *Römer* 48/52, 246/255, 257/266; cf. 42/46). Thus, it is the theme of the antithetical realms of Adam and Christ which determines Käsemann's view of salvation history (*PP* 119 f./67). He finds confirmation for this in the antithetical pairing of Isaac and Ishmael, and Jacob and Esau (*Römer* 258/267; cf. *PP* 123/69).

[136] There would appear to be an error in the German here (*Denn Gott hat nach Röm. 11, 32 alle . . . unter dem Gehorsam* [presumably *Ungehorsam*] *beschlossen, auf daß sich aller in der Aufrichtung des Glaubensgehorsams erbarme.*).

[137] These are constant themes of Käsemann's critique of the legacy of German idealism (e.g., *EVB* ii. 191/179; *PP* 20 f./8 f., 120–5/67–70, 152–5/86–8, 171/98; *Römer* 7/9, 98/104, 110 f./117, 112/118 f., 120/127, 143/151, 246/255, 298/308, 309/319).

[138] *Unheilsgeschichte* presents a problem for Käsemann's translators: cf. 'the history of perdition' (ET of the Romans commentary, 52), 'a history of the absence of salvation' (255), and a 'history of ruin' (266).

If this is the fundamental pattern of salvation history, it can also be divided into the competing 'worlds' of Adam, Abraham, Moses, Christ, and of the resurrection (*PP* 21/8). These are not related in a simple chronological sequence but are the pattern of God's plan of salvation (*Heilsplan*). Käsemann adopts *Heilsplan* as an alternative to *Heilsgeschichte* because the former is not associated in his mind with the ideas of an immanent process within history which human beings can depend on or 'calculate' (*PP* 112 f./63). In his use the term does not imply the notion of predestination but of a particular pattern in history: 'Abraham and Christ are parallel, Moses and Christ antithetic, and Adam and Christ dialectically related to one another' (*Römer* 120/127).

God's promise is the underlying factor in salvation history and runs through it in hidden form, only to be revealed by the gospel at the end-time (121/127). The hiddenness of the promise means that human beings cannot find a false certainty of salvation (*Heilssicherheit*, 112/118 f.) through the medium of salvation history. For the participants themselves salvation history is ambiguous and full of catastrophes. On the model of Abraham in Rom. 4, it is created by God's call to leave the old certainties: 'Sarah's laugh is faith's constant companion' (*PP* 123/69). Käsemann sums up with an oblique reference to the theme of God's lordship: 'For Paul, salvation history is therefore exodus under the sign of the Word and in the face of Sarah's justifiable laughter. Its continuity is paradoxical because it can only endure when God's word, contrary to the earthly realities, creates for itself children and communities which stand under the first beatitude'[139] (124/70). Further, promise and gospel are not to be related as promise and fulfilment, as promise is the anticipation or complement of the gospel (referring to Gal. 3: 8), is materially identical with it, and is another aspect of the revelation of the word (*PP* 158 f./90). Promise is 'the gospel pre-given in salvation history, its historical concealment, whereas the

[139] The ET has 'communities of the pure in spirit' which is a good example of a translation which is technically correct and idiomatic but can be highly misleading: Käsemann is not concerned with the 'pure in spirit' (a phrase which carries moral and religious overtones in the Anglo-Saxon world) but with the promise and claim of God's kingdom (and thus with eschatology; cf. his understanding of the first commandment, p. 27 above).

gospel itself is the promise eschatologically revealed and open to the day' (158/90). The eschatological events of promise and gospel break into real history, designating it as the sphere in which the divine creativity and direction (ET: 'providence') have always ruled. History and eschatology do not coincide but are united through the word of the divine self-address (*Selbstzusage*; ET: 'self-promise'; ibid.). Here Käsemann again takes up the debate about the theological relevance of history which was at the heart of the question of the historical Jesus.[140] The antithesis between history and eschatology is no longer useful to New Testament studies: 'The two are joined in a singular dialectic in which the eschatological view first encroaches on mere history [*Historie*] and what it understands as such, and turns the past into eschatology's dimension in depth . . .' (*PP* 164 f./94). The same dialectic continues after Paul, even if, in the post-Pauline period, eschatology is 'historicized' and salvation history comes to be understood as a process of development. Paul himself is not concerned with the interpretation of history (ET: 'historical interpretation') as such. His concern is with the identity of the God who reveals himself in history, who remains the creator and true to himself (164/95; ET: 'the eternal faithfulness of God'). Käsemann returns again to the question of the doctrine of God which underlies Paul's theology and to criticism of Bultmann: 'The apostle's theology involves a definite salvation-historical perspective. The interpreter who denies this is forced to reduce the Lord of history to the creator of the particular moment and hence to do violence to the Pauline doctrine of God' (*Römer* 21/23, commenting on Rom. 1: 16*c*; cf. 240/255 f.).

If the major emphases in Käsemann's interpretation of salvation history are on discontinuity and paradox, it is also necessary to speak of a certain type of continuity. In general theological terms, Käsemann argues that continuity is created only by God's word (and not by a force immanent within salvation history); consequently, this continuity is designated 'miracle' (*Wunder*). (At the same time, in an implied criticism of pietism, this view assures that the term 'miracle' is not used

[140] See the bibliography in ch. 1 n. 39 above, and Sauter 1976: 87–9.

merely of phenomena which are regarded as 'supernatural'.) At the level of the interpretation of Paul, Käsemann treats the subject of continuity in salvation history through the idea of the remnant. In contrast to Jewish Christianity, the idea of the remnant is not central to Paul's view (*EVB* ii. 190/177, 196/185; *Römer* 95/101, 110/117), though he does employ it in a paradoxical manner in Rom. 9: 27 ff., 11: 4 ff., and 13 ff. (*PP* 153/87; *Römer* 253 f./263). The remnant is as much the result of a divine miracle as the faith of the Gentiles and both are preceded by God's judgement (*Römer* 266/275). 'For Paul the idea of the remnant is inseparably related to that of judgment and therefore to new creation' (290/300). This means that the remnant is the Jewish Christianity which does not trust in works but solely in the faithfulness of the creator to his creation (ibid.). Again the faithfulness of God is the true continuum (246/255, 298/308). The idea of the remnant is not the basis of Paul's ecclesiology but is used by him solely to elucidate the relationship of Jewish Christianity to Judaism and to the new people of God (266/276). This point is taken up again in Käsemann's interpretation of Paul's ecclesiology.

PAUL'S HERMENEUTICS: THE SPIRIT AND THE LETTER

In the essay 'Geist und Buchstabe'[141] Käsemann turns to the subject of Paul's hermeneutics. Against contemporary views that Paul's theology has neither a system, nor a firm methodology, Käsemann argues that, at the least, it has a 'dominating centre' or 'central message'. Consequently, for the first time in Christian history an approach to a theological hermeneutic is developed: the principle of the spirit and the letter determines Paul's use of the Old Testament as a whole. While the explicit textual basis is acknowledged to be slight (the pair γράμμα–πνεῦμα occurs only in Rom. 2: 27–9, 7: 6; 2 Cor. 3: 6), Käsemann offers an interpretation of Rom. 10: 5–13 as a test case for his view (*PP* 237–9/138 f.).

[141] *PP* 237–85/138–66 (cf. 'Probleme' 144 and *Römer* 6–72/74–7, 284–7). Ehler expounds this topic at length and gives an account of its background in Luther's understanding of the task of interpreting scripture (1986: 71–118).

For Käsemann the starting-point for interpretation is the breakdown of the idealistic view in which the letter was understood as an external, contingent, arbitrary factor which cannot be assimilated to the internal, spiritual life. By contrast, in Paul, the letter is one of the functions of the Mosaic law. On the basis of Rom. 2: 25–7, he argues that it is 'the Mosaic Torah in its written documentation, which is claimed by the Jews as saving privilege and which for Paul (as the essential portion and aspect of the Old Testament) is identical with scripture as a whole' (245/143). Thus 'letter' is interchangeable with law in its negative senses and particularly relates to the Old Testament in its fixed form. The term only occurs in eschatological declarations and its background is the two-aeons teaching: 'letter' always relates to the old aeon and 'spirit' to the new (ibid.). In Rom. 7: 6 the letter is what Jewish interpretation and tradition have made out of the divine will: it is the perversion of the divine will into the demand for works, which drives human beings into transgression, hubris, and despair (252/147). As such it has the character of power. In 2 Cor. 3: 6 the letter and the spirit appear as cosmic powers which coincide with the old and new covenants (253 f./147 f., 259/151).

In opposition to the letter is the spirit which is, first, the divine energy, expressed in miracle and ecstasy, and then the power which sets human beings in the presence of the exalted lord on earth, freeing them from striving after their own righteousness. Thus, the spirit is defined christologically (or from the doctrine of justification). This point is of particular importance for Paul's critique of the views of the enthusiasts who understood the spirit as an uncontrolled ecstatic power and a guarantee of salvation. Käsemann restates his basic point and then outlines its programmatic significance: 'The spirit and the letter . . . part company under the insignia of the message of justification. This is the criterion which distinguishes between the spirits and the powers' (261/152; *die Unterscheidung der Geister und Mächte*; ET: 'which divides the principalities and powers'). 'Distinguishing between the spirits' is the catchphrase which Käsemann uses of the theological task of distinguishing between law and gospel, the piety of achievement and the righteousness of faith.[142] The same test is to be applied to contemporary theology which replaces this christological criterion with the ideas of 'the facts of salvation' (*Heilstatsachen*) and a prolongated or restored incarnation (278 f./162). In summary, although Paul did not develop a dogmatic system, his theology is determined by an *articulus stantis et cadentis ecclesiae*—the doctrine of justification—which he applied with the greatest systematic boldness and clarity (274/160).

The idealist interpretation is again incorrect when it regards the spirit and the letter as synonyms for spirit and tradition. Both scripture and tradition can speak the word, and both are the documentation of the spirit. Thus, when Paul interprets the Old Testament, he asks where the voice of the righteousness of faith, and not that of the piety of achievement, is to be heard (271–4/258–60, 285/166, with reference to Rom. 10: 6). In fact Paul can quote Moses as the representative of the righteousness of works in v. 5 and as a witness to the righteousness of faith in v. 6, thus showing that his attitude to the Old Testament and the law is governed by a unique dialectic (*eigenartige Dialektik*; ET: 'curious dialectic', 282/164). In the Old Testament Paul finds law both as the demand for works and as promise. Because he applies this dialectic, based on the doctrine of justification, to the Old Testament as a whole, it is not going too far to speak of a canon within the canon (281 f./164 f.). This treatment of Paul's use of the Old Testament is the exegetical basis of Käsemann's contribution to the question of the nature of the New Testament canon.[143]

[142] On Luther's view that the true task of theology is the spirit-given division of spirit and letter in scripture, see Ehler 1986: 112.

[143] Ehler argues that Käsemann's insistence on justification as the centre of scripture, and on the necessity of 'distinguishing the spirits', arises in the first place from his commitment to the heritage of the Reformation, and only secondly as an interpretation of Paul (1986: 108).

'GOD'S RIGHTEOUSNESS': LORDSHIP, THEOLOGICAL INTERPRETATION, CRITICISM

Käsemann's interpretation of the doctrine of justification in Paul can be summed up in three points. He objects to the view which regards 'God's righteousness' solely as the gift of God, arguing that this is a partial aspect which is not to be divorced from the aspect of God's power. It is essential to speak, not only of God's gift of justification, but also of his entering into the earthly arena. Secondly, the doctrine of justification does not merely concern the individual but God's claim on the world. This is part of Käsemann's 'apocalyptic' reading of Paul. Thirdly, the statement that the doctrine of justification is Paul's true christology must not be expounded only in terms of the gospel addressing human beings as individuals and their consequent new self-understanding, but in terms of the lordship of Christ which is the 'content' of God's righteousness. However, Käsemann does not only debate with Bultmann and his followers. He also criticizes attempts to dislodge the doctrine of justification from the centre of Paul's theology, particularly by those who see salvation history as its central theme.

It has now been shown that the doctrine of justification, approached through the interpretation of the *δικαιοσύνη θεοῦ* motif, is the centre of Käsemann's interpretation of Paul.[144] It

[144] *Contra* Kerr (1981*a* and 1981*b*) who argues that Käsemann's interpretation of Romans (and by implication of Paul) is 'open to review and patient of analysis without much explicit reference to the doctrine of justification', even though Käsemann himself regards justification as the key to Paul (1981*b*, 148). The vague 'without much explicit reference' allows Kerr plenty of room for manœuvre and he does mention the connection between justification and salvation history (1981*a*: 109). However, he is not able to account for Käsemann's highly unified account of Paul's theology without a full acknowledgement of the key place of justification within it. Another incorrect view is given by Osborn: 'The theme of the letter is anticipated in 1: 7, where the love of God is the ground of grace and peace: because God is really our Father and Christ is really our Lord' (1975: 29). This does not take account of Käsemann's criticism of interpretation which focuses on the love of God. By contrast the key role of christology/the doctrine of justification is well brought out by Riches: 'Ultimately then what holds Käsemann's view of Paul's theology together is his insistence on the centrality to it of Paul's christology. The real mark of that christology is the way in which it opens up on to a deeper understanding of both God and man. In it God is revealed as the God who creates *ex nihilo*, who justifies the

is central in the sense that Käsemann believes that all Paul's other important themes are determined by it or reflect it, and thus it gives Paul's theology its coherence. It is also central in the sense that it is the essence of his message. The question therefore remains how the doctrine of justification is related to the theme of the lordship of Christ. In fact, as has already been seen, the two are very closely related. The material covered in this chapter contributes several new aspects to the lordship of Christ construct which underlies Käsemann's interpretation of Paul:

1. The concept of 'boasting' is related to Käsemann's understanding of Paul's anthropology: by the object of their boasting, human beings indicate to whom they belong, i.e., to which lord they belong.

2. Negatively, the works of the law and the assumption of privilege allow human beings to deny God's lordship over them. This is the characteristic of the *homo religiosus*. Instead of submitting to God's lordship, human beings use the law to make a claim over against God. This state can only be overcome by the critical power of the gospel which reduces human beings to nothing (*redigi ad nihilum*) and creates them anew (*creatio ex nihilo*).

3. Positively, God's righteousness is not simply a status conferred on a human being but God himself entering the arena in his gift. (More generally Käsemann can say that we experience God's lordship in his gifts.) God's righteousness is therefore the manifestation of his power (in his gift) to which human beings must become obedient (by faith). Expressed christologically, the lordship of Christ is the content of God's righteousness in that the latter is realized in the proclamation and continuing presence of Christ's lordship. From a different aspect, Paul's teaching on justification is said to give a clear definition of the lordship of Christ. These statements again make it clear that Käsemann is using a construct which carries particular theological themes with it when he speaks of the lordship of Christ. In historical terms, Käsemann understands δικαιοσύνη θεοῦ as a variation of the primitive

godless and who raises the dead; man is revealed as the one who is most deeply at odds with himself in his disobedience to God and who finds freedom and hope in his obedience to his lord Jesus Christ' (1976: 567; cf. Morgan 1975: 69 f.).

Christian proclamation of the kingdom of God. However, this thesis is left at the level of a theological continuity in primitive Christian proclamation and is not related, with the exception of the briefest discussion of 1 Cor. 15: 24, to Paul's (extremely limited)[145] use of the motif of the kingdom of God.

4. God's righteousness is his legal 'right' or claim as creator on his world. Like the previous point which emphasizes the theology pole of the theology–anthropology dialectic, this point continues Käsemann's 'apocalyptic' interpretation of Paul. The cosmic scope of Christ's lordship is again prominent when Käsemann argues that Paul reinterprets the notion of God's 'covenant faithfulness' so that it becomes his 'faithfulness to creation'. The same theme is also present in the discussion of salvation history. Human beings are not isolated individuals but stand in a particular world; they do not exist in isolated segments of time, nor on account of their repeated individual decisions, but within a history. This history is primarily determined by the antithetical realms (and, thus, lordships) of Adam and Christ. These two lordships are not connected in a simple chronological sequence and so there is no immanent law of history. The change of lordship from one to the other is the work of the creator alone, who acts in the justification of the ungodly. The continuity of salvation history is provided by his action and is, therefore, designated 'miracle'.

5. Käsemann's contribution to the debate on the correct approach to Paul's soteriology is the occasion for a closer definition of the theme of the lordship of Christ. While Paul does not divorce the cross and the resurrection of Christ, it is critical for the correct understanding of his theology that the cross should determine the resurrection, and not vice versa. The cross is the 'real' theme of Paul's theology. By this Käsemann means that all aspects of Paul's theology are determined by the doctrine of justification or the *δικαιοσύνη θεοῦ* motif with its dialectic of gift and power, grace and judgement. In the gift and claim of the gospel, the crucified lord continues to be present and to exercise his lordship. The resurrection issues in a theology of the word by which the

[145] Rom. 14: 17; 1 Cor. 4: 20, 6:9–10, 15: 50; cf. 15: 24; Gal. 5: 21; cf. 1 Thess. 2: 12; 2 Thess. 1: 5.

crucified one continues to be present as lord. The lordship of Christ is and remains the lordship of the crucified.

The most prominent feature of Käsemann's understanding of the task of interpretation in the area of Pauline theology covered by this chapter is the extensive use which he makes of the history-of-traditions method, not merely for historical purposes, but for contemporary theological restatement of the Christian faith. Thus, for example, against both Catholic and (conservative, pietistic) Protestant interpretation, he argues that while sacrificial motifs occur in Paul's writings, they are merely traditional and do not express Paul's own theology. (At this point, it is Paul's supposedly radical interpretation of early Christian traditions which is held to be normative for Christian faith.) Similar use is made of the history-of-religions method. Against Bultmann's view of Paul's eschatology, that what is future for the Jews is (also) a present reality for Paul, Käsemann uses the new evidence of the Dead Sea Scrolls to argue that the present–future dialectic is common to the two, as is the idea of *sola gratia*, but that Paul sharpens the *sola gratia* so that it becomes *justificatio impii*. Thus, on these points, what is distinctive about Paul is regarded as theologically important.

However, it is also the case that Käsemann urges the continuing theological significance of some aspects of Paul's theology which the latter shares with Jewish tradition. The power character of the gift, the putative technical term *δικαιοσύνη θεοῦ*, and the cosmic scope of Paul's theology are all derived from its 'apocalyptic' background and are employed against Bultmann's views. Thus, in this debate with Bultmann and others, Käsemann does not consistently take up a particular level of the Pauline text as theologically normative, though there is a strong tendency to find theological relevance in what is distinctively Pauline.

The fundamental significance of Käsemann's decision to interpret *δικαιοσύνη θεοῦ* with the aid of a conceptuality drawn from his earlier studies of Paul's participatory themes (and especially his understanding of the spirit) has already been stated. It is above all this argument which leads to his highly unified interpretation of Paul. Although aspects of Käsemann's programme have been noted before, the decisive role played by this conceptuality in the solution of the problem of the unity of Paul's thought, and the comprehensive nature of Käsemann's attempt to overcome the dichotomies postulated by late nineteenth-century research, have not been appreciated. In addition to offering a resolution of the standard question of the eschatological, participatory, and juridical elements of Paul's theology, it has been seen in this chapter that Käsemann integrates the topics of salvation history and hermeneutics within this view of Paul's theology. Both topics are said to be determined by the doctrine of justification.

Apart from the fundamental questions raised by recent research into the relationship between Paul and Judaism (which challenges the very notion of a Pauline 'doctrine of justification'), there are very serious problems in Käsemann's discussion of this area of Paul's thought. His treatment of the law is hampered by the dominant concept of 'piety', and by an inability to discuss the notion of salvation history without seeing this theme (anachronistically) in terms of immanent continuity. Secondly, his use of the history-of-traditions and history-of-religions methods is overambitious with regard to the δικαιοσύνη θεοῦ motif and theologically reductive in the discussion of the variety of Paul's soteriological motifs. Finally, his case that Paul extends the idea of God's faithfulness to the covenant to his faithfulness to creation is not convincing.

5

The Lordship of Christ in the Church and in the Christian Life

As was seen in Chapter 2, in the pre-1950 period Käsemann concentrated on the ecclesiological themes in Paul's thought. These themes continue to be important to him in the post-1960 period, alongside the new themes of 'apocalyptic' and the centrality of the doctrine of justification. It now remains to be seen how these new themes are carried through in his understanding of Paul's ecclesiology and ethics.

THE BODY OF CHRIST: THE LORDSHIP OF CHRIST OVER THE CHURCH

In the post-1960 period Käsemann returned to the theme of the body of Christ in the essay 'Das theologische Problem des Motivs vom Leibe Christi' (*PP* 178–210/102–21) and in the Romans commentary. He interacts with the debate on this subject which had continued since his dissertation and his early essays, but his main concerns are, firstly, to argue that the theme of the body of Christ expresses Paul's lordship christology and, secondly, to defend this view, historically and theologically, against other views of the body of Christ theme and of Paul's ecclesiology as a whole.

The body of Christ as a real entity: history-of-religions background and Pauline usage

In his dissertation Käsemann had argued strongly for the importance of the gnostic background of the body of Christ motif, and thus, by implication, for the determining influence of history-of-religions questions for interpretation. By contrast, his studies of the post-1960 period show that a clear methodological shift has taken place. He now argues that: 'Generally speaking, it is possible to shed light on Paul's meaning even without detailed investigation into the history of religion' (*PP* 179 f./103; cf. his pessimistic statement about the possibility of solving the history-of-religions question, *Römer* 325/338). History-of-religions questions are no longer the starting-point; they are worked in with other questions where Käsemann thinks that they are helpful. The body of Christ motif is now to be understood primarily in the light of Paul's new Adam christology (*PP* 188/108, 194 f./112, 203/117; *Römer* 325 f./338).

Käsemann's major initial concern is to reject the view that the body of Christ is a 'beautiful metaphor' (*PP* 179/103): Paul is speaking of 'an actually existing reality' (181/104). 'The exalted Christ really has an earthly body, and believers with their whole being are actually [*realiter*] incorporated into it and have therefore to behave accordingly' (182/104). Käsemann repeats his arguments that *οὕτως καὶ ὁ Χριστός* breaks out of the comparative language of 1 Cor. 12: 12*ab*, and should be translated 'so it is with Christ himself'; and that to be incorporated into the body of Christ by baptism (12: 13) implies that there is a real entity into which a person can be baptized. Paul's sacramental language is 'realistic' and the sacrament effects a change of existence which is to be understood as an exchange of lords. While Paul makes both comparative and identity statements about the body of Christ (e.g., 'for just as the body is one . . .' and 'we are one body in Christ' respectively), 'the comparison unfolds . . . the reality which is envisaged in the identity statements by applying them to the concrete life of the community' (182/104; ET modified). The idea of organism which Paul takes up in the comparative statements presupposes a mythological conception which he presses into service in his paraenesis (ibid.). While these arguments were previously used in an overall case for gnostic influence in Paul's ecclesiology, they now serve the argument that in Paul the exalted Christ really has an earthly body into which believers are incorporated and over which he rules.

With regard to the technical history-of-religions question Käsemann's position changes slightly between 1969 and

1973/4. In 1969 he argues that three ideas (organism, corporate personality, and the *anthropos* myth)[1] were probably combined syncretistically, even if decisive importance is to be ascribed to the third (*PP* 180 f./103). Apart from the history-of-religions argument, there is a further reason why the *anthropos* myth is to be regarded as dominant: unlike the organism idea or the notion of corporate personality, it alone can secure the primacy of christology over ecclesiology (202 f./117). Once again Käsemann implies that a particular theological pattern determines even the history-of-religions questions.[2]

In the Romans commentary Käsemann makes a different threefold analysis of the history-of-religions hypotheses. He now subsumes both the *anthropos* myth (which is no longer discussed) and the organism idea under the general category of the gigantic body of the cosmos. (It is surprising that the *anthropos* myth is not discussed here, even though Käsemann re-emphasizes the connection between the body of Christ and the Adam–Christ typology which he does relate back to the Jewish *anthropos-sophia* figure; see p. 166 above.) Secondly, there is the notion of corporate personality. Thirdly, an inner-Christian derivation is considered: the church is the body of the crucified and resurrected one, and is joined to Christ by the sacraments (*Römer* 325/337).

Käsemann adds further reasons for connecting the body of Christ and the new Adam christology. This connection is clearly made in the deutero-Pauline epistles, the first interpretations of the Pauline passages. Secondly, the baptismal

[1] In the light of his earlier commitment to *gnostic* influence on Paul's theology, it is possible to assume that Käsemann is continuing with this view in the 1969 essay (e.g. Wedderburn 1971: 83 and 90). Käsemann's dismissal of the pre-Christian gnostic primal-man hypothesis first appeared in print in 1972, and Käsemann does not make it clear in the 1969 essay that he is not talking about the *gnostic* primal man. The ambiguity is increased because he continues to speak of the 'heavenly world-embracing *anthropos*' (193/111) and of Christ's body which 'penetrates and embraces the earth' (202/116). This language is strongly reminiscent of the gnostic redeemer with his gigantic body which encompasses the earth. By contrast the Romans commentary rules out the possibility of the gnostic view (see below).

[2] Wedderburn rebuts Käsemann's point that the *anthropos* myth is theologically necessary by arguing that corporate personality, properly defined, is also theologically viable (1971: 85). However, it is not correct that Käsemann's objection to corporate personality is that it is unintelligible (ibid.) but that it does not guarantee the primacy of christology over ecclesiology.

terminology in the statement about the παλαιὸς ἄνθρωπος in Rom. 6: 6 is understood to allude to Adam, who is contrasted with the one renewed in the image of Christ in Col. 3: 10. Thirdly, in Gal. 3: 27 f. the unity of the community derives from putting on Christ, 'obviously as the new man', and this is taken up in the exhortation of Rom. 13: 14. Fourthly, 1 Cor. 12: 13 and 1 Cor. 10: 16 relate incorporation into Christ to baptism and the Lord's supper respectively (325 f./338). Thus, Käsemann attempts to demonstrate that the themes of the new Adam and the body of Christ are interlocked in Paul's theology: both are expressions of Paul's fundamental concern for the lordship of Christ. He concedes that in terms of the history-of-religions it is not clear how the lordship of Christ came to be called the body of Christ, nor on what presupposition Adam and Christ could be contrasted under the common denominator of *anthropos* in 1 Cor. 15: 45 ff. so that the church could be called 'the body of the eschatological Adam' (326/338).[3]

With regard to the history of the body of Christ motif itself, Käsemann argues against the consensus represented by E. Schweizer[4] that Paul coined the term himself. The sparsity of its use, and then in paraenetic contexts, indicates that it is pre-Pauline. The body of Christ is the ecclesiological formula with which hellenistic Christianity armed itself for world-wide

[3] Käsemann is followed by his student, Klaiber, who assumes but does not defend the connection between the two themes (1982: 113 f.). The case against it is put concisely by Wilckens: the collective body concept is missing in the Adam and Christ passages, as is any reference to Adam in Rom. 12: 4 f. (1982: 13 f.; cf. Wedderburn 1971: 90), or, it can be added, in the other passages in which σῶμα occurs as an ecclesiological term. Thus, it is arbitrary to connect the opposition of the universal 'lordships' of Rom. 5 with the ecclesiological 'body' motif which only occurs in specifically ecclesiological contexts. Similarly, while Rom. 6: 6 may allude to Adam in the phrase παλαιὸς ἄνθρωπος (though Paul speaks of 'our' old nature), neither it, nor the immediate context, refers to the body of Christ or any specific ecclesiological entity. Consequently it is difficult to see the relevance of this observation to the interpretation of Paul's ecclesiology. Despite Paul's use of baptismal motifs in Rom. 6, the focus is on the wider struggle between sin and life. Käsemann's case looks stronger than it is because (1) he is able to appeal to other baptismal traditions (especially 1 Cor. 12: 13) which do contain the ecclesiological σῶμα motif, though Paul is not necessarily referring to the body of Christ on every occasion he mentions baptism, and (2) he makes extensive use of deutero-Pauline texts. Elsewhere I hope to develop the case that Paul's ecclesiological motif is not 'the body of Christ' but 'one body' (ἓν σῶμα).

[4] Schweizer 1961*a*, 1961*b*, and 1964*a*.

mission (183/105). Käsemann speculates that the mythological view of the body of Christ was known to Paul's readers and, *therefore*, he was able to modify it in paraenetic contexts in the direction of popular philosophy (*PP* 183/105). Here Käsemann begins to broach a major subject of the essay, an explanation of Paul's limited use of the motif.

The centre of Paul's ecclesiology: the body of Christ or the people of God?

In a second line of argument in the essay of 1969, Käsemann enters and intensifies the debate concerning the relative importance for Paul's ecclesiology of the body of Christ motif and the people of God theme.[5] While the latter does occur more frequently in Paul, this alone does not mean that it is his characteristic ecclesiology.[6] Against the weight of statistics ought to be set the general trend towards a body of Christ ecclesiology in the deutero-Pauline epistles; the point that Paul did not find the idea of the people of God, which was to hand, sufficient; and the influence of modern interest in salvation history, which is closely connected with the people of God theme (*PP* 186 f./107). Above all, Käsemann's case is based on the conviction, which dominates the essay, that the body of Christ is the concept of the church which most adequately corresponds to Paul's work and message:[7] 'No other concept of the church represents his work and message more adequately, because no other concept characterises the world in the same way as the sphere of lordship claimed by

[5] Käsemann discusses this for the first time in his review of Oepke 1950 (*VF* 5 (1951/2), 217).

[6] The ET reverses Käsemann's meaning at a crucial point when it translates 'This [the people of God] being the constitutive idea of Pauline ecclesiology', where it should read 'which in fact from time to time is taken as constitutive for Pauline ecclesiology' (*PP* 185/106).

[7] H. F. Weiss argues that the church as the eschatological people of God is constitutive for Paul and that the body of Christ (with its christological accent) has only a complementing function. However, Weiss then comes much nearer to Käsemann when he states that because what is new in Paul's ecclesiology, over against Jewish Christianity, is the christological basis of his body of Christ idea, this in fact corresponds better to Paul's understanding of the church (Weiss 1977: 411–20). Even if Weiss does not intend 'constitutive' in Käsemann's sense ('theologically central') his argument is self-contradictory.

Christ' (*die Welt als das von Christus beanspruchte Herrschaftsgebiet*; 185/106, ET modified).

Käsemann then argues that the frequent occurrence of the people of God theme ought not to be regarded as decisive as it occurs only in particular contexts. It is used exclusively in paraenesis or in connection with Old Testament quotations or in polemic against Judaism. This last point accounts for the antithesis of Moses and Christ, the retreat of the remnant idea, and the absence of the theme of Israel's restoration. In the dispute about the law, Paul uses this motif to prove that the church is the people of God and that Israel must be justified among the ungodly (187 f./107 f.). However, whereas Käsemann here attempts to play down the people of God theme because it occurs only in these contexts, elsewhere he argues that the polemic against the law, the justification of the ungodly, and Israel's place among them stand at the heart of Paul's gospel.

Käsemann also argues—in what must be seen as another major concession against his case—that Paul is unwilling to let go of his Jewish heritage because the promise, unlike the law, is not made obsolete by Christ. The eschatological people of God remains to this extent a feature of Paul's ecclesiology. However, its centre does not lie here but in the contrast of the two aeons of Adam and Christ. This dualism cannot be expressed by the people of God theme, but is expressed by the body of Christ/new Adam theme. It is Paul's new Adam christology which prevents the theme of the people of God from taking the ascendancy it would otherwise have in Paul—as it has in later Catholic views where the church becomes 'the prolongation and representative of her Lord, in whom she integrates herself, though as her author and head' (195 f./112). While the people of God theme deals with the sacred past, the body of Christ motif expresses Paul's concern for Christ's 'universal rule' (*Weltherrschaft*) and his rule over the church (196/113). Thus, Paul's ecclesiology is determined by his 'exclusively christological viewpoint' (ET: 'christological consideration'; 189/109).

These views show how Käsemann's interpretation of Paul's ecclesiology expresses his own theological concerns in this second period. The doctrine of justification (or Paul's christology) determines salvation history and ecclesiology, and not vice versa. Further, the point that the body of Christ is the sphere in which the universal lordship claimed by Christ is already manifested is in line with his 'apocalyptic' reading of Paul, whose theology is orientated to the world and is subject to the eschatological reservation.

The crucified and the ecclesiological body of Christ

Given Käsemann's thesis that Paul's ecclesiology is christologically determined, it is important to him to give a precise account of the relationship of Christ and the church. (The theological background to this question is, of course, extremely important: on the one hand, Käsemann wishes to maintain and restate a Protestant insistence on Christ over the church; on the other hand, he himself contributed to the Lutheran rediscovery of the theme of the church earlier in the century.) He pursues the question by taking up the question of the relationship of the crucified body of Christ[8] (*Kreuzesleib*) and the church as the body of Christ (*Christusleib der Kirche*).[9] Käsemann polemicizes against those who read 'ecclesiological metaphysics' into Paul. This is done in a variety of ways by those who associate the ecclesiological body of Christ with the crucified body, regard the crucified body as the prolepsis of the ecclesiological body, or see the two as coinciding or as identical (*PP* 191 f./110 with bibliography). He repeats his interpretation of 1 Cor. 10: 16 f., laying particular emphasis on Paul's theological interpretation of hellenistic Christian belief: the hellenistic 'mysterious' incorporation of the participant into the destiny[10] of Jesus' death becomes the Pauline

[8] This translation does not bring out the direct reference to the theology of the cross which *Kreuzesleib* intends.

[9] This curious phrase occurs in Käsemann's 1937 essay, where it denotes the ecclesiological body of Christ in distinction to the eucharistic body of Christ ('Abendmahl' 85–8), and again here in the 1969 essay where the relation of the crucified body and the ecclesiological body are under discussion. It means no more than 'the church as the body of Christ' (*PP* 194/112), although it clearly was a problem for Käsemann's translator ('the body of Christ in [!] the church', 192/110; 'the church in its character as the body of Christ', 194/111; and 'the body of Christ in the form of the church', 197/113).

[10] The ET omits the mention of 'destiny' (*Todesschicksal*) and thus obscures the already cryptic reference to the idea of the participation of the devotee in the destiny of the lord who is worshipped in the cult (*PP* 181/104, 193/111).

doctrine of incorporation into the body of the exalted lord. A careful distinction is to be made. The crucified body of Jesus is his alone, and no one is incorporated into it. The church as the body of Christ is created and held together by the spirit, and thus only comes into existence after Easter and Pentecost, or the exaltation of Christ (193 f./111 f.). The church is the place of Christ's presence but only through the spirit and not in its own right, nor in such a way that it can become independent of its lord. This careful distinction between the crucified body of Christ and the church as the body of Christ means that the church is not given undue importance (196 f./113).

Käsemann then gives an account of the relationship of the crucified, eucharistic, and ecclesiological 'bodies'. Christians are drawn into the death of Christ by the eucharistic gifts (1 Cor. 10: 16 f.), baptism (Rom. 6: 3 f.), and mission (2 Cor. 4: 10 f.). Thus, the church is *subsequently* made a partaker of the event of the cross by the risen one. The church portrays (*darstellen*) his earthly body after his exaltation. Conformed into the likeness of the crucified one, like him it manifests (*bekunden*) life *sub contrario* as God's work in its own corporeal dying. In this way, while the crucified, eucharistic, and ecclesiological 'bodies' are related, the church is kept distinct from its lord. Christ's death does not lead to the exaltation or self-transcendence of the church; rather, his exaltation makes the church the instrument (ET: 'means') whereby Christ's earthly destiny cannot be forgotten (197/113). 'Pauline ecclesiology is part of the apostle's theology of the cross and to that degree can only be understood in the light of his Christology' (197/113 f.).

Käsemann does not, however, succeed in making a close connection between the crucified body and the church as the body of Christ.[11] The church is said to take part subsequently 'in the event of the cross', a formulation which does not relate specifically to the crucified body. Secondly, the church as the body of Christ lives a re-enactment of the crucified body of Christ in its own corporeal dying and as such is a living 'proclamation'. It constantly 'portrays' or 'manifests' (*darstellen, bekunden*) his death. Here Käsemann draws on his earlier

[11] Güttgemanns 1966: 259.

interpretation of ἀνάμνησις. His choice of expression prevents an identification of Christ and the church—while emphasizing the reality of the presence and lordship of Christ in the church.[12] The church is the locus of Christ's lordship in the world—because Christ is and remains her lord, and is present in her by the spirit. In this section it has again been noticeable that Käsemann employs his earlier exegetical arguments for explicitly theological purposes.

Σῶμα as the possibility of communication between Christ, the church, and the world

As has been seen, for Käsemann, *σῶμα* is the 'piece of world' which Christ claims and which we have to offer (pp. 59 f. and 158–61 above). If *σῶμα* is the possibility of communication, and the body of Christ is the sphere of Christ's lordship on earth into which Christians are incorporated, then the church is the sphere of communication between Christ, his own, and the world (199/115). The means of communication are the sacraments, the word, and faith. This is one reason why Paul deals so little with the church in his letters: the individual Christian and congregation em*body* (*sich ver*leib*lichen*) Christ in the world. Consequently, Bultmann's theme of 'detachment from the world' (*Entweltlichung*; ET: 'unworldliness', 200/115), is highly dangerous because Christ wants documentation of his lordship in the world (197–201/114–16).[13]

The church as the instrument of the crucified lord

The heart of Käsemann's interpretation of the body of Christ motif is reached on the basis of the observation that Paul, unlike his interpreters, does not speak of 'the body of the church': 'It is the religio-historical, historical and theological problem of our motif that it is not talking about the body of a collective (i.e., the body of the messianic community) but the

[12] Cf. Käsemann's objections to Schlier's interpretation of the ecclesiology of Ephesians based on the body of Christ motif (*EVB* ii. 253–61). For his response to Schlier's view of the ecclesiology of 1 Cor., see p. 251 below.

[13] Käsemann indicates that he is not criticizing Bultmann's concept in itself when he adds 'although it certainly has its particular meaning'. On *Entweltlichung*, see Bultmann 1951: 181, 351 f., and p. 157 above.

body of an individual, namely Christ' (201/116). Käsemann argues that Paul's thought is to be understood in the following order. Firstly, in terms of the history-of-religions derivation, it is decisive that Paul does not begin, on the Stoic model, from a plurality and see Christ as the inner unity; rather, the heavenly Christ has a body which penetrates (*durchdringen*; ET: 'fills') and comprehends the world. The next step is to identify Christ's body with the church, and finally, and only after these points have been made, the relationship between the members is described, by means of a comparison, as mutual and general solidarity (201 f./116; cf. *Römer* 326/338).

Käsemann's argument here posits the priority of the history-of-religions question, even though he sharply reduces the importance of this approach in his opening methodological remarks. Further, he has not shown on the basis of Paul's statements, but only from the presupposition of the *anthropos* myth, that Christ has a body which penetrates and comprehends the world. The most that Käsemann can say on the basis of Pauline statements is that 'it is with Christ himself as it is with the body' and that ' "in Christ" the church is a body' (*PP* 180/103). These points do not imply either that Christ has a body, or that his body penetrates and comprehends the world. Thus, while Käsemann here admits that the motif itself is used only in comparisons, he argues that Paul's concern, i.e., his theological concern,[14] is with the world-wide body of the exalted Christ. The motif of the body of Christ and the supposed theological concern are not closely connected.[15] There is the strong suspicion that, although the gnostic model has been abandoned in theory, its conceptuality (the body of the redeemer which penetrates and comprehends the world) continues to determine Käsemann's interpretation.

Käsemann adds an argument which he uses in other contexts: the stress in σῶμα Χριστοῦ lies on the genitive which speaks of Christ's power in the gift (202/116; cf. on δικαιοσύνη θεοῦ, pp. 195 ff. above). The aspect of Christ's power is of

[14] Käsemann here uses *es geht um* . . . with the same meaning as *sachlich*.

[15] The same can be said of Klaiber's attempt to argue that the conception of the world-wide, missionary body of Christ, which he admits first appears in Col. and Eph., nevertheless underlies the passages in Rom. and 1 Cor. because the 'decisive elements' are present (1982: 110).

theological importance: 'Christ is there before the church and he is not absorbed into the church. As creator and judge, he remains the one who stands over against [*das Gegenüber*] his members' (202/116 f., ET corrected; cf. 214/124). Christ in his power stands in relation to the church—but this is only correctly understood if it is seen that, fundamentally, he stands over against the church (on Christ as *das Gegenüber*, see ch. 3 n. 76 above). Here Käsemann emphasizes the lordship of Christ over the church and picks up a theme from his interpretation of the Lord's supper in which the participants encounter Christ as saviour and judge.

Moving to the contemporary theological level, Käsemann argues that, unlike trends in ecumenical ecclesiology, Paul does not use the connection between christology and ecclesiology to glorify the church: 'the body [i.e., the church] is destined for service and only participates in the glory of the exalted Lord in so far as it remains his instrument in earthly lowliness' (203/227). This distinguishes Pauline Christianity from the mystery religions which promised participation in the glory of the cult god. 'The whole context of Rom. 12.3 ff. and 1 Cor. 12.12 ff. is clearly directed against an enthusiastic *theologia gloriae*' (ibid.). The church must remain a part of the world's everyday life (*Alltag*) and not fly from the lowliness which was the mark of its lord before his resurrection (ibid). Käsemann sums up with respect to the theological convictions which have motivated and guided his interpretation. Paul is not, *contra* Catholic Christianity, interested in the church *per se*; nor, *contra* pietism, is he interested in it as a religious group. Paul is only concerned with the church as the means whereby Christ reveals himself on earth and embodies himself in the world through the spirit (200/115). The body of Christ is the sphere of Christ's lordship on earth in which he finds obedience before the parousia (204/117).

Paul's use of the body of Christ motif

It is to Käsemann's credit that he turns, in the last section of his essay to deal with Paul's theology, to the pressing question of why, if the body of Christ theme is so important to Paul's theology, he did not treat the theme thematically or other than in paraenetic contexts. If Paul's usage is compared with Colossians and Ephesians, where the body of Christ is spoken of 'doxologically', a 'decisive distinction' is to be observed (204/118). The first two points have already been mentioned:

1. If the view based on the *anthropos* myth was already current, it can be argued that Paul modified the motif in the direction of the popular philosophical tradition.

2. Paul is not interested in the church *per se* because the individual Christian and the congregation are to embody Christ in the world.

3. The objection that Käsemann's interpretation depends on the presupposition that Paul developed the body of Christ motif theologically in his preaching (even though he does not in his extant letters) is incontrovertible, but equally this objection cannot be established conclusively. Paul did treat some important topics thematically and it is difficult to see why the topic of church is not dealt with in this way.[16]

4. However, this state of affairs becomes understandable if the functional character of the body of Christ motif in Paul is noted: 'Everything that is important in his ecclesiology then expresses itself in the relation of Christology to the spirit, word, service, faith and sacrament and to the concrete state of affairs in the churches. Thus paraenesis remains the proper place for an explicit discussion on the theme of the church' (205/118). Because of his paraenetic concerns Paul pursues his argument largely through the idea of organism and in the form of comparison. Further, theological reflection takes second place to existence lived in the body of Christ. If solidarity is the most important concern of paraenesis, then this can be made clear from the aspect of anthropology (ibid.).

In effect Käsemann is here putting the case that the interpreter needs to invoke a body of Christ theology in order to understand and bring together other aspects of Paul's theology. But if all that is important in Paul's ecclesiology expresses itself in the relation between christology and the spirit and other themes, or can be made clear from the

[16] It could be asked whether Paul deals thematically with discipleship or suffering (two of Käsemann's examples) any more than with the church. Probably Käsemann means that Paul does not deal thematically with the body of Christ, which in his view is the centre of Paul's understanding of the church.

anthropological angle, there is no need to invoke another concept to express the whole. In fact Käsemann is left in the difficult position of arguing both that Paul has a fully worked out theology of the body of Christ which is central to his ecclesiology and is determined by his fundamental theological convictions, and that everything that is significant in his ecclesiology is contained elsewhere in his theology.

Despite Käsemann's thesis concerning the primacy of christology over ecclesiology, his interpretation of Paul's ecclesiology has some Catholic emphases. Thus, against typically Protestant views, he argues for the importance of the doctrine of the church in Paul, for an effective view of the sacraments which are said to incorporate partakers into the church, and he repeatedly emphasizes that Christ is present in the church. (The last two points are made without repeated reference to the efficacy of the word.) He commends the Catholic view of the mystical body of Christ for preventing the Pauline theologoumenon from being understood in a purely pictorial or metaphorical sense, although the metaphysical basis of this view removes the existential grounding of Paul's motif. The incorporation of Christians *realiter* into the body also gives support to Catholic interpretation (*PP* 182 f./105). These points are very much in line with the Catholic tendencies within Käsemann's earlier work on Paul (pp. 106 ff. above). As with the case of the gift–power conceptuality, Käsemann integrates his earlier views while setting them firmly within a Protestant doctrinal framework. Finally, as has been seen repeatedly in this chapter, in comparison with his earlier work on Paul's ecclesiology, Käsemann now puts his exegetical hypotheses to work in the cause of explicit contemporary theological concerns.[17]

[17] Another important example of this is to be found in the case of Bultmann and Käsemann's views on σῶμα Χριστοῦ and ἐν Χριστῷ. Bultmann initially paid little attention to body of Christ (1930*a*: 164; remarkably he does not mention the motif in his reviews of either Schweitzer 1930 or Käsemann's *Leib*, Bultmann 1931 and 1936 respectively). His view of ἐν Χριστῷ first follows Bousset (the formula is to be understood in the light of the relationship between πνεῦμα and κύριος, and hence of Paul's christology and with regard to the cult; Bultmann 1922*b*: 194) and then he arrives at his own view: it is an eschatological formula, 'the new existential possibility that is determined by Christ' (1930*a*: 168; cf. 1926*c*: 274; 1932*b*: 158). After Käsemann's *Leib* he adopts the 'ecclesiological' interpretation (ἐν Χριστῷ is derived from σῶμα Χριστοῦ, it refers to the state of having being incorporated into the body of

CHARISMA: GIFT, TASK, AND LIMIT IN CHRISTIAN MINISTRY AND ETHICS

Käsemann's understanding of the meaning and function of charisma in Paul's theology was outlined in Chapter 2 where it was studied with a view to its contribution to the overall shape of his interpretation of Paul. A charisma is the individuation and concretion of grace, the specific part an individual has in the lordship of Christ. As such it both is a gift (as the individuation and concretion of grace) and makes a claim (the charismata are the mode of the *cosmocrator*'s claim on the world). In this way the doctrine of charisma is the projection of the doctrine of justification into the area of ecclesiology. It now remains to give an account of the contribution of the charisma idea to Käsemann's interpretation of Paul's ecclesiology and ethics.[18]

Käsemann's view of ministry is shaped by R. Sohm's distinction between theories of church order based on law and those based on love.[19] Just as Käsemann seeks to overcome other dichotomies in Paul's thought, he seeks to show that this dichotomy is overcome in the dialectic of gift and task.

Christ; 1951: 310 f.). Having persuaded Bultmann to give ἐν Χριστῷ an ecclesiological interpretation, Käsemann changed his own view of the phrase. In 1950 he emphasizes its soteriological character (*EVB* i. 91/84) and in 1969 he rejects the ecclesiological view because it endangers the primacy of christology over ecclesiology (*PP* 174/99). '"In Christ" is the state of those who through the gospel are called out of the old world and who only belong to the new creation in so far as they continue to be confronted with the Lord who justifies the ungodly' (177/101). This is a summary of Käsemann's view of the centre of Paul's theology, and indicates, once again, that the determination of Pauline motifs by the supposed centre of his theology weighs far more heavily with him than the exegesis of the Pauline texts in which the motifs occur. However, this view is given some exegetical support in *Römer* 212–15/220–3. An interesting new point is made, but not followed up: 'in Christ' is Paul's correction of an enthusiastic formula, 'in the spirit'. A major problem with this entire debate is that the theological labels which are employed are not precise enough to indicate the nuances of the various positions. Bultmann's 'ecclesiological' view is also 'existential' and 'eschatological', and Käsemann's final 'christological' view includes all these aspects, now determined by the theme of the justification of the ungodly.

[18] After the 1949/1960 essay, Käsemann returned to the charisma theme in *EVB* ii. 202–4/192–5; *PP* 206–8/118–120; and *Römer*, especially 320–3/333–5. For Paul's ecclesiology in general, in addition to the material already cited in this chapter, the essays 'Paulus und der Frühkatholizismus' (*EVB* ii. 23–52/236–51) and 'Der gottesdienstliche Schrei nach der Freiheit' (*PP* 211–36/122–37), and *Freiheit* chs. 3 and 4 should be consulted.

[19] Sohm 1892.

Secondly, he is concerned to oppose, on the one hand, Catholic church order, based on the principles of tradition, legitimization, and hierarchy,[20] and, on the other hand, the egalitarianism of the enthusiasts.

As the specific part that the individual has in the lordship of Christ, a charisma is both a gift and a call to service. Its structure is parallel to that of 'God's righteousness' which is both a gift and a power. Because of this, the charismata do not isolate those who receive them (as happened among the enthusiastic Corinthians whose multiplicity of gifts led to religious anarchy), but call them to obedience and allows each to contribute to the building up of the church.

Paul is in agreement with the Corinthians on the multiplicity of the gifts. The church must reflect the multiplicity of the charismata and must not be characterized by uniformity or forced conformity (*Uniformität und Gleichschaltung*, the latter with its National Socialist overtones; ET: 'rationalization'; *EVB* i. 115/70; cf. *PP* 206/118 f.; *Römer* 367/379). Within the church the very multiplicity of gifts leads to the possibility of mutual service, and hence to the building up of the church. This has the consequence that there can be no division between active and passive members in the church; the priesthood of all believers is proclaimed (*EVB* i. 115/70). This diversity is not a temporary feature. The body of Christ is characterized by the extreme antitheses of Jew and Greek, male and female, slave and free. These conditions of life become a charismatic status when they are accepted under the lord: 'My condition of life, whatever it is [*mein jeweiliger Stand*; ET: 'previous condition'], becomes charisma only when I recognize that the Lord has given it to me and that I am to accept this gift as his calling and command to me' (*EVB* i. 116/72).[21]

[20] Thus, the 1949/1960 essay was initially a response to Schlier's interpretation of the ecclesiology of 1 Cor. (*EVB* i. 109 n. 1/63 n. 1). Schlier argues that the charismatic understanding of the church which is read from 1 Cor. and defended today as the true understanding of the church is in fact opposed by Paul. God's revelation appears primarily and fundamentally in objective apostolic kerygma whose material and formal substance is received and handed on in the apostolic paradosis of the church. It is office alone which makes the genuine charisma possible (1948/9: 465, 467).

[21] Schulz highlights the social conservatism of Käsemann's interpretation of charisma: along with Paul's expectation of the end, his doctrine of the natural order, and his anti-enthusiastic front, the charisma doctrine means that Paul maintains the

Käsemann then turns to questions concerning the authenticity of the charismata. The criterion of a genuine charisma is not the fact of its existence (*Faktizität*), as the Corinthians thought, but the mode of its use (*Modalität*; 112/67, 116/72). In the midst of diversity, the unity given in baptism is maintained only *in actu*, in love and service (ibid.). Faced with enthusiastic congregations which were tearing themselves apart on account of the 'multiplicity of gifts, possibilities and demonstrations', Paul has the task of giving a theological reason for unity in the midst of multiplicity. The watchword is solidarity, not uniformity (*PP* 206/118).

Paul's teaching on charisma also has implications for the relationship between the church and the world. The church must remain polyform and its members nonconformist if it is to continue to serve a polyform and nonconformist world:[22] 'The necessity and blessing of Christian liberty as the state of being in the presence of Christ is not to give everyone the same thing but to give and allow everyone what is his' (*PP* 206/119; cf. *Römer* 326/338 f.). The relationship of the church to the world will be touched on again when the nature of Christian worship is examined.

If Paul is in initial agreement with the Corinthian pneumatics on the multiplicity of the gifts, he is highly critical of them in other respects. He devotes 1 Cor. 14 to the idea of testing the spirits (*EVB* i. 112/66 f.) and makes significant use of the catchwords of popular philosophy to defend the true diversity of the church against the threat of religious chaos, and against the elevation of the arbitrary (*die Willkür*) which characterizes the enthusiasts' actions and beliefs. Thus, the catchword 'useful' (presumably referring to *συμφέρει* in 1 Cor. 6: 12) comes to mean 'that which builds up the church' (112/67). The phrase 'to each his own' (Rom. 12: 3; 1 Cor. 3: 5; 11: 18; 12: 7) proclaims that everyone has their charisma

subjection of Christian slaves, etc. The concrete subordination of Christians in their present status does not affect their charismatic activity which can be offered as service within the orders of the world. Schulz protests that this is correct but not sufficient: only the activity of the *freed* slave is charismatic service (1976: 460). Käsemann does not allow the negative statements of Gal. 3: 28 any weight (contrast the discussions of Betz 1979: 18–201, Schüssler Fiorenza 1983: 205–41, and p. 256 below).

[22] The first sentence of the ET on *PP* 206/119 ought to read 'It can only pervade the world, whose reality is everyday life, by not becoming conformist.'

from God. This rules out egalitarianism because there is differentiation in God's generosity, which leads, as has been seen, to mutual service. Just as gift and task go together, so do freedom and order, and thus the concept of charisma contains within itself the notion of limit, a notion which Paul used extensively against the Corinthian enthusiasts.[23] A charisma is accompanied by the corresponding *μέτρον πίστεως* (Rom. 12: 3). For Käsemann the converse of the catch-phrase 'All is yours' (1 Cor. 3: 21) is 'Let each person remain before God in the condition in which they received their call' (7: 24). My charisma is always the only ethical possibility open to me (Barth; 119 f./76 f.). Another catch-phrase is 'For one another' (1 Cor. 12: 23). For the Christian the gift frees people from themselves and from determination by others so that they can become servants to all.[24] Paul also makes use of the catch-phrase 'Submit yourself to one another in the fear of Christ' (Rom. 12: 10; Phil. 2: 3). Here the idea is of the obedience which is due because of an order or hierarchy (*τάγμα*). The Christian must submit to the charisma of the other, and thus authority and charisma go together. (Conversely, against Catholic views, authority is not to be located in ecclesiastical office or hierarchy but only in the charisma and in the actual exercise of ministry; *EVB* i. 121/77 f.) The same anti-enthusiastic slant is to be detected behind Paul's use of *σωφρονεῖν* (Rom. 12: 3, the soberness which keeps to the right measure; *Römer* 320/332), conscience, and reason (the critical faculty which is renewed by the spirit; 318/330). To sum up, the pneumatic is given earthly responsibility, and the Christian who receives the gift is thereby called away from striving for autonomy into the freedom of self-offering (322/334). 'Paul was able to take up the catch-phrases of contemporary popular philosophy in order to test the spirits and to bring the enthusiasts back into the sphere of humanity' (*Freiheit* 149).

This brings Käsemann to the discussion of the relationship of 'ministerial office' and 'community' in Paul[25] which again is

[23] Schrage develops the idea of limit with respect to the charisma of the unmarried state (1961: 141–6).

[24] *EVB* i. 121/77; see *Freiheit* 130 and ch. 4 as a whole ('Service in Freedom'), for Käsemann's use of Luther's theme of 'The Freedom of a Christian' (1520).

[25] The ET of the title, 'Ministry [*Amt*, office] and Community in the New Testament' partially obscures that this is the central question of the 1949/1960 essay.

based on the charisma concept. He starts from a very important negative point:

> a situation in which all Christians are regarded as charismatics [ET: 'endowed with charisma'] is a situation which does not admit the possibility of sacred space, sacred time, the right of representative action in the cultus, of sacred persons in the sense of both Judaism and the pagan religions—in fact, the whole possibility of objects or persons thought of as specially privileged in the realm of the holy by reason of their connection with the *temenos*. (*EVB* i. 121/78)

This does not mean that the holy is profaned but that grace has invaded the world and its everyday life (*Alltag*; ibid.). In this context all the baptized are 'office-bearers' (*Amtsträger*; 123/80) because each has his charisma and responsibility. Thus, charisma and office are not antithetical (*Römer* 323/335), and charisma as the individuation of grace is the basis of the priesthood of all believers (*EVB* i. 123/80; *PP* 207/119; *Römer* 323/335). This is not to be understood in terms of the believer's individual and private relationship to God (*EVB* i. 123/80) but of public, official ministry, however much this may clash with the Protestant and modern Lutheran conception of ecclesiastical office (123 f./81). No individual possessor of a charisma (not even the commissioned preacher, Käsemann adds, with an eye to his own tradition) has a special prerogative over the body of Christ. All are to serve in word and deed as office-bearers, notwithstanding Paul's concern for good order in 1 Cor. 14 (ibid.).

The universal obligation to service does not, however, imply the equality of all. There are some signs of fixed offices in the letters, and the lists of gifts show signs of grading (124/81 f.). They can be categorized under the headings of kerygmatic (apostles, prophets, evangelists, teachers, inspiration, and ecstasy),[26] diaconic (deacons, deaconesses, those who give alms and tend the sick, miraculous healing, and exorcism), and cybernetic (i.e., administrative; the 'first fruits' of Rom. 16: 5 and 1 Cor. 16: 15; 'those who are over you', 1 Thess. 5: 12; the 'bishops', Phil. 1: 1; charismatic suffering, 2 Cor. 4: 7 ff.; 114/69). Of course, the Pauline letters do show the beginnings of what would now be called fixed offices

[26] Käsemann does not defend this classification of the last two mentioned.

(bishops, deacons, the deaconess Phoebe, the functions listed in Rom. 12: 6–8, 124/81 f.; cf. *Römer* 328/341) but Paul's theory of order is not a static one resting on offices and institutions. For him authority rests only in the concrete act of ministry in which the *kyrios* announces his lordship and presence (*EVB* i. 125/83). Sohm's antithesis of love and law is not adequate for Paul's theology in which gift and demand, freedom and order, belong together (125 f./83).

Käsemann sums up, first from the point of view of the individual Christian and then of the church: 'In a sentence—every Christian in his own place, in his particular situation, with his specific capacities and weaknesses, may and must be a "place holder" for Christ [*Platzhalter Christi*] to the point of death' (not simply temporally, 'until death' [ET]; *PP* 207/119). As with the relation of Christ and the church, the relation of Christ and the Christian must be clearly defined: the Christian is not a substitute for or representative (*Stellvertreter*) of Christ, but 'the place where we stand is to be kept open for him' (207/119). If all do this, solidarity is born, which is 'the unity of those who are different, who as those who belong to the same Lord, endure the tensions which otherwise exist between them and let them become fruitful for the whole and for the world around them. Thus is expressed in the midst of the world the lordship of him who creates a new world, the one body out of many members' (207 f./119 f., ET modified).[27]

Käsemann's understanding of charisma in Paul has come under severe exegetical criticism. Brockhaus notes that Käsemann takes up Sohm's approach, credits him with having best understood Sohm, but argues that, precisely for this reason, he has got into the deepest trouble with this

[27] Käsemann's views on church order and charisma (in conjunction with Schweizer 1946 and von Campenhausen 1953) have been highly influential in both Protestant and Catholic circles, as even the titles of the following studies show: Eichholz (*Was heißt charismatische Gemeinde?*) 1960; Dombois (*Das Recht der Gnade: Oekumenisches Kirchenrecht*, i) 1961; Schürmann ('Die geistlichen Gnadengaben in der paulinischen Gemeinde') 1966, which first appeared in the commentary to *Lumen gentium*; Hasenhüttl (*Charisma—Ordnungsprinzip der Kirche*) 1969; Dreier (*Das kirchliche Amt: Eine kirchenrechtstheoretische Studie*) 1972; and Herten ('Charisma—Signal einer Gemeindetheologie des Paulus') 1976. Heinz 1974: 351–410, discusses Käsemann, and shows how many of his concerns can be organized around the theme of the church.

approach. He has not resolved the tension in this approach but moved it to the dialectical level.[28] Brockhaus argues that there is no evidence in Paul for the hostility to office (*Amtsfeindschaft*) which underlies Käsemann's views. The earliest elements of office are present (duration, order of rank, limitation of function). Further, it is not correct that Paul bases his view of office on the charisma concept; rather, he integrates official functions into the list of charismata without emphasizing them, positively or negatively, in comparison with the other functions. In addition, Käsemann fails to notice the difference between the lists of charismata. 1 Cor. 12: 8–10 lists the pneumatic, enthusiastic gifts which are repeated in 12: 28–30 with the addition of some 'authoritative functions', while Rom. 12: 6–8 retains only prophecy from the pneumatic gifts and goes on to ethical charismata. Moreover, other Pauline concepts (love, *οἰκοδομή*, the weaker brother) cannot be made a part of a concept of community based solely on the idea of charisma.[29]

Brockhaus also notes Käsemann's expansion of the charisma doctrine into the sphere of ethics. Here he argues that, while Käsemann's views do not go against the direction of Paul's statements, he takes them further than Paul did. Paul did regard abstinence enabled by unmarried status as a charisma, but not marriage itself. The charismata and the parallel antitheses of 1 Cor. 12: 13 and Gal. 3: 28 should be kept apart, as Paul makes no use of the parallel antitheses in his teaching on charisma. With Merk,[30] Brockhaus argues that the 'conditions of life' lose their significance in the community, and are only considered under the aspect of their disappearance and the consequent unity of the community. By contrast the charismata are the wealth of the community and their diversity is characterized by mutual completion.[31] While Paul's tendency is towards an extension of the lists, this is to include activities, talents, and functions, not sexual, social, and religious givens.[32] Similarly unpauline is the narrowing of the basis of ethics to the charisma principle, which should be understood as one principle among many.[33]

[28] Brockhaus 1972: 39 n. 214, 41.

[29] Ibid. 214–19.

[30] Merk 1968: 110 n. 198, 160.

[31] Brockhaus 1972: 225.

[32] Cf. Schrage 1982: 170.

[33] Brockhaus 1972: 222–6.

However, Brockhaus does not point to the source of the problem in Käsemann's view of charisma. As was seen above (p. 101), Käsemann's starting-point was an interpretation of Rom. 6: 23, in which he argued that all the charismata are dependent on the one charisma. All the charismata are 'concrete forms' (*Konkretionen*) of the comprehensive gift of salvation (*Römer* 177/185). It is on this basis that Käsemann polemicizes against the translation of charisma as gift, a point which supports his general conviction that the gift must never be separated from the Giver. However, as the contrast of *τὸ χάρισμα* with *τὰ ὀψώνια* makes clear, charisma does mean precisely 'free gift' here,[34] which is its normal meaning in the few occurrences outside of the New Testament. It is highly unlikely that Paul has any connection with the charismata in mind in Rom. 6. If this is correct, and the criticisms made above are borne in mind, Käsemann's attempt to find a unified meaning for the word (based on the power–gift dialectic) must be rejected.[35]

CHRISTIAN ETHICS UNDER THE LORDSHIP OF CHRIST

Many of the principles of Käsemann's interpretation of Paul's ethical teaching have been touched upon in previous sections. In addition to the themes of the body of Christ and of charisma, which have already been noted, apostleship was understood as the discipleship of the crucified one, a perspective which is equally applicable to the life of every Christian. There remains the task of considering Käsemann's view of the nature of Paul's ethics in general and some specific topics.

The nature of Paul's ethics

In criticism of interpretation informed by the ethics of German idealism, Käsemann argues that Paul's ethics were

[34] Brockhaus 1972: 132 f.; cf. Conzelmann 1973: 393 f. (who in his article on charisma in Kittel fails to mention Käsemann's essay of 1949/1960); Schlier 1977: 213; and Wilckens 1980: 40, who all discuss whether a more specific reference to charisma as the *donativum*, the special payment made to soldiers on extraordinary occasions, is intended. On this last point caution is advocated by Cranfield 1975: 330.

[35] So also Grau 1946 and Schweizer 1946.

not developed from one ethical principle. In Paul the spirit always calls for the concrete act of service in a particular situation. Two points are emphasized. The spirit lays demands on each individual, claiming people completely and concretely in their particular relationships, and making them capable of a new manner of life. However, this does not happen in isolation and, thus, secondly, in their action individuals show themselves to be members of the community (*Römer* 312/324).

On another front it is also incorrect to regard Paul's ethics as a system of casuistry (in criticism of Catholic tendencies in interpretation): the motif of order plays a very subordinate role and comprehensive discussion of ethical possibilities is only a feature of later Christian ethics. Paul falls back, without inhibition, on contemporary models (lists of virtues and vices, household codes, penitential practice, and rules for the community; 312 f./324 f.). In general, early Christian ethics were marked by a remarkable degree of syncretism which had a genuine theological basis: they are 'grounded in the conviction that God's will is [ET: 'was'] not completely unknown to anybody, that Christian obedience is constitutively the freedom to adapt existing moral insights, and that to that extent it is the fulfilment of authentic humanity' (312/324). Käsemann sums up against the two fronts of an ethics derived from a single principle and ethics as a system of casuistry: 'If the avoidance of both principles and casuistry is noted, one may maintain that primitive Christian exhortation deals with what is required at any particular time [*das jeweils Erförderliche*] only by way of example'[36] (313/325, ET modified).

Paul's contribution is that he is the first Christian thinker to have reflected on exhortation from a theological standpoint. He was probably forced to do this by the problems at Corinth, but the systematic argument in Romans shows that this also derives from his theology. As has already been seen, Käsemann argues that Paul makes extensive use of the doctrines of the body of Christ and of charisma for this purpose. Further, he concentrates on 'basic motifs' (*Grundmotive*) of moral action

[36] Käsemann's *exemplarisch* can mean more than 'by way of example' when it refers, not merely to an example, but to that which is exemplary (*EVB* ii. 196/186; *PP* 261/152; *Römer* 175/184; cf. the related phrase, *repräsentativ*, 301/311). Käsemann's interpretation is followed by Schrage 1961: 127.

which are set within his christological, eschatological, and sacramental perspectives and which derive their specifically Christian obligation from their setting in Paul's theology.[37]

In Romans, Paul sets the heading of 12: 1–2 over the general paraenesis that follows, and concludes with the summary in 13: 8–14. The particular problems of 14–15: 13 are solved by the catch-phrase of mutual acceptance on a christological foundation. Whatever traditions are taken up and irrespective of whether they are successfully co-ordinated, the whole is a logically developed sketch in which Paul gives something like a model of Christian conduct and mentions certain main emphases which stand in material sequence.[38] Even in the decision to make exhortation form the conclusion of Romans, the apostle draws the consequence of his message of the justification of the ungodly[39] in the everyday life of the community (ibid.).

If the theme of justification is to be related to ethics, then the division, common in Protestant orthodoxy, between justification as the beginning of the Christian life and sanctification as a separate process which follows it must be abandoned. Paul does not limit the event of justification in time, and the new life is also the work of grace. Such a division separates the gift from the giver by regarding justification as a gift to the believer which does not bring with it the continuing presence of the giver who calls to service. Secondly, it understands justification in an anthropological perspective instead of viewing it christologically as 'transferal to the lordship [ET: 'dominion'] of Christ' (*Römer* 164/172).[40] The

[37] With reference to Schrage 1961: 122, 187.

[38] The ET has 'projection' for sketch (*Entwurf*), 'image' for model (*Leitbild*), and 'points of difficulty' for main emphases (*Schwerpunkte*).

[39] Keck works out this basic theme with regard to ethical theory in the Käsemann Festschrift (Keck 1976).

[40] The grounding of this point in Käsemann's theology of lordship is particularly clear in a passage in his recent, unpublished lecture 'Gottesgerechtigkeit bei Paulus': 'In the light of the gospel, sanctification is nothing other than having one lord who has to hold and carry us in body, soul, spirit, time, and eternity. Sanctification is exclusively confirmation of the first commandment in a world in which many lords and gods present themselves, promise salvation, and wish to incorporate us in the ranks of the powerful, the wise, the rich, and the pious, where they pretend to set us on our own feet . . . According to Luther's explanation of the second article of faith, "that Jesus Christ is my lord" is Christian sanctification, and nothing but that, and the Heidelberg Catechism expounds this with the words "that I, in life and death,

key word, ἁγιασμός, is drawn from baptismal vocabulary (cf. 1 Thess. 4: 7; 1 Cor. 6: 11), but an originally cultic word has come to have ethical and eschatological meaning: the conflict of the two aeons is continually decided afresh in the lives of Christians. In short, sanctification is 'the daily task of the living out of justification', 'an existence for God manifesting itself bodily in the secular world and in the face of temptation [*Anfechtung*]' (175/183, ET modified).

Here again Käsemann takes up Bultmann's views and subjects them to his characteristic criticism. In his classic essay of 1924 Bultmann had argued that Paul's ethics are to be understood in an eschatological dimension, and not as mere ethics or within the context of 'mysticism'. Paul is not concerned with sinlessness as freedom from guilt but as freedom from the power of sin, nor with development to perfection but with the constant grasping afresh of the once-for-all eschatological event. Further, the 'indicative', the statement of the gift of salvation, does not merely precede the 'imperative' of moral demand; rather the two paradoxically coincide.[41] Bultmann can sum up his view in Pindar's phrase, 'Become what you are' (165/173).[42] While this view was consciously critical of earlier views influenced by German idealism (which started, not from eschatology, but from the essence of a human being),[43] Käsemann argues that Bultmann is still determined by that tradition. The catch-phrase 'become what you are' leads to an intolerable formalization of the problem, which belies the point that Paul spends so much

belong to my true saviour Jesus Christ and am his own".' (*Heiligung ist evangelisch nichts anderes, als dieses: einen einzigen Herrn zu haben, der leiblich, seelisch, geistig, zeitlich und ewig uns tragen und erhalten muß. Heiligung ist ausschließlich Bewährung des ersten Gebotes in einer Welt, in der viele Herren und Götter sich uns anbieten, uns Heil versprechen, uns in die Reihen der Mächtigen, Weisen, Reichen, Frommen eingliedern wollen, wo sie uns auf die eigenen Beine zu stellen . . . vorgeben. 'Daß Jesus Christus sei mein Herr' ist nach Luthers Erklärung zum zweiten Glaubensartikel die christliche Heiligung, sonst nichts, und der Heidelberger Katechismus hat das mit den Worten verdeutlicht, 'daß ich im Leben und im Sterben meinem getreuen Heilande Jesus Christus gehöre und sein eigen bin'.*

[41] Bultmann started from the genuine connection between statements which form an antinomy (e.g., Gal. 5: 25) and concluded that it belonged to the manner of existence of the justified to stand under the imperative—a paradox which could only be fully understood by faith (1924*a*: 36, 53 f.; cf. Barth 1922: 187 f.). Cf. *Römer* 166/174. Käsemann's contribution to this debate is set in a wider context by Schrage (1982: 156–76).

[42] Bultmann 1951: 332.

[43] Bultmann 1924*a*: 41.

time on concrete exhortation (ibid.).[44] Secondly, this catch-phrase does not break free from the restriction of an anthropological perspective, and 'leaves the possibility open of interpreting the Pauline imperative as a summons to Christian "self-realization"' (166/174). This cautiously formulated criticism indicates that Bultmann himself is probably not open to this last charge (cf. *EVB* ii. 188/176).

To avoid these dangers, account must be taken of the (Catholic) line of interpretation which speaks of union with Christ and grounds Paul's ethics in his understanding of the sacraments. Ethical demands arise out of the sacramentally grounded *σὺν Χριστῷ* and the interchangeable *ἐν Χριστῷ* and *ἐν πνεύματι*. Or again, with regard to the structure of Romans, the coherence of chapters 5 (justification) and 6 (with its sacramental theme) is achieved by describing participation in the *regnum Christi* as the gift of salvation (*Römer* 166 f./174 f.). Interpretation along the lines of union with Christ, while it runs the risk of not protecting the primacy of christology by fusing the believer and the lord, makes it clear that the gift cannot be separated from the giver himself (167/175). The catch-phrase 'become what you are' should be reformulated: 'Abide by the Lord who has been given to you and by his lordship' (*EVB* ii. 188/176). Käsemann sums up, emphasizing, firstly, the concrete quality of Paul's ethics under the heading of discipleship and, secondly, the christological determination of his theology:

> The so-called imperative is integrated into the indicative and does not stand paradoxically alongside it, since the Kyrios remains Kyrios only for the one who serves him. Gift and task coincide in the fact that both designate standing under Christ's lordship, which only inadequately, namely, from the truncated anthropological view, can be brought under the idealistic formula: 'Become what you are'. The point is that the lordship of the exalted one be declared in the following [*Nachfolge*, discipleship] of the crucified one . . . Paul's ethics cannot be independent of either dogmatics or the cultus. It is part of his eschatology. More exactly, it is the anthropological reverse side of his christology. (*Römer* 167 f./175 f.)

[44] This question was followed up by Schrage (1961).

Everyday life as the sphere of Christian obedience

In Rom. 12: 1 Paul restricts the demands made on the Christian to a single theme: 'Presenting the body is the [ET: 'a'] central demand of God resulting from the message of justification. Having made us members of Christ's kingdom, God wants us to give visible confirmation of this' (*Römer* 315/327; cf. *EVB* ii. 199/189). What is at issue is not just our private existence but our earthly ability to communicate with the creator who does not give up his claim on the world. Thus, *σῶμα* means 'our being in relation to the world' (*unser auf die Welt bezogenes Sein*).[45]

For Käsemann the most significant point is that Paul uses cultic language (*παρίστημι, θυσία, ἅγιος, εὐάρεστος, λατρεία*) but transposes it into the sphere of eschatology (*Römer* 315/327),[46] i.e., into the secular, corporeal reality determined by the new aeon. Paul calls for a living sacrifice manifest in everyday life (*Alltag*)[47] and in the corporeal sphere, the sphere of creation. The same theme continues in v. 2 where baptismal paraenesis is probably employed (cf. Phil. 4: 18; 1 Pet. 2: 2 and 5). 'What was previously cultic is now extended to the secularity of our earthly life as a whole' (315/327; on this theme in the New Testament in general, cf. 'Versöhnung' 54/58).[48] For Käsemann this means that there has been a replacement of cultic thinking, even though worship and the sacraments are not disparaged but are now not separated from everyday life ('Versöhnung' 54/58; *EVB* ii. 201/191 f.). The anti-Catholic slant of his interpretation is particularly clear in the comment that the *temenos* of the ancient world is shattered, and while ritual is retained, if in a drastically reduced form, it loses its threatened isolation and no longer works *ex opere operato* (*Römer* 316/328; *EVB* ii. 201/191). 'The universal priesthood of all believers, called forth and manifested in the whole range of its activity, now appears as the

45 Cf. Bauer 1971: 179.

46 As early as 1949 Käsemann touched on this theme in his criticism of the idea of holy places ('Gemeinde' 1).

47 The emphases on the concreteness of the divine demand and on 'everyday life' are both present in Barth (1922: 411).

48 Käsemann takes up and radicalizes the anti-cultic position of Bultmann 1948: 114–16.

eschatological worship of God which puts an end to every other cultus' (*EVB* ii. 201/191). Christian worship and ethics merge at this point.

The theme of 'everyday life' is also intended to be critical of sectarian tendencies within Protestantism which seek to make a sharp distinction between the community of believers, as the place of God's presence, and the world (*PP* 69/37, 120 f./68; cf. pp. 269 ff. below on the church's solidarity, even in its worship, with unredeemed creation). Paul is concerned with service in everyday life and the secular world. Christian existence is not a private matter but has eschatological, i.e., public, character which is important for the world. It is only such an existence which does justice to Christ's lordship, which claims, not the individual, nor the religious sphere, but the world (*Römer* 317 f./329 f.). Thus, this part of Käsemann's interpretation of Paul's ethics is informed by a critique of the flight from reality and into the sacred or cultic by the 'enthusiast' and the 'Catholic'. The Christian is called to serve in the midst of the world and its life.

'Ἀνάγκη as the mark of apostolic existence

The subject of apostleship was returned to by Käsemann in his inaugural lecture at Tübingen in 1959.[49] This essay, which focuses on 1 Cor. 9: 14–18, is programmatic in the sense that it sets out Käsemann's view of the task of interpretation: the interpretation of scripture determined by the gospel (or 'Protestant interpretation of scripture', *evangelische Schriftauslegung*) is constantly accompanied and tempted by nomism and enthusiasm, or again, by liberal or Catholic tendencies (*EVB* ii. 231/226).[50]

[49] 'Eine paulinische Variation des "amor fati"', *EVB* ii. 223–39/217–35.

[50] Käsemann does not say that he is going to repeat some previous work (ET) but that he is going to practise his profession, i.e., as an exegete (*Lassen Sie mich meinem Handwerk jetzt so nachgehen . . .*; 223/217). Nor is the theme of the lecture 'the contradictory attitude of the apostle . . . gracious, and yet extremely dialectical', but 'the apparently contradictory and in any case highly dialectical behaviour of the apostle' (ibid.). The rendering of *Verhalten* (behaviour) with 'attitude' in an essay devoted to the critique of idealist interpretation is, at the least, unfortunate. The ET of 1 Cor. 9: 14–18 omits the main verb in v. 15*b* ('to die'); and Käsemann's translation of v. 17 does not speak of 'discharging a trust' but of being entrusted with a commission, nor of 'my rights as a preacher' (v. 18) but my right in the gospel (ibid.).

Turning to his Pauline theme, Käsemann pleads for the importance of the ἀνάγκη concept, the destiny (*Schicksal*) which lays hold of a person (232/228). Recent interpretation has either, under the influence of liberalism, watered down this concept to an inner psychological drive,[51] or has been determined by Catholic apologetic for a doctrine of reward for works. For Käsemann the question is how the apostle can claim a right to boast while remaining true to the doctrine of justification by faith alone. The apostle is confronted with the power of grace; his commission, and the compulsion arising out of it, originate with the lord (v. 16*cd*; 233/229). The power character (*Machtcharakter*) of God's grace, and of his other 'attributes', is again stressed. Thus, the ἀνάγκη motif contains the dialectics of grace and judgement, gift and demand: '*Ananke* here describes the power of God's will which radically challenges man, prevails over him with its demand and which makes its servant into its instrument' (234/230, ET modified).

With regard to the history-of-religions background of ἀνάγκη, Käsemann argues that there is both continuity and modification. Paul the Jew, unlike the Greek (ἀνάγκη) or the Roman (*fatum*), cannot speak of the anonymous force of blind fate (*Verhängnis*) or chance. If, nevertheless, he uses the Greek concept, he does so to characterize God's power as sovereign, inexorable, and ineluctable. To oppose this power means to experience it as a curse which leads to destruction. By contrast, the Christian experiences this power within the dialectics of obedience and love, slavery and freedom. Here Käsemann again takes up the dialectic of Luther's 'Freedom of the Christian' (238/234 f.). In the context of 1 Cor. 9, the point is that, because the gospel exercises a force on the apostle like that of destiny, he is not free in his action, nor can he claim a reward, financial or otherwise (235/231, 236/233).

Having established the meaning and importance of v. 16*cd*, Käsemann turns to the interpretation of the passage as a whole. There are three stages in Paul's line of thought:

1. Paul cannot accept financial support as he would then lose his boast and reward.

[51] Käsemann follows Maurer 1956 in the criticism of the psychological view of this passage.

2. Because the gospel exercises a force on him like that of destiny, he is not free in his action.
3. Nevertheless, he is blessed in his action.

Most recent interpretation jumps from (1) to (3), or at the most gives (2) psychological significance. But Paul is not concerned with disinterested love or the categorical imperative. For him, those who love will give up their fully justified rights if they wish to be and to remain those who love and serve. Thus, the fundamental problem of the passage is 'How can the one who experiences, as destiny, the compulsion of the gospel to serve ['to serve' is omitted by the ET], at the same time be and remain the one who loves?' (237/233; ET modified) For Paul compulsion does not exclude love because destiny (*Schicksal*) is not fate (*Verhängnis*) but issues in obedience and love. The power of grace invades a person's life and takes it into its service. Thus, joy is the mark of the apostle because 'the sacrifice consists in what God gave us' (Schlatter;[52] quoted on 239/235). The distinguishing mark of the apostle's love is not disinterest but engagement. The slave of the gospel also experiences the freedom of the children of God. Paul cannot and will not give up the sign of this love, his renunciation of financial support from the Corinthians, because it is his boast and his reward. In this position Paul is close to the Stoic ideal of the *amor fati*, but, unlike the Stoic, he does not boast of the autonomy of the spirit within a scheme of cosmic necessity, but of the liberating power of the gospel. The passage is an 'evangelical' variation of the *amor fati* (238/234).

The emphasis on compulsion or destiny which rules Käsemann's interpretation is to be accepted. This note is strong in v. 16, and not just in the use of ἀνάγκη. If καύχημα, a ground for boasting, is read without Lutheran connotations, then Paul states that such a ground for boasting does not exist because a commission has been entrusted to him (v. 17*b*).[53] Conversely, a curse will fall on him if he does not fulfil this calling (v. 16*d*). However, there is no reason (apart from the

[52] Schlatter 1926: 6.

[53] Cf. Lietzmann 1907: 43 ('Ἀνάγκη because he is commissioned by God . . .') and Barrett 1968/1971: 209. ('All Paul says is that preaching is no credit to him, because he has no choice about it. He cannot but preach.')

prior theological question as to how Paul can affirm the ideas of boasting and reward) to relate the passage to *sola fide* or *redigi ad nihilum*. Käsemann is able to introduce these themes because of the occurrence of *καύχημα*, in which, following Bultmann, he sees a key term in Paul's critique of the doctrine of justification by works. However, all the other key terms for Käsemann's interpretation (righteousness, law, faith, etc.) are not present, and *μισθός* does not mean the future reward for good works by which human beings can secure their own salvation. As Käsemann notes, v. 18 is highly paradoxical, and the paradox is that Paul's 'reward' is not his legitimate 'pay' as an apostle (with a play on words on *μισθός*), but making the gospel available free of charge, and thus assisting it in its progress. If Paul were to make full use of his right in the gospel he might obstruct its course.[54]

A second criticism of Käsemann's interpretation of this passage is to be levelled against the introduction, without argumentation, of the theme of love. This allows him to speak of the dialectic of love and obedience, in line with Luther's 'Freedom of the Christian', but does not arise from the text. The terms of the argument of the chapter up to this point have been freedom (v. 1), status ('Am I not an apostle?', v. 1), right (*ἐξουσία*, vv. 4, 11, and 12), authority (*Μὴ κατὰ ἄνθρωπον ταῦτα λαλῶ*; v. 8), sowing and reaping (v. 11), the authority of the law (v. 8), and of the commandment of Christ (v. 14). The idea of love—whether disinterested or engaged—plays no part. Käsemann appears to be a prisoner to the history of interpretation here, and, ironically, to the continuing power of the idealist tradition.

Romans 13: 1–7 as anti-enthusiastic paraenesis

In the interpretation of Rom. 13: 1–7[55] Käsemann finds himself at the centre of a direct conflict between Lutheran

[54] Cf. Barrett 1968/1971: 207–11, who emphasizes Paul's wish not to put an obstacle in the path of the preaching of the gospel (v. 12).

[55] 'Römer 13,1–7 in unserer Generation', *ZThK* 56 (1959), 316–76 ('Römer 13'); 'Grundsätzliches zur Interpretation von Römer 13' (1961), *EVB* ii. 204–22/196–216; and *Römer* 337–47/350–9; reviews of L. Hick, *Die Staatsgewalt im Lichte des Neuen Testaments* (1948), *VF* 4 (1949/50), 200–2, and C. Morrison, *The Powers That Be: Earthly Rulers and Demonic Powers in Rom. 13, 1–7* (1960), *ThLZ* 87 (1962), 516.

tradition (which found support in this passage for its emphasis on obedience to the civil authorities as ordained by God) and the German experience under Hitler. In order to criticize the Lutheran tradition, Käsemann debates at great length with the history of interpretation ('Römer 13' 316–73) and works hard to relativize the significance of the passage by arguing that it is aimed at a particular view of primitive Christian enthusiasm.

After a preliminary discussion of the nature of New Testament paraenesis, Käsemann emphasizes the uniqueness of this passage in Paul. The theme of relations with political powers, otherwise at the most (*sonst allenfalls*; ET: 'although') touched on elsewhere, is surprising because Christian contacts with authority were relatively few and, for the most part, passive (*Römer* 338/350). In another context Paul can disparage secular courts (1 Cor. 6: 1 ff.) and this indicates that his exhortation here is not theoretically derived (*Römer* 345/357; cf. 'Römer 13' 34–51).

The passage is to be understood within the section 12: 1–13: 14, and is not connected directly with the specifically Christian love command in 12: 20 f. and 13: 8–10 (*EVB* ii. 206 f./199; *Römer* 339 f./352). In the same way Paul's characteristic 'eschatological reservation' (as appears, for example, in vv. 11 f.) is missing. The passage is an independent or even alien body in Paul's exhortation which is to be expounded, first, in terms of itself, and only then, in the light of 12: 1, as an instruction on the theme of Christian worship (or service)[56] in everyday life (*Römer* 339 f./352).

The leading idea of the passage is provided by the ταγ-stem. Paul uses this with an anti-enthusiastic thrust in other passages, for example, against the emancipatory tendencies of Christian women and slaves. 'For the apostle the obedience owed to God demonstrates itself in earthly form in not leaving the state of subordination but in taking account of ταπεινοφροσύνη as the mark of a Christian life' (339/351; cf. *EVB* ii. 215–18/208–12). The new age does not create the island of the blessed, as the Corinthians thought; rather, it creates the possibility of service which is universal and corporeal (*leibhaftig*;

[56] Here and elsewhere Käsemann plays on the fact that the word *Gottesdienst* (worship) contains the word *Dienst* (service).

ET: 'alive') because it declares God's rightful lordship over the earth in the midst of the old age and thus preserves the world as divine creation (*EVB* ii. 218/211 f.).

The limited scope of the passage is further demonstrated by the fact that its vocabulary is thoroughly secular, and contains many words taken from the realm of hellenistic administration. 'Put pointedly, Paul takes up the jargon of hellenistic bureaucracy' ('Römer 13' 361).[57] The text is basically exhortatory; the accent is not on theological or metaphysical thought but on the injunction to be subordinate to the political authorities. Paul says nothing about the state or the Roman empire itself; he has local or regional authorities in mind, tax collectors, police, magistrates, Roman officials (*Römer* 341 f./354). It is with such officialdom that Christians might be expected to have dealings. Against this historical context, Paul exhorts those who, like the Corinthians, are prone to treat earthly authorities with indifference or contempt because of their heavenly citizenship (338/351). In terms of the history of religions, the piece is to be located within the Diaspora synagogue (342/354 f., with references).

Käsemann sums up, emphasizing the limited nature of the passage and the coherence of this section with Paul's anti-enthusiastic theology:

> Paul neither demonizes rulers nor glorifies them. The vocabulary of Hellenistic administration, the motifs borrowed from Jewish tradition, and the emphasis on exhortation must correspond to a sober exposition. The problem of political force does not come into view. This is the real problem [*Aporie*] of the passage. It can be explained only out of the one-sided front against a feared enthusiasm which emerges in 12: 3 and 1 Cor 7: 24, where each is directed to remain in

[57] Following Strobel 1956, the following terms and themes are adduced: *ἐξουσίαι τεταγμέναι*, prominent Roman officials—and with this falls the vogue for seeing a reference here to angelic powers (cf. 'Römer 13' 351–61); *λειτουργός*, the authorized representative of an administrative body; *ἀρχή*, a municipal authority; *ἔκδικος*, the agent (*Anwalt*) who acts as a representative of the governor of a community; *τοῦ θεοῦ διαταγή* as a characteristic of the power of the state; *διαταγή* (*Anordnung*), understood, not as an abstract order, but as a concrete regulation; *ὑποτάσσεσθαι*, denoting the relation of subjects to the *ὑπερέχοντες* defined in terms of obligation; the power of the sword (v. 4); which was at least in part transferred to Caesar's deputies; *ἔπαινος*, referring to the honouring of citizens and communities in official correspondence; and *καλός* and *ἀγαθός*, characterizing political conduct, such as fulfilling duties and paying taxes ('Römer 13' 361; *EVB* ii. 212/204; *Römer* 341 f./353 f.).

the state in which God has placed him. As elsewhere the apostle uses themes from popular philosophy to call the enthusiasts to order, he does it here by adopting the Hellenistic ideal of the state and the citizen. We cannot escape daily life. We meet the will of God there. The political sphere is certainly provisional. But only enthusiasts fail to see that our worship is to be accomplished in provisional things by doing what has to be done in the given situation. (346 f./359)

Going beyond the text, Käsemann broaches the question of the limits of the obedience which can be demanded of a Christian. This occurs when, and only when, further service becomes impossible. Christians cannot be asked to deny their existence as Christians, though this should not be confused with the maintenance of traditional forms of Christian existence and organization. The charismatic is able to distinguish between the tradition and the opportunity of the hour (*EVB* ii. 221/214). The Christian task is to authenticate (*bewähren*; see ch. 3 n. 63 above) Christ as the hidden lord of the world. However, this hiddenness is reserved for Christ; his followers cannot serve anonymously (221/215). Käsemann does not explicate or support this point. Finally, the question of Christian participation in revolution is raised. The Christian's right as a citizen to partake in revolution cannot be denied when every act of service takes on the character of participation in common self-destruction (231 f./215 f.). This discussion highlights the crucial role of service in Käsemann's understanding of Christian existence.

WORSHIP IN SOLIDARITY WITH CREATION

As was seen above, Käsemann regards Rom. 8 as part of Paul's anti-enthusiastic theology. This perspective is applied even to the worship of the church as it is understood in Käsemann's essay on Rom. 8: 26 f.[58] The passage is marked by Paul's distinctive view of the spirit. Although Paul shares the presuppositions of the hellenistic enthusiasts that the spirit is the end-time gift *per se* which is manifested in ecstasy and miracle, he modifies this view. His doctrine of the spirit is

[58] 'Der gottesdienstliche Schrei nach der Freiheit', *PP* 211–36/122–37; cf. *VF* 7 (1956), 149 (which contains a eulogy of Schniewind) and *Römer* 231–4/23–43.

determined by his christology, so that there is a practical identity between 'in Christ' and 'in the spirit'. However, Paul offers three safeguards against the danger of enthusiasm. The power of the risen Christ is to be proved in everyday life as the *nova oboedientia*. Secondly, the spirit is regarded as the power of standing fast in temptation (*Anfechtung*) and suffering. Thirdly, the spirit is an earnest and is thus set under the eschatological reservation (*PP* 211–15/122–4). It is against this background that Paul speaks about prayer in Rom. 8: 26 f.

The statement that Christians do not know how to pray as they ought is unique in the New Testament which is otherwise marked by a supreme confidence in this area. Interpretation either attempts to weaken this point or to interpret it in terms of an inner inability to pray. But the text speaks of *ἀσθένεια* and of the vicarious or representative (*stellvertretend*) intercession of the spirit (220/128). This point is strengthened in the Romans commentary: *ἀσθένεια* is not an inner inability but the state of external assault (*Anfechtung*) which characterizes Christian existence (*Römer* 231 f./240). The phrase *στεναγμοὶ ἀλάλητοι* does not mean wordless sighs but unspeakable sighs, the nearest parallel being the *ἄρρητα ῥήματα* of 2 Cor. 12: 4. The phenomenon which Paul is writing about must be highly noticeable, public and not private, and hence the glossolalia which was characteristic of the worship of the Pauline congregations (*PP* 221–6/12–31).

Käsemann then contrasts Paul's estimation of glossolalia with that of the enthusiasts by interpreting these verses against their immediate context: 'the apostle describes as sighs what the church considers and praises as the manifestation of heavenly tongues and thus compares them with the sighs of the creature and the sighing for redemption from bodily temptation [*Anfechtung*] which is familiar to every Christian' (227 f./132). The cries of glossolalia in the congregation's worship are not the songs of the angels, but the proof that believers still have to join the choir of the depths which can be heard by unredeemed creation (231/134). Even in worship, which in enthusiastic circles is often an escape from earthly reality, the church is in a deep, if tension filled, solidarity with the world (234/136). The *theologia gloriae* of the enthusiasts has been thoroughly demythologized into a *theologia viatorum* by Paul (ibid.). This corresponds to the central themes of Paul's theology, the humanization of humanity (*die Menschwerdung des Menschen*; see p. 146 above), and the revelation of God's power *sub contrario* in 'God's righteousness'.[59] This understanding of prayer is orientated to the first beatitude[60] according to which only the poor receive salvation.

It is not only the doctrine of justification which leads Paul to demythologize the view of the spirit held by the enthusiasts; his 'apocalyptic' also contributes to this process. Typically Käsemann integrates the two themes: 'When it is a matter of the justification of the ungodly, God does not just want a new religiosity but a renewed creation under the cosmocrator Christ' (*Römer* 234/242). The present time is the time of the messianic woes, the birth-pangs of the new age, from which Christians are not excepted. In Paul's view, the apparently supernatural gift of glossolalia is nothing other than the cry of the assailed for freedom, a freedom which will only be attained when the hidden cosmocrator changes this world into the sphere of his lordship (*PP* 233–5/135 f.). If this perspective is lost, then the hidden *cosmocrator* becomes merely the lord of the cult, and the church, which is meant to be the beginning of the new world, a conventicle (235/136 f.). Thus, Käsemann again argues that Paul's theology (here his understanding of the spirit and of prayer) is determined by the central doctrine of justification in its 'apocalyptic' horizon.

[59] Käsemann acknowledges his debt to Schniewind for this point: 'Prayer is described in Rom. 8: 26 f. as it is formed from the δικαιοσύνη θεοῦ' (Schniewind 1952: 91 quoted on *PP* 232/134). In fact Käsemann's article is a rethinking of the question from Schniewind's starting-point with the addition of his own particular emphases. Thus, the eschatological understanding of justification, in which 'eschatology' refers to the events of the end (Schniewind), becomes the 'apocalyptic' horizon of the doctrine of justification (Käsemann). This leads into Käsemann's new point that, even in worship, the church is in solidarity with unredeemed creation. Schniewind and Käsemann also share a concern for the christological determination of pneumatology. Schniewind criticizes Fuchs's monograph *Christus und der Geist bei Paulus* (1932) for diminishing the christological kerygma in favour of anthropological categories (1952: 96–103), and thus his argument anticipates Käsemann's criticisms of Bultmann. Schniewind was unable to complete his essay before his death and so the section on Christ as the incarnate one (which is regarded as the criterion for the differentiation between the spirit and Christ in Paul) is missing.

[60] Käsemann claims the support of Barth 1922: 330 f. here, though this is not obvious on the surface. Schniewind reviews Luther, Barth, and Schlatter's interpretation of this passage in the light of the doctrine of justification (1952: 94–6).

THE CHURCH AND THE CHRISTIAN LIFE: LORDSHIP, THEOLOGICAL INTERPRETATION, CRITICISM

It has now been shown that Käsemann's interpretation of Paul's understanding of the church and the Christian life is determined throughout by the doctrine of justification in its 'apocalyptic' horizon, and thus by the centre of Paul's theology (as this is interpreted by Käsemann). The motif of the body of Christ, and not that of the people of God, is regarded as the centre of Paul's ecclesiology because it alone can protect the doctrinal pattern of the primacy of christology over ecclesiology. The ἐν Χριστῷ motif means the state of being continually confronted by the lord who justifies the ungodly. Paul's ecclesiology and ethics are governed by the charisma concept which is the projection of the doctrine of justification into these areas.[61] Paul, as an apostle, is compelled by a force like destiny because God's righteousness is both gift and power. Even the teaching to obey secular authorities is to be understood in the light of Paul's critique of enthusiasm, a critique which stems from his doctrine of justification and the 'apocalyptic' character of his theology, and which calls the enthusiast back to earthly reality as the sphere of Christian service. Paul is particularly concerned with concrete acts of service, which, if considered theologically, are the living out of the doctrine of justification, the *nova oboedientia*.

The cosmic scope of the doctrine of justification is again apparent in Käsemann's treatment of the church and ethics. Thus 'the Body of Christ proved attractive to Paul because it expressed better than the notion of the "People of God" the motif of a new creation with a world-wide dimension'.[62] Again, the body of Christ is the sphere of Christ's lordship through which the *cosmocrator* claims the world. In Christian worship—and even when using the gift of glossolalia—the church expresses its solidarity with unredeemed creation as it awaits its final liberation. In the area of ethics, Paul is

[61] Cf. Schütz's summary of Käsemann's view: 'The Church is the embodiment of the gospel understood as the doctrine of justification' (1975: 256 f.).

[62] Harrington 1971*a*: 247, referring to *PP* 188 f./108.

concerned, not with the acts and decisions of the individual, but with the 'confirmation' of Christ's lordship in the world, the preservation of this world as God's creation.

With the consistent emphasis on the centrality of the doctrine of justification goes the continued 'battle on two fronts'. In the area of ecclesiology, Käsemann is particularly concerned with Catholic and enthusiastic, or egalitarian, interpretation. Against Catholic views, he argues that Paul's ecclesiology is not based on the principles of hierarchy, tradition, and legitimization, nor on the concepts of sacred office, persons, or places. Instead, Paul's understanding of the church is based on the charisma concept, the priesthood of all believers, and the invasion of the secular by grace.[63] Against the enthusiasts are urged the themes of service within the 'conditions of life' of this world, the call to responsibility, and, again, the call out of the community of the pious into the secular, the sphere of God's action. Against the related error of egalitarian interpretation, he sets Paul's understanding of charisma in which people are given differing gifts which complement each other, thereby creating the opportunity of mutual interdependence and the building up of the community.

As much of Käsemann's pre-1950 work was in the area of ecclesiology, many of the elements of the lordship of Christ construct in this area, and the related area of ethics, have already been noted above. However, some points are modified in the post-1960 period, and some new ones added:

1. In *Leib und Leib Christi* Käsemann argued for the importance of the gnostic aeon concept, and, for example, interpreted the body of Christ in terms of a world-encompassing aeon. In the post-1960 period the focus moves away from history-of-religions questions to the explicitly theological question of which motif best expresses Paul's theological concerns. Käsemann's main aim is to uphold the view that while Christ is present in the church, he is present as lord and judge. Christ and the church must not be identified; Christ's lordship over the church must not be reversed. (The 1947/8 article on the

[63] Harrington comments correctly that it is difficult to avoid the impression that Käsemann plays Paul's theology off against that of 'early catholicism' on the analogy of the authentic Lutheran teaching on justification and the institutional (better, Catholic) churches (1971*b*: 366).

Lord's supper, with its emphasis on Christ's presence in the sacrament as saviour and judge, thus marks a middle point between Käsemann's views of 1933 and 1969.)

2. The theme of apostleship is also broached again in the post-1960 period. Through the discussion of *ἀνάγκη* Käsemann argues that the apostle experiences the power of grace as a force like destiny. The controlling idea here is the dialectic of gift and power, as in the interpretation of 'God's righteousness' and of charisma. Surprisingly, Käsemann does not relate the *ἀνάγκη* concept to the theme of the lordship of Christ explicitly.

3. The *ἐν Χριστῷ* motif sums up 'the state of those who through the gospel are called out of the old world and who only belong to the new creation in so far as they continue to be confronted with the Lord who justifies the ungodly'. This interpretation is a concise summary of Käsemann's view of Paul's theology: the lordship of Christ is defined in its eschatological nature, cosmic intention, and in its connection with the doctrine of justification. By this interpretation the integration of Paul's juridical, eschatological, and participatory categories is completed: the phrase *ἐν Χριστῷ* belongs to the category of participation but is here set in an eschatological perspective and interpreted in the light of the doctrine of justification. It is this integration of the different sides of Paul's thought which allows Käsemann to argue against the separation of the doctrines of justification and sanctification.

4. The theme of everyday life as the sphere of Christian service means that there is no area which is beyond Christ's lordship. The barriers which are inherent in the idea of cult have been demolished; all creation in its secularity is open to the attack of grace, the claim of Christ's lordship on the world.

5. Christian worship, and even the gift of glossolalia, is not proof of the church's heavenly status but, paradoxically, the sign that it is still under assault (*Anfechtung*) and in solidarity with unredeemed creation. The worship of the church is the cry of the assailed for eschatological freedom. (Here Paul demythologizes the *theologia gloriae* of the enthusiasts into a *theologia viatorum*.) Thus, even this aspect of the church's life is determined by the theme of God's righteousness in its 'apocalyptic' perspective. In this instance the connection with

the lordship theme is through the doctrine of justification and the idea of the eschatological reservation.

6. Even the theme of submission to civil authority (Rom. 13: 1–7) is to be related to the lordship of Christ. Service within the order of the world, including obedience to secular authorities, declares God's rightful lordship over the earth in the midst of the old age and preserves the world as God's creation.

In this part of Käsemann's interpretation of Paul's theology the most noticeable feature of his methodology has already been commented on, namely the consistent use of explicitly theological models drawn from the period of the Reformation. Käsemann carries through his programme of interpreting Paul's ecclesiology in the light of his doctrine of justification very thoroughly, thereby setting Christ over the church. The shift from an approach focusing on history-of-religions questions to one that is led by theological concerns, within which history-of-religion insights may or may not contribute, is particularly clear in the discussion of the body of Christ. However, history-of-religions categories continue to have a role in Käsemann's theological work. The hellenistic idea of the identification of the devotee with the destiny of the lord is said to be taken up by Paul and interpreted as the doctrine of the incorporation of the believer into the body of the exalted lord, the sphere of Christ's lordship. Again, the concept of *ἀνάγκη*, while not being accepted by Paul in the sense of blind fate, speaks of the ineluctable will of God and challenges theologies which retreat into psychological categories. Thus, Käsemann again takes up history-of-religions categories and makes use of them in theological work.

The main weaknesses of Käsemann's depiction of Paul's ecclesiology and ethics are directly related to his use of theological models for interpretation. In two important cases it is necessary to criticize Käsemann's use of the gift–power dialectic, an idea which goes back to the connection between gift and giver in Schlatter and Barth. The attempt to link the *χαρίσματα* of 1 Cor. 12 and Rom. 12 to the one *χάρισμα* of Rom. 6: 23 (and thus to the gift–power dialectic of Käsemann's interpretation of justification) is not convincing. The same is true of the view that the compelling destiny which drives the apostle in 1 Cor. 9: 16 is to be seen as an expression of the dialectic of freedom and obedience (Luther). Equally, Käsemann's attempt to safeguard 'the primacy of christology over ecclesiology' by demoting the theme of the people of God, in favour of the body of Christ motif, is not successful. Finally, the key exegetical argument that the body of Christ motif should be connected to Paul's new Adam christology, and hence interpreted along the lines of a sphere of power of world-wide scope, was rejected.

6

Conclusion

If Käsemann's interpretation of Paul's theology in its entirety is surveyed, the consistency of his views across five decades is remarkable. Thus, while Käsemann changed his understanding of what constituted the 'centre' of Paul's theology after the publication of his dissertation, and of the history-of-religions background to Paul's theology in the 1950s, perhaps surprisingly these major changes did not fundamentally alter his interpretation. The underlying consistency of his views is due to two characteristics which mark his approach throughout his career: firstly, the approach to Paul's theology in terms of dialectical tension, particularly the dialectic of gift and power; secondly, the constant search for a unifying interpretation of Paul, an interpretation which seeks to take account of elements which are often seen as mutually exclusive.

The constant search for a unified interpretation outweighs the difference over where the centre of Paul's thought is to be found. In *Leib und Leib Christi*, Käsemann had argued that the participatory themes of the spirit, the sacraments, and the 'in Christ' were central. In the post-1960 period, Käsemann interprets Paul's theology from a central nexus of themes which can be summed up as the doctrine of justification in its 'apocalyptic' orientation. However, in the course of this study it has become clear that Käsemann's early work is of great significance for understanding his later views. For while he soon gave up his earlier view of what constituted the centre of Paul's theology, many of the key insights of the dissertation are retained, including his distinctive approach to the different lines of Paul's thought. In the dissertation, the participatory theme of the spirit is interpreted, at one point, in terms of the doctrine of justification, a juridical theme. In all his later work, the different types of conceptuality (especially the juridical, the participatory, and the eschatological) are interpreted in the light of one another. Thus, while Paul's theology is construed in different ways, the underlying approach is similar.

This feature of Käsemann's approach can be further illustrated from two important examples. God's righteousness is not understood (in line with the traditional Lutheran view) solely as the gift of a righteous status granted to a human being; it is also a power at work in a human being, issuing in the new obedience. Here the doctrine of justification (a juridical theme) is interpreted by means of the gift–power dialectic, a dialectic which Käsemann first applies to the understanding of the spirit (a participatory theme). Conversely, Käsemann understands the idea of charisma (a participatory theme) as the projection of the doctrine of justification into the sphere of ecclesiology: a charisma both is a gift and exerts the power of the giver. If it is to retain its character as such, it cannot be claimed by human beings as their own work or achievement. Recipients of the charismata allow the giver to work through them, thereby living out the doctrine of justification. In this way, the participatory theme of the spirit is interpreted in the light of the juridical theme of justification, and vice versa. (Käsemann's interpretation assumes from first to last that Paul's theology is determined throughout by his eschatology, a point which also contributes to the consistency of his view of Paul.) Consequently, what is held to constitute the centre of Paul's theology changes, but this has only a limited effect on Käsemann's interpretation. The approach whereby the various lines of thought in Paul's theology are used to interpret each other ensures a remarkable degree of consistency in Käsemann's interpretation throughout his career.

A second factor which accounts for the consistency of Käsemann's interpretation is the persistence of his use of the gift–power dialectic. The theological antecedent of this dialectic is to be located ultimately in Luther's understanding of the gospel: Christ is both God's gift to us and our lord. At the same time Käsemann finds the same dialectic in the experience of the gift and claim of the spirit in primitive Christianity. At this crucial point, theological and historical judgements coincide.

The dialectic of gift and power can also be related to

Käsemann's (and Luther's) theme that the gospel is always at war on the two fronts of legalism and enthusiasm. Against legalism, the critical power of the gospel reduces human beings to nothing and creates them anew by the gift of justification. This cannot be earned by works but must be received as a gift in faith. On the second front, the gospel confronts the enthusiast with its claim. The gospel is not simply a gift to be enjoyed by the recipient but a power which brings about the new obedience.[1]

The gift–power dialectic is also significant for contemporary theology, and, perhaps surprisingly, for ecumenical debate. While Käsemann's championing of the doctrine of justification appears, at times, to be simply an aggressively Protestant stance, the fact that he interprets this doctrine in terms of the gift–power dialectic allows him to incorporate Catholic emphases, including the 'make righteous' theme.[2] The same approach, whereby Catholic themes are incorporated within a Protestant doctrinal framework, was noted in the discussion of ecclesiology and the sacraments.

In the light of this analysis, Käsemann's fundamental exegetical decision is to interpret the supposedly technical term *δικαιοσύνη θεοῦ* (through which he interprets the doctrine of justification) in terms of concepts first applied in the study of the participatory themes. These include not only the dialectic of gift and power, but also the spatial and dynamic concept of a 'sphere of power' discussed below.

Käsemann's view of Paul can also be summarized in his catch-phrase 'the lordship of Christ'. When he uses this catch-phrase he is not referring to an exegetical hypothesis based, for instance, on Paul's use of *κύριος*, though his debt to Bousset's *Kyrios Christos* is important. The catch-phrase functions on three levels. Firstly, Käsemann finds this theme

[1] Although it is correct that Käsemann opposes 'the notion of personality as the vehicle of transcendence, and the idea of a measurable, demonstrable continuity in history' (Harrisville 1985: 256), the primary targets in the 'war on two fronts' are not these but legalism and enthusiasm. It is not accurate either to sum up Käsemann's theology in the one word, *Anfechtung* (ibid.). While one of the main aspects of legalism, the tendency to rely on God's gifts as a guarantee of salvation, is criticized by the *Anfechtung* theme, the other main aspect, reliance on one's own works, is not.

[2] This is noted by Kerr (1981*b*: 148), despite his curious attempt to dispute the importance of the doctrine of justification for Käsemann (ch. 4 n. 144 above).

present in a great variety of the individual themes and topics of Paul's letters.[3] These are listed in the conclusions to the preceding chapters and form the exegetical basis of Käsemann's interpretation. They provide the material for what we have called the lordship of Christ construct. Secondly, the lordship of Christ functions as a theologoumenon which is independent of particular Pauline texts, and is free to provide connections between topics which are not specifically related in the text. Thirdly, at the level of contemporary theological debate, the catch-phrase is a summary of Käsemann's own theology, in which he takes up Luther's theology of the cross and argues that christology (understood in the closest connection with the doctrine of justification) must be given the dominant and determining position within Christian doctrine.

This complex situation explains why Käsemann can assert, in various contexts, that 'God's righteousness', the doctrine of justification, Paul's christology, the dialectic of gift and power, and the lordship of Christ (understood as a sphere of power) are the 'centre' of Paul's theology. 'God's righteousness' is the Pauline motif through which the central doctrine of justification is expounded. Paul's christology is determined by the cross and hence by his doctrine of justification. The gift–power dialectic is used to expound the doctrine of justification and is said to underlie the whole of Paul's theology. The lordship of Christ is the catch-phrase which sums up Käsemann's theological programme and enables him to relate the individual themes of his interpretation to its doctrinal centre.[4]

Käsemann's interpretation of Paul is self-consciously a theological interpretation. In his dissertation this meant focusing on Pauline concepts and the myths which he

[3] 'To this theme of God's *Basileia*, seizing the world through the event of the cross, Käsemann proceeded to warp everything he thought and wrote, and by their allegiance to this theme marked his enemies and his friends' (Harrisville 1985: 256). Gibbs is, therefore, incorrect to say that there has been no attempt (before his own) to interpret Paul's theology from the interpretative centre of the lordship of Christ (1971: 25).

[4] N. M. Watson, who acknowledges his debt to Käsemann, continues in this tradition when he argues that the model of 'centre' is too static for Paul's theology and suggests the trinitarian model of 'coinherence'. The different elements of Paul's thought inhere in one another, in the sense of belonging to one another, and require one another for their adequate comprehension (1983: 394).

employed, and interpreting them existentially. In turn, these concepts and myths become the 'building blocks' for constructing Paul's theology. (These 'building blocks' are often signalled by the use of transliterations: *cosmocrator*, *kaine diatheke*, etc.; see p. 115 above.) In the post-1960 period this approach is integrated into and subordinated to an explicitly theological approach,[5] in which the doctrinal shape and the coherence of Paul's theology are the key questions. Käsemann does not abandon historical-critical methods, but they are not the driving force of his work.[6] Thus, to take the central example, despite Käsemann's attempt to argue that *δικαιοσύνη θεοῦ* is a fixed formula which Paul inherited from Jewish 'apocalyptic' (and his caution on this point, in contrast with Stuhlmacher, is to be noted), in the final analysis his interpretation of this phrase depends on the point that the gift–power dialectic is characteristic of Paul's theology as a whole, and not on a history-of-religions derivation. And, as has been seen, the gift–power dialectic has both theological and historical antecedents.

In the course of his interpretation of Paul, Käsemann makes use of historical methods in a variety of ways for the purposes of theological interpretation. He takes no systematic stand with regard to the place of the 'results' of historical research in contemporary theology. At a general level he uses the history-of-religions approach to avoid a premature modernizing of the text. However, at the same time, he argues that certain themes in the history of religion (which as such provide only the framework of Paul's theology) are of permanent significance for Christian theology. The most prominent example here is the cosmic scope and future

[5] Thus, this study offers some support for Ritschl's unsubstantiated hypothesis on the course of German theology (exegesis) since 1945 (1982, 135 f.): (1) 1945–55: an almost exclusive emphasis on exegesis. In Käsemann's case this is the period of concentration on historical and form-critical questions. (2) 1955–*c.* 1965: an emphasis on hermeneutical and methodological questions and a growing interest in ethics. For Käsemann this meant a concern with the doctrinal shape of Paul's theology and the subordination of the history-of-religions approach to theological questions. (3) 1965–*c.* 1975: a fragmentation of the theological endeavour into socio-political ethics versus conservative trends. Käsemann played his part in the attack on the latter, and has developed his theology in the direction of political theology, particularly in the collection *Kirchliche Konflikte*, i (1969–83).

[6] Harrisville 1985: 257.

orientation of the 'apocalyptic' perspective. He also employs historical methods to criticize conservative views, sometimes to the detriment of historical interpretation. The positing of liturgical fragments and of traditional motifs in Paul's letters is used as a powerful lever against Catholic, conservative Protestant, or pietist appeal to the Pauline text.

In addition, Käsemann takes up concepts drawn from the history-of-religions approach and uses them for contemporary theological purposes. Particularly important here are such concepts as 'sphere of lordship' or power (*Herrschaftssphäre*, *Machtbereich*, etc.). Initially Käsemann understood a sphere of power along the lines of a gnostic aeon and in terms of the dynamics of participation in the primitive Lord's supper. The concept is spatial, relational, and dynamic: human beings stand within a sphere of power, they are under the power of a particular lord. In the post-1960 period the emphasis shifts to the Pauline theme of the antithetical lordships of Adam and Christ, in which each determines his own 'sphere of power'. Again, the earlier view is not jettisoned but it is integrated with the new—even though the theory of the influence of a pre-Christian gnosticism has been abandoned.

If the evolution of these concepts in Käsemann's work is complex, so also is the use to which he puts them, as this is not limited to the area of historical interpretation. Because Käsemann uses the notion of a 'sphere of power' to expound his understanding of Paul's theology, and believes that this has a particular theological thrust (the doctrinal pattern of the primacy and determining role of christology over all other themes), the notion itself takes on the same doctrinal colouring. Finally, this complex concept also has a role in contemporary theological debate. It is used by Käsemann to criticize both Bultmann's individualistic view of Christianity and Catholic views which do not subordinate the corporate, sacramental aspects of Christianity to the doctrinal pattern implied by the primacy of christology. What is so unusual in Käsemann's approach is the use, for theological purposes, of what was, at least in the first instance, a history-of-religions concept. In this way it is not simply the 'results' of historical scholarship which affect the theological process but the concepts by which these are articulated.

The key role of the concept of a 'sphere of power' in Käsemann's interpretation of Paul raises the question of how his interpretation is to be classified. In the light of his own background and the influence of Barth and Bultmann on him, it is natural to assume that he regards Paul's theology as a theology of the word. And indeed there are statements in his work to this effect:

> It [Paul's theology] is a theology of the Word because it is only through the word of the cross that Jesus' death remains present, remains grace, remains promise and obligation [*Verpflichtung*; ET: 'covenant']; and it is the work of the one who is risen to let this Word manifest itself in preaching, in the sacraments and in the Christian life. (*PP* 106/59)

In its subordination of all other themes to the word, this statement is consistent with the tradition of Protestant neo-orthodoxy within which Käsemann stands. Further, he sets the theology of the word over against theologies which focus on the facts of redemption (90/50), manifestations (92 f./51) or history (125/70). It is particularly in criticism of this last view that Käsemann speaks of the word. He also integrates this concept of the word with his other main themes. God's word is his creative power which is incalculable and not at our disposal. It sets us in Christ's lordship and deprives us of our autonomy. Our response to it is the obedience of faith which must prove itself in the Christian life (*PP* 145/82).

However, Käsemann's statements about the role of the sacraments keep the question about the nature of his interpretation open. The subordination of preaching to the sacraments in his dissertation is in line with the emphasis on the sacramental nature of Paul's religion in Bousset and Heitmüller but is highly surprising by the standards of Barth and Bultmann's views of Paul. And while a more orthodox Protestant line is taken in all his later publications, his earlier view is not simply ignored or reversed. He continues to argue that the sacraments (both baptism and the Lord's supper) incorporate participants—and not only believers who have responded to the word—into Christ and his body. Nevertheless, the Catholic idea of mystical union is not regarded as the appropriate model with which to understand the relationship between Christ and Christians. In its place Käsemann puts the theme of lordship: 'His [Paul's] concern is that we take the place occupied by the earthly Jesus and thus declare the lordship of the exalted One. To the extent that this is not done exclusively by the word, it is indisputable that Paul held the sacraments as constitutive and irreplaceable for every Christian' (*Römer* 161/169).

Apart from the telling lack of precision in this statement ('to the extent that this is not done exclusively by the word'), in another context Käsemann argues that word and sacrament are to be regarded as complementary, and both are brought under the theme of the lordship of Christ: 'As the sacrament displays the externality of the act of revelation and protects it against spiritualizing, the word stresses the fact that relations are established and protects against an impersonalizing [*Verdinglichung*] of revelation. In both cases the central concern is not the individual but the lordship of Christ . . .' (174/182). In addition to these statements, the present study has shown that Käsemann's interpretation of Paul is by no means exclusively orientated to the word. Much more important to his interpretation as a whole are the theme of the lordship of Christ and the concept of a sphere of power. In this respect there is a sharp contrast with Bultmann, and a measure of continuity with the history-of-religions school with its emphasis on the importance of the sacraments in Paul. Thus, there is a tension between Käsemann's statements (which regard Paul's theology as a theology of the word) and his actual interpretation. On the basis of the latter, it is to be concluded that his interpretation is based on the theme of lordship (understood as a sphere of power) and is expounded by means of the gift–power dialectic.

Käsemann's place in the history of Pauline interpretation is to be understood in the light of his attempt to bring together the two divergent traditions of interpretation to which he is heir: on the one hand, the tradition of the historical-critical exegesis of mid- to late nineteenth-century German Protestantism (especially Baur, Lüdemann, and the history-of-religions school) and, on the other hand, the tradition of an explicitly theological interpretation, drawing on Lutheran and Reformed perspectives, in the third and fourth decades of this century (especially Barth, Schlatter, and Bultmann). His interpretation attempts to overcome the fragmented view of Paul common at the turn of the century (as exemplified in the three lines of thought in Schweitzer's analysis of Paul) by integrating the insights of historical-critical exegesis within an interpretation with a dominating, doctrinal centre. Similarly, the salvation-historical element in Paul's thought, emphasized by Baur but minimized in most Protestant interpretation, is affirmed but firmly subordinated to the doctrine of justification. At the same time, Käsemann integrates the insights of interpretations which focused on Paul's *religion* (the sacraments, confession of the lord in the worship of the community) within an interpretation which deals with Paul's *theology*.

Käsemann's place in the history of interpretation can also be viewed in the context of the dominant interpretations of his own time. Firstly, and most importantly, he debates with Bultmann's view of Paul (and of Christian theology) on four main theological points. On all four points he moves the emphasis from the first pole of a theological dialectic, where Bultmann had set it, to the second pole:

1. Accepting Bultmann's starting-point on the interrelation in theology of 'anthropology' and 'theology', Käsemann argues that the emphasis should be laid, not with Bultmann on the anthropological pole, but with Barth and Schlatter on the theological pole. It is not sufficient to speak of 'human being in faith'; the theologian must speak of God, the creator who does not give up his claim on creation but justifies the ungodly, raises the dead, and calls into existence the things which do not exist.

2. Correspondingly, while taking up Bultmann's second dialectic concerning the interrelation in theology of soteriology and christology, Käsemann argues against Bultmann's (and Melanchthon's) soteriological orientation and for the christological orientation of theology. Christian theology must proclaim the lordship of Christ, not merely the salvation of human beings. On this point Käsemann regards himself as correcting a distortion within Lutheran tradition by restoring a proper understanding of Luther to the tradition.

3. With regard to the dialectic of the individual and the world, Paul's theology is not primarily orientated to the individual but to the world.

4. In the debate about realized and future eschatology in Paul, despite the presence and importance of realized eschatology in the apostle's theology, this must be contained within a future perspective, namely the hope of Christ's final triumph.

In addition to these 'corrections' to Bultmann, Käsemann keeps up a constant and wide-ranging critique on the two fronts of 'Catholic' and 'enthusiastic' interpretation.

To sum up Käsemann's place in the history of interpretation, it can be said that, inspired by theological themes from Barth and Schlatter, Käsemann puts forward a view of Paul which is basically indebted to Barth and offers a 'correction' of Bultmann. As an interpreter of the New Testament, he gives his views better (though not unflawed) historical and exegetical foundations than Barth did, and integrates the results of nineteenth-century research on the church and sacraments which the latter ignored. By doing so, Käsemann pointed (with Schweitzer) to the apocalyptic background of Paul and the New Testament, and thus to an important part of their Jewish background.

If it is important to give an account of Käsemann's place in the history of nineteenth- and twentieth-century German-language theology, it is also worth reflecting on the relative lack of influence that his work has today. The weakening of the tradition of a historically informed, theological exegesis within the neo-orthodox theological tradition has been noticeable since the mid-1970s. The social and political upheaval in the years after 1968 certainly raised very serious questions about the abstract quality of neo-orthodox theology, and about its apolitical stance. In general much of the vitality of the movement had been lost over the fifty years since the publication of Barth's Romans commentary. Thus, Käsemann's Romans, the *magnum opus* which sums up his life's work as an interpreter of Paul, appeared precisely at the point at which the tradition which it represents was going into decline. This is reflected to a small extent in the reception of the Romans commentary.[7] From within the Bultmann school, W. Schmithals argued that the work does not open up a new epoch in interpretation but closes, impressively, that opened by Barth.[8] His argumentation for this judgement[9] reflects his own interests rather than the course of Pauline studies in the following decade but, none the less, the judgement is correct in itself. H. D. Betz, anticipating a large number of positive reviews, strikes a considerable note of caution with regard to historical method, as has already been noticed (ch. 3 n. 5). This is a small but significant pointer to the fact that Käsemann's theological approach to the letter goes against contemporary concern for the primacy of the task of understanding Paul within his own religious culture. However, these criticisms ought to be understood as attempts to correct the tradition from within, i.e., as attempts to redress the balance between historical and theological factors in interpretation.

Another reason for the relative lack of influence of Käsemann's work today is the point that it did not lead to the setting up of a 'school' of interpreters inspired by his approach. There was perhaps the beginning of such a school in the doctoral work of Käsemann's pupils, P. Stuhlmacher, C. Müller, W. Schrage, and W. Klaiber,[10] but of these scholars only the last two could be said to have continued to work with the approach used by Käsemann. Of the two most eminent scholars in this list, Schrage has concentrated his attention on an area only touched on by his teacher, namely, ethics, while Stuhlmacher's theological position has moved in

[7] In addition to the reviews commented on below, the following substantive reviews ought to be noted: Strecker, 1974, Giblin 1975, Morgan 1975, Riches 1976. Sauter 1976, Kerr 1981*a* and 1981*b*, Wright 1982.

[8] On the fundamental relationship to Barth's Romans, cf. the title of Lohse's newspaper article on Käsemann's commentary: 'The great bell rings again' (1973*b*)—a reference to Barth's own remark that his Romans commentary had been like a man in a dark tower who had grasped the bell rope without knowing what he was doing.

[9] Schmithals believes that Käsemann has not paid attention to the historical problem of the lack of unity of Romans (1974: 151), an interest he shares with O'Neill (1975). Schmithals's accusation of a 'liberal disregard' for historical questions on Käsemann's part is unfair; rather, Käsemann and Schmithals disagree on the solution to the problem of the unity of the epistle, the former finding it in a theological synthesis, the latter in disputing the integrity of the epistle.

[10] Schrage 1961 (his articles of 1964 1969, and 1980 also take up Käsemann's questions); Müller 1964; Stuhlmacher 1965 (cf. 1968); and Klaiber 1982.

a much more conservative direction. Käsemann's Festschrift certainly shows signs of his influence on a wide range of German-speaking scholars but this is no more than would be expected. The same is true of the fact that his contributions to many individual issues of Pauline scholarship continue to be debated. In more recent years Käsemann's work has, perhaps, been held in higher regard abroad, particularly by some American scholars, than in Europe.[11] Nevertheless, in general terms it cannot be said that his approach to Paul has been particularly influential. Certainly there has been no new 'Tübingen School'.[12]

A further, more important, point concerns the significant shift in the history of Pauline interpretation which has made much of Käsemann's work look prematurely dated. Three years after the final edition of the Romans commentary, E. P. Sanders published his influential work *Paul and Palestinian Judaism* (1977). While many of Sanders's concerns were shared by other scholars, as was seen in Chapter 4, this book can be regarded as a landmark in Pauline and New Testament studies. Sanders professes no theological interest in Paul; certainly he is not motivated by the quest for the continuing theological relevance of the Pauline message. Rather, he concentrates on the historical question of locating Paul within his Jewish context, and the wider motivation for his study is to be seen in the unmasking of an erroneous Christian understanding of Jewish religion. Thus, while Käsemann portrays Paul against his Jewish background with particular reference to the apocalyptic themes, and often emphasizes the contrast between Paul and contemporary Judaism, Sanders focuses on Paul's Jewishness and on a correction of a Christian, and, more specifically, an Augustinian-Lutheran, perception of ancient Judaism.

On this last point Sanders's challenge to the Lutheran understanding of the law in ancient Judaism and in Paul strikes at one of the central themes of Käsemann's view of

[11] Harrisville 1985 and Scroggs 1985 provide retrospective views of Käsemann's career.

[12] The question mark in the title of Wright's article 'A New Tübingen School? Ernst Käsemann and his Commentary on Romans; is significant. However, he does not actually discuss the idea contained in his title in the following article.

Paul. Following Luther and Bultmann, Käsemann assumes that Paul has a doctrine of justification which turns on a contrast between law and grace. On the apparently assured ground of this assumption, he set himself the task of demonstrating that this doctrine ought not to be interpreted purely in relation to the individual but in its 'apocalyptic' horizon, i.e., Paul's eschatology is cosmic in scope and future in orientation. The paradox is that while many scholars have accepted Käsemann's 'corrections' of Bultmann's view of Paul, the same scholars have undermined the underlying assumptions about Paul's supposed doctrine of justification with its fundamental contrast between law and grace which Käsemann built on. Thus, Käsemann's view of Paul has dated very rapidly because one of his key assumptions about what constitutes the centre of Paul's theology has, unexpectedly, been successfully challenged in the period immediately after he retired from New Testament scholarship. Further, while it might be thought that this would leave much of his work untouched, for example, the studies of Paul's ecclesiology, this is not the case. Käsemann's later work on Paul is dedicated to the proposition that all aspects of Paul's theology are determined by the supposed doctrine of justification. If the latter has been put under the severest challenge, then Käsemann's work on other aspects of Paul's theology is also challenged. When the renewed interest in Paul's religion (as opposed to his theology) and in sociological and psychological approaches to Paul (as opposed to theological ones) is added to the points already made, it is not difficult to see why contemporary Pauline studies seem so far removed from the summary of Pauline theology which Käsemann offered in the Romans commentary less than twenty years ago. At the same time it is remarkable how many of these contemporary interests are similar to those of the history-of-religions school against which the neo-orthodox understanding of a historically informed theological exegesis was developed.

The major problems with Käsemann's interpretation of Paul are directly related to his ambitious project to interpret Paul historically and theologically. Firstly, his use of theological models (Christ as a gift and as lord; the twofold understanding of 'piety'; the presumption in favour of the body of Christ motif over the people of God theme, or in favour of the *justificatio impii* theme over sacrificial and cultic models in soteriology) was found to lead to exegetical distortion. Secondly, considerable confusion arises from the use of labels which have both historical and theological connotations, especially the term 'apocalyptic'. Again, the use of the transliteration *cosmocrator* gives the impression of being a historical term relating to linguistic usage in antiquity; in fact it carries Käsemann's theological concern about Christ's lordship over the world. Thirdly, there is a tendency for historical questions to be solved by theological reasoning, or at the level of the reconstruction of Paul's theology, without adequate reference to particular historical texts. The interpretation of *δικαιοσύνη θεοῦ* falls into this category: Käsemann's view depends on a theory about Pauline (and Christian) theology in general, the dialectic of gift and power, and not on exegesis of Paul's use of the phrase or its history-of-religions derivation.[13]

Finally, the precise character of Käsemann's interpretation of Paul needs to be determined. Käsemann intends his interpretation to be theologically committed and historically defensible. Thus, in the tradition of the prefaces to Barth's Romans, it is crucial that we do not hear only what Paul had to say to his contemporaries, but also what he has to say to all people of every age. Interpretation of the New Testament is not true to its final subject-matter, God, if it is not theological, or if it lacks contemporary theological significance. The greatest challenge is the attempt to combine this goal with that of an interpretation which is defensible on strictly historical grounds. In such an undertaking it is almost inevitable that one or other goal will finally take precedence. In the last analysis, and when his professional and committed engagement with the historical questions concerning the interpretation of Paul has been taken into account, this is the case with Käsemann. The theological demands made on the Pauline text (specifically the desire to find a particular doctrinal pattern in Paul) are, finally, more important to him

[13] Noteworthy among more general criticisms of Käsemann's view of Paul is the problem of his attempt to interpret Paul's theology with such a large degree of dependence on the contents and structure of Romans (e.g., Strecker 1974: 285 f.).

than the limits imposed by the strict application of historical methods. The achievement and the main problem of his interpretation can be described in the words of another Bultmann pupil who learnt from Barth's prefaces, H. Schlier. In his *Grundzüge einer paulinischen Theologie*, Schlier makes a distinction between, on the one hand, the theology of Paul which is reconstructed historically and, on the other, a contemporary theology which is determined in content by the Pauline kerygma and has a material connection with the theology of the apostle. The latter is called a 'Pauline theology' and its task is not merely the description of the apostle's theology but a contemporary theological reflection which is constantly related to the kerygma of the Pauline epistles. As such it is a contemporary statement *with* Paul.[14] Käsemann's interpretation of Paul is a great achievement as a 'Pauline theology' in this sense, but at the same time it seeks to be defensible as a historical interpretation of the theology underlying the apostle's letters. It is a theological achievement which, because of its dual goals, is particularly vulnerable to historical criticism. This is the risk inherent in the project.

[14] Schlier 1978: 9. The last point picks up Barth's call to speak *with* Paul, not *of* or *against* him (see ch. 1 n. 127 above).

Bibliography of Cited Works

1. ERNST KÄSEMANN

The following bibliography is based on that given in the Käsemann Festschrift (Lang 1976, but see ch. 1 n. 4 above). Unless otherwise indicated below, page references in the text are to the latest version cited here.

(a) Unpublished work

1945 'Die evangelische Kirche im deutschen Zusammenbruch: Vortrag vor evang. Akademikern Gelsenkirchen am 4.12.1945'.

1942/8 'Der Dienst der Frau an der Wortverkündigung nach dem NT' (1942); circulated in manuscript form in 'Die Frau im geistlichen Amt in der evangelischen Kirche', Evangelische Frauenarbeit in Deutschland, n.d. (*c.*1948), 8–38.

1949 'Zur Frage der Entmythologisierung: Vortrag am 7.12.1949 in Darmstadt'.

'Vom Leben der paulinischen Gemeinde: Referat im Propädeutikum am 21.6.1949'.

1952 'Die zweite Bitte des Vaterunsers', dated 1 Dec. 1952.

n.d. 'Theologie des Neuen Testaments, Vorlesungsnachschrift' [1960s].

'Gottesgerechtigkeit bei Paulus' [1980s].

'Das Motiv der Leiblichkeit bei Paulus' [1980s].

Universitätsbibliothek Tübingen, letters from the 'Nachlaß Rudolf Bultmann'.

(b) Published work

1933 *Leib und Leib Christi: Eine Untersuchung zur paulinischen Begrifflichkeit*, BHTh 9 (Tübingen, 1933).

1936 'Gustav Adolf-Arbeit als Dienst aller evangelischen Christenheit', in *Jahres-Bericht des Westfälischen Hauptvereins der Gustav Adolf-Stiftung über das Kalenderjahr 1936*, 14–22.

1937 'Das Abendmahl im Neuen Testament', in H. Asmussen *et al.* (eds.), *Abendmahlsgemeinschaft?* BEvTh 3 (Munich, 1937), 60–93.

1939 *Das wandernde Gottesvolk: Eine Untersuchung zum Hebräerbrief*, FRLANT 55 (NS 37) (Göttingen, 1939; 2nd edn., 1957).

ET of the 2nd edn.: *The Wandering People of God: An Investigation of the Letter to the Hebrews* (Minneapolis, 1984).
rev. of W. Oehler, *Das Wort des Johannes an die Gemeinde* (1938), *ThLZ* 64 (1939), 411–12.

1942 'Die Legitimität des Apostels: Eine Untersuchung zu II Korinther 10–13', *ZNW* 41 (1942), 33–71; published as a book, Libelli 33 (Darmstadt, 1956); repr. in Rengstorf 1964: 475–521 (page references to this edn.).

1946 rev. of H. W. Bartsch, *Gnostisches Gut und Gemeindetradition bei Ignatius von Antiochen* (1940), *VF* [3] (1946/7), 131–6.
rev. of R. Bultmann, *Das Evangelium des Johannes* (1941), *VF* [3] (1946/7), 182–201.

1947 'Anliegen und Eigenart der paulinischen Abendmahlslehre', *EvTh* 7 (1947/8), 263–83; repr. in *EVB* i. 11–34. ET: 'The Pauline Doctrine of the Lord's Supper', *ENTT* 108–35.
'7. Sonntag nach Trinitatis: 1 Korinther 6, 19–20', *GPM* 2 (1947/8), 40–3; repr. in *EVB* i. 276–9.

1948 rev. of M. Barth, *Der Augenzeuge: Eine Untersuchung über die Wahrnehmung des Menschensohnes durch die Apostel* (1946), *ThLZ* 73 (1948), 665–70.
'2. Sonntag nach Epiphanias: 1 Korinther 2, 6–16', *GPM* 3 (1948/9), 28–35; repr. in *EVB* i. 267–79.

1949 'Eine urchristliche Taufliturgie', in E. Wolf (ed.), *Festschrift Rudolf Bultmann zum 65. Geburtstag überreicht* (Stuttgart, 1949), 133–48; repr. in *EVB* i. 34–51. ET: 'A Primitive Christian Baptismal Liturgy', *ENTT* 14–67.
rev. of E. Percy, *Die Probleme der Kolosser- und Epheserbriefe* (1946), *Gn* 21 (1949), 342–7.
'Aus der neutestamentlichen Arbeit der letzten Jahre', *VF* [4] (1949/50), 195–223.

1950 'Kritische Analyse von Phil. 2, 5–11', *ZThK* 47 (1950), 313–60; repr. in *EVB* i. 51–95. ET: 'A Critical Analysis of Philippians 2: 5–11', *JTC* 5 (1968), 45–88.
'Zum Verständnis von Römer 3, 24–26', *ZNW* 43 (1950/1), 150–4; repr. in *EVB* i. 96–100.

1951 'Ketzer und Zeuge: Zum johanneischen Verfasserproblem', *ZThK* 48 (1951), 292–311; repr. in *EVB* i. 168–87.
'Begründet der neutestamentliche Kanon die Einheit der Kirche?' *EvTh* 11 (1951/2), 13–21; repr. in *EVB* i. 214–223 and *Das Neue Testament als Kanon* (see below: 1970), 124–33. ET: 'The Canon of the New Testament and the Unity of the Church', *ENTT* 95–107.
'Ein neutestamentlicher Überblick', *VF* 5 (1951/52), 191–218.

1952 'Eine Apologie der urchristlichen Eschatologie', *ZThK* 49 (1952), 272–96; repr. in *EVB* i. 135–57. ET: 'An Apologia for Primitive Christian Eschatology', *ENTT* 16–95.

'Probleme neutestamentlicher Arbeit in Deutschland', in K. E. Logstrup *et al.* (eds.), *Die Freiheit des Evangeliums und die Ordnung der Gesellschaft*, BEvTh 15, (Munich, 1952), 133–52.

'Die Johannesjünger in Ephesus', *ZThK* 49 (1952), 144–54; repr. in *EVB* i. 158–68. ET: 'The Disciples of John the Baptist in Ephesus', *ENTT* 136–48.

'Lätare: Philipper 2, 12–18', *GPM* 7 (1952/3), 7–82; repr. in *EVB* i. 293–8.

'2. Sonntag nach Trinitatis: 1. Kor. 12, 4–11', *GPM* 7 (1952/3), 144–7.

1954 'Das Formular einer neutestamentlichen Ordinationsparänese', in W. Eltester (ed.), *Neutestamentliche Studien für Rudolf Bultmann*, BZNW 21 (Berlin, 1954), 261–8; repr. in *EVB* i. 101–8.

'Das Problem des historischen Jesus', *ZThK* 51 (1954), 125–53; repr. in *EVB* i. 187–214. ET: 'The Problem of the Historical Jesus', *ENTT* 15–47.

'Sätze heiligen Rechtes im Neuen Testament', *NTS* 1 (1954/5), 248–60; repr. in *EVB* ii. 69–82. ET: 'Sentences of Holy Law in the New Testament', *NTQT* 66–81.

1956 'Hinweise auf neuere neutestamentliche Forschung', *VF* 7 (1956), 148–68.

'Christus, das All und die Kirche: Zur Theologie des Epheserbriefes' (rev. of F. Mussner, *Christus, das All und die Kirche*, 1955), *ThLZ* 81 (1956), 585–90.

rev. of C. H. Dodd, *The Interpretation of the Fourth Gospel* (1953), *Gn* 28 (1956), 321–6; repr. in 'Johannes-Interpretation in England', *EVB* ii. 148–55.

'7. Sonntag nach Trinitatis: Römer 6, 19–23', *GPM* 10 (1956/57), 184–6; repr. in *EVB* i. 263–6.

1957 rev. of W. F. Howard, *The Fourth Gospel in Recent Criticism and Interpretation* (rev. by C. K. Barrett, London, 1955) and C. K. Barrett, *The Gospel according to St. John* (New York, 1955), *Göttingische Gelehrte Anzeigen* (Göttingen), 211 (1957), 145–60; rev. edn. in 'Johannes-Interpretation in England', *EVB* ii. 131–48.

'Aufbau und Anliegen des johanneischen Prologs', in W. Matthias (ed.), *Libertas Christiana: Friedrich Delekat zum 65. Geburtstag*, BEvTh 26 (Munich, 1957); rev. edn. in *EVB* ii. 151–81. ET: 'The Structure and Purpose of the Prologue to John's Gospel', *NTQT* 138–67.

'Neutestamentliche Fragen von heute', *ZThK* 54 (1957), 1–21; repr. in *EVB* ii. 11–31. ET: 'New Testament Questions of Today', *NTQT* 1–22.

1958 'Epheserbrief', *RGG*, 3rd edn., 2 (1958), 517–20.

'Formeln II: Liturgische Formeln im NT', *RGG*, 3rd edn., 2 (1958), 993–6.

'Geist IV: Geist und Geistesgaben im NT', *RGG*, 3rd edn., 2 (1958), 1272–9.

1959 'Kolosserbrief', *RGG*, 3rd edn., 3 (1959), 1727–8.

'Römer 13, 1–7 in unserer Generation', *ZThK* 56 (1959), 316–76.

'Eine paulinische Variation des "amor fati"', *ZThK* 56 (1959), 138–54; repr. in *EVB* ii. 223–39. ET: 'A Pauline Version of the "Amor Fati"', *NTQT* 217–35.

1960 'Liturgie II: Im NT', *RGG*, 3rd edn., 4 (1960), 402–4.

Exegetische Versuche und Besinnungen, i (Göttingen, 1960). ET: *Essays on New Testament Themes*, SBT 41 (London, 1964; ET of selected essays from EVB i). Published here for the first time: 'Amt und Gemeinde im Neuen Testament', *EVB* i. 10–34 (page references to this edn.); repr. in K. Kertelge (ed.), *Das kirchliche Amt im Neuen Testament*, WdF 439 (Darmstadt, 1977), 173–204; ET: 'Ministry and Community in the New Testament', *ENTT* 63–94.

'Die Anfänge christlicher Theologie', *ZThK* 57 (1960), 162–85; repr. in *EVB* ii. 82–104. ET: 'The Beginnings of Christian Theology', *NTQT* 82–107 (page references to this edn.) and *JTC* 6 (1969), 17–46.

'Gottesdienst im Alltag der Welt: Zu Römer 12', in W. Eltester (ed.), *Judentum, Urchristentum, Kirche: Festschrift für J. Jeremias*, BZNW 26 (1960), 165–71; repr. in *EVB* ii. 198–204. ET: 'Worship and Everyday Life: A Note on Romans 12', *NTQT* 188–95.

1961 'Gottesgerechtigkeit bei Paulus', *ZThK* 58 (1961), 367–78; enlarged edn. in *EVB* ii. 181–93. ET: '"The Righteousness of God" in Paul', *NTQT* 168–82 (page references to this edn.) and 'God's Righteousness in Paul', *JTC* 1 (1964), 100–10.

'Paulus und Israel', in H. J. Schultz (ed.), *Juden, Christen, Deutsche* (Stuttgart, 1961), 307–11; repr. in *EVB* ii. 194–7. ET: 'Paul and Israel', *NTQT* 183–7.

'Grundsätzliches zur Interpretation von Römer 13', in K. G. Steck *et al.* (eds.), *Unter der Herrschaft Christi*, BEvTh 32 (Munich, 1961), 37–55; repr. in *EVB* ii. 204–22. ET:

'Principles of the Interpretation of Romans 13', *NTQT* 196–216.
'Das Interpretationsproblem des Epheserbriefs' (rev. of H. Schlier, *Der Brief an die Epheser*, 2nd edn., 1958), *ThLZ* 86 (1961), 1–8; repr. in *EVB* ii. 252–61.
1962 'Zum Thema der urchristlichen Apokalyptik', *ZThK* 59 (1962), 257–84; repr. in *EVB* ii. 105–31. ET: 'On the Subject of Primitive Christian Apocalyptic', *NTQT* 108–37 (page references to this edn.) and 'On the Task of Primitive Christian Apocalyptic', *JTC* 6 (1969), 9–133.
'Zum gegenwärtigen Streit um die Schriftauslegung', in F. Viering (ed.), *Das Wort Gottes und die Kirchen*, Schriften des Ev. Bundes in Westfalen 4 (Göttingen, 1962), 7–32; repr. in *EVB* ii. 268–90.
1963 'Wunder IV: Im NT', *RGG*, 3rd edn., 6 (1963), 1835–7.
'Einführung' in K. Scholder (ed.), *F. C. Baur: Ausgewählte Werke in Einzelausgaben*, i: *Historisch-kritische Untersuchungen zum Neuen Testament* (Stuttgart, 1963), pp. viii–xxv.
'Paulus und der Frühkatholizismus', *ZThK* 60 (1963), 75–89; repr. in *EVB* ii. 23–52. ET: 'Paul and Nascent Catholicism', *JTC* 3 (1967), 14–27, and 'Paul and Early Catholicism', *NTQT* 236–51 (page references to this edn.).
'Neutestamentlicher Sammelbericht II', *VF* 10 (1963/5), 78–94.
'Unity and Diversity in New Testament Ecclesiology', *NovT* 6 (1963), 290–7. German: 'Einheit und Vielfalt in der neutestamentlichen Lehre von der Kirche', *Ökumenische Rundschau*, 13 (Stuttgart, 1964), 58–63; repr. in *EVB* ii. 262–7. ET: 'Unity and Multiplicity in the New Testament Doctrine of the Church', *NTQT* 252–9 (page references to this edn.).
1964 'Einheit und Wahrheit: Bericht über die Faith-and-Order-Konferenz in Montreal 1963', *Monatsschrift für Pastoraltheologie*, 53 (1964), 65–75.
'Erwägungen zum Stichwort "Versöhnungslehre im Neuen Testament"', in E. Dinkler (ed.), *Zeit und Geschichte: Dankesgabe an R. Bultmann zum 80. Geburtstag* (Tübingen, 1964), 47–59. ET: 'Some Thoughts on the Theme "The Doctrine of Reconciliation in the NT"', in J. M. Robinson (ed.), *The Future of our Religious Past: Essays in Honour of Rudolf Bultmann* (London, 1971), 4–64.
'Der gottesdienstliche Schrei nach der Freiheit', in W. Eltester (ed.), *Apophoreta: Festschrift für E. Haenchen zu*

seinem 70. Geburtstag, BZNW 30 (Berlin, 1964), 142–55; repr. in *PP* (Tübingen, 1969), 211–36. ET: 'The Cry for Liberty in the Worship of the Church', *PoP* 122–37.

Exegetische Versuche und Besinnungen, ii (Göttingen, 1964). ET: *New Testament Questions for Today*, The New Testament Library (London, 1969; ET of selected essays from *EVB* ii). Published here for the first time: 'Sackgassen im Streit um den historischen Jesus', *EVB* ii. 31–68; ET: 'Blind Alleys in the "Jesus of History" Controversy', *NTQT* 23–65.

1965 'Konsequente Traditionsgeschichte?' *ZThK* 62 (1965), 137–52.

rev. of E. Jüngel, *Paulus und Jesus* (1962), *ThLZ* 90 (1965), 184–7.

rev. of F. Amiot, *Die Theologie des Heiligen Paulus* (1962), *ThLZ* 90 (1965), 355–6.

1966 *Jesu letzter Wille nach Johannes 17* (Tübingen, 1966; rev. edn. 1971). ET of the edn. of 1966, *The Testament of Jesus: A Study of the Gospel of John in the Light of Chapter 17* (Philadephia, 1968).

'Ephesians and Acts', in L. E. Keck and J. L. Martyn (eds.), *Studies in Luke–Acts: Essays Presented in Honor of P. Schubert* (Nashville, 1966), 288–97.

rev. of *Studiorum Paulinorum Congressus Internationalis Catholicus 1961* (2 vols., 1963), *ThLZ* 91 (1966), 186–7.

1967 'Die Heilsbedeutung des Todes Jesu bei Paulus', in F. Viering (ed.), *Zur Bedeutung des Todes Jesu* (Gütersloh, 1967), 11–34; repr. in *PP* 61–107. ET: 'The Saving Significance of the Death of Jesus in Paul', *PoP* 32–59.

'Erwiderung an Ulrich Asendorf', *Lutherische Monatshefte*, 6 (1967), 595–7.

'Vom theologischen Recht historisch-kritischer Exegese', *ZThK* 64 (1967), 25–81.

rev. of R. P. Martin, *Phil. II. 5–11 in Recent Interpretation and in the Setting of Early Christian Worship* (1967), *ThLZ* 93 (1968), 665–6.

1968 *Der Ruf der Freiheit* (Tübingen, 1st edn., 1968; rev. 3rd edn., 1968; 5th enlarged edn., 1972). ET of the 3rd edn.: *Jesus Means Freedom* (London, 1969).

1969 *Paulinische Perspektiven* (Tübingen, 1969). ET: *Perspectives on Paul*, The New Testament Library (London, 1971). Published here for the first time: 'Zur paulinischen Anthropologie', 9–60; ET: 'On Paul's Anthropology', 1–31. 'Rechtfertigung und Heilsgeschichte im Römerbrief', 108–39; ET: 'Justification and Salvation History in the Epistle to the Romans', 60–78. 'Der Glaube Abrahams in Römer 4', 140–77; ET: 'The Faith of Abraham in Romans 4', 7–101. 'Das theologische Problem des Motivs vom Leibe Christi', 178–210; ET: 'The Theological Problem Presented by the Motif of the Body of Christ', 102–21. 'Geist und Buchstabe', 237–85; ET: 'The Spirit and the Letter', 138–66.

1970 'Das Thema des Neuen Testaments', *1845–1970 Almanach: 125 Jahre Chr. Kaiser Verlag München* (Munich, 1970), 66–83.

Das Neue Testament als Kanon: Dokumentation und kritische Analyse zur gegenwärtigen Diskussion (Göttingen, 1970).

1972 'The Problem of a New Testament Theology', *NTS* 19 (1972/3), 235–45.

1973 *An die Römer*, HNT 8*a* (Tübingen, 1973; 4th edn., 1980). ET: *Commentary on Romans* (London, 1973; second impression with corrections, 1982).

1975 'Die neue Jesus-Frage', in J. Dupont (ed.), *Jésus aux origines de la christologie*, Bibliotheca Ephemeridum Theologicarum Lovaniensium 40 (Louvain, 1975), 47–57.

'Das Evangelium und die Frommen', in H. J. Schütz (ed.), *Wir werden lachen—die Bibel: Überraschungen mit dem Buch* (Berlin, 1975), 125–34. ET: 'The Gospel and the Pious', *ABR* 30 (1982), 1–9.

1977 'Tod im argentinischen Dschungel: Geschichte und Deutung einer Ermordung', *Evangelischer Kommentar*, 10 (1977), 46–71.

1980 rev. of B. Ulrich, *Zur frühchristlichen Theologiegeschichte* (1976), *ThLZ* 105 (1980), 432–3.

1982 *Kirchliche Konflikte*, i (Göttingen, 1982). Published here for the first time: 'Aspekte der Kirche', 7–36. 'Was ich als deutscher Theologe in fünfzig Jahren verlernte' (Lecture to the Theology Faculty of the University of Marburg on the occasion of the fiftieth anniversary of receiving his doctorate, 25 Nov. 1981), 233–44.

1985 Preface to T. Thun, *Menschenrechte und Aussenpolitik: Bundesrepublik Deutschland–Argentinien 1976–1983*, Wissenschaftliche Publikationen zur Politik, Ökonomie und Kultur in der Dritten Welt (Bremen, 1985), 9–12.

2. GENERAL

ACHTEMEIER, P. J. (1976), rev. of E. Käsemann, *An die Römer* (1974), *Int* 30 (1976), 190–3.

Althaus, P. (1922/1957), *Die letzten Dinge: Lehrbuch der Eschatologie*, Studien des apologetischen Seminars, 9 (Gütersloh, 1922; 7th edn., 1957).

—— (1938/1951), *Paulus und Luther über den Menschen: Ein Vergleich*, Studien der Luther-Akademie 14 (Göttingen, 1938; 2nd enlarged edn., 1951).

—— (1959), *Der Brief an die Römer*, NTD 6 (9th edn., Göttingen, 1959).

Amiot, F. (1962), *Die Theologie des Heiligen Paulus* (Mainz, 1962).

Asendorf, U. (1967), 'Zum Kreuzesverständnis bei Ernst Käsemann', *Lutherische Monatshefte*, 6 (1967), 545–6, 549–50.

—— (1971), *Gekreuzigt und Auferstanden: Luthers Herausforderung an die moderne Christologie*, Arbeiten zur Geschichte und Theologie des Luthertums, 25 (Hamburg, 1971).

Barbour, R. S. (1972), *Traditio-Historical Criticism of the Gospels: Some Comments on Current Methods* (London, 1972).

Barrett, C. K. (1957), *A Commentary on the Epistle to the Romans*, BNTC (London, 1957).

—— (1962), *From First Adam to Last: A Study in Pauline Theology* (London, 1962).

—— (1968/1971), *A Commentary on the First Epistle to the Corinthians*, BNTC (London, 1968; 2nd edn., 1971).

—— (1973), *A Commentary on the Second Epistle to the Corinthians*, BNTC (London, 1973).

Barth, K. (1922), *Der Römerbrief* (Zurich, 1922; page references to this edition). ET: *The Epistle to the Romans* (Oxford, 1933).

—— (1924), *Die Auferstehung der Toten: Eine akademische Vorlesung über 1. Kor. 15* (Munich, 1924; page references to this edition). ET: *The Resurrection of the Dead: A Commentary on 1 Corinthians XV* (London, 1933).

—— (1928), *Erklärung des Philipperbriefes* (Zurich, 1928). ET: *The Epistle to the Philippians* (London, 1962).

—— (1940), *Die kirchliche Dogmatik 2* (Die Lehre von Gott), i (Zurich, 1940). ET: *Church Dogmatics 2* (The Doctrine of God), i (Edinburgh, 1957).

—— (1952*a*), *Christus und Adam nach Röm. 5: Ein Beitrag zur Frage nach dem Menschen und der Menschheit*, ThSt 35 (Zurich, 1952). ET: *Christ and Adam: Man and Humanity in Romans 5*, SJT Occasional Papers, 5 (Edinburgh, 1956).

—— (1952*b*), *Rudolf Bultmann: Ein Versuch, ihn zu verstehen*, ThSt 34 (Zurich, 1952). ET: 'Rudolf Bultmann: An Attempt to Understand Him', in Bartsch 1952: 83–132.

Bartsch, H. W. (1948) (ed.), *Kerygma und Mythos* (Hamburg, 1948). ET: *Kerygma and Myth: A Theological Debate* (London, 1953).

—— (1952) (ed.), *Kerygma und Mythos*, ii (Hamburg, 1952). ET: *Kerygma and Myth: A Theological Debate*, ii (London, 1962).

BAUER, K.-A., (1971), *Leiblichkeit das Ende aller Werke Gottes: Die Bedeutung der Leiblichkeit bei Paulus*, StNT 4 (Gütersloh, 1971).

BAUER, W., ARNDT, W. F., GINGRICH, F. W., and DANKER, F. W. (1979), *A Greek–English Lexicon of the New Testament and Other Early Christian Literature* (Chicago, 1957; 2nd edn., 1979 = ET and adaption of W. Bauer's *Griechisch–Deutsches Wörterbuch zu den Schriften des Neuen Testaments und der übrigen urchristlichen Literatur*, 5th edn., 1957).

BAUMGARTEN, J. (1975), *Paulus und die Apokalyptik: Die Auslegung apokalyptischer Überlieferungen in den echten Paulusbriefen* (Neukirchen-Vluyn, 1975).

BAUR, F. C. (1845), *Paulus, der Apostel Jesu Christi: Sein Leben und Wirken, seine Briefe, und seine Lehre: Ein Beitrag zu einer kritischen Geschichte des Urchristenthums* (Stuttgart, 1845). ET: *Paul, the Apostle of Jesus Christ: His Life and Works, his Epistles and Teachings: A Contribution to a Critical History of Primitive Christianity* (London, 1873).

BECKER, J. (1964), *Das Heil Gottes: Heils- und Sündenbegriffe in den Qumrantexten und im Neuen Testament*, StUNT 3 (Göttingen, 1964).

—— (1970), 'Erwägungen zur apokalyptischen Tradition in der paulinischen Theologie', *EvTh* 30 (1970), 593–609.

BEHM, J. (1912), *Der Begriff διαθήκη im Neuen Testament* (Leipzig, 1912).

BEKER, J. C. (1980), *Paul the Apostle: The Triumph of God in Life and Thought* (Edinburgh, 1980).

—— (1982), *Paul's Apocalyptic Gospel. The Coming Triumph of God* (Philadelphia, 1982).

BENOIT, P. (1977), 'L'Évolution du language apocalyptique dans le corpus paulien', in L. Monloubou (ed.), *Apocalypses et théologie d'espérance*, Lectio divina, 95 (Paris, 1977), 29–335.

BERGER, K. (1977), 'Neues Material zur "Gerechtigkeit Gottes"', *ZNW* 68 (1977), 266–75.

BETZ, H. D. (1975), rev. of E. Käsemann, *An die Römer* (1974), *SEÅ* 40 (1975), 143–5.

—— (1979), *Galatians: A Commentary on Paul's Letter to the Churches in Galatia*, Hermeneia (Philadelphia, 1979).

BLACK, M. (1973), *Romans*, New Century Bible (London, 1973).

BOER, M. C. DE (1988), *The Defeat of Death: Apocalyptic Eschatology in 1 Corinthians 15 and Romans 5*, JSNT Supplement Series 22 (Sheffield, 1988).

BÖHMER, H. (1905/1918), *Luther im Lichte der neueren Forschung: Ein kritische Bericht von Heinrich Böhmer* (Leipzig, 1905; 5th edn., 1918).

BORNKAMM, G. (1939), 'Taufe und neues Leben', *ThBl* 18 (1939), 233–42; repr. in Bornkamm 1952*a*: 34–50. ET: 'Baptism and New Life in Paul: Romans 6', *Early Christian Experience* (London, 1969; page references to the ET), 71–86.

—— (1950), 'Christus und die Welt in der urchristlichen Botschaft', *ZThK* 47 (1950), 212–26; repr. in Bornkamm 1952*a*: 157–72; ET: 'Christ and the World in the Early Christian Message', in *Early Christian Experience* (London, 1969; page references to the ET), 14–28.

—— (1952*a*), *Das Ende des Gesetzes: Paulusstudien*, BEvTh 16 (Munich, 1952).

—— (1952*b*), 'Paulinische Anakoluthe im Römerbrief', in Bornkamm 1952*a*, 76–92.

—— (1969), *Paulus* (Stuttgart, 1969). ET: *Paul* (London 1971; page references to the ET).

BOUSSET, W. (1904), 'Das Neue Testament und die Religionsgeschichte', *ThR* 8 (1904), 265–77, 311–18, 353–65.

—— (1907), *Hauptprobleme der Gnosis*, FRLANT 10 (Göttingen, 1907).

—— (1913/1921), *Kyrios Christos: Geschichte des Christusglaubens bis Irenaeus* (Göttingen, 1913; 2nd edn., 1921; 5th edn., with a preface by R. Bultmann, 1965); ET: *Kyrios Christos: A History of the Belief in Christ from the Beginnings of Christianity to Irenaeus* (New York, 1970; page references to the ET).

—— (1915), *Jesus der Herr: Nachträge und Auseinandersetzungen zu Kyrios Christos*, FRLANT 25 (Göttingen, 1915).

—— and GRESSMANN, H. (1903/1926), *Die Religion des Judentums im späthellenistischen Zeitalter*, HNT 21 (Tübingen, 1903; 3rd edn., rev. by H. Gressmann, 1926).

BRANDENBURGER, E. (1962), *Adam und Christus: Exegetisch-religionsgeschichtliche Untersuchung zu Röm. 5: 12–21 (1 Kor. 15)*, WMANT 7 (Neukirchen, 1962).

BRAUCH, M. T. (1977), 'Perspectives on "God's Righteousness" in Recent German Discussion', in Sanders 1977: 523–42.

BROCKHAUS, U. (1972), *Charisma und Amt: Die paulinische Charismenlehre auf dem Hintergrund der frühchristlichen Gemeindefunktion* (Wuppertal, 1972).

BRUCE, F. F. (1963), *The Epistle of Paul to the Romans: An Introduction and Commentary*, Tyndale New Testament Commentaries (London, 1963).

BULTMANN, R. (1915), 'Neutestamentliche Theologie', (rev. of J. Behm's (1912) and E. Lohmeyer's (1913) books on διαθήκη) *ThR* 18 (1915), 264–7.

—— (1922*a*), 'Karl Barths Römerbrief in zweiter Auflage', *ChW* 36

(1922), 320–3, 330–4, 358–61, 36–73; repr. in Moltmann 1962: 11–42 (page references to this edition). ET in Robinson 1968: 236–56.

—— (1922*b*), rev. of K. Deissner, *Paulus und die Mystik seiner Zeit* (2nd edn., 1921), *ThLZ* 47 (1922), 193–4.

—— (1924*a*), 'Das Problem der Ethik bei Paulus', *ZNW* 23 (1924), 123–40; repr. in Rengstorf 1964: 17–99 (page references to this edition) and Bultmann 1967: 36–54.

—— (1924*b*), 'Die liberale Theologie und die jüngste theologische Bewegung', *ThBl* 3 (1924), 73–86; repr. in Bultmann 1933*e*: 1–25. ET: 'Liberal Theology and the Latest Theological Movement', in Bultmann 1969, 28–52 (page references to the ET).

—— (1925*a*), 'Das Problem einer theologischen Exegese des N.T.', *ZZ* 3 (1925), 334–57; repr. in Moltmann 1963: 47–72 and Strecker 1975: 24–77 (page references to this edition). ET: 'The Problem of a Theological Exegesis of the New Testament', in Robinson 1968: 236–56.

—— (1925*b*), 'Welchen Sinn hat es, von Gott zu reden?' *ThBl* 4 (1925); repr. in Bultmann 1933*e*, 26–37. ET: 'What Does it Mean to Speak of God?' in Bultmann 1969: 53–65.

—— (1926*a*), 'Wilhelm Heitmüller', *ChW* 40 (1926), 20–13.

—— (1926*b*), 'Karl Barth: Die Auferstehung der Toten', *ThBl* 5 (1926), 1–14; repr. in Bultmann 1933*e*: 38–64 (page references to this edition). ET: 'Karl Barth, The Resurrection of the Dead', in Bultmann 1969: 66–94.

—— (1926*c*), rev. of A. Deissmann, *Paulus* (2nd edn., 1925), *ThLZ* 51 (1926), 273–8.

—— (1928), 'Die Bedeutung der dialektischen Theologie für die neutestamentlichen Wissenschaft', *ThBl* 7 (1928), 157–67; repr. in Bultmann 1933*e*: 114–33. ET: 'The Significance of "Dialectical Theology" for the Scientific Study of the New Testament', in Bultmann 1969: 145–64 (page references to the ET).

—— (1929*a*), 'Zur Geschichte der Paulus-Forschung', *ThR* (NS) 1 (1929), 26–59; repr. in Rengstorf 1964: 304–37 (page references to this edition).

—— (1929*b*), 'Kirche und Lehre im NT', *ZZ* 7 (1929), 9–43; repr. in Bultmann 1933*e*: 153–87. ET: 'Church and Teaching in the New Testament', in Bultmann 1969: 184–219.

—— (1929*c*), 'Die Bedeutung des geschichtlichen Jesus für die Theologie des Paulus', *ThBl* 8 (1929), 137–51; repr. in Bultmann 1933*e*: 188–213. ET: 'The Significance of the Historical Jesus for the Theology of Paul', in Bultmann 1969: 220–46 (page references to the ET).

—— (1930*a*), 'Paulus', *RGG* (2nd edn.), 4 (Tübingen, 1930), 101–

45. ET: 'Paul', in Bultmann 1961: 130–72 (page references to the ET).

Bultmann, R. (1930*b*), rev. of E. Lohmeyer's *Kyrios Jesus* (1928) and *Der Brief an die Philipper* (1928), *DLZ* 51 (1930), 774–80.

—— (1931), rev. of A. Schweitzer, *Die Mystik des Apostels Paulus* (1930), *DLZ* 52 (1931), 1153–8.

—— (1932*a*), 'Römer 7 und die Anthropologie des Paulus', in W. Schneemelcher (ed.), *Imago Dei: Festschrift für Gunther Dehn* (Giessen, 1932), 53–62; repr. in Bultmann 1967: 198–209. ET: 'Romans VII and the Anthropology of Paul', in Bultmann 1961: 173–85.

—— (1932*b*), rev. of K. Mittring, *Heilswirklichkeit bei Paulus* (1929), *ThLZ* 57 (1932), 156–9.

—— (1933*a*), 'Die Christologie des NT', in Bultmann 1933*e*: 245–67. ET: 'The Christology of the New Testament', in Bultmann 1969: 262–85.

—— (1933*b*), '*αφίημι κτλ*'. *TDNT* 1 [1933], 50–12.

—— (1933*c*), 'Der Begriff des Wortes Gottes im NT', in Bultmann 1933*e*: 268–93. ET: 'The Concept of the Word of God in the New Testament', in Bultmann 1969: 286–312.

—— (1933*d*), 'Das Problem der "Natürlichen Theologie"', in Bultmann 1933*e*: 294–312. ET: 'The Problem of "Natural Theology"', in Bultmann 1969: 313–31.

—— (1933*e*), *Glauben und Verstehen: Gesammelte Aufsätze*, i (Tübingen, 1933).

—— (1936), 'Neueste Paulusforschung', *ThR* (NS) 6 (1936), 22–46.

—— (1938*a*), '*θάνατος κτλ*'. *TDNT* 3 [1938], 7–25.

—— (1938*b*), '*καύχημα κτλ*'. *TDNT* 3 [1938], 648–52.

—— (1939), 'Johannes Weiss zum Gedächntnis', *ThBl* 18 (1939), 242–6.

—— (1940), 'Christus des Gesetzes Ende', in R. Bultmann and H. Schlier, *Christus des Gesetzes Ende*, BEvTh 1 (Munich, 1940); repr. in *Glauben und Verstehen*, ii: *Gesammelte Aufsätze* (Tübingen, 1952), 32–58. ET: 'Christ the End of the Law', in *Essays Theological and Philosophical* (London 1955), 36–66.

—— (1941*a*), *Das Evangelium des Johannes*, KEK 2 (10th edn., Göttingen, 1941). ET: *The Gospel of John: A Commentary* (Oxford 1971).

—— (1941*b*), 'Neues Testament und Mythologie', in *Offenbarung und Heilsgeschehen*, BEvTh 7 (Munich, 1941); repr. in Bartsch 1948: 15–53. ET: 'New Testament and Mythology', in S. M. Ogden (ed.), *New Testament and Mythology and Other Basic Writings* (London, 1985; page references to this edition), 1–43.

—— (1948), *Theologie des Neuen Testaments*, part I (Tübingen, 1948). ET: *Theology of the New Testament*, i (London, 1952; page references to the ET).

—— (1949), *Das Urchristentum im Rahmen der antiken Religionen* (Zurich, 1949). ET: *Primitive Christianity in its Contemporary Setting* (London, 1956).

—— (1950), 'Ursprung und Sinn der Typologie als hermeneutischer Methode', in *Pro regno pro sanctuario: Festschrift für G. van der Leeuw* (Nijkerk, 1950), 8–100; repr. in Bultmann 1967: 36–80 (page references to this edition).

—— (1951), *Theologie des Neuen Testaments*, part II (Tübingen, 1951). ET: *Theology of the New Testament*, i (London 1952; page references to the ET).

—— (1953), *Theologie des Neuen Testaments*, part III (Tübingen, 1948). ET: *Theology of the New Testament*, ii (London 1955; page references to the ET).

—— (1956), 'Lebenslauf'; first published as 'Autobiographical Reflections', in Bultmann 1961: 335–41.

—— (1957), *History and Eschatology* (Edinburgh, 1957). German: *Geschichte und Eschatologie* (Tübingen, 1958).

—— (1959), 'Adam und Christus nach Römer 5', *ZNW* 50 (1959), 14–65; repr. in Bultmann 1967: 424–44. ET: 'Adam and Christ according to Romans 5', in W. Klassen and G. F. Snyder (eds.), *Current Issues in New Testament Interpretation* (New York, 1962), 143–65.

—— (1961), *Existence and Faith: Shorter Writings of Rudolf Bultmann*, ed. S. M. Ogden (London, 1961).

—— (1964*a*), '*δικαιοσύνη θεοῦ*', *JBL* 83 (1964), 12–16; repr. in Bultmann 1967: 470–5 (page references to this edition).

—— (1964*b*), 'Ist die Apokalyptik die Mutter der christlichen Theologie? Eine Auseinandersetzung mit Ernst Käsemann', in W. Eltester (ed.), *Apophoreta: Festschrift für Ernst Haenchen* (Berlin, 1964), 64–9; repr. in Bultmann 1967: 476–82 (page references to this edition).

—— (1967), *Exegetica: Aufsätze zur Erforschung des Neuen Testament*, ed. E. Dinkler (Tübingen, 1967).

—— (1969), *Faith and Understanding*, i, ed. R. W. Funk (London, 1969).

Burton, E. de W. (1920), *A Critical and Exegetical Commentary on the Epistle to the Galatians*, ICC (Edinburgh, 1920).

Busch, E. (1975), *Karl Barth: Lebenslauf: Nach seinen Briefen und autobiographischen Texten* (Munich, 1975). ET: *Karl Barth: His Life from Letters and Autobiographical Texts* (London, 1976; page references to the ET).

CADMAN, W. H. (1964), 'Δικαιοσύνη in Romans 3, 21–26', in F. L. Cross (ed.), *Studia evangelica*, ii (Berlin, 1964), 532–5.

CAMBIER, J. (1967), *L'Évangile de Dieu selon l'épître aux Romains: Exégèse et théologie biblique*, i: *L'Évangile de la justice et de la grâce*, Studia Neotestamentica, 3 (Bruges, 1967).

CAMPENHAUSEN, H. VON (1953), *Kirchliches Amt und geistlicher Vollmacht in den ersten drei Jahrhunderten*, BHTh 14 (Tübingen, 1953). ET: *Ecclesiastical Authority and Spiritual Power in the Church of the First Three Centuries* (London, 1969).

CLOSE, W. J. (1972), 'The Theological Relevance of History: The Role, Logic and Propriety of Historical Understanding in Theological Reflection, Considered in the Context of the Debate on the Historical Jesus between Rudolf Bultmann and Ernst Käsemann', unpublished dissertation (Basle, 1972).

COLLANGE, J.-F. (1973), *L'Épître de saint Paul aux Philippiens*, CNT 10*a* (Neuchâtel, 1973). ET: *The Epistle of St Paul to the Philippians* (London, 1979; page references to the ET).

COLLINS, J. J. (1979), 'Introduction: Towards the Morphology of a Genre', *Semeia*, 14 ['Apocalypse: The Morphology of a Genre'] (Missoula, 1979), 1–20.

COLPE, C. (1961), *Die religionsgeschichtliche Schule: Darstellung und Kritik ihres Bildes vom gnostischen Erlösermythos*, FRLANT (NS) 60 (Göttingen, 1961).

CONZELMANN, H. (1966*a*), 'Heutige Probleme der Paulus-Forschung', *Der evangelische Erzieher*, 18 (Frankfurt, 1966), 241–52. ET: 'Current Problems in Pauline Research', *Int* 22 (1968; page references to the ET), 171–86.

—— (1966*b*), 'Zur Analyse der Bekenntnisformel 1. Kor. 15, 3–5', *EvTh* 25 (1966), 1–11; repr. in Conzelmann 1974: 131–41. ET: 'On the Analysis of the Confessional Formula in 1 Corinthians 15: 3–5', *Int* 20 (1966), 15–25.

—— (1967), *Grundriß der Theologie des Neuen Testaments*, Einführung in der evangelischen Theologie 2 (Munich, 1967). ET: *An Outline of the Theology of the New Testament* (London, 1969; page references to the ET).

—— (1968), 'Die Rechtfertigung des Paulus: Theologie oder Anthropologie?' *EvTh* 28 (1968), 38–404 (page references to this edition); repr. in Conzelmann 1974: 191–206. ET: 'Paul's Doctrine of Justification. Theology or Anthropology?', in F. Herzog (ed.), *Theology of the Liberating Word* (Nashville, 1971), 108–23.

—— (1969), *Der erste Brief an die Korinther*, KEK 5 (11th edn., Göttingen, 1969). ET: *1 Corinthians: A Commentary on the First Epistle to the Corinthians*, Hermeneia (Philadelphia, 1975; page references to the ET).

—— (1973), 'χάρισμα κτλ'. *TDNT* 9 (1973), 393–7.

—— (1974), *Theologie als Schriftauslegung: Aufsätze zum Neuen Testament*, BEvTh 65 (Munich, 1974).

Cranfield, C. E. B. (1975), *A Critical and Exegetical Commentary on the Epistle to the Romans*, i, ICC (Edinburgh, 1975).

—— (1979), *A Critical and Exegetical Commentary on the Epistle to the Romans*, ii, ICC (Edinburgh, 1979).

Cullmann, O. (1936), 'Le Caractère eschatologique du devoir missionaire et de la conscience apostolique de S. Paul. Étude sur le *κατέχον (-ων)* de 2. Thess. 2: 6–7', *RHPhR* 16 (1936), 210–45.

—— (1946/1962), *Christus und die Zeit, die urchristliche Zeit- und Geschichtsauffassung* (Zurich, 1946; 3rd edn., 1962). ET: *Christ and Time* (London, 1962).

—— (1965), *Heil als Geschichte: Heilsgeschichtliche Existenz im Neuen Testament* (Tübingen, 1965). ET: *Salvation in History* (London, 1967).

Cumont, F. (1919), 'Mithras ou Sarapis *ΚΟΣΜΟΚΡΑΤΩΡ*', *Académie des inscriptions et belles-lettres: Comptes rendus des séances de l'année 1919* (Paris, 1919), 313–28.

Dahl, N. A. (1953), 'The Problem of the Historical Jesus', first published in *Rett laeve og kjetterske meninger* (Oslo, 1953). ET in C. E. Braaten and R. A. Harrisville (eds.), *Kerygma and History* (Nashville, 1962); and in *The Crucified Messiah* (Minneapolis, 1974), 48–90.

Dantine, W. (1966), 'Rechtfertigung und Gottesgerechtigkeit', *VF* 11 (1966), 68–100.

Davies, W. D. (1948/1955), *Paul and Rabbinic Judaism: Some Rabbinic Elements in Pauline Theology* (London, 1948; 2nd edn., 1955; with a new introduction and additional appendix, 1970).

Deissmann, A. (1892), *Die neutestamentliche Formel 'in Christo Jesu'* (Marburg, 1892).

Delling, G. (1972), *Der Kreuzestod in der urchristlichen Verkündigung* (Göttingen, 1972).

Dibelius, M. (1909), *Die Geisterwelt im Glauben des Paulus* (Göttingen, 1909)

—— (1923/1937), *An die Thessalonicher: An die Philipper*, HNT 11 (Tübingen, 2nd edn., 1923; 3rd edn., 1937).

Dittenberger, W. (1903–1905) (ed.), *Orientis Graeci inscriptiones selectae*, 2 vols. (Leipzig, 1903–5).

—— (1915–24) (ed.), *Sylloge inscriptionum Graecarum*, 4 vols. (Leipzig, 3rd edn. 1915–24).

Dombois, H. (1961), *Das Recht der Gnade: Oekumenisches Kirchenrecht*, i (Witten, 1961).

Donfried, K. P. (1977), (ed.), *The Romans Debate* (Minneapolis, 1977).

Dreier, R. (1972), *Das kirchliche Amt: Eine kirchenrechtstheoretische Studie*, JusEcc 15 (Munich, 1972).

Dunn, J. D. G. (1980), *Christology in the Making: A New Testament Inquiry into the Origins of the Incarnation* (London, 1980; rev. edn. with a new preface, 1989).

—— (1983), 'The New Perspective on Paul', *BJRL* 65 (1983), 95–122.

—— (1988*a*), *Romans 1–8*, WBC 38*a* (Dallas, 1988).

—— (1988*b*), *Romans 9–16*, WBC 38*b* (Dallas, 1988).

Ebeling, G. (1961), 'Der Grund christlicher Theologie', *ZThK* 58 (1961), 227–44 (page references to this edition). ET: 'The Ground of Christian Theology', *JTC* 6 (1969), 47–68.

Ehler, B. (1986), *Die Herrschaft des Gekreuzigten: Ernst Käsemanns Frage nach der Mitte der Schrift*, BZNW 46 (Berlin, 1986).

Eichholz, G. (1960), *Was heißt charismatische Gemeinde?* TEH (NS) 77 (Munich, 1960).

Eichhorn, A. (1898), *Das Abendmahl im Neuen Testament*, Supplements to *ChW* 36 (Leipzig, 1898).

Ewing, A. C. (1934), *Idealism: A Critical Survey* (London, 1934; 3rd edn., 1961).

Fellechner, E. L. (1978), 'Petersons theologischer Weg', in A. Schindler (ed.), *Monotheismus als politisches Problem? Erik Peterson und die Kritik der politischen Theologie*, Studien zur evangelischen Ethik, 14 (Gütersloh, 1978), 76–120.

Findeisen, S., Frey, H., and Johanning, W. (1967), *Das Kreuz Jesu und die Krise der Evangelischen Kirche: Fragen, die uns die Theologie Ernst Käsemanns aufgibt*, Liebenzeller Studienhefte, 5 (Bad Liebenzell, 1967).

Fitzer, G. (1966), 'Der Ort der Versöhnung nach Paulus', *ThZ* 22 (1966), 161–83.

Fitzmyer, J. A. (1974), rev. of E. Käsemann, *An die Römer* (1973), *TS* 13 (1974), 744–7.

—— (1975), 'Reconciliation in Pauline Theology', in J. W. Flanagan and A. W. Robinson (eds.), *No Famine in the Land: Studies in Honor of John L. Mackenzie* (Missoula, Mo., 1975), 155–77.

Foster, S. A. (1976), 'The Canons of Historical Authenticity in the Writings of R. Bultmann, G. Bornkamm and E. Käsemann', unpublished dissertation, (Edinburgh, 1976).

Friedrich, J., Pöhlmann, W., and Stuhlmacher, P. (1976), (eds.), *Rechtfertigung: Festschrift für Ernst Käsemann zum 70. Geburtstag* (Tübingen and Göttingen, 1976).

FROITZHEIM, F. (1979), *Christologie und Eschatologie bei Paulus*, Forschung zur Bibel, 35 (Würzburg, 1979).

FUCHS, E. (1932), *Christus und der Geist bei Paulus*, UNT 23 (Leipzig, 1932).

—— (1949), *Die Freiheit des Glaubens: Römer 5–8 ausgelegt*, BEvTh 14 (Munich, 1949).

—— (1961), 'Über die Aufgabe einer christlichen Theologie', *ZThK* 58 (1961), 245–67. ET: 'On the Task of a Christian Theology', *JTC* 6 (1969), 6–98.

FURNISH, V. P. (1964/5), 'The Jesus–Paul Debate: From Baur to Bultmann', *BJRL* 47 (1964/5), 342–81.

GÄUMANN, N. (1967), *Taufe und Ethik: Studien zu Römer 6*, BEvTh 47 (Munich, 1967).

GEORGI, D. (1964), 'Der vorpaulinische Hymnus, Phil. 2, 6–11', in E. Dinkler (ed.), *Zeit und Geschichte (Dankesgabe an R. Bultmann zum 80. Geburtstag)* (1964, Tübingen), 263–93.

GIBBS, J. G. (1971), *Creation and Redemption: A Study in Pauline Theology*, Supplements to *NovT* 26 (Leiden, 1971).

GIBLIN, C. H. (1975), rev. of E. Käsemann, *An die Römer* (1973), *RB* 82 (1975), 118–25.

GISEL, P. (1977), *Vérité et histoire: La Théologie dans la modernité. Ernst Käsemann*, Théologie historique, 41 (Paris, 1977).

GLASSON, T. F. (1981), 'What is Apocalyptic?' *NTS* 27 (1981), 98–105.

GOGARTEN, F. (1924), 'Theologie und Wissenschaft: Grundsätzliche Bemerkungen zu Karl Holls "Luther"', *ChW* 38 (1924), 34–42, 71–80, 121–4.

GOPPELT, L. (1968), 'Versöhnung durch Christus', in *Christologie und Ethik: Aufsätze zum Neuen Testament* (Göttingen, 1968), 117–32.

GRAU, F. (1946), 'Die neutestamentliche Begriff χάρισμα, seine Geschichte und seine Theologie', unpublished dissertation (Tübingen, 1946).

GUNDRY, R. H. (1976), *Sôma in Biblical Theology: With Emphasis on Pauline Anthropology*, SNTSMS 29 (Cambridge, 1976).

GUNKEL, H. (1888), *Die Wirkungen des heiligen Geistes, nach der populären Anschauung der apostolischen Zeit und nach der Lehre des Apostels Paulus: Eine biblische-theologische Studie* (Göttingen, 1888). ET: *The Influence of the Holy Spirit: The Popular View of the Apostolic Age and the Teaching of the Apostle Paul* (Philadelphia, 1978; page references to the ET).

—— (1895), *Schöpfung und Chaos in Urzeit und Endzeit: Eine religionsgeschichtliche Untersuchung über Gen 1 und Ap Joh 15* (Göttingen, 1895).

—— (1903), *Zum religionsgeschichtlichen Verständnis des Neuen Testaments*,

FRLANT 1 (Göttingen, 1903). ET: 'The Religio-historical Interpretation of the New Testament', *Monist* (Chicago, 1903), 398–455.

GUNKEL, H. (1913), 'Mythen und Mythologie in Israel', *RGG*, (1st edn.), 4 (1913), cols. 621 ff.

GÜTTGEMANNS, E. (1966), *Der leidende Apostel und sein Herr: Studien zur paulinischen Christologie*, FRLANT 90 (Göttingen, 1966).

—— (1967), 'Literatur zur Neutestamentlichen Theologie: Randglossen zu ausgewählten Neuerscheinungen', *VF* 12 (1967), 61–79.

—— (1971), '"Gottesgerechtigkeit" und strukturale Semantik: Linguistische Analyse zu δικαιοσύνη θεοῦ', *Studia linguistica Neotestamentica*, BEvTh 60 (Munich, 1971), 5–98.

HALL, D. R. (1983), 'Rom. 3: 1–8 Reconsidered', *NTS* 29 (1983), 183–197.

HANSON, P. D. (1975), *The Dawn of Apocalyptic* (Philadelphia, 1975).

HÄRING, H. (1972), *Kirche und Kerygma: Das Kirchenbild in der Bultmannschule*, ÖF 1. 6 (Freiburg, 1972).

HARNACK, A. VON (1921), *Marcion: Das Evangelium vom fremden Gott: Eine Monographie zur Geschichte der Grundlegung der katholischen Kirche*, TU 45 (Leipzig, 1921).

HARRINGTON, D. J. (1971*a*), 'Ernst Käsemann on the Church in the NT: I', *HJ* 12 (1971), 246–57.

—— (1971*b*), 'Ernst Käsemann on the Church in the NT: II', *HJ* 12 (1971), 365–76.

—— (1974), rev. of E. Käsemann, *An die Römer* (1973), *Bib* 55 (1974), 583–7.

HARRISVILLE, R. A. (1985), 'Crux sola nostra theologia: A Retrospective Review of the Work of Ernst Käsemann', *RSR* 11 (1985), 256–9.

HASENHÜTTL, G. (1969), *Charisma: Ordnungsprinzip der Kirche*, ÖF 5 (Freiburg, 1969).

HAUFE, G. (1971), 'Exegese als Provokation', *Die Zeichen der Zeit: Evangelische Monatsschrift für Mitarbeiter der Kirche*, 25 (Berlin, 1971), 258–64.

HAWTHORNE, G. F. (1983), *Philippians*, WBC 44 (Waco, Tex., 1983).

—— (1987), *Word Biblical Themes: Philippians* (Waco, Tex., 1987).

HEIDLER, F. (1934), rev. of E. Käsemann, *Leib und Leib Christi* (1933), *Neues sächsisches Kirchenblatt* (Leipzig, 2 Sept. 1934), 559.

HEINZ, G. (1974), *Das Problem der Kirchenentstehung in der deutschen protestantischen Theologie des 20. Jahrhunderts*, Tübinger Theologische Studien, 4 (Mainz, 1974).

HEITMÜLLER, W. (1903), *Taufe und Abendmahl bei Paulus: Darstellung und religionsgeschichtliche Beleuchtung* (Göttingen, 1903).

—— (1908), 'Abendmahl', in *RGG* (1st edn.) 1 (Tübingen, 1908), 20–52.

—— (1911), *Taufe und Abendmahl im Urchristentum*, RV 1. 22/3 (Tübingen, 1911).

—— (1912), 'Zum Problem Paulus und Jesus', *ZNW* 13 (1912), 320–37; repr. in Rengstorf 1964, 124–43.

—— (1917), *Luthers Stellung in der Religionsgeschichte des Christentums: Rede zur 400 jährigen Reformations-Feier der Philipps-Universtität*, Marburger Akademische Reden, 38 (Marburg, 1917).

HELLHOLM, D. (1983), (ed.), *Die Apokalyptik in Mittelmeerraum und im Vorderen Orient: International Colloquium on Apocalypticism, Uppsala, 1979* (Tübingen, 1983).

HERTEN, J. (1976), 'Charisma: Signal einer Gemeindetheologie des Paulus', in J. Hainz (ed.), *Kirche im Werden* (Munich, 1976), 58–89.

HICK, L. (1948), *Die Staatsgewalt im Lichte des Neuen Testaments* (Aachen, 1948).

HODGSON, P. C. (1966), *The Formation of Historical Theology: A Study of F. C. Baur*, Makers of Modern Theology (New York, 1966).

HOFIUS, O. (1976), *Der Christushymnus Philipper 2, 6–11: Untersuchungen zu Gestalt und Aussage eines urchristlichen Psalms*, WUNT 17 (Tübingen, 1976).

HOLL, K. (1921), *Gesammelte Aufsätze zur Kirchengeschichte*, i: *Luther* (Tübingen, 1921).

—— (1924), 'Gogartens Lutherauffassung: Eine Erwiderung', *ChW* 38 (1924), 307–14.

HOLMSTRÖM, F. (1926), *Das eschatologische Denken der Gegenwart* (Gütersloh, 1926).

HOMMEL, H. (1953/4), 'Pantokrator', *Theologia Viatorum: Jahrbuch der kirchlichen Hochschule Berlin*, 5 (Berlin, 1953/4), 322–78; repr. in *Schöpfer und Erhalter* (1956), 87–137, and *Sebasmata: Studien zur antiken Religionsgeschichte und zum frühen Christentum*, i, WUNT 31 (Tübingen, 1983), 131–77.

HÜBNER, H. (1974/5), 'Existentiale Interpretation der paulinischen "Gerechtigkeit Gottes". Zur Kontroverse Rudolf Bultmann–Ernst Käsemann: Rudolf Bultmann zum 90. Geburtstag', *NTS* 21 (1974/5), 462–88.

—— (1979/80), 'Pauli Theologiae Proprium', *NTS* 26 (1979/80), 445–73.

—— (1978/1982), *Das Gesetz bei Paulus: Ein Beitrag zum Werden der paulinischen Theologie*, FRLANT 180 (Göttingen, 1978; 3rd edn., 1982). ET: *Law in Paul's Thought*, Studies in the New Testament and its World (Edinburgh, 1984).

HULTGREN, A. J. (1985), *Paul's Gospel and Mission: The Outlook from his Letter to the Romans* (Philadelphia, 1985).

HUNTER, A. M. (1961), *Paul and his Predecessors* (rev. edn., London, 1961).

INCE, G. (1987), 'Creation, Justification, Resurrection: An Exposition and Critique of Käsemann's Romans', unpublished Ph.D. dissertation (Edinburgh, 1987).

ITTEL, G. W. (1958), 'Die Hauptgedanken der "Religionsgeschichtlichen Schule"', *ZRGG* 10 (1958), 61–78.

IWAND, H. J. (1930), *Rechtfertigungslehre und Christusglaube: Eine Untersuchung zur Systematik der Rechtfertigungslehre Luthers in ihren Anfängen* (Leipzig, 1930); repr. as Theologische Bücherei, 14 (Munich, 1966).

—— (1956), 'Vom Primat der Christologie', in E. Wolf, C. von Kirschbaum, and R. Frey (eds.), *Antwort: K. Barth zum 70. Geburtstag* (Zurich, 1956), 172–89.

JAMPEN, E. W. (1937), rev. of E. Käsemann, *Leib und Leib Christi* (1933), *KBRS* 93 (Basle, 1937), 10–10.

JASPERT, B. (1971), (ed.), *Karl Barth–Rudolf Bultmann: Briefwechsel 1922–1966*, Karl Barth-Gesamtausgabe 5, Briefe (Zurich, 1971).

JENTSCH, W. (1968), *Zwischenbemerkung: Neuralgische Punkte zwischen Universitätstheologie und Gemeindefrömmigkeit* (Neukirchen, 1968).

JEREMIAS, J. (1949), 'Zwischen Karfreitag und Ostern', *ZNW* 42 (1949), 194–201.

—— (1953), 'Zur Gedankenführung in den paulinischen Briefen', in *Studia Paulina in honorem J. de Zwaan* (Haarlem, 1953), 146–54.

JERVELL, J. (1960), *Imago Dei: Gen. 1, 26f. im Spätjudentum, in der Gnosis und in den paulinischen Briefen*, FRLANT 76 (Göttingen, 1960).

JEWETT, R. (1971), *Paul's Anthropological Terms: A Study of their Use in Conflict Settings*, Arbeiten zur Geschichte des antiken Judentums und des Urchristentums, 10 (Leiden, 1971).

—— (1980), 'Major Impulses in the Theological Interpretation of Romans since Barth', *Int* 34 (1980), 17–31.

JOHNSON, R. A. (1974), *The Origins of Demythologizing: Philosophy and Historiography in the Theology of R. Bultmann*, Studies in the History of Theology (Leiden, 1974).

JÜLICHER, A. (1908/1917), 'Der Brief an die Römer', Die Schriften des Neuen Testaments (Göttingen, 1908; 3rd edn., 1917).

—— (1920), 'Ein moderner Paulus-Ausleger' (rev. of K. Barth's *Der Römerbrief* (1919)), *ChW* 34 (1920), 466–8; repr. in Moltmann 1962: 87–98 (page references to this edition).

JÜNGEL, E. (1962), *Paulus und Jesus: Eine Untersuchung zur Präzisierung der Frage nach dem Ursprung der Christologie*, HUNT 2 (Tübingen, 1962).

—— (1963), 'Das Gesetz zwischen Adam und Christus: Eine theologische Studie zu Röm 5,12–21', *ZThK* 60 (1963), 42–68; repr. in Jüngel 1972: 145–72.

—— (1968), 'Gottes umstrittene Gerechtigkeit: Eine reformatorische Besinnung zum paulinischen Begriff *δικαιοσύνη θεοῦ*', in E. Jüngel and M. Geiger, *Zwei Reden zum 450. Geburtstag der Reformation*, ThSt 93 (Zurich, 1968), 3–26; repr. in Jüngel 1972: 60–79.

—— (1972), *Unterwegs zur Sache: Theologische Bemerkungen*, BEvTh 61 (Munich, 1972).

Kabisch, R. (1893), *Die Eschatologie des Paulus in ihren Zusammenhängen mit dem Gesamtbegriff des Paulinismus* (Göttingen, 1893).

Kähler, M. (1892/1896), *Der sogenannte historische Jesus und der geschichtliche, biblische Christus* (Leipzig, 1892; 2nd edn., 1896; repr. in Theologische Bücherei. Neudrucke und Berichte aus dem 20. Jahrhundert 2, Systematische Theologie, Munich, 1969). ET: *The So-called Historical Jesus and the Historic Biblical Christ* (Philadelphia, 1964).

—— (1911), *Das Kreuz: Grund und Maß für die Christologie*, BFChTh 15. 1 (Gütersloh, 1911).

Keck, L. E. (1976), 'Justification of the Ungodly and Ethics', in Friedrich *et al.* 1976, 199–210.

Kelsey, D. H. (1975), *The Uses of Scripture in Recent Theology* (London, 1975).

Kerr, F. (1981*a*), 'The Theology of Ernst Käsemann—I. Commentary on Romans by Ernst Käsemann', *NBl* 62 (1981), 100–13.

—— (1981*b*), 'The Theology of Ernst Käsemann—II.', *NBl* 62 (1981), 148–57.

Kertelge, K. (1967), *Rechtfertigung bei Paulus: Studien zur Struktur und zum Bedeutungsgehalt des paulinischen Rechtfertigungsbegriffs*, NTA (NS) 3 (Münster, 1967).

—— (1977) (ed.), *Das kirchliche Amt im Neuen Testament*, WdF 439 (Darmstadt, 1977).

Kim, S. (1981), *The Origin of Paul's Gospel*, WUNT 4 (Tübingen, 1981, and Grand Rapids, Mich., 1982).

Klaiber, W. (1978), 'Kommentare zu den Paulusbriefen (III): Der Römerbrief', *Theologie für die Praxis: Aus dem Theologischen Seminar der Evangelisch-methodistischen Kirche*, iv (Reutlingen, 1978), 10–15.

—— (1982), *Rechtfertigung und Gemeinde: Eine Untersuchung zum paulinischen Kirchenverständnis*, FRLANT 127 (Göttingen, 1982).

Klappert, B. (1967), (ed.), *Diskussion um Kreuz und Auferstehung: Zur gegenwärtigen Auseinandersetzung in Theologie und Gemeinde* (Wuppertal, 1967).

Klatt, W. (1969), *Hermann Gunkel, zu seiner Theologie der Religionsgeschichte und zur Entstehung der formgeschichtlichen Methode*, FRLANT 100 (Göttingen, 1969).

KLEIN, G. (1963), 'Römer 4 und die Idee der Heilsgeschichte', *EvTh* 23 (1963), 424–47; repr. in Klein 1969: 145–69.

—— (1964), 'Exegetische Probleme in Römer 3, 21–4, 25. Anwort an U. Wilckens', *EvTh* 24 (1964), 676–83; repr. in Klein 1969: 170–9.

—— (1967), 'Gottes Gerechtigkeit als Thema der neuesten Paulusforschung', *VF* 12 (1967), 1–11 (page references to this edition); repr. in Klein 1969: 225–36.

—— (1969), *Rekonstruktion und Interpretation: Gesammelte Aufsätze zum Neuen Testament*, BEvTh 50 (Munich, 1969).

—— (1973), 'Apokalyptische Naherwartung bei Paulus', in H. D. Betz and L. Schottroff (eds.), *Neues Testament und christliche Existenz: Festschrift für Herbert Braun zum 70. Geburtstag am 4. Mai 1973* (Tübingen, 1973), 241–62.

—— (1976), 'Righteousness in the New Testament', *The Interpreter's Dictionary of the Bible*, Supplementary volume (Nashville, 1976), 750–2.

KNOX, J. (1964), 'Romans 15: 14–33 and Paul's Conception of his Apostolic Mission', *JBL* 83 (1964), 1–11.

KOCH, H. (1971), 'Römer 3, 21–31 in der Paulusinterpretation der letzten 150 Jahre', unpublished dissertation (Göttingen, 1971).

KOCH, K. (1970), *Ratlos vor der Apokalyptik: Eine Streitschrift über der schädlichen Auswirkungen auf Theologie und Philosophie* (Gütersloh, 1970). ET: *The Rediscovery of Apocalyptic*, SBT 2. 22 (London 1972).

KÖGEL, J. (1908), *Christus der Herr: Erläuterungen zu Philipper 2, 5–11*, BFChTh 12. 2 (Gütersloh, 1908).

KOPFERMANN, W. (1967), 'Wie christlich ist Ernst Käsemann? Kritische Kommentare I', *Lutherischer Rundblick*, 3 (Wiesbaden, 1967), 168–70.

KRODEL, G. (1965), 'Enthusiasm (*Schwärmerei*)', in J. Bodensieck (ed.), *The Encyclopaedia of the Lutheran Church*, i (Minneapolis, 1965), 783–8.

KUHN, K. G. (1950a), 'Neutestamentliche Sektion (Bericht K. G. Kuhn)', *ThLZ* 75 (1950), 226.

—— (1950b), 'Die in Palästina gefundenen hebräischen Texte und das NT', *ZThK* 47 (1950), 192–211.

—— (1966), *Enderwartung und gegenwärtiges Heil. Untersuchungen zu den Gemeindeliedern von Qumran, mit einem Anhang über Eschatologie und Gegenwart in den Verkündigung Jesu*, StUNT 4 (Göttingen, 1966).

KÜMMEL, W. G. (1952), 'πάρεσις und ἔνδειξις', *ZThK* 49 (1952), 154–67.

—— (1958), *Das Neue Testament: Geschichte der Erforschung seiner Probleme* (Freiburg, 1958). ET: *The New Testament: The History of the Investigation of its Problems* (London, 1973; page references to the ET).

—— (1970), *Das Neue Testament im 20. Jahrhundert, ein Forschungsbericht*, SBS 50 (Stuttgart, 1970).

—— (1974), 'Die Botschaft des Römerbriefs' (rev. of E. Käsemann, *An die Römer*, 1973), *ThLZ* 99 (1974), 481–8.

—— (1976), 'Albert Schweitzer als Paulusforscher', in Friedrich *et al.* 1976: 26–89.

—— (1982), 'Ein Jahrhundert Erforschung der Eschatologie des Neuen Testaments', *ThLZ* 107 (1982), 81–96.

—— (1984), 'Rudolf Bultmann als Paulusforscher', in B. Jaspert (ed.), *Rudolf Bultmanns Werk und Wirkung* (Darmstadt, 1984), 174–93.

KÜNNETH, W. (1933/1951), *Theologie der Auferstehung*, FGLP 6. 1 (Munich, 1933; 4th edn., 1951). ET: *The Theology of the Resurrection* (London, 1965).

—— (1966), *Entscheidung heute: Jesu Auferstehung—Brennpunkt der theologischen Diskussion* (Hamburg, 1966).

KUSS, O. (1957/1963), *Der Römerbrief*, i (Regensburg, 1957; 2nd edn., 1963).

LANG, F. G. (1976), 'Bibliographie Ernst Käsemann 1933–75', in Friedrich *et al.* 1976: 593–604.

LARSSON, E. (1962), *Christus als Vorbild: Eine Untersuchung zu den paulinischen Tauf- und Eikontexten*, ASNU 23 (Uppsala, 1962).

LAWLOR, H. J., and OULTON, J. E. L. (1927) (eds.), *Eusebius: The Ecclesiastical History and the Martyrs of Palestine*, i: *Translation* (London, 1927).

LEWANDOWSKI, G. A. (1974), 'An Introduction to Ernst Käsemann's Theology', *Encounter*, 35 (Indianapolis, 1974), 222–42.

LIETZMANN, H. (1906/1933), *An die Römer*, HNT 8 (Tübingen, 1906; 4th edn., 1933).

—— (1907), *An die Korinther I/II*, HNT 9 (Tübingen, 1907).

—— (1909), *Der Weltheiland: Eine Jenaer Rosenvorlesung mit Anmerkungen* (Bonn, 1909).

LJUNGMAN, H. (1964), *Pistis: A Study of its Presuppositions and its Meaning in Pauline Use*, Acta r. societatis humaniorum litterarum Lundensis, 64 (Lund, 1964).

LOHMEYER, E. (1913), *Der Begriff διαθήκη, ein Beitrag zur Erklärung des neutestamentlichen Begriffs*, UNT 2 (Leipzig, 1913).

—— (1928*a*), *Kyrios Jesus: Eine Untersuchung zu Phil 2, 5–11*, Sitzungsberichte der Heidelberger Akademie der Wissenschaften, Philosophisch-historische Klasse, Jahrgang 1927/8, 4. Abhandlung (Heidelberg, 1928).

LOHMEYER, E. (1928*b*), *Der Brief an die Philipper*, KEK 9. 1 (Göttingen, 8th edn., 1928).

—— (1929*a*), *Grundlagen der paulinischen Theologie*, BHTh 1 (Tübingen, 1929).

—— (1929*b*), *Die Briefe an die Kolosser und an Philemon*, KEK 9. 2 (Göttingen, 8th edn. 1929).

LOHSE, E. (1955/1963), *Märtyrer und Gottesknecht: Untersuchungen zur urchristlichen Verkündigung von Sühnetod Jesu Christi*, FRLANT 61 (Göttingen, 1955; 2nd edn., 1963).

—— (1971), 'Apokalyptik und Christologie', *ZNW* 62 (1971), 48–67 (page references to this edition); repr. in Lohse 1973*c*: 125–44.

—— (1973*a*), 'Die Gerechtigkeit Gottes in der paulinischen Theologie', in Lohse 1973*c*: 20–27.

—— (1973*b*), 'Die große Glocke läutet wieder: Ein Ereignis neutestamentlicher Forschung: Käsemanns Römerbriefkommentar', *Deutsches Allgemeines Sonntagsblatt* (14 Oct. 1973).

—— (1973*c*), *Die Einheit des Neuen Testaments: Exegetische Studien zur Theologie des Neuen Testaments* (Göttingen, 1973).

LÜCKE, F. (1820/1852), *Commentar über die Schriften des Evangelisten Johannis IV, 1: Versuch einer vollständiger Einleitung in die Offenbarung Johannis und in die gesamte apokalyptische Literatur* (Bonn, 1820; 2nd edn., 1852).

LÜDEMANN, G. (1987), 'Die Religionsgeschichtliche Schule', in B. Moeller (ed.), *Theologie in Göttingen: Eine Vorlesungsreihe*, Göttinger Universitätsschriften, Series A, No. 1 (Göttingen, 1987), 325–61.

—— and SCHRÖDER, M. (1987), *Die Religionsgeschichtliche Schule: Eine Dokumentation* (Göttingen, 1987).

LÜDEMANN, H. (1872), *Die Anthropologie des Apostels Paulus und ihre Stellung innerhalb seiner Heilslehre: Nach den vier Hauptbriefen dargestellt* (Kiel, 1872).

LÜHRMANN, D. (1965), *Das Offenbarungsverständnis bei Paulus und in den paulinischen Gemeinden*, WMANT 16 (Neukirchen, 1965).

—— (1970), 'Rechtfertigung und Versöhnung: Zur Geschichte der paulinischen Tradition', *ZThK* 67 (1970), 437–52.

—— (1976), 'Christologie und Rechtfertigung', in Friedrich *et al.* 1976: 351–64.

LÜTGERT, W. (1908), *Freiheitspredigt und Schwarmgeister in Korinth: Ein Beitrag zur Charakteristik der Christuspartei*, BFChTh 12. 3 (Gütersloh, 1908).

—— (1909), *Die Vollkommenen im Philipperbrief und Die Enthusiasten in Thessalonich*, BFChTh 13. 6 (Gütersloh, 1909).

LUTHER, M. (1515/16), *Luther: Lectures on Romans*, ed. W. Pauck,

Library of Christian Classics (Philadelphia, 1961); lectures first given 1515/16.

—— (1520), *The Freedom of a Christian*, in *Martin Luther: Selections from his Writings*, ed. J. Dillenberger (New York, 1961), 42–85; 1st pub. 1520.

—— (1522), 'Preface to the Epistle of St. Paul to the Romans', in *Martin Luther: Selections from his Writings*, ed. J. Dillenberger (New York, 1961), 1–34; 1st pub. 1522.

—— (1535), *A Commentary on St Paul's Epistle to the Galatians: Based on Lectures Delivered by Martin Luther at the University of Wittenberg in the year 1531 and First Published in 1535*, ed. P. S. Watson (London, 1953).

LYONNET, S. (1957), 'Notes sur l'exégèse de l'épître aux Romains', *Bib* 38 (1957), 35–61.

MCGRATH, A. (1986), *Iustitia Dei: A History of the Christian Doctrine of Justification: The Beginnings to the Reformation* (Cambridge, 1986).

MACQUARRIE, J. (1955), *An Existentialist Theology: A Comparison of Heidegger and Bultmann* (London, 1955; page references to the Pelican edn. of 1980).

MARSHALL, I. H. (1978), 'The Meaning of "Reconciliation"', in R. A. Guelich (ed.), *Unity and Diversity in New Testament Theology: Essays in Honor of George E. Ladd* (Grand Rapids, Mich., 1978), 117–32.

MARTIN, R. P. (1967), *Carmen Christi: Philippians ii, 5–11 in Recent Interpretation and in the Setting of Early Christian Worship*, SNTSMS 4 (Cambridge, 1967).

—— (1976), *Philippians*, New Century Bible Commentaries (London, 1976; rev. edn., 1980).

—— (1981), *Reconciliation: A Study of Paul's Theology* (London, 1981).

MAURER, C. (1956), 'Grund und Grenze apostolischer Freiheit: Exegetisch-theologische Studie zu 1. Korinther 9', in E. Wolf, C. von Kirschbaum, and R. Frey (eds.), *Antwort: Karl Barth zum 70. Geburtstag am 10. Mai 1956* (Zurich, 1956), 630–41.

—— (1974), rev. of E. Käsemann, *An die Römer* (1973), *KBRS* 130 (1974), 193.

MERK, O. (1968), *Handeln aus Glauben: Die Motivierungen der Paulinischen Ethik*, MThSt 5 (Marburg, 1968).

—— (1972), *Biblische Theologie des Neuen Testaments in ihrer Anfangszeit: Ihre methodischen Probleme bei Johann Philipp Gabler und Georg Lorenz Bauer und deren Nachwirkungen*, MThSt 9 (Marburg, 1972).

METZGER, B. M. (1971), *A Textual Commentary on the Greek New Testament* (London, 1971).

MEYER, B. F. (1983), 'The Pre-Pauline Formula in Rom 3: 25–26a', *NTS* 29 (1983), 198–208.

MICHAELIS, W. (1933), rev. of E. Käsemann, *Leib und Leib Christi* (1933), *Theologisches Literatur Blatt*, 25 (Leipzig, 1933), 387–90.

—— (1935), *Der Brief des Paulus an die Philipper*, ThHK (Leipzig, 1935).

—— (1938), '*κοσμοκράτωρ*', *TDNT* 3 (1938), 913.

MICHEL, O. (1955/1979), *Der Brief an die Römer*, KEK 4. 10 (Göttingen, 1955; 5th edn., 1979).

—— (1966), rev. of C. Müller, *Gottes Gerechtigkeit und Gottes Volk* (1964), *ThLZ* 91 (1966), 187–8.

MOLTMANN, J. (1962), (ed.), *Anfänge der dialektischen Theologie*, i, Theologische Bücherei, Neudrucke und Berichte aus dem 20. Jahrhundert, 17/1 Systematische Theologie (Munich, 1962).

—— (1963), (ed.), *Anfänge der dialektischen Theologie*, ii, Theologische Bücherei, Neudrucke und Berichte aus dem 20. Jahrhundert, 17/2 Systematische Theologie (Munich, 1963).

MORGAN, R. C. (1973), *The Nature of New Testament Theology: The Contribution of William Wrede and Adolf Schlatter*, SBT 2. 25 (London, 1973).

—— (1975), rev. of E. Käsemann, *An die Römer* (1973), *HJ* 16 (1975), 68–70.

—— (1977), 'F. C. Baur's Lectures on New Testament Theology', *ExT* 88 (1977), 202–6.

—— (1978), 'Biblical Classics II. F. C. Baur: Paul', *ExT* 90 (1970), 4–10.

—— (1982), 'The Significance of "Paulinism"', in M. D. Hooker and S. G. Wilson (eds.), *Paul and Paulinism: Essays in Honour of C. K. Barrett* (London, 1982), 320–38.

—— (1985), 'Ferdinand Christian Baur', in N. Smart *et al.* (eds.), *Nineteenth Century Religious Thought in the West*, i (Cambridge, 1985), 261–89.

MORRISON, C. (1960), *The Powers That Be: Earthly Rulers and Demonic Powers in Rom. 13. 1–7*, SBT 29 (London, 1960).

MOULE, C. F. D. (1981), rev. of E. Käsemann, *Commentary on Romans* (1980), *JTS* NS 32 (1981), 498–502.

MÜLLER, C. (1964), *Gottes Gerechtigkeit und Gottes Volk: Eine Untersuchung zu Römer 9–11*, FRLANT 86 (Göttingen, 1964).

MÜLLER, K. (1905), 'Beobachtungen zur paulinischen Rechtfertigungslehre', in F. Giesebrecht *et al.* (eds.), *Theologische Studien Martin Kähler zum 6. Jan. 1905* (Leipzig, 1905), 87–110.

MUNCK, J. (1954), *Paulus und die Heilsgeschichte* (Copenhagen, 1954). ET: *Paul and the Salvation of Mankind* (London, 1959).

—— (1956), *Christus und Israel: Eine Auslegung von Röm. 9–11* (Aarhus, 1956). ET: *Christ and Israel: An Interpretation of Romans 9–11* (Philadelphia, 1967).

MUSSNER, F. (1974), *Der Galaterbrief*, HThK 9 (Freiburg, 1974).

NEUENZEIT, P. (1960), *Das Herrenmahl: Studien zur paulinischen Eucharistieauffassung* (Munich, 1960).

NEUGEBAUER, F. (1961), *In Christus: ΕΝ ΧΡΙΣΤΩΙ: Eine Untersuchung zum Paulinischen Glaubensverständnis* (Göttingen, 1961).

NORDEN, E. (1913), *Agnostos Theos: Untersuchung zur Formengeschichte religiöser Rede* (Leipzig, 1913).

—— (1924), *Die Geburt des Kindes: Geschichte einer religiösen Idee*, Studien der Bibliothek Warburg 3 (Leipzig, 1924).

OEPKE, A. (1950), *Das neue Gottesvolk in Schriftum, Schauspiel, bildender Kunst und Weltgestaltung* (Gütersloh, 1950).

—— (1953), '*ΔΙΚΑΙΟΣΥΝΗ ΘΕΟΥ* bei Paulus in neuer Beleuchtung', *ThLZ* 78 (1953), 257–64.

—— (1954), 'Leib Christi oder Volk Gottes bei Paulus?' *ThLZ* 79 (1954), 363–8.

O'NEILL, J. C. (1975), *Paul's Letter to the Romans* (Harmondsworth, 1975).

OSBORN, E. F. (1975), 'Käsemann on Romans: Article on Ernst Käsemann, *An die Römer* (Tübingen: J. C. B. Mohr, 1974)', *ABR* 23 (1975), 2–31.

PERCY, E. (1942), *Der Leib Christi (Σῶμα Χριστοῦ) in den paulinischen Homologumena und Antilegomena* (Lund, 1942).

—— (1946), *Die Probleme der Kolosser- und Epheserbriefe* (Lund, 1946).

PERRIN, N. (1967), *Rediscovering the Teaching of Jesus* (London, 1967).

PETERSON, E. (1926), *Εἷς θεός: Epigraphische, formgeschlichtliche und religionsgeschichtliche Untersuchungen*, FRLANT 24 (Göttingen, 1926).

PLUTA, A. (1969), *Gottes Bundestreue: Ein Schlüsselbegriff in Röm. 3, 25a*, SBS 34 (Stuttgart, 1969).

PLUTTA-MESSERSCHMIDT, E. (1973), *Gerechtigkeit Gottes bei Paulus: Eine Studie zu Luthers Auslegung von Römer 3: 5*, HUNT 14 (Tübingen, 1973).

RÄISÄNEN, H. (1978), 'Paul's Theological Difficulties with the Law', in E. A. Livingstone (ed.), *Studia biblica 1978*, iii, JSNT Supplement 3 (Sheffield, 1980), 301–20.

—— (1980), 'Legalism and Salvation by the Law', in S. Pedersen (ed.), *Die paulinische Literatur und Theologie*, Scandinavische Beiträge (Aarhus, 1980), 63–83.

—— (1983), *Paul and the Law*, WUNT 29 (Tübingen, 1983).

Reitzenstein, R. (1904), *Poimandres: Studien zur griechisch-ägyptischen und frühchristlichen Literatur* (Leipzig, 1904).

—— (1910/1927), *Die hellenistischen Mysterienreligionen nach ihren Grundgedanken und Wirkungen* (Leipzig, 1910; 3rd. edn., 1927). ET: *The Hellenistic Mystery-Religions*, Pittsburg Theological Monographs, 15 (Pittsburgh, Pa., 1978).

—— (1921), *Das iranische Erlösungsmysterium* (Bonn, 1921).

—— (1929), *Die Vorgeschichte der christlichen Taufe* (Leipzig, 1929).

Rengstorf, K. H. (1964), *Das Paulusbild in der neueren deutschen Forschung*, WdF 24 (Darmstadt, 1964).

Reumann, J. (1966), 'The Gospel of the Righteousness of God: Pauline Reinterpretation in Romans 3: 21–31', *Int* 20 (1966), 432–52.

Riches, J. K. (1976), rev. of E. Käsemann, *An die Römer* (1973), *SJT* 29 (1976), 557–74.

Ritschl, D. (1982), 'How I See German Theology', in S. Sykes (ed.), *England and Germany: Studies in Theological Diplomacy*, Studien zur interkulturellen Geschichte des Christentums, 25 (Berlin, 1982).

Robinson, J. A. T. (1952), *The Body: A Study in Pauline Theology*, SBT 5 (London, 1952).

Robinson, J. M. (1959), *A New Quest of the Historical Jesus*, SBT 25 (London, 1959). German: *Kerygma und historischer Jesus* (Zurich, 1960; rev. and enlarged edn., 1967).

—— (1968) (ed.), *The Beginnings of Dialectical Theory*, i (Virginia, 1968).

Rohde, E. (1890), *Psyche, Seelencult und Unsterblichkeitsglaube der Griechen*, i (Freiburg i.B., 1890).

Rollins, W. G. (1970), 'The New Testament and Apocalyptic', *NTS* 17 (1970), 454–76.

Rowland, C. C. (1982), *The Open Heaven: A Study of Apocalyptic in Judaism and Early Christianity* (London, 1982).

Rudolf, K. (1971), 'Gnosis und Gnostizismus, ein Forschungsbericht', *ThR* NS 36 (1971), 1–61, 89–124.

—— (1977), *Die Gnosis: Wesen und Geschichte einer spätantiken Religion* (Leipzig, 1977). ET: *Gnosis: The Nature and History of an Ancient Religion* (Edinburgh, 1983; page references to the ET).

Sanday, W. and Headlam, A. C. (1895/1902), *A Critical and Exegetical Commentary on the Epistle to the Romans*, ICC (Edinburgh, 1895; 5th edn., 1902).

Sanders, E. P. (1977), *Paul and Palestinian Judaism: A Comparison of Patterns of Religion* (London, 1977). German translation with a new foreword, *Paulus und das palästinische Judentum: Ein Vergleich zweier Religionsstrukturen*, StUNT 17 (Göttingen, 1985).

—— (1983), *Paul, the Law and the Jewish People* (Philadelphia, 1983).

SANDIFER, D. W. (1979), 'History and Existential Interpretation: The Debate between Ernst Käsemann and Rudolf Bultmann', unpublished dissertation (Emory University, 1979).

SASS, G. (1939), *Apostelamt und Kirche: Eine theologisch-exegetische Untersuchung des paulinischen Apostelbegriffs*, FGLP 9. 2 (Munich, 1939).

SAUTER, G. (1976), 'Systematische Gesichtspunkte in Ernst Käsemanns Römerbrief-Kommentar', *VF* 21 (1976), 80–94.

SCHADE, H.-H. (1981), *Apokalyptische Christologie bei Paulus: Studien zum Zusammenhang von Christologie und Eschatologie in den Paulusbriefen*, GTA 18 (Göttingen, 1981).

SCHAEFER, P. (1938), rev. of E. Käsemann, *Leib und Leib Christi* (1933), *Eine heilige Kirche: Zeitschrift für Kirchenkunde und Religionswissenschaft* (= vol. 20 of *Hochkirche*) (Munich, 1938), 67–9.

SCHENKE, H.-M. (1962), *Der Gott 'Mensch' in der Gnosis: Ein religionsgeschichtlicher Beitrag zur Diskussion über die paulinische Anschauung von der Kirche als Leib Christi* (Göttingen, 1962).

—— (1973), 'Die neutestamentliche Christologie und der gnostische Erlöser', in K.-W. Tröger (ed.), *Gnosis und Neues Testament: Studien aus Religionswissenschaft und Theologie* (Berlin, 1973), 205–29.

SCHILLE, G. (1965), *Frühchristliche Hymnen* (Berlin, 1965).

—— (1975), 'Das Recht des Schöpfers: Zur Theologie Ernst Käsemanns', Theologische Versuche, 5 (Berlin, 1975), 71–82.

SCHLATTER, A. (1917), *Luthers Deutung des Römerbriefs* (Stuttgart, 1917).

—— (1922), 'Karl Barths "Römerbrief"', *Die Furche: Akademische Monatsschrift*, 12 (Berlin, 1922), 142–7; repr. in Moltmann 1962: 228–32 (page references to this edition).

—— (1926), *Das Gott wohlgefällige Opfer* (Bethel, 1926).

—— (1929), 'Das Kreuz Jesu, unsere Versöhnung mit Gott', in *Gesunde Lehre: Reden und Aufsätze* (Velbert, 1929), 7–14.

—— (1935), *Gottes Gerechtigkeit: Ein Kommentar zum Römerbrief* (Stuttgart, 1935; 4th edn., 1965).

—— (1952), *Adolf Schlatters Rückblick auf seine Lebensarbeit*, ed. T. Schlatter, BFChTh Sonderheft (Gütersloh, 1952).

SCHLIER, H. (1930), *Christus und die Kirche im Epheserbrief*, BHTh 6 (Tübingen, 1930).

—— (1948/9), 'Über das Hauptanliegen des 1. Briefes an die Korinther', *EvTh* 9 (1948/9), 462–73.

—— (1949/1971), *Der Brief an die Galater*, KEK 7 (Göttingen, 10th edn., 1949; 14th edn., 1971).

—— (1958), *Der Brief an die Epheser* (Düsseldorf, 2nd edn., 1958).

—— (1977), *Der Römerbrief*, HThK 6 (Freiburg, 1977).

SCHLIER, H. (1978), *Grundzüge einer paulinischen Theologie* (Freiburg, 1978).

SCHMIDT, J. M. (1969), *Die jüdische Apokalyptik: Die Geschichte ihrer Erforschung von den Anfängen bis zu den Textfunden von Qumran* (Neukirchen-Vluyn, 1969).

SCHMITHALS, W. (1974), 'Der Römerbrief des Apostels Paulus: Anmerkungen zu einem neuen Römerbriefkommentar', *Reformierte Kirchenzeitung*, 115 (Neukirchen-Vluyn, 1974), 150–1.

SCHMITZ, H. J. (1977), *Frühkatholizismus bei Adolf von Harnack, Rudolph Sohm und Ernst Käsemann*, Themen und Thesen der Theologie (Düsseldorf, 1977).

SCHMITZ, O. (1924), *Die Christus-Gemeinschaft des Paulus im Lichte seines Genitivgebrauchs*, NTF, 1st ser.: Paulusstudien, 2 (Gütersloh, 1924).

SCHNEIDER, J. (1934), rev. of E. Käsemann, *Leib und Leib Christi* (1933), *Zeitschrift für Kirchengeschichte*, 53 (Stuttgart, 1934), 348–51.

SCHNELLE, U. (1982), *Gerechtigkeit und Christusgegenwart: Vorpaulinische und paulinische Tauftheologie*, GTA 24 (Göttingen, 1982).

SCHNIEWIND, J. (1952), 'Das Seufzen des Geistes: Röm. 8, 26.27', in *Julius Schniewind: Nachgelassene Reden und Aufsätze*, ed. E. Kähler (Berlin, 1952), 81–103.

SCHOEPS, H. J. (1959), *Paulus: Die Theologie des Apostels im Lichte der jüdischen Religionsgeschichte* (Tübingen, 1959). ET: *Paul: The Theology of the Apostle in the Light of Jewish Religious History* (Philadelphia, 1961).

SCHOLDER, K. (1977), *Die Kirchen und das Dritte Reich*, i: *Vorgeschichte und Zeit der Illusionen 1918–1934* (Frankfurt, 1977). ET: *The Churches and the Third Reich*, i: *Preliminary History and the Time of Illusions, 1918–1934* (London 1987).

SCHRAGE, W. (1961), *Die konkreten Einzelgebote in der paulinischen Paränese: Ein Beitrag zur neutestamentlichen Ethik* (Gütersloh, 1961).

—— (1964), 'Die Stellung zur Welt bei Paulus, Epiktet und in der Apokalyptik: Ein Beitrag zu 1 Kor 7, 2–31', *ZThK* 61 (1964), 125–54.

—— (1969), 'Römer 3, 21–26 und die Bedeutung des Todes Jesu Christi', in P. Rieger (ed.), *Das Kreuz Jesu* (Göttingen, 1969), 65–88.

—— (1980), 'Ist die Kirche das "Abbild seines Todes"? Zu Röm 6, 5', in D. Lührmann and G. Strecker (eds.), *Kirche: Festschrift für Günther Bornkamm zum 75. Geburtstag* (Tübingen, 1980), 205–19.

—— (1982), *Ethik des Neuen Testament*, NTD Ergänzungsreihe, Grundriss zum Neuen Testament, 4 (Göttingen, 1982). ET: *The Ethics of the New Testament* (Edinburgh, 1988).

—— (1979), *Das Evangelium von der Versöhnung in Christus* (Stuttgart, 1979).

Talbert, C. H. (1966), 'A Non-Pauline Fragment at Romans 3, 24–26?' *JBL* 85 (1966), 287–96.

Theissen, G. (1974*a*), 'Soziale Integration und Sakramentales Handeln: Eine Analyse von 1 Kor. 11: 17–34', *NovT* 16 (1974), 17–206; repr. in *Studien zur Soziologie des Urchristentums*, WUNT 19 (Tübingen, 1979), 290–317. ET: 'Social Integration and Sacramental Activity: An Analysis of 1 Cor. 11: 17–34', in *The Social Setting of Pauline Christianity: Essays on Corinth*, Studies in the New Testament and its World (Edinburgh, 1982), 145–74 (page references to this edition).

—— (1974*b*), 'Soteriologische Symbolik in den paulinischen Schriften: Ein strukturalistischer Beitrag', *KuD* 20 (1974), 282–302.

Thieme, K. (1935), rev. of E. Käsemann, *Leib und Leib Christi* (1933), *Sanctificatio nostra: Religiöse Monatsschrift für den katholischen Klerus*, 6 (Kevelaer, 1935), 46.

Thiselton, A. C. (1980), *The Two Horizons: New Testament Hermeneutics and Philosophical Description with Special Reference to Heidegger, Bultmann, Gadamer, and Wittgenstein* (Exeter, 1980).

Thun, T. (1985), *Menschenrechte und Aussenpolitik: Bundesrepublik Deutschland–Argentinien 1976–1983*, Wissenschaftliche Publikationen zur Politik, Ökonomie und Kultur in der Dritten Welt (Bremen, 1985).

Thyen, H. (1970), *Studien zur Sündenvergebung im Neuen Testament und seinen alttestamentlichen und jüdischen Voraussetzungen*, FRLANT 96 (Göttingen, 1970).

—— (1984), 'Rudolf Bultmann, Karl Barth und das Problem der "Sachkritik"', in B. Jaspert (ed.), *Rudolf Bultmanns Werk und Wirkung* (Darmstadt, 1984), 44–52.

Trillhaas, W. (1967), 'Regnum Christi: Zur Geschichte der Idee im Protestantismus', *LR* 17 (1967), 51–73. ET: 'Regnum Christi: On the History of the Concept in Protestantism', *LW* 14 (1967), 40–58 (page references to the ET).

Verheule, A. F. (1973), *Wilhelm Bousset: Leben und Werk: Ein theologiegeschichtlicher Versuch* (Amsterdam, 1973).

Volz, P. (1934), *Die Eschatologie der jüdischen Gemeinde im neutestamentlichen Zeitalter* (Tübingen, 1934; = 2nd edn., of *Jüdische Eschatologie von Daniel bis Akiba*, 1903).

Wagner, G. (1962), *Das religionsgeschichtliche Problem von Römer 6*, AThANT 39 (Zurich, 1962). ET: *Pauline Baptism and the Pagan Mysteries* (Edinburgh, 1967).

Watson, F. (1986), *Paul, Judaism and the Gentiles: A Sociological Approach*, SNTSMS 56 (Cambridge, 1986).

WATSON, N. M. (1970), 'Justification: A New Look', *ABR* 18 (1970), 31–44.

—— (1983), '". . . To Make Us Rely Not On Ourselves But On God Who Raises The Dead": 2 Cor. 1: 9b as the Heart of Paul's Theology', in U. Luz and H. Weder (eds.), *Die Mitte des Neuen Testaments: Einheit und Vielfalt neutestamentlicher Theologie: Festschrift für Eduard Schweizer zum siebzigsten Geburtstag* (Göttingen, 1983), 384–98.

WEDDERBURN, A. J. M. (1971), 'The Body of Christ and Related Concepts in 1 Corinthians', *SJT* 24 (1971), 74–96.

—— (1983), 'Hellenistic Christian Traditions in Rom. 6?' *NTS* 29 (1983), 337–55.

WEGENAST, K. (1962), *Das Verständnis der Tradition bei Paulus und in den Deuteropaulinen*, WMANT 8 (Neukirchen, 1962).

WEISS, H. F. (1977), '"Volk Gottes" und "Leib Christi": Überlegungen zur paulinischen Ekklesiologie', *ThLZ* 102 (1977), 411–20.

WEISS, J. (1909), *Paulus und Jesus* (Berlin, 1909). ET: *Paul and Jesus* (London, 1909; page references to the ET).

—— (1910/1925), *Der erste Korintherbrief*, KEK 5 (Göttingen, 9th edn. 1910; 10th edn. 1925).

WENGST, K. (1972), *Christologische Formeln und Lieder des Urchristentums*, StNT 7 (Gütersloh, 1972).

WERNLE, P. (1901), *Die Anfänge unserer Religion* (Tübingen, 1901).

WIKENHAUSER, A. (1934), 'Zur paulinischen Lehre vom "Leibe Christi"' (rev. of E. Käsemann, *Leib und Leib Christi*, 1933), *Theologische Revue*, 33 (Münster, 1934), 265–73.

WILCKENS, U. (1961), 'Die Rechtfertigung Abrahams nach Röm. 4', in R. Rendtorff and K. Koch (eds.), *Studien zur Theologie der alttestamentlichen Überlieferungen: Festschrift für Gerhard von Rad* (Zurich and Neukirchen, 1961), 111–27; repr. in Wilckens 1974: 33–49.

—— (1964), 'Zur Römer 3, 21–4, 25: Antwort an G. Klein', *EvTh* 11 (1964), 586– 610; repr. in Wilckens 1974: 50–76.

—— (1969), 'Was heißt bei Paulus: "Aus Werken des Gesetzes wird kein Mensch gerecht"?', *EKK Vorarbeiten*, 1 (Zurich and Neukirchen, 1969), 51–77; repr. in Wilckens 1974: 77–109.

—— (1974), *Rechtfertigung als Freiheit: Paulusstudien* (Neukirchen, 1974).

—— (1978), *Der Brief an die Römer*, EKK 6. 1 (Zurich and Neukirchen, 1978).

—— (1980), *Der Brief an die Römer*, EKK 6. 2 (Zurich and Neukirchen, 1980).

—— (1982), *Der Brief an die Römer*, EKK 6. 3 (Zurich and Neukirchen, 1982).

Williams, S. K. (1980), 'The "Righteousness of God" in Romans', *JBL* 99 (1980), 241–90.

Willi-Plein, I. (1975), rev. of E. Käsemann, *An die Römer* (2nd edn., 1974), *Judaica: Beiträge zum Verständnis des judischen Schicksals in Vergangenheit und Gegenwart*, 31 (Zurich, 1975), 41–2.

Winter, M. (1975), *Pneumatiker und Psychiker in Korinth: Zum religionsgeschichtlichen Hintergrund von 1. Kor. 2, 6–3, 4*, MThSt 12 (Marburg, 1975).

Wissmann, E. (1926), *Das Verhältnis von πίστις und Christusfrömmigkeit bei Paulus*, FRLANT (NS) 23 (Göttingen, 1926).

Wolf, E. (1933), 'Über neuere Lutherliteratur und den Gang der Lutherforschung', *CuW* 9 (1933), 201–26.

—— (1934), 'Über neuere Lutherliteratur und den Gang der Lutherforschung', *CuW* 10 (1934), 6–21, 203–19, 259–73, and 437–57.

Wrede, W. (1897), *Über Aufgabe und Methode der sogennanten neutestamentlichen Theologie* (Göttingen, 1897). ET: 'The Tasks and Methods of "New Testament Theology"', in Morgan 1973: 68–116 and 182–93.

—— (1904), *Paulus*, RV 1. 5–6 (Halle, 1904); repr. in Rengstorf 1964: 1–97 (page references to this edition). ET: *Paul* (London, 1907).

Wright, N. T. (1978), 'The Paul of History and the Apostle of Faith', *TynB* 29 (1978), 61–88.

—— (1980), 'The Messiah and the People of God', unpublished dissertation (Oxford, 1980).

—— (1982), 'A New Tübingen School? Ernst Käsemann and his Commentary on Romans', *Themelios*, 7 (Harrow, 1982), 6–16.

Young, N. H. (1974), 'Did St Paul Compose Romans III 24 f.?' *ABR* 22 (1974), 23–32.

Zeller, D. (1968), 'Sühne und Langmut: Zur Traditionsgeschichte von Röm. 3, 24–26', *ThPh* 43 (1968), 51–75.

—— (1973), *Juden und Heiden in der Mission des Paulus: Studien zum Römerbrief*, Forschung zur Bibel, 1 (Stuttgart, 1973).

Ziesler, J. A. (1972), *The Meaning of Righteousness in Paul: A Linguistic and Theological Enquiry*, SNTSMS 20 (Cambridge, 1972).

—— (1989), *Paul's Letter to the Romans*, Trinity Press International New Testament Commentaries (London, 1989).

Index of Textual References

Index of Authors